CHRISTIANITY
HISTORY, BELIEF, AND PRACTICE

CHRISTIANITY
HISTORY, BELIEF, AND PRACTICE

EDITED BY MATT STEFON,
ASSISTANT EDITOR, RELIGION

Britannica®
Educational Publishing
IN ASSOCIATION WITH

ROSEN
EDUCATIONAL SERVICES

Published in 2012 by Britannica Educational Publishing
(a trademark of Encyclopædia Britannica, Inc.)
in association with Rosen Educational Services, LLC
29 East 21st Street, New York, NY 10010.

Distributed exclusively by Rosen Educational Services.
For a listing of additional Britannica Educational Publishing titles, call toll free (800) 237-9932.

First Edition

Britannica Educational Publishing
Michael I. Levy: Executive Editor
J.E. Luebering: Senior Manager
Adam Augustyn, Assistant Manager, Encyclopaedia Britannica
Marilyn L. Barton: Senior Coordinator, Production Control
Steven Bosco: Director, Editorial Technologies
Lisa S. Braucher: Senior Producer and Data Editor
Yvette Charbonneau: Senior Copy Editor
Kathy Nakamura: Manager, Media Acquisition
Matt Stefon: Assistant Editor, Religion

Rosen Educational Services
Alexandra Hanson-Harding: Editor
Nelson Sá: Art Director
Cindy Reiman: Photography Manager
Nicole Russo: Designer
Matthew Cauli: Cover Design
Introduction by Matt Stefon

Library of Congress Cataloging-in-Publication Data

Christianity: history, belief, and practice / edited by Matt Stefon. — 1st ed.
    p. cm. — (The Britannica guide to religion)
"In association with Britannica Educational Publishing, Rosen Educational Services."
Includes bibliographical references and index.
ISBN 978-1-61530-493-6 (library binding)
1. Christianity. I. Stefon, Matt. II. Britannica Educational Publishing.
BR121.3.C475 2012
230—dc22

2010046428

Manufactured in the United States of America

Front cover, page 3: Crucifix in St. Peter's Basilica, Vatican, Rome, Italy. *Godong/Robert Harding World Imagery/Getty Images*

Back cover: Cross on a hill. *Shutterstock.com*

On pages 1, 15, 53, 82, 108, 127, 159, 180, 199, 232, 258, 282, 333, 362: The "Christ the Redeemer" statue atop the Corcovado mountain in Rio de Janeiro, Brazil. *AFP/Getty Images.*

Interior page borders image © www.istockphoto.com / MichaelSvoboda

CONTENTS

2

33

36

48

65

83

137

152

182

197

214

237

264

287

309

330

334

363

INTRODUCTION

Christianity is the largest of the world's religions, comprising about one-third of the human population. Yet it is one of the great traditions for more reasons than its sheer number of adherents. Christianity is one of the great cultural as well as spiritual forces in the world. Its impact on human history, whether positive or negative, cannot be underestimated or ignored, and a general awareness of its beliefs and practices and of the context in which these emerged and developed is an essential component of an understanding of world affairs. This volume presents a general outline of the history of Christianity, of its beliefs and practices, and of its major (and of many minor) branches.

The ministry of Jesus of Nazareth seems to have gone largely unnoticed in the early 1st century AD to the world outside what is now Israel and was then occupied by Rome. To his disciples, however, the appearance of Jesus was an extraordinary event of world-transforming significance. Jesus's moral pronouncements about the kingdom of God, his performance of miracles and healings, and his apocalyptic (or, revelatory) pronouncements about the end of time were enough to convince his followers that he was the Christ—from *christos*, the Greek equivalent to the Hebrew term *messiah*, or "anointed")—sent by God to redeem Israel and reinstate its glory and stature. Jesus himself appeared to have

authority from God, whom he called his heavenly Father, and declared that he was coming to "fulfill" the Torah (the Jewish moral teaching, also known as The Law). After his death the gospels, the biblical accounts of his ministry and life, declare that a remarkable thing happened. Three days after his death and interment, the tomb in which Jesus had been laid was empty, and Jesus himself appeared to his disciples. Further, though they do not perfectly agree, the gospels proclaim the resurrected Jesus's imminent return, or Second Coming.

Through the two millennia that followed, those who have proclaimed themselves to be the followers of Jesus's teaching, known as "Christians," have placed tremendous hope in his Resurrection and promised return. Some of these followers have interpreted the resurrection figuratively, placing their hopes in a resurrection or rebirth of the human spirit or of the will and courage to persevere in the midst of suffering. Most others take the Resurrection to be a historical event. To them, Jesus Christ not only was but is both a human and a divine being who conquered death and promised to return to earth to rescue those who believe in him, giving them everlasting life. Despite this disagreement over whether the truth of the Resurrection is figurative or historical, all Christians view Jesus as the saviour either through example or through existence and act.

Members of The Bay Ridge Christian Center Pentecostal Church pray during a two-hour church service on April 10, 2005, in Brooklyn, New York. Robert Nickelsberg/Getty Images

A unique feature of mainstream, orthodox Christianity is the doctrine of the Holy Trinity. Christianity is a monotheistic religion—like Judaism, from which it arose, it holds that there is one supreme God who created and is the Lord of everything. Yet the majority of Christians believe that God works in the world in three persons: the Father, the Son (Jesus), and the Holy Spirit. Each of these three is a distinct entity, a point leading some non-Christians to charge Christianity of being a polytheistic tradition, or one that reveres several or many gods. Even some Christians disagree with the mainstream of Christian tradition on this point, and advocate Unitarianism, or the belief that God is ultimately a single entity. Yet Trinitarian Christians hold that all three members of the Trinity are modes of the one God and are united in the Godhead.

The first two persons of the Trinity receive most of the attention of laypersons and of theologians. God the Father is generally the Creator and giver of life, and specifically the father of Jesus Christ. God the Son is the figure of Jesus not merely as Jesus of Nazareth, the charismatic preacher, healer, and moral reformer—the Son is also the Christ, the anointed, who through the mystery of the Incarnation is both fully human and fully God. Various Christologies (theories about Christ) proclaim different views of resurrection, of salvation, and of the Son's relationship to the Father. Yet a generally held Christian belief is that God became flesh and took on humanity as a means of expiating human sin.

The third person of the Trinity is the Holy Spirit. The origins of the doctrine of the Spirit may be found in Genesis, the first book of the Hebrew Scriptures (which some Christians call the "Old Testament"). In the first verse of Genesis, the Spirit, likened to a wind, moved upon the primordial waters before creation. The Hebrew word *ruach*, which also means "breath," was translated as *pneuma* ("breath" or "spirit") into Greek and as *spiritus* ("spirit" but also implying "breath") into Latin. The Spirit appears many times not only in the Hebrew Bible but also in the Christian Scriptures, or New Testament, particularly in reference to the founding of the church. The Acts of the Apostles portrays the Holy Spirit as descending on Pentecost as a "violent wind" upon the apostles and manifesting as "divided tongues, as of fire," enabling them to speak various languages and spread the Gospel. The Gospel of John describes the Spirit as the Paraclete, or "comforter," whose presence attends to the faithful until the Second Coming.

Conceptions of the Spirit and of his role in Christian life became one of several points of contention among different major branches of the faith, in large part because the conception of the nature and role of the Spirit influences that of the nature and role of the Father and the Son, and thus informs attitudes toward human salvation and the church's role in it. The Nicene Creed, a declaration of the Christian faith upheld by all of the major historical churches, mentions all three persons of the Trinity; however, distinct versions of the creed portray different, conflicting views of the relationship between the persons of the Godhead. The Western churches—whether Catholic or Protestant or independent—contain a clause called the *Filioque*, Latin for "and of the Son," which declares that the Spirit proceeds from both the Father and the Son. The Eastern Orthodox and Oriental Orthodox churches reject the Filioque, believing that it may be interpreted as creating an unnecessary hierarchy within the Godhead by subordinating the Spirit to the Father and the Son.

However they envision God, Christians have many ways of constructing a personal relationship with the divine. Monasticism is one of the oldest institutions of the church, tracing its roots back to the 3rd century. An Egyptian holy man named St. Anthony moved to the desert to live a pious life. More believers followed, and in a relatively short time, monasteries arose as places where Christians devoted their lives to contemplation.

Contemplation of divine works, of the life of Jesus Christ, and of the relationship of the Godhead to creation—and particularly to human life—itself inspired various methods. Christianity arose from Hellenized Judaism, which owed much to the philosophical and theological concepts of the ancient Greco-Roman world. Concepts of the nature of God, of the divine Word (Logos—an untranslatable Greek term meaning such things as "word" and "reason" and "logic" and "order" simultaneously), of the

relationship of the soul to the body, and of the ultimate fate of the soul blended (not always perfectly) with such Israelite beliefs in a personal, national God and, after the mid-1st millennium BC, the resurrection of the body. Neoplatonism, a system of thought whose proponents considered themselves disciples of the Greek thinker Plato, was perhaps the most influential philosophical school on Western and Eastern Orthodox Christianity for much of their first two millennia. It provided a view of the universe in which all creatures were generated by and derived their existence from a perfect, transcendent entity called the One.

Philosophy has therefore been one of the most prominent dimensions of Christian life. The Apostle Paul, who expanded the church in non-Jewish areas of the Roman Empire, was well versed in Stoic philosophy. Justin Martyr, a 2nd-century Christian convert, was famous for his apologies (explanations) of Christian ideas against the critiques of pagan philosophers. St. Anselm of Canterbury emphasized a "faith [that is] seeking understanding." St. Thomas Aquinas synthesized all of the eleven centuries of Christian theology along with Greek thought (largely the writings of Aristotle, which had been preserved by Muslim thinkers) in laying the groundwork for natural theology, or for a way of determining divine truths by arguing from nature to God through the exercise of one's innate reason. The work of the Austrian mathematician and philosopher Ludwig Wittgenstein has invited speculation into the relationship of language and religious belief.

Mysticism is another major aspect of Christianity. Many forms of Christian mysticism are related to and draw from philosophy—Neoplatonism has long held appeal to mystics, particularly because of its emphasis on the aspects of the One that were inaccessible through language and logic. Such a "negative theology," so called because it eschews reason and celebrates the intangible and mysterious, pervades the tradition. The *Confessions* of St. Augustine of Hippo, a former Neoplatonist, speak of his conversion and declare the inscrutability of God's will. The medieval German mystic Johannes Eckhart, more popularly known as Meister Eckhart, promoted an attitude of detachment from the transient, created world and toward the Godhead. Other mystical beliefs include the Quaker "Inner Light," the presence of the Spirit that speaks to each believer in silence.

No introduction to a religious tradition would be complete without a survey of its divisions. A curious trait of Christianity is just how susceptible it has been to divisions, or schisms. The so-called "Great Schism" of 1054, in which the pope and the patriarch of Constantinople excommunicated each other, is one of the two prime examples of schism in Christian history, as it is often viewed through the telescope of history as the final break between Roman Catholicism and Eastern Orthodoxy. The rise of Protestantism in the 15th and 16th century in England and among the Reformers such as Martin Luther and John Calvin is often viewed as the next major schism. Yet schisms have long been a part of Christian history, as one group of believers has endeavoured to have its own interpretation of doctrine as the essence of Christianity. For example, in the wake of the Council of Chalcedon (451), many churches in Egypt, Ethiopia, India, Syria, and Armenia (the first nation to embrace Christianity) that rejected the council's Christological platform, which became orthodoxy in the Catholic and Eastern Orthodox churches, were branded as heretics—the disagreements between the "Chalcedonian" and Oriental Orthodox churches were largely put to rest only in the mid-to-late 20th century.

Even major churches were not always able to maintain a straight house. The Roman Catholic Church is under the temporal jurisdiction of the pope. Several national Eastern European and Middle Eastern churches are under the primacy of the pope but enjoy much ecclesiastical freedom, including the freedom to maintain their own liturgical rites and languages. After the First Vatican Council (1869-70) proclaimed papal infallibility, several churches claiming to better represent Catholic tradition than the mainstream Catholic church did, broke away and formed the Old Catholic church movement. Although they proclaim their Catholic heritage, most in the early 21st century strongly resemble Protestant churches. The Eastern Orthodox churches

cephalous (eccle-
) churches whose
ry primacy to the
Constantinople.
ox churches are
that are united in
h each other—they
s and some, such
thodox Tewahedo
in the past 75 years
ephalocy. Last, but
all of the Protestant
have expanded

exponentially beyond Lutheranism, the Reformed and Presbyterian (Calvinist), and Anglican traditions to include such movements as evangelicalism, fundamentalism, and Pentecostalism (arguably the world's fastest-growing Christian movement).

In short, Christianity has come a long, long way since the ministry of Jesus of Nazareth. The story of how he became revered by many as the Christ, the saviour of humankind, the one God made flesh, is the narrative that drives this book.

CHAPTER 1

THE ESSENCE AND IDENTITY OF CHRISTIANITY

Christianity is at the very least the faith tradition that focuses on the figure of Jesus Christ. In this context, faith refers both to the believers' act of trust and to the content of their belief. As a tradition, Christianity is more than a system of religious belief. It also has generated a culture, a set of ideas and ways of life, practices, and artifacts that have been handed down from generation to generation since Jesus first became the object of faith. Christianity is thus both a living tradition of faith and the culture that the faith leaves behind. The agent of Christianity is the church, the community of people who make up the body of believers.

To say that Christianity "focuses" on Jesus Christ is to say that somehow it brings together its beliefs and practices and other traditions in reference to a historic figure. Few Christians, however, would be content to keep this reference merely historical. The vast majority of Christians focus their faith in Jesus Christ as someone who is also a present reality. They may include many other references in their tradition and thus may speak of "God" and "human nature" or of "church" and "world," but they would not be called Christian if they did not bring their attentions first and last to Jesus Christ.

While there is something simple about this focus on Jesus as the central figure, there is also a complexity that is revealed by the thousands of separate churches, sects, and denominations that make up the modern Christian tradition. To project these separate bodies against the background of their development in the nations of the world is to suggest a bewildering variety. To picture people expressing their adherence to that tradition in their prayer life and church-building, in their quiet worship or their strenuous efforts to change the world, is to suggest even more of that variety.

Given such complexity, it is natural that throughout Christian history both those in the tradition and those surrounding it have made attempts at simplification. Two ways to do this have been to concentrate on the "essence" of

the faith, and thus on the ideas that are integral to it, or to be concerned with the "identity" of the tradition, and thus on the boundaries of its historical experience.

Modern scholars have located the focus of this faith tradition in the context of monotheistic religions. Christianity addresses the historical figure of Jesus Christ against the background of, and while seeking to remain faithful to, the experience of one God. It has consistently rejected polytheism and atheism.

A second element of the faith tradition of Christianity, with rare exceptions, is a plan of salvation or redemption. That is to say, the believers in the church picture themselves as in a plight from

The face of Christ is painted on the ceiling of the 12th century Our Lady of Naya Church in Kfarchleiman, Lebanon. Early Christians transformed a rocky reservoir into this monastic complex. Joseph Eid/AFP/Getty Images

which they need rescue. For whatever reason, they have been distanced from God and need to be saved. Christianity is based on a particular experience or scheme directed to the act of saving—that is, of bringing or "buying back," which is part of what redemption means, these creatures of God to their source in God. The agent of that redemption is Jesus Christ.

It is possible that through the centuries the vast majority of believers have not used the term *essence* to describe the central focus of their faith. The term is itself of Greek origin and thus represents only one part of the tradition, one element in the terms that have gone into making up Christianity. Essence refers to those qualities that give something its identity and are at the centre of what makes that thing different from everything else. To Greek philosophers it meant something intrinsic to and inherent in a thing or category of things, which gave it its character and thus separated it from everything of different character.

If most people are not concerned with defining the essence of Christianity, in practice they must come to terms with what the word *essence* implies. Whether they are engaged in being saved or redeemed on the one hand, or thinking and speaking about that redemption, its agent, and its meaning on the other, they are concentrating on the essence of their experience. Those who have concentrated from within the faith tradition have also helped to give it its identity. It is not possible to speak of the essence of

a historical tradition without referring to how its ideal qualities have been discussed through the ages. Yet one can take up the separate subjects of essence and identity in sequence, being always aware of how they interrelate.

EARLY VIEWS

Jesus and the earliest members of the Christian faith tradition were Jews, and thus they stood in the faith tradition inherited by Hebrew people in Israel and the lands of the Diaspora. They were monotheists devoted to the God of Israel. When they claimed that Jesus was divine, they had to do so in ways that would not challenge monotheism.

Insofar as they began to separate or be separated from Judaism, which did not accept Jesus as the Messiah, the earliest Christians expressed certain ideas about the one on whom their faith focused. As with other religious people, they became involved in a search for truth. God, in the very nature of things, was necessarily the final Truth. In a reference preserved in the Gospel According to John, however, Jesus refers to himself not only as "the way" and "the life" but also as "the Truth." Roughly, this meant "all the reality there is" and was a reference to Jesus's participation in the reality of the one God.

It has been suggested that the best way to preserve the essence of Christianity is to look at the earliest documents—the four Gospels and the letters that make up much of the New Testament—which contain the best account of what the earliest Christians remembered, taught, or believed about Jesus Christ. It is presumed that "the simple Jesus" and the "primitive faith" emerge from these documents as the core of the essence. This view has been challenged, however, by the view that the writings that make up the New Testament themselves reflect Jewish and Greek ways of thinking about Jesus and God. They are seen through the experience of different personalities, such as the apostle Paul or the nameless composers—traditionally identified as Matthew, Mark, Luke, and John—of documents that came to be edited as the Gospels. Indeed, there are not only diverse ways of worship, of polity or governance of the Christian community, and of behaviour pictured or prescribed in the New Testament; there are also diverse theologies, or interpretations of the heart of the faith. Most believers see these diversities as complementing each other and leave to scholars the argument that the primal documents may compete with and even contradict each other. Yet there is a core of ideas that all New Testament scholars and believers would agree are central to ancient Christian beliefs. One British scholar, James G. Dunn, says they would all agree that "the Risen Jesus is the Ascended Lord." In other words, there would have been no faith tradition and no scriptures had not the early believers thought that Jesus was "Risen," raised from the dead, and, as "Ascended," somehow above the ordinary plane of mortal and temporal experience. From that simple assertion

early Christians could begin to complicate the search for essence.

An immediate question was how to combine the essential focus on Jesus with the essential monotheism. At various points in the New Testament and especially in the works of the Apologists, late 1st- and 2nd-century writers who sought to defend and explain the faith to members of Greco-Roman society, Jesus is identified as the "preexistent Logos." That is, before there was a historical Jesus born of Mary and accessible to the sight and touch of Jews and others in his own day, there was a Logos—a principle of reason, an element of ordering, a "word"—that participated in the Godhead and thus existed, but which only preexisted as far as the "incarnate" Logos, the word that took on flesh and humanity (John 1:1–14), was concerned.

In searching for an essence of truth and the way of salvation, some primitive Jewish Christian groups, such as the Ebionites, and occasional theologians in later ages employed a metaphor of adoption. Much as an earthly parent might adopt a child, so the divine parent, the one Jesus called abba (Aramaic: "daddy," or "father"), had adopted him and taken him into the heart of the nature of what it is to be God. There were countless variations of themes such as the preexistent Logos or the concept of adoption, but they provide some sense of the ways the early Apologists carried out their task of contributing to the definition of the essence of their Jesus-focused yet monotheistic faith.

LOGOS

The word Logos (Greek: "word," "reason," or "plan") indicates the divine reason implicit in the cosmos, ordering it and giving it form and meaning. It became particularly significant in Christian writings and doctrines to describe or define the role of Jesus Christ as the principle of God active in the creation and the continuous structuring of the cosmos and in revealing the divine plan of salvation to humankind. It thus underlies the basic Christian doctrine of the pre-existence of Jesus.

The idea of the logos in Greek thought harks back at least to the 6th-century-BC philosopher Heracleitus, who discerned in the cosmic process a logos analogous to human reason. Later, the Stoics, philosophers who followed the teachings of the thinker Zeno of Citium (4th–3rd century BC), defined the logos as an active rational and spiritual principle that permeated all reality. They called the logos providence, nature, God, and the soul of the universe, which is composed of many seminal logoi that are contained in the universal logos. Philo of Alexandria, a 1st-century-AD Jewish philosopher, taught that

"Jesus Before the Gates of Jerusalem," manuscript illumination by Liberale da Verona, 1470-74; in the Piccolomini Library, Siena, Italy. SCALA/Art Resource, New York

the logos was the intermediary between God and the cosmos, being both the agent of creation and the agent through which the human mind can apprehend and comprehend God. According to Philo and the Middle Platonists, philosophers who interpreted in religious terms the teachings of the 4th-century-BC Greek master philosopher Plato, the logos was both immanent in the world and at the same time the transcendent divine mind.

In the first chapter of The Gospel According to John, Jesus Christ is identified as "the Word" (Greek logos) incarnated, or made flesh. This identification of Jesus with the logos is based on Hebrew Bible concepts of revelation, such as occurs in the frequently used phrase "the Word of the Lord"—which connoted ideas of God's activity and power—and the Jewish view that Wisdom is the divine agent that draws humanity to God and is identified with the word of God. The author of The Gospel According to John used this philosophical expression, which easily would be recognizable to readers in the Hellenistic world, to emphasize the redemptive character of the person of Christ, whom the author describes as "the way, and the truth, and the life." Just as Jews had viewed the Torah as preexistent with God, so also the author of John viewed Jesus, but Jesus came to be regarded as the personified source of life and illumination of mankind. John interprets the logos as inseparable from the person of Jesus and does not simply imply that the logos is the revelation that Jesus proclaims.

The identification of Jesus with the logos was further developed in the early church but more on the basis of Greek philosophical ideas. This development was dictated by attempts made by early Christian theologians and apologists to express the Christian faith in terms that would be intelligible to the Hellenistic world and to impress their hearers with the view that Christianity was superior to, or heir to, all that was best in pagan philosophy. Thus, in their apologies and polemical works, the early Christian Fathers stated that Christ as the preexistent logos (1) reveals the Father to mankind and is the subject of the Old Testament manifestations of God; (2) is the divine reason in which the whole human race shares, so that the 6th-century-BC philosopher and others who lived with reason were Christians before Christ; and (3) is the divine will and word by which the worlds were framed.

While it is easier to point to diversity than to simplicity or clarity among those who early expressed faith, it must also be said that from the beginning the believers insisted that they were united in their devotion to the essence of their faith tradition. In their eyes, there could not have been many final truths, and there were not many legitimate ways of salvation. It was of the essence of their tradition to reject other gods and other ways, and most defining of essence and identity occurred as one set of Christians was concerned lest others might deviate from the essential faith and might, for example, be attracted to other gods or other ways.

While Jesus lived among his disciples and those who ignored or rejected him, to make him the focus of faith or denial presented one type of issue. After the "Risen Jesus" had become the "Ascended Lord" and was no longer a visible physical presence, those at the head of the tradition had a different problem. Jesus remained a present reality to them,

and when they gathered to worship they believed that he was "in the midst of them." He was present in their minds and hearts, in the spoken word that testified to him, and also in some form when they had their sacred meal and ingested bread and wine as his "body and blood." They created a reality around this experience.

The search for the essence of Christianity led people in the Greek world to concentrate on ideas. The focus on Jesus narrowed to ideas, to "beliefs about" and not only "belief in," and to doctrines. The essence began to be cognitive—referring to what was known—or substantive. As debates over the cognitive or substantive aspects of Jesus's participation in God became both intense and refined, the pursuit of essences became almost a matter of competition in the minds of the Apologists and the formulators of doctrines in the 3rd through the 6th centuries. During this time Christians met in council to develop statements of faith, confessions, and creeds. The claimed essence was used in conflict and rivalry with others. Christian Apologists began to speak, both to the Jews and to the other members of the Greco-Roman world, in terms that unfavourably compared their religions to Christianity. The essence also came to be a way to define who had the best credentials and was most faithful. The claim that one had discerned the essence of Christianity could be used to rule out the faithless, the apostate, or the heretic. The believers in the essential truth and way of salvation saw themselves as insiders and others as outsiders. This concept became important after the Christian movement had triumphed in the Roman Empire, which became officially Christian by the late 4th century. To fail to grasp or to misconceive what was believed to be the essence of faith might mean exile, harassment, or even death.

In the early stages of the development of their faith, Christians did something rare if not unique in the history of religion: they adopted the entire scriptural canon of what they now saw to be another faith, Judaism, and embraced the Hebrew Scriptures, which they called the Old Testament. But while doing so, they also incorporated the insistent monotheism of Judaism as part of the essence of their truth and way of salvation, just as they incorporated the Hebrew Scriptures' story as part of their own identity-giving narrative and experience.

This narrowing of focus on Jesus Christ as truth meant also a complementary sharpening of focus on the way of salvation. There is no purpose in saving someone who does not need salvation. Christianity therefore began to make, through its councils and creeds, theologians and scholars, some attempts at definitive descriptions of what it is to be human. Later some of these descriptions were called "original sin," the idea that all humans somehow inherited from Adam, the first-created human, a condition that made it impossible for them to be perfect or to please a personal God on their own. While Christians never agreed on a specific teaching on original sin, they did describe as the essence of Christianity the fact that something limited humans and led them to need redemption. Yet the concentration always returned to Jesus Christ as belonging more to the essence of Christianity than did any statements about the human condition.

The essence of Christianity eventually included statements about the reality to God. Christians inherited from Judaism a relatively intimate picture of a God who made their young and small universe and then carried on discourse with humans, making covenants with them and rewarding or punishing them. But the Greek part of their tradition contributed the concept of a God who was greater than any ideas of God but who had to be addressed through ideas. Indeed, it was during this time that words such as *essence, substance,* and *being*— terms that did not belong to the Hebrew Bible or New Testament traditions—came to be wedded to biblical witness in the creeds. Christians used the vocabulary and repertory of options then available to them in speaking of the all-encompassing and the ineffable and grafted these onto the witness to God that was essential to their faith.

MEDIEVAL AND REFORMATION VIEWS

For a thousand years, the essence of Christian faith was guarded differently than it had been in the first three centuries, before Christianity became official. Throughout the Middle Ages the understanding of the essence evolved. In the 4th and 5th centuries, theologians including Ambrose, Augustine of Hippo, and Jerome laid the foundations for the development of Christian thought. By the 5th century, the bishop of Rome, the pope, as a result of conciliar decisions and unique events in Rome, had become the leading spokesman for the faith in Latin, or Western, Christendom. This position would assume greater institutional strength in later periods of the Middle Ages. In the Eastern churches, despite the claims of the patriarch of Constantinople, no single pontiff ruled over the bishops, but they saw themselves just as surely and energetically in command of the doctrines that constituted the essence of Christianity.

The Western drama, especially after the year 1000, was more fateful for Christianity in the modern world. The pope and the bishops of Latin Christendom progressively determined the essence through doctrines and canons that enhanced the ancient grasp of faith. As they came to dominate in Europe, they sought to suppress contrary understandings of the essence of the faith. In the 14th and 15th centuries, Jews were confined to ghettos, segregated and self-segregated enclaves where they did not and could not share the full prerogatives of Christendom. When sects were defined as heretical—Waldenses, Cathari, and others—because of their repudiation of Roman Catholic concepts of Christian essence, they had to go into hiding or were pushed into enclaves beyond the reach of the custodians of official teaching. The essence of Christianity had become a set of doctrines and laws articulated and controlled by a hierarchy that saw those doctrines as a divine deposit of truth. Theologians might argue about the articulations with great subtlety and intensity, but in that millennium few would have chosen to engage in basic disagreement over the official teachings, all of which were seen to be corollaries of the basic faith in Jesus Christ as participating in the truth of God and providing the way of salvation.

Through these centuries there was also increasing differentiation between the official clergy, which administered the sacraments and oversaw the body of the faithful, and the laity. Most of what was debated centuries later about the essence of medieval Christianity came from the records of these authorities.

As more is learned about the faith of the ordinary believers, it becomes more evident in the records of social history that people offered countless variations on the essence of the faith. Many people used the church's officially legitimated faith in the power of saints' relics to develop patterns of dealing with God that, according to the Protestant Reformers, detracted from the uniqueness of Jesus Christ as the only agent of salvation.

During this thousand years in both Western and Eastern Christianity, when the faith had a cultural monopoly, there was an outburst of creativity and a fashioning of a Christian culture that greatly enhanced and complicated any once-simple notions of an essence. Christianity was as much a cultural tradition as it was a faith tradition, an assertion that the leadership of the medieval church would not have regarded as diminishing or insulting. Christianity as a cultural tradition is perhaps most vividly revealed in the magnificent cathedrals and churches that were built in the Middle Ages and in the illuminated manuscripts of the period.

As Christian culture grew ever more complex, however, there arose a constant stream of individual reformers who tried to get back to what they thought was its

Girolamo Savonarola preaching to a crowd in Florence, Italy. Kean Collection/Archive Photos/ Getty Images

original essence. Among these was St. Francis of Assisi, who in his personal style of devotion and simple way of life was often seen as capturing in his person and teachings more of the original essence of Jesus's truth and way of salvation than did the ordained authorities in the church and empires. Unlike the Waldenses and members of other dissident groups, Francis accepted the authority of the ordained clergy and contributed to a reform and revival of the broader church.

In the late Middle Ages a number of dissenters emerged—such as Jan Hus in Bohemia, John Wycliffe in England, and Girolamo Savonarola in Florence—who challenged the teachings of the church in more radical ways than someone like St. Francis did. For all their differences, they were united in their critique of what they thought complicated the essence of Christianity. On biblical prophetic grounds they sought simplicity in the cognitive, moral, and devotional life of Christianity.

When the Protestant Reformation divided Western Christianity—as Eastern Christians, already separated since the 11th century, looked on—the 16th-century European world experienced a foretaste of the infinite Christian variety to come. The reforms that gave rise to the many Protestant bodies—Lutheran, Anglican, Presbyterian, Reformed, Anabaptist, Quaker, and others—were themselves debates over the essence of Christianity. Taken together, they made it increasingly difficult for any one to claim a monopoly on the custodianship of that essence, try as they might. Each new sect offered a partial discernment of a different essence or way of speaking of it, even if the vast majority of Protestants agreed that the essence could be retrieved best, or, indeed uniquely, through recovery of the central message of the Holy Scriptures.

After the ferment of the Reformation, most of the dissenting groups found it necessary, as they established themselves in various nations, to engage in their own narrowing of focus, rendering of precise doctrines, and understanding of divine truth and the way of salvation. Within a century theologians at many Protestant universities were adopting systems that paralleled the old scholasticisms against which some reformers had railed. Those who had once thought that definition of doctrine failed to capture the essence of Christianity were now defining their concept of the essence in doctrinal terms.

The belief that there is a faith that has been held by everyone, always, and everywhere lived on through the proliferation of Protestant denominations and Roman Catholic movements and, in sophisticated ways, has helped animate the modern ecumenical movement. Thus some have spoken of that movement as a reunion of churches—an idea that carries an implication that they had once been "one"—and a further hint that one included an essence on which people agreed. Reunion would therefore entail a stripping away of accretions, a reducing of the number of arguments, and a refocusing on essentials.

MODERN VIEWS

The modern church and world brought new difficulties to the quest for defining an essence of Christianity. Both as a result of Renaissance humanism, which gloried in human achievement and encouraged human autonomy, and of Reformation ideas that believers were responsible in conscience and reason for their faith, an autonomy in expressing faith developed. Some spoke of Protestantism as being devoted to the right of private judgment. Roman Catholics warned that believers who did not submit to church authority would issue as many concepts of essence as there were believers to make the claims.

In the 18th century the Western philosophical movement called the Enlightenment further obscured searches for the essence of Christianity. The Enlightenment proclaimed optimistic views of human reach and perfectibility that challenged formerly essential Christian views of human limits. The deity became a benevolent if impersonal force, not an agent that arranged a way of salvation to people in need of rescue. The Enlightenment also urged a view of human autonomy and of the use of reason in a search for truth. But, in the view of Enlightenment thinkers, reason did not need to be responsive to supernatural revelation, as contained in the Old and New Testaments. Indeed, reason questioned the integrity of those scriptures themselves through methods of historical and literary criticism. No longer should one rely on the word of priests who passed on notions of essential Christianity.

While many Westerners moved out of the orbit of faith as a result of the Enlightenment and the rise of criticism, many others—in Germany, France, England, Scotland, and, eventually, the Americas—remained Christians, people of faith if now of faith differently expressed. Some Christians, the Unitarians, rejected the ideas of both a preexistent Logos made incarnate in Christ and a Jesus adopted into Godhead. Jesus was seen as the great teacher or exemplar. They thus also tested the boundaries of essential teaching about a way of salvation. Meanwhile, Deist Christianity was at heart a view of God that remained "mono-" in that it was devoted to a single principle. Yet as "deist" instead of "theist" it departed from the ancient picture of a personal God engaged in human affairs.

In the 19th century philosophical and historical criticism inspired some Christians to renew the search for essences. For example, in the wake of the German Idealist philosopher G.W.F. Hegel, so-called "Hegelian" thinkers tried to rescue Christianity by viewing it as an unfolding of "absolute spirit." They followed Christian history through a constant dialectic, a series of forces and counterforces producing new syntheses. A problem with the Hegelian approach arose as the historical Jesus came to be seen merely as one stage in the unfolding of absolute spirit; he was not a decisive agent of the way of salvation "once for

Georg Wilhelm Friedrich Hegel. Spencer Arnold/Hulton Archive/Getty Images

all," as the biblical Letter to the Hebrews had claimed him to be.

Soon biblical scholars such as David Friedrich Strauss were speaking of the historical Jesus as a myth of a certain set of people in one moment of the dialectical unfolding. The Christian faith itself began to dissolve, and many Hegelians began to reject the God of the Christian faith along with the historical Jesus.

Another group of 19th-century theologians took the opposite course. In the spirit of the 18th-century German philosopher Immanuel Kant, these neo-Kantians spoke not of the noumenal world, the unseen realm of essences beyond visible reality, but of the phenomenal realm, the world of history in which things happened. Theologians in this school engaged in a century-long "quest for the historical Jesus," in which they sought the simple essence of Christianity. Significantly, the greatest exemplar of this historical tradition, the German theologian Adolf von Harnack, wrote one of the best-known modern books on the essence of Christianity, *Das Wesen des Christentums* (1900; *What Is Christianity?*). The call had come to purge Christianity of what Harnack called traces of "acute Hellenization," of the Greek ideas of essence, substance, and being that were introduced into the Christian tradition in its early history. The focus shifted to the Fatherhood of God and the announcement of the Kingdom, as Jesus had proclaimed in the Gospels. While this approach matched the thirst for simplification in the minds of many of the Christian faithful, it also diminished the concept of God. The result was a form of Christian humanism that more traditional Christians regarded as a departure from the essence of Christianity. This view claimed to be based on the historical Jesus, but scholars could not agree on the details.

Throughout the modern period some thinkers took another route toward expressing the essence of Christianity. The notion that the theologians would never find the essence of Christianity grew among German Pietists, among the followers of John Wesley into Methodism, and in any number of Roman Catholic or Protestant devotional movements. Instead, according to these groups, the Christian essence was discernible in acts of piety, closeness to the fatherly heart of God as shown in the life of Jesus, and intimate communion with God on emotional or affective—not cognitive, rational, or substantial (i.e., doctrinal)—grounds. Although these pietisms have been immensely satisfying to millions of modern believers, they have been handicapped in the intellectual arena when pressed for the definitions people need in a world of choice.

Some modern Christians have shifted the topic from the essence of Christianity to its absoluteness among the religions. They have been moved by what the Germans called *Religionswissenschaft*, the study of world religions. In that school, the focus fell on the sacred, what the German theologian Rudolf Otto called "the idea of the Holy." On those terms, as the German scholar Ernst Troeltsch showed, it was more difficult to speak of the "absoluteness" of Christianity and its truth; one had to speak of it on comparative terms. Yet some early 20th-century comparativists, such as the Swedish Lutheran archbishop Nathan Söderblom, applied their understanding of the study of religion to help animate the movement for Christian reunion.

The modern ecumenical movement is based upon the belief that the church has different cultural expressions that must be honoured and differing confessional or doctrinal traditions designed to express the essential faith. These traditions demand criticism, comparison, and perhaps revision, with some possible blending toward greater consensus in the future. At the same time, supporters of the movement have shown that, among Christians of good will, elaborations of what constitutes the essence of Christianity are as confusing as they are inevitable and necessary.

Despite this confusion, the ecumenical movement was an important development in the 20th century. It took institutional form in the World Council of Churches in 1948, which was composed of Protestant and Eastern Orthodox churches. The World Council emerged out of two organizations that offered distinct approaches to the essential concepts of the faith. One approach was devoted first to "Life and Work," a view that the essentials of Christianity could be best found and expressed when people followed the way or did the works of Christ, since this constituted his essence. The other approach, concerned with "Faith and Order," stressed the need for comparative study of doctrine, with critical devotion to the search for what was central. By no means did these groups cling any longer to the notion that when they found unity they would have found a simple essence of Christianity. Yet they believed that they could find compatible elements that would help to sustain them on the never-ending search for what was central to the faith tradition.

Some modern scholars—for example, the British theologian John Hick—viewing the chaos of languages dealing with the essentials of the faith and the complex of historical arguments, pose the understanding of the essence in the future. They speak of "eschatological verification," referring to the end, the time beyond history, or the time of fulfillment. In that future, one might say, it will have become possible to assess the claims of faith. Theologians of these schools argue that such futuristic notions motivate Christians and the scholars among them to clarify their language, refine their historical understandings, and focus their devotion and spirituality.

THE QUESTION OF CHRISTIAN IDENTITY

These comments on the search for the essence of Christianity, the task of defining the core of the faith tradition, demonstrate that the question of Christian identity is at stake at all times. In the midst of change, Christians strive to have some "inner sameness and continuity" through the focus on Jesus Christ and the way of salvation. At the same time, Christians posit that this identity will be discoverable by and useful to those who are not part of the tradition: secularists, Buddhists, Communists, or other people who parallel or rival Christian claims about truth and salvation.

It is necessary for the scholar to put his own truth claims in a kind of suspension and to record faithfully, sorting out large schools of coherence and pointing to major strains. It is not difficult to state that something was a majority view if the supporting data are present. For example, it is not difficult to say what Roman Catholics at particular times have regarded as the essence of Christianity or what the various Protestant confessions regard as the true way of salvation. It remains safe to say that Christian identity begins and ends with a reference to Jesus in relation to God's truth and a way of salvation.

CHAPTER 2

CHRISTIAN HISTORY

Christianity began as a movement within Judaism at a period when Jews had long been dominated culturally and politically by foreign powers and had found in their religion (rather than in their politics or cultural achievements) the linchpin of their community. From Amos (8th century BC) onward the religion of Israel was marked by tension between the concept of monotheism, with its universal ideal of salvation (for all nations), and the notion of God's special choice of Israel. In the Hellenistic age (323 BC–3rd century AD), the dispersion of Jews throughout the kingdoms of the eastern Mediterranean and the Roman Empire reinforced this universalistic tendency. But the attempts of foreign rulers, especially the Syrian king Antiochus IV Epiphanes (in 168–165 BC), to impose Greek culture in Palestine provoked zealous resistance on the part of many Jews, leading to the revolt of Judas Maccabeus against Antiochus. In Palestinian Judaism the predominant note was separation and exclusiveness. Jewish missionaries to other areas were strictly expected to impose the distinctive Jewish customs of circumcision, kosher food, and sabbaths and other festivals. Other Jews, however, were not so exclusive, welcoming Greek culture and accepting converts without requiring circumcision.

THE EARLY CHURCH

The relationship of the earliest Christian churches to Hellenistic Judaism turned principally on two questions: (1)

the messianic role of Jesus of Nazareth and (2) the permanent validity of the Mosaic (Jewish) Law for all. Note that some of the issues and controversies covered in this chapter will appear in greater depth later in this book.

THE RELATION OF THE EARLY CHURCH TO LATE JUDAISM

The Hebrew Scriptures viewed history as the stage of a providential drama eventually ending in a triumph of God over all present sources of frustration (e.g., foreign domination or the sins of Israel). God's rule would be established by an anointed prince (the Messiah) of the line of David, king of Israel in the 10th century BC. The proper course of action leading to the consummation of the drama, however, was the subject of some disagreement. Among the diverse groups were the aristocratic and conservative Sadducees, who accepted only the five books of Moses (the Pentateuch) and whose lives and political power were intimately associated with Temple worship, and the Pharisees, who accepted the force of oral tradition and were widely respected for their learning and piety. The Pharisees not only accepted biblical books outside the Pentateuch but also embraced doctrines—such as those on resurrection and the existence of angels— of recent acceptance in Judaism, many of which were derived from apocalyptic expectations that the consummation of history would be heralded by God's intervention in the affairs of men in dramatic,

Moses expounding the law, illuminated manuscript page from the Bury Bible, about 1130. In Corpus Christi College, Cambridge. Courtesy of the Master and Fellows of Corpus Christi College, Cambridge

cataclysmic terms. The Sanhedrin (central council) at Jerusalem was made up of both Pharisees and Sadducees. The Zealots were aggressive revolutionaries known for their violent opposition to Rome and its polytheisms. Other groups were the Herodians, supporters of the client kingdom of the Herods (a dynasty that supported Rome) and abhorrent to the Zealots, and the Essenes, a quasi-monastic dissident group, probably including the sect that preserved the Dead Sea Scrolls. This latter sect did not participate in the Temple worship at Jerusalem and observed another religious calendar; from their desert retreat they awaited divine intervention and searched prophetic writings for signs indicating the consummation.

What relation the followers of Jesus had to some of these groups is not clear. In the canonical Gospels (those accepted as authentic by the church) the main targets of criticism are the scribes and Pharisees, whose attachment to the tradition of Judaism is presented as legalistic and pettifogging. The Sadducees and Herodians likewise receive an unfriendly portrait. The Essenes are never mentioned. Simon, one of Jesus's 12 disciples, was or had once been a Zealot. Jesus probably stood close to the Pharisees.

Under the social and political conditions of the time, there could be no long future either for the Sadducees or for the Zealots: their attempts to make apocalyptic dreams effective led to the desolation of Judaea and the destruction of the Temple after the two major Jewish revolts against the Romans in 66–70 and 132–135. The choice for many Jews, who were barred from Jerusalem after 135, thus lay between the Pharisees and the emerging Christian movement. Pharisaism as enshrined in the Mishna (oral law) and the Talmud (commentary on and addition to the oral law) became normative Judaism. By looking to the Gentile (non-Jewish) world and carefully dissociating itself from the Zealot revolutionaries and the Pharisees, Christianity made possible its ideal of a world religion, at the price of sacrificing Jewish particularity and exclusiveness. The fact that Christianity has never succeeded in gaining the allegiance of more than a small minority of Jews is more a mystery to theologians than to historians.

THE RELATION OF THE EARLY CHURCH TO THE CAREER AND INTENTIONS OF JESUS

The prime sources for knowledge of Jesus of Nazareth are the four canonical Gospels in the New Testament. There are also a number of noncanonical sources, notably the apocryphal gospels, which contain stories about Jesus and sayings attributed to him. The *Gospel of Thomas*, preserved and found about 1945 in Egypt, contains several such sayings, besides some independent versions of canonical sayings. At certain points the Gospel tradition finds independent confirmation in the letters of the apostle Paul. Although the allusions in non-Christian sources (the Jewish historian Josephus, the Roman historians Tacitus and Suetonius, and Talmudic texts) are almost negligible, they refute the unsubstantiated notion that Jesus might never have existed.

The chronology of the life of Jesus is one of the matters of uncertainty. Matthew places the birth of Jesus at least two years before Herod the Great's death late in 5 BC or early in 4 BC. Luke connects Jesus's birth with a Roman census that, according to Josephus, occurred in

SYNOPTIC GOSPELS

Since the 1780s the first three books of the New Testament—the Gospels According to Matthew, Mark, and Luke—have been called the Synoptic Gospels because they are so similar in structure, content, and wording that they can easily be set side by side to provide a synoptic comparison of their content. The Gospel of John has a slightly alternate arrangement of pattern and content and offers a somewhat different perspective on the ministry and significance of Jesus Christ. It appears richer in theological interpretation but may also preserve good historical information. The striking similarities between the first three Gospels prompt questions regarding the actual literary relationship that exists between them. Mark was probably used by Matthew and Luke, who may also have used the Q Gospel (so-called from the German Quelle, "source"; Q is the hypothetical Gospel that is the origin of common material in later Gospels). This question, called the Synoptic problem, has been elaborately studied in modern times.

The Gospels are not detached reports but were written to serve the religious needs of the early Christian communities. Legendary and

St. Mark, illuminated manuscript page from the Gospel Book of the Court School of Charlemagne, c. 810. Stadtbibliothek, Trier, Ger.

apologetic (defensive) motifs, and the various preoccupations of the communities for which they were first produced, can readily be discerned as influences upon their narratives. Although many details of the Gospels remain the subject of disagreement and uncertainty, the scholarly consensus accepts the substance of the Gospel tradition as a truthful account.

AD 6–7 and caused a revolt against the governor Quirinius. Luke could be right about the census and wrong about the governor. The crucifixion under Pontius Pilate, prefect of Judaea (AD 26–36), was probably about the year 29–30, but again certainty is impossible.

Jesus's encounter with John the Baptist, the ascetic in the Judaean Desert who preached repentance and baptism in view of God's coming Kingdom, marked a decisive moment for his career. He recognized in John the forerunner of the kingdom that his own ministry proclaimed. The first preaching of Jesus, in his home region of Galilee, took the form of vivid parables and was accompanied by miraculous healings. The Synoptic writers describe a single climactic visit of Jesus to Jerusalem at the end of his career; but John may be right (implicitly supported by Luke 13:7) in representing his visits as more frequent and the period of ministry as lasting more than a single year. Jesus's attitude to the observance of the law generated conflict with the Pharisees; he also aroused the fear and hostility of the ruling Jewish authorities. A triumphal entry to Jerusalem at Passover time (the period celebrating the Exodus of the Hebrews from Egypt in the 13th century BC) was the prelude to a final crisis. After a last supper with his disciples he was betrayed by one of them, Judas Iscariot. Arrest and trial followed, first before the Sanhedrin and then before Pilate, who condemned him to crucifixion. According to the Evangelists, Pilate condemned Jesus reluctantly, finding no fault in him. Their version of the condemnation was an attempt to keep Jesus from appearing guilty in Roman eyes, and it was a means for the early Christian community to find its way in the Roman world. In any event, Jesus was executed in a manner reserved for political or religious agitators. It was a universal Christian belief that three days after his death he was raised from the dead by divine power.

Jesus preached the imminent presence of God's Kingdom, in some texts as future consummation, in others as already present. The words and acts of Jesus were believed to be the inauguration of a process that was to culminate in a final triumph of God. His disciples recognized him as the Messiah, the Anointed One, though there is no record of him using the word (except indirectly) in reference to himself. The titles Prophet and Rabbi also were applied to him. His own enigmatic self-designation was "Son of man," sometimes in allusion to his suffering, sometimes to his future role as judge. This title is derived from the version of the Book of Daniel (7:13), where "one like a son of man," contrasted with beast figures, represents the humiliated people of God, ascending to be vindicated by the divine Judge. In the developed Gospel tradition the theme of the transcendent judge seems to be most prominent.

Apocalyptic hope could easily merge into messianic zealotry. Moreover, Jesus's teaching was critical of the established order and encouraged the poor and oppressed, even though it contained an implicit rejection of revolution. Violence was viewed as incompatible with the ethic of the Kingdom of God. Whatever contacts there may have been with the Zealot movement (as the narrative of feeding 5,000 people in the desert may hint), the Gospels assume the widest distance between Jesus's understanding of his role and the Zealot revolution.

With this distance from revolutionary idealism goes a sombre estimate of human perfectibility. The gospel of repentance presupposes deep defilement in individuals and in society. The sufferings and pains of humanity under the power of evil spirits calls out for compassion and an urgent mission. All the acts of a disciple must express love and forgiveness, even to enemies, and also detachment from property and worldly wealth. To Jesus, the outcasts of society (prostitutes, the hated and oppressive tax agents, and others) were objects of special care, and censoriousness was no virtue. Though the state is regarded as a distant entity in certain respects, it yet has the right to require taxes and civic obligations: Caesar has rights that must be respected and are not incompatible with the fulfillment of God's demands.

Some of the futurist sayings, if taken by themselves, raise the question whether Jesus intended to found a church. A negative answer emerges only if the authentic Jesus is assumed to have expected an immediate catastrophic intervention by God. There is no doubt that he gathered and intended to gather around him a community of followers. This community continued after his time, regarding itself as the specially called congregation of God's people, possessing as covenant signs the rites of baptism and Eucharist (Lord's Supper) with which Jesus was particularly associated—baptism because of his example, Eucharist because the Last Supper on the night before the crucifixion was marked as an anticipation of the messianic feast of the coming age.

A closely related question is whether Jesus intended his gospel to be addressed to Jews only or if the Gentiles were also to be included. In the Gospels Gentiles appear as isolated exceptions, and the choice of 12 Apostles has an evident symbolic relation to the 12 tribes of Israel. The fact that the extension of Christian preaching to the Gentiles caused intense debate in the 40s of the 1st century is decisive proof that Jesus had given no unambiguous directive on the matter. Gospel sayings that make Jews' refusal to recognize Jesus's authority as the ground for extending the Kingdom of God to the Gentiles must, therefore, have been cast by the early community.

THE GENTILE MISSION AND ST. PAUL

Saul, or Paul (as he was later called), was a Pharisee who persecuted the primitive church. Born at Tarsus (Asia Minor), he had come to Jerusalem as a student of the famous Rabbi Gamaliel and had harried a Christian group called by Luke the "Hellenists," who were led by Stephen (the first Christian martyr) and who regarded Jesus as a spiritual reformer sent to purge the corrupt worship of Jerusalem. While on a mission to Damascus to persecute the followers of Jesus, Paul was suddenly converted to faith in Christ and, simultaneously, to a conviction that the Gospel must pass to the non-Jewish world under conditions that dispensed with exclusively and distinctively Jewish ceremonies. Paul was disapproved by Christian Jews and remained throughout his career a controversial figure. He gained recognition for the converts of the Gentile mission by the Christian community in Jerusalem; but his work was considered an affront to Jewish traditionalism. He saw clearly that the universal mission of the church to all humanity, implicit in the coming of the Messiah, or Christ, meant a radical break with rabbinical traditions.

Owing to the preservation of some weighty letters, Paul is the only vivid figure of the apostolic age (1st century AD). Like his elder contemporary Philo of Alexandria, also a Hellenized Jew of the dispersion, he interpreted the Hebrew Bible allegorically and affirmed the primacy of spirit over letter in a manner that was in line with Jesus's freedom with regard to the sabbath. The crucifixion of Jesus he viewed as the supreme redemptive act and also as the means of expiation for the sin of mankind. Salvation is, in Paul's thought, therefore, not found by a conscientious moralism but rather is a gift of grace, a doctrine in which Paul was anticipated by Philo. But Paul linked this doctrine with his theme that the Gospel represents liberation from the Mosaic Law. The latter thesis created difficulties at Jerusalem, where the Christian community was led by James, the brother of Jesus, and the circle of the intimate disciples of Jesus. James, martyred at Jerusalem in 62, was the primary authority for the Christian Jews, especially those made anxious by Paul; the canonical letter ascribed to James opposes the antinomian (anti-law) interpretations of the doctrine of justification by faith. A middle position seems to have been occupied by Peter. All the Gospels record a special commission of Jesus to Peter as the leader among the 12 Apostles. But Peter's biography can only be dimly constructed. According to early tradition, he died in Rome in Nero's persecution (64) about the same time as Paul.

The supremacy of the Gentile mission within the church was ensured by the effects on Jewish Christianity of the fall of Jerusalem (70) and Hadrian's exclusion of all Jews from the city (135). Jewish Christianity declined and became the faith of a very small group without links to either synagogue or Gentile church. Some bore the title Ebionites, "the poor" (compare Matthew 5:3), and did not accept the tradition that Jesus was born of a virgin.

In Paul's theology, the human achievement of Jesus was important because his obedient fidelity to his vocation gave moral and redemptive value to his self-sacrifice. A different emphasis appears in The Gospel According to John, written (according to 2nd-century tradition) at Ephesus. John's Gospel partly reflects local disputes, not only between the church and the Hellenized synagogue but also between various Christian groups. John's special individuality lies in his view of the relation between the historical events of the tradition and the Christian community's present experience of redemption. The history is treated symbolically to provide a vehicle for faith. John's conception of the preexistent Logos being made flesh in Jesus, because it is less attached to the contingent events of a particular man's life, made Jesus's universal significance intelligible to the Hellenistic world. In antiquity, divine presence had to be understood as either inspiration or incarnation. If the Synoptic Gospels suggest inspiration, The Gospel According to John chooses incarnation. The tension between these two types of Christology, or doctrines of Christ, first became acute in the debate between the schools of Antioch and Alexandria in the late 4th century.

THE CONTEMPORARY SOCIAL, RELIGIOUS, AND INTELLECTUAL WORLD

Many Palestinian Jews appreciated the benefits of Roman rule in guaranteeing peace and order. The Roman government tolerated regional and local religious groups and found it convenient to control Palestine through client kings like the Herods. The demand that divine honours be paid not only to the traditional Roman or similar gods but also to the emperors was not extended to Judaea except under the emperor Caligula (reigned 37–41), whose early death prevented desecration of Jerusalem's holy sites and social unrest. It was enough that Jews dedicated temple sacrifices and synagogues in the emperor's honour. The privileges of Roman citizenship were possessed by some Jewish families, including that of the apostle Paul.

In his letter to the Romans, Paul affirmed the providential role of government in restraining evil. Christians did not need to be disaffected from the empire, though the deification of the emperor was offensive to them. Moreover, although as an agency of social welfare the church offered much to the downtrodden elements in society, the Christians did not at any stage represent a social and political threat. After the example of their master, the Christians encouraged humility and patience before wicked men. Even the institution of slavery was not the subject of fundamental Christian criticism before the 4th century. The church, however, was not lost in pious mysticism. It provided for far more than the cultic (liturgical) needs of its members. Inheriting a Jewish moral ideal, its activities included food for the poor, orphans, and foundlings; care for prisoners; and a community funeral service.

Christianity also inherited from Judaism a strong sense of being holy, separate from idolatry and pagan eroticism. As polytheism permeated ancient society, a moral rigorism severely limited Christian participation in some trades and professions. At baptism a Christian was expected to renounce his occupation if that implicated him in public or private compromise with polytheism, superstition, dishonesty, or vice. There was disagreement about military service, however. The majority held that a soldier, if converted and baptized, was not required to leave the army, but there was hesitation about whether an already baptized Christian might properly enlist. Strict Christians also thought poorly of the teaching profession because it involved instructing the young in literature replete with pagan ideals and what was viewed as indecency. Acting and dancing were similarly suspect occupations, and any involvement in magic was completely forbidden.

The Christian ethic therefore demanded some detachment from society, which in some cases made for economic difficulties. The structure of ancient society was dominated not by class but by the relationship of patron and client. A slave or freedman depended for his livelihood and prospects upon his patron, and a man's power in society was reflected in the extent of his dependents and supporters. In antiquity a strong patron was indispensable if one was negotiating with police or tax authorities or law courts or if one had ambitions in the imperial service. The authority of the father of the family was considerable. Often, Christianity penetrated the social strata first through women and children, especially in the upper classes. But once the householder was a Christian, his dependents tended to follow. The Christian community itself was close-knit. Third-century evidence portrays Christians banking their money with fellow believers; and widely separated groups helped one another with trade and mutual assistance.

Women in ancient society—Greek, Roman, or Jewish—had a domestic, not a public, role; feminine subordination was self-evident. To Paul, however, Christian faith transcends barriers to make all free and equal (Galatians 3:28). Of all ancient writers Paul was the most powerful spokesman for equality. Nevertheless, just as he refused to harbour a runaway slave, so he opposed any practice that would identify the church with social radicalism (a principal pagan charge against it). Paul did not avoid self-contradiction (1 Corinthians 11:5, 14:34–35). His opposition to a public liturgical role for women decided subsequent Catholic tradition in the East and West. Yet in the Greek churches (though not often in the Latin) women were ordained as deacons—in the 4th century by prayer and imposition of hands with the same rite as male deacons—and had a special responsibility at women's baptism. Widows and orphans were the neediest in antiquity, and the church provided them substantial relief. It also encouraged vows of virginity, and by AD 400 women from wealthy or politically powerful families acquired prominence as superiors of religious communities. It seemed natural to elect as abbess a woman whose family connections might bring benefactions.

The religious environment of the Gentile mission was a tolerant, syncretistic (fused) blend of many cults and myths. Paganism was concerned with success; the gods were believed to give victory in war, good harvests, success in love and marriage, and sons and daughters. Defeat, famine, civil disorder, and infertility were recognized as signs of cultic pollution and disfavour. People looked to religion for help in mastering the forces of nature rather than to achieve moral improvement. Individual gods cared either for specific human needs or for specific places and groups. The transcendent God of biblical religion was, therefore, very different from the numerous gods of limited power and local significance. In Asia Minor Paul and his coworker Barnabas were taken to be gods in mortal form because of their miracles. To offer sacrifice on an altar seemed a natural expression of gratitude to any dead, or even living, benefactor. Popular enthusiasm could bestow divine honours on such heroes as dead pugilists and athletes. In the Roman Empire it seemed natural to offer sacrifice and burn incense to the divine emperor as a symbol of loyalty, much like standing for a national anthem today.

Traditional Roman religion was a public cult, not private mysticism, and was upheld because it was the received way of keeping heaven friendly. To refuse participation was thought to be an expression of disloyalty. Jews were granted exemption for their refusal because their monotheism was an ancestral national tradition. The Christians, however, did everything in their power to dissuade people from following the customs of their fathers, whether Gentiles or Jews, and thereby seemed to threaten the cohesion of society and the principle that each group was entitled to follow its national customs in religion.

If ancient religion was tolerant, the philosophical schools were seldom so. Platonists, Aristotelians, Stoics, Epicureans, and Skeptics tended to be very critical of one another. By the 1st century BC, an eclecticism emerged—that is, doctrines were selected from different systems of thoughts without adopting the whole parent system for each doctrine—and by the 2nd century AD, there developed a common stock of philosophy shared by most educated people and by some professional philosophers, which derived metaphysics (the philosophical study whose object is to determine the real nature of things and determine their meaning, structure, and principles) involving theories on the nature of Being from Plato, ethics from the Stoics, and logic from Aristotle. This eclectic Platonism provided an important background and springboard for early Christian apologetics (defences of the faith). Its main outlines appear already in Philo of Alexandria, whose thought influenced not only perhaps the writer of the anonymous letter to the Hebrews, traditionally held to be Paul, in the New Testament but also the great Christian thinkers Clement of Alexandria, Origen, and Ambrose of Milan. Because of this widespread philosophical tendency in ancient society, the Christian could generally assume some belief in Providence and assent to high moral imperatives among his pagan contemporaries. Platonism in particular provided a metaphysical framework within which the Christians could interpret the entire pattern of creation, the Fall of humanity, the incarnation, redemption, the church, sacraments, and last things.

THE INTERNAL DEVELOPMENT OF THE EARLY CHRISTIAN CHURCH

In the first Christian generation, authority in the church lay either in the kinsmen of Jesus or in those whom he had commissioned as Apostles and missionaries. The Jerusalem church under James, the brother of Jesus, was the mother church. Paul admitted that if they had refused to grant recognition to his Gentile converts he would have laboured in vain. If there was an attempt to establish a hereditary family overlordship in the church, it did not succeed. Among the Gentile congregations, the Apostles sent by Jesus enjoyed supreme authority. As long as the Apostles lived, there existed a living authoritative voice to which appeal could be made. But once they all had died, there was an acute question regarding the locus of authority.

THE PROBLEM OF JURISDICTIONAL AUTHORITY

The earliest documents of the 3rd and 4th Christian generations are mainly concerned with this issue: what is the authority of the ministerial hierarchy? The apostolic congregations had normally been served by elders (Greek *presbyteroi*, "priests") or overseers (*episkopoi*, "bishops"), assisted by attendants (*diakonoi*, "deacons"). The clergy were responsible for preaching, for administering baptism and Eucharist, and for distributing aid to the poor. In each city the senior member of the college (assembly) of presbyters, the bishop, naturally had some special authority; he corresponded with other churches and would attend the ordinations of new bishops as the representative of his own community and as a symbol of the catholicity—the universality and unity—of the church of Christ.

Ignatius, bishop of Antioch early in the 2nd century, wrote seven letters on his way to martyrdom at Rome that indicate how critical the centrifugal forces in the church had made the problem of authority. The bishop, he insisted, is the unique focus of unity without whose authority there is no sacrament and no church.

A few years earlier the letter of Bishop Clement of Rome (c. AD 95) to the church at Corinth based the hierarchy's authority on the concept of a historical succession of duly authorized teachers. Clement understood the clergy and laity to be essentially distinct orders within the one community, just as in the Hebrew Bible there were high priests, priests, Levites (Temple functionaries), and laymen. The principles of Clement and Ignatius became important when the church was faced by people claiming recognition for their special charismatic (spiritual) gifts and especially by a prominent group of heretics known as the Gnostics claiming to possess secret oral traditions whispered by Jesus to his disciples and not contained in publicly accessible records such as the Gospels. Indeed, in his conflicts with the Gnostics in the late 2nd century, Irenaeus of Lyons promoted the

Saint Ignatius, bishop of Antioch and Roman martyr, being killed in a lion's den in AD 107. Apic/ Hulton Archive/Getty Images

idea of apostolic succession, the teaching that the bishops stand in a direct line of succession from the Apostles.

The authority of the duly authorized hierarchy was enhanced by the outcome of another 2nd-century debate, which concerned the possibility of absolution for sins committed after baptism. The *Shepherd of Hermas*, a book that enjoyed canonical status in some areas of the early church, enforced the point that excessive rigorism produces hypocrisies. By the 3rd century the old notion of the church as a society of holy people was being replaced by the conception that it was a school for frail sinners. In spite of protests, especially that of the schism led by the theologian and schismatic pope Novatian at Rome in 251, the final consensus held that the power to bind and loose (compare Matthew 16:18–19), to excommunicate and absolve, was vested in bishops and presbyters by their ordination.

Early Christianity was predominantly urban; peasants on farms were deeply attached to old ways and followed the paganism favoured by most aristocratic landowners. By AD 400 some landowners had converted and built churches on their property, providing a "benefice" for the priest, who might often be one of the magnate's servants. In the East and in North Africa each township normally had its own bishop. In the Western provinces bishops were fewer and were responsible for larger areas, which, from the 4th century onward, were called by the secular term *dioceses* (administrative districts). In the 4th century pressure to bring Western custom into line with Eastern and to multiply bishops was resisted on the ground that it would diminish the bishops' social status. By the end of the 3rd century the bishop of the provincial capital was acquiring authority over his colleagues: the metropolitan (from the 4th century on, often entitled archbishop) was chief consecrator of his episcopal colleagues. The bishops of Rome, Alexandria, and Antioch in the 3rd century were accorded some authority beyond their own provinces, in part because the first bishop of each of those cities was thought to have been one of the Apostles. Along with Jerusalem and Constantinople (founded in 330), these three sees (seats of episcopal authority) became the five patriarchates. The title *papa* ("father") was for 600 years an affectionate term applied to any bishop to whom one's relation was intimate; it began to be specially used of bishops of Rome from the 6th century and by the 9th century was almost exclusively applied to them.

From the beginning, Christians in Rome claimed for themselves special responsibilities to lead the church. About AD 165, memorials were erected at Rome to the Apostles Peter—traditionally considered the first bishop of Rome—and Paul: to Peter in a necropolis on the Vatican Hill and to Paul on the road to Ostia. The construction reflects a sense of being guardians of an apostolic tradition, a self-consciousness expressed in another form when, about 190, Bishop Victor of Rome threatened with excommunication Christians in Asia Minor who, following local custom, observed Easter on the day of the Jewish Passover rather than (as at Rome) on the Sunday after the first full moon after the spring equinox. Stephen of Rome (256) is the first known pope to base claims to authority on Jesus's commission to Peter (Matthew 16:18–19).

Bishops were elected by their congregations—i.e., by the clergy and laity assembled together. But the consent of the laity decreased in importance as recognition by other churches increased. The metropolitan and other provincial bishops soon became just as important as the congregation as a whole; and, though they could never successfully impose a man on a solidly hostile community, they could often prevent the appointment falling under the control of one powerful lay family or faction. From the 4th century on, the emperors occasionally intervened to fill important sees, but such occurrences were not a regular phenomenon (until the 6th century in Merovingian Gaul).

THE PROBLEM OF SCRIPTURAL AUTHORITY

After the initial problems regarding the continuity and authority of the hierarchy, the greatest guarantee of true continuity and authenticity was found in the Scriptures. Christians inherited (without debate at first) the Hebrew Bible as the Word of God to the people of God at a now superseded stage of their pilgrimage through history. If St. Paul's Gentile mission was valid, then the Old Testament Law was viewed as no longer God's final word to his people. Thus, the Hebrew Bible began to be called the "old" covenant. There was some hesitation in the church about the exact books included. The Greek version of the Hebrew Bible (Septuagint) included books (such as the Wisdom of Solomon, Ecclesiasticus, and others) that were not accepted in the Hebrew canon. Most, but not all, Gentile Christian communities accepted the Septuagintal canon. The 3rd-century Alexandrian theologian Origen and especially the Latin biblical scholar Jerome (4th–5th century) believed it imprudent to base theological affirmations on books enjoying less than universal recognition. The fact that in many English Bibles the parts of the Hebrew Bible accepted in the Septuagint but not in the Hebrew canon are often printed separately under the (misleading) title Apocrypha is a tribute to these ancient hesitations.

The growth of the New Testament is more complex and controversial. The earliest Christians used oral tradition to pass on the story of Jesus's acts and words, often told in the context of preaching and teaching. As the first generation passed away, however, the need for a more permanent and lasting tradition of the life of Jesus became apparent. Mark first conceived the plan of composing a connected narrative, probably in the decade before—or at some time near—AD 70, when the Temple was destroyed by the Romans. The Gospels that traditionally were thought to have been written by Matthew and Luke borrowed from Mark and were compiled in the generation after his Gospel. Toward the end of the first century, and reflecting the persecutions of the emperor Domitian (who ruled 81-96), The Gospel According to John was written. Nevertheless, even after the Gospels were in common circulation, oral tradition was still current; it may even have been preferred. The Gospels themselves, which were probably intended for pastoral uses, did not immediately assume the status of scripture. Well into the 3rd century, new gospels were being compiled, such as the Gospel of Thomas and the Gospel of Judas, which were not incorporated into the canonical New Testament. The Synoptic Gospels seem to have been used by early church philosopher Justin Martyr at Rome about AD 150 in the form of an early harmony (or synthesis of the Gospels); to this, Justin's Syrian pupil Tatian added The Gospel According to John to make his *Diatessaron* (according to the four), a harmony of all four Gospels so successful that in Mesopotamia (Tatian's homeland) it virtually ousted the separate Gospels for 250 years. And in the late 2nd century, Irenaeus accepted as the standard version of the Christian scriptures the four Gospels and several other texts that would become part of the canonical New Testament.

On a second level of authority stood the apostolic letters, especially those of Paul. The first of the letters appeared about AD 50, and well before AD 90 the main body of his correspondence was circulating as a corpus (body of writings). Paul's letters were the earliest texts of the Christian Scriptures. In addition to them, there are the seven so-called Catholic Letters (i.e., James, 1 and 2 Peter, 1, 2, and 3 John, and Jude), which were among the last of the literature to be accepted as part of the canonical New Testament.

Paul's antitheses of law and grace, justice and goodness, and the letter and the spirit were extended further than Paul intended by the radical heretic Marcion of Pontus (c. 140–150), who taught that the Old Testament came from the inferior vengeful Jewish God of justice and that the New Testament told of the kindly universal Father. As the current texts of Gospels and letters presupposed some divine revelation through the Old Testament, Marcion concluded that they had been corrupted and interpolated by Judaizers. Marcion therefore established a fixed canon of an edited version of Luke's Gospel, some of the Pauline Letters (expurgated), and none of the Hebrew Scriptures.

The orthodox reaction by such theologians as Justin, Irenaeus, and Tertullian in the 2nd century was to insist on the Gospel as the fulfillment of prophecy and on creation as the ground of redemption. Reasons were found for accepting the four already current Gospels, the full corpus of Pauline Letters, Acts of the Apostles, John's Apocalypse (Revelation), and the Catholic Letters. On the authorship of the Letter to the Hebrews there were doubts: Rome rejected it as non-Pauline and Alexandria accepted it as Pauline. The list once established was a criterion (the meaning of "canon") for the authentic Gospel of the new covenant and soon (by transference from the old) became entitled the New Testament. (The Greek word *diathēkē* means both "covenant" and "testament.") The formation of the canon meant that special revelation ended with the death of the Apostles and that no authority could be attached to the apocryphal gospels, acts, and apocalypses proliferating in the 2nd century.

THE PROBLEM OF THEOLOGICAL AUTHORITY

Third, a check was found in the creed, an authoritative profession of the faith. At baptism, after renouncing "the devil and his pomps," initiates declared their faith in response to three questions of the form:

Do you believe in God the Father almighty? Do you believe in Jesus Christ his Son our Lord…? Do you believe in the Holy Spirit in the church and in the Resurrection?

In time, these interrogations became the basis of declaratory creeds, adapted for use by clergy who felt themselves required to reassure colleagues who were not especially confident of their orthodoxy. The so-called Apostles' Creed, a direct descendant of the baptismal interrogation used at Rome by AD 200, is similar to the creed used in Rome in the 3rd and 4th centuries. Each church (or region) might have its own variant form, but all had the threefold structure.

The internal coherence given by creed, canon, and hierarchy was necessary both in the defense of orthodox Christianity against Gnostic theosophical speculations and also in confronting pagan society. The strong coherence of the scattered congregations was remarkable to pagan observers.

EARLY HERETICAL MOVEMENTS

Gnosticism, from the Greek *gnōstikos* (one who has *gnōsis*, or "secret knowledge"), was an important movement in the early Christian centuries—especially the 2nd—that offered an alternative to emerging orthodox Christian teaching. Gnostics taught that the world was created by a demiurge or satanic power—which they often associated with the God of the Hebrew Bible—and that there is total opposition between this world and God. Redemption was viewed as liberation from the chaos of a creation derived from either incompetent or malevolent powers, a world in which the elect are alien prisoners. The method of salvation was to discover the Kingdom of God within one's elect soul and to learn how to pass the hostile powers barring the soul's ascent to bliss. The gnostics held a Docetist Christology, in which Jesus only appeared to assume the flesh. Although

not assuming material form according to the gnostics, Jesus, nonetheless, was the redeemer sent by God to reveal His special *gnōsis*. Irenaeus and other Christian theologians, as well as the 3rd-century Neoplatonic philosopher Plotinus, dismissed gnosticism as a pretentious but dangerous nonsense.

Along with Irenaeus and others, the writers of the later New Testament books seem to have opposed early gnosticism. The supporters of what would become orthodox Christianity stressed the need to adhere to tradition, which was attested by the churches of apostolic foundation. A more hazardous reply was to appeal to ecstatic prophecy. About AD 172 a quasi-pentecostal movement in Phrygia was led by Montanus with two prophetesses, Prisca and Maximilla, reasserting the imminence of the end of the world. He taught that there was an age of the Father (corresponding to that of the Old Testament), an age of the Son (recounted in the New Testament), and an age of the Spirit (heralded by the prophet Montanus). Montanism won its chief convert in Tertullian. Its claim to supplement the New Testament was generally rejected, and the age of prophecy was held to have ended in the time of the apostles.

RELATIONS BETWEEN CHRISTIANITY AND GRECO-ROMAN CULTURE

The Christians were not respectful toward ancestral pagan customs, and their preaching of a new king sounded like revolution. The opposition of Jews to them led to breaches of the peace. Thus, the Christians could very well be unpopular, and they often were. Paul's success at Ephesus provoked a riot to defend the cult of the goddess Artemis.

CHURCH-STATE RELATIONS

In AD 64 a fire destroyed much of Rome; the emperor Nero, in order to escape blame, killed a "vast multitude" of Christians as scapegoats. For the first time, Rome was conscious that Christians were distinct from Jews. But there probably was no formal senatorial enactment proscribing Christianity at this time. Nero's persecution, which was local and short, was condemned by Tacitus as an expression of the emperor's cruelty rather than as a service to the public good. Soon thereafter, however, the profession of Christianity was defined as a capital crime—though of a special kind, because one gained pardon by apostasy (rejection of a faith once confessed) demonstrated by offering sacrifice to the pagan gods or to the emperor. Popular gossip soon accused the Christians of secret vices, such as eating murdered infants (due to the secrecy surrounding the Lord's Supper and the use of the words *body* and *blood*) and sexual promiscuity (due to the practice of Christians calling each other "brother" or "sister" while living as husband and wife).

Early persecutions were sporadic, caused by local conditions and dependent on the attitude of the governor. The fundamental cause of persecution was the Christians' conscientious rejection of the gods whose favour was believed to have brought success to the empire. But distrust was increased by Christian detachment and reluctance to serve in the imperial service and in the army. At any time in the 2nd or 3rd centuries, Christians could find themselves the object of unpleasant attention. Violence against them could be precipitated by a bad harvest, a barbarian attack, or a public festival of the emperor cult. Yet, there were also long periods of peace, and the stability provided by the empire and its network of roads and communications may have facilitated Christianity's growth. The ambivalence of official policy is perhaps best revealed in the exchange between Pliny the Younger, governor of Bithynia, and the emperor Trajan in 111. Pliny executed Christians who were brought before him and who refused to worship the emperor and Roman gods but then sought the emperor's advice on how to treat Christians in his province. Trajan responded that Christians legitimately brought before Pliny should be punished but that the governor should not seek out Christians for persecution. The Christians should be left alone as long as they did not stir up trouble.

Organized, empire-wide persecutions occurred, however, at moments of extreme crisis and as a response to the growth of the faith. During the 3rd century, economic collapse, political chaos, military revolt, and barbarian invasion nearly destroyed the empire. Christians were blamed for the desperate situation because they denied the gods who were thought to protect Rome, thereby bringing down their wrath. To regain divine protection, the emperors introduced the systematic persecution of Christians throughout the empire. The emperor Decius (reigned 249–251) issued an edict requiring all citizens to offer sacrifice to the emperor and to obtain from commissioners a certificate witnessing to the act. Many of these certificates have survived. The requirement created an

Statue of Diocletian's tetrarchy, red porphyry, c. AD 300, brought to Venice in 1258. Alinari/Art Resource, New York

issue of conscience, especially because certificates could be bought. The great bishop-theologian Cyprian of Carthage was martyred during the next great wave of persecutions (257–259), which was aimed at eradicating the leaders of the church. The persecuting emperor Valerian, however, became a Persian prisoner of war, and his son Gallienus issued an edict of toleration restoring confiscated churches and cemeteries.

Beginning in February 303, the church faced the worst of all persecutions under the co-emperors Diocletian and Galerius. The reasons for this persecution are uncertain, but they have been ascribed, among other things, to the influence of Galerius, a fanatic follower of the traditional Roman religion; Diocletian's own devotion to traditional religion and his desire to use Roman religion to restore complete unity in the empire; and the fear of an alienation of rebellious armies from emperor worship. After Diocletian's retirement, Galerius continued the persecutions until 311, when he was stricken by a painful disease, described in exquisite detail by the church historian Eusebius, who believed it was an act of revenge by the Christian God. Galerius died shortly after ending the persecutions. The situation of the early church improved further the following year, when the emperor Constantine, prior to a battle against a rival emperor, experienced a vision of the cross in the heavens with the legend "In this sign, conquer." Constantine's victory led to his eventual conversion to Christianity.

In 313, the joint emperors Constantine and Licinius issued the Edict of Milan, a manifesto of toleration, which, among other things, granted Christians full legal rights.

The persecutions had two lasting consequences. Although the blood of the martyrs, as contemporaries declared, had helped the church to grow, schism eventually arose with those who had yielded to imperial pressure. Groups such as the Donatists in North Africa, for example, refused to recognize as Christians those who had sacrificed to the emperor or turned over holy books during the persecutions.

CHRISTIANITY AND CLASSICAL CULTURE

The attitude of the earliest Christians toward paganism and the imperial government was complicated by their close association with Greco-Roman literary and artistic culture: it was difficult to attack the former without seeming to criticize the latter. Nevertheless, the Christian opinion of other religions, except Judaism, was generally very negative. All forms of paganism—the mystery (salvational) religions of Isis, Attis, Adonis, and Mithra, as well as the traditional Greco-Roman polytheisms and

A Christian pilgrim child is baptized in the Jordan River during a mass baptism ceremony at Yardenit in northern Israel on September 06, 2010. Approximately 100,000 Christians make their pilgrimage to the Holy Land each year. Jack Guez/AFP/Getty Images

the cult of the emperor—were regarded as the worship of evil spirits. Like Jews, Christians, unless gnostic, were opposed to the fusion of diverse religious beliefs and practices. With the exception of the notion of baptism as a rebirth, Christians generally and significantly avoided the characteristic vocabularies of the mystery religions.

Many Christians also rejected the literary traditions of the classical world, denouncing the immoral and unethical behaviour of the deities and heroes of ancient myth and literature. Reflecting this position, Tertullian once asked, "What has Athens to do with Jerusalem?" Despite this hostility, many Christians recognized the value of ancient letters. St. Paul could quote such pagan poets as Aratus, Menander, and Epimenides. Clement of Rome cited the dramatists Sophocles and Euripides. Educated Christians shared this literary tradition with educated pagans. The defenders of Christianity against pagan attack (especially Justin Martyr and Clement of Alexandria in the 2nd century) welcomed classical philosophy and literature; they wished only to reject all polytheistic myth and cult and all metaphysical and ethical doctrines irreconcilable with Christian belief (e.g., Stoic materialism and Platonic doctrines of the transmigration of souls and the eternity of the world). Clement of Alexandria, the second known head of the catechetical school at Alexandria, possessed a wide erudition in the main classics and knew the works of Plato and Homer intimately. His successor at Alexandria, Origen, showed less interest in literary and aesthetic matters but was a greater scholar and thinker; he first applied the methods of Alexandrian philology (the study of disciplines relevant to literature or to language as used in the text of the Bible). Augustine held that although classical literature contained superstitious imaginings, it included references to moral truths and learning that could be used in the service of God. The great church father compared classical literature to the gold of the Egyptians, which God permitted the Hebrews to use on their journey to the Promised Land even though it had once been used in pagan religious practice.

THE APOLOGISTS

The Christian Apologists of the 2nd century were a group of writers who sought to defend the faith against Jewish and Greco-Roman critics. They refuted a variety of scandalous rumours, including allegations of cannibalism and promiscuity. By and large, they sought both to make Christianity intelligible to members of Greco-Roman society and to define the Christian understanding of God, the divinity of Christ, and the resurrection of the body. To accomplish this, the Apologists adopted the philosophical and literary vocabulary of the broader culture to develop a more refined expression of the faith that could appeal to the sophisticated sensibilities of their pagan contemporaries.

Second-century Platonists, for example, found it easy to think of Mind (*nous*) or Reason (Logos) as divine power immanent within the world. Philo of Alexandria had spoken of the Logos as mediating between the transcendent God and the created order. Although some of their coreligionists were offended by the use of Greek philosophical ideas, the Apologists made important advances in the development of Christian thought and were the first of the Christian theologians.

THE EARLY LITURGY, THE CALENDAR, AND THE ARTS

Paul's letters mention worship on the first day of the week. In John's Apocalypse, Sunday is called "the Lord's day." The weekly commemoration of the Resurrection replaced for Christians the synagogue meetings on Saturdays; the practice of circumcision was dropped, and initiation was by baptism; and continuing membership in the church was signified by weekly participation in the Eucharist. Baptism in water in the name of Father, Son, and Holy Spirit was preceded by instruction (catechesis) and fasting. Persons about to be baptized renounced evil and, as they made the declaration of faith, were dipped in water; they then received by anointing and by the laying on of hands (confirmation) the gift of the Holy Spirit and incorporation within the body of Christ. Only the baptized were allowed to be admitted to the Eucharist, when the

words of Jesus at the Last Supper were recalled; the Holy Spirit was invoked upon the people of God making the offering, and the consecrated bread and wine were distributed to the faithful. Accounts of these rites are given in the works of Justin (*c.* 150) and especially in the *Apostolic Tradition* of Hippolytus of Rome (*c.* 220).

Before the 4th century, worship was in private houses. A house church of AD 232 has been excavated at Doura-Europus on the Euphrates. Whereas pagan temples were intended as the residence of the god, churches were designed for the community. The rectangular basilica with an apse (semicircular projection to house the altar), which had been used for Roman judicial buildings, was found especially suitable. The Doura-Europus church has Gospel scenes on the walls. But many heroes from the Hebrew Scriptures also appear in the earliest Christian art; Jewish models probably were followed. The artists also adapted conventional pagan forms (good shepherd; praying persons with hands uplifted). Fishing scenes, doves, and lyres also were popular. In themselves neutral, they carried special meaning to the Christians. The words of several pre-Constantinian hymns survive (e.g., "Shepherd of tender youth," by Clement of Alexandria), but only one with musical notation (Oxyrhynchus papyrus 1786 of the 3rd century).

The earliest Christians wrote to convert or to edify, not to please. Their literature was not produced with aesthetic intentions. Nevertheless, the pulpit offered scope for oratory (as in Melito of Sardis's *Homily on the Pascha*, c. 170). Desire for romance and adventure was satisfied by apocryphal Acts of the Apostles, recounting their travels, with continence replacing love. Justin and Irenaeus did not write for high style but simply to convey information. Apologists hoping for well-educated readers, however, could not be indifferent to literary tastes. By AD 200 the most graceful living writer of Greek literature was Clement of Alexandria, the liveliest writer of Latin, Tertullian. Wholly different in temperament (Clement urbane and allusive, Tertullian vigorous and vulgar), both men wrote distinguished prose with regard to form and rhetorical convention.

By the 3rd century the Bible needed explanation. Origen of Alexandria set out to provide commentaries and undertook for the Old Testament a collation of the various Greek versions with the original Hebrew. Many of his sermons and commentaries were translated into Latin between 385 and 400 by Tyrannius Rufinus and Jerome; their learning and passionate mystical aspiration shaped Western medieval exegesis (critical interpretive methods).

THE ALLIANCE BETWEEN CHURCH AND EMPIRE

In the 4th century, the Roman emperor and Christian convert Constantine the Great (reigned 306-337)was regarded as

Marble colossal head of Constantine the Great, part of the remains of a giant statue from the Basilica of Constantine, in the Roman Forum, c. AD 313. Hirmer Fotoarchiv, München

the great revolutionary, especially in religion. He did not make Christianity the religion of the empire, but he granted important concessions to the church and its bishops, and his conversion encouraged other Roman citizens to become Christian. His foundation of the city of Constantinople in 330 (conceived to be the new Rome) as a Christian city untainted by pagan religion profoundly affected the future political and ecclesiastical structure of the empire and the church. Relations with old Rome, whether in matters of church or of state, were not to be cordial.

Constantine completely altered the relationship between the church and the imperial government, thereby beginning a process that eventually made Christianity the official religion of the empire. Many new converts were won, including those who converted only with the hope of advancing their careers. The church was also faced by a new form of governmental interference when Constantine presided at the Council of Nicaea (325), which addressed a debate over the nature of the Son of God that became known as the Arian controversy. The council provided the definition of the relationship between God the Father and God the Son that is still accepted by most Christians today. Despite this turmoil, and the outright hostility toward Christianity of the emperor Julian the Apostate (reigned 361–363), the church survived, and the adherents of the traditional Roman religion relapsed into passive resistance. The quietly mounting pressure against paganism in the 4th century culminated in the decrees of Emperor Theodosius I (reigned 379–395), who made Catholic Christianity the official religion of the empire and who closed many pagan temples. By the end of the 4th century, therefore, Christianity had been transformed from a persecuted sect to the dominant faith of the empire, in the process becoming intertwined with the imperial government.

The link between church and state was expressed in the civil dignity and insignia granted to bishops, who also began to be entrusted with ambassadorial roles. Constantine himself appointed bishops, and he and his successors convened councils of bishops to address important matters of the faith. By 400 the patriarch of Constantinople (to his avowed embarrassment) enjoyed precedence at court before all civil officials. The emperors issued a number of rulings that afforded greater privilege and responsibility to the bishops, enhancing their position in both church and society. The close relations between the empire and the church in the 4th century were reflected in the writings of Ambrose (bishop of Milan, 374–397), who used "Roman" and "Christian" almost as synonyms. After Theodosius ordered the massacre of the citizens of Thessalonica, however, Ambrose demanded that the emperor undergo penance, thereby enforcing upon Theodosius submission to the church as its son, not its master.

A new movement took shape in the late 3rd and 4th centuries that was a response to both the tragedy of the final persecutions and to the triumph of Constantine's conversion. Monasticism is an institutionalized religious movement whose members are bound by vows to an ascetic life of prayer, meditation, or good works. Members of monastic orders, called monks, are usually celibate and live apart from society either in a community of monks or nuns or as religious recluses. The earliest Christian monastic communities were founded in the deserts of Egypt, most notably by the hermit St. Anthony of Egypt (251–356). It began in response to contemporary social conditions, but it had scriptural roots and reflected the attraction of the ascetic life that had long been part of the Christian and philosophical traditions.

The church was significantly slow to undertake missionary work beyond the frontiers of the empire. The Goth Ulfilas converted the Goths to Arian Christianity (*c.* 340–350) and translated the Bible from Greek to Gothic—omitting, as unsuitable, warlike passages of the Old Testament. The Goths passed their Arian faith on to other Germanic tribes, such as the Vandals. (Sometime between 496 and 508 the Franks, under their great king Clovis, became the first of the Germanic peoples to convert to Catholic Christianity; they were soon followed by the Visigoths.) In the 5th century the Western provinces were overrun by Goths, Vandals, and Huns, and the imperial succession was ended when a German leader, Odoacer, decided to rule without an emperor (476). The position of the papacy was enhanced by the decline of state power, and this prepared the way for the popes' temporal sovereignty over parts of Italy (which they retained from the 7th to the 19th century).

THEOLOGICAL CONTROVERSIES OF THE 4TH AND 5TH CENTURIES

Until about 250, most Western Christian leaders (e.g., Irenaeus and Hippolytus) spoke Greek, not Latin. As the Western and Eastern churches began to develop distinct theological ideas, Latin rose in prominence in the churches closer to Rome, while Greek retained its primacy in the East.

WESTERN CONTROVERSIES

The main Latin theology came primarily from such figures as Tertullian and Cyprian (bishop of Carthage, 248–258) rather than from any figure in Rome. Tertullian wrote *Against Praxeas*, in which he discussed the doctrines of the Trinity and the person of Christ. But in 251 Novatian's schism at Rome diverted interest away from speculative theology to juridical questions about the membership of the church and the validity of sacraments. Differences of opinion over similar issues in the 4th century led to a schism between Rome and the churches of North Africa. One such conflict, known as the Donatist controversy, which raised questions about the validity of the sacraments, dominated all North African church life. Cyprian and the Donatists said that the validity of the sacraments depended on the worthiness of the minister; Rome and North African Christians in communion with Rome said that it did not, because the sacraments received their validity from Christ, not man. Much of the great theologian Augustine's energies as bishop of Hippo (from 396 to 430) went into trying to settle the Donatist issue, in which he finally despaired of rational argument and reluctantly came to justify the use of limited coercion.

The other major controversy of the Western Church was a more confused issue, namely, whether faith is acquired through divine grace or human freedom. In response to his perception of the teachings of the British monk Pelagius, Augustine ascribed all credit to God. Pelagius, however, protested that Augustine was destroying human responsibility and denying the capacity of humans to do what God commands. Augustine, in turn, responded in a series of treatises against Pelagius and his disciple Julian of Eclanum. Pelagianism was later condemned at the councils of Carthage (416), Milevis (416), and Ephesus (431) and by two bishops of Rome, Innocent I in 416 and Honorius I in 418.

EASTERN CONTROVERSIES

As mentioned earlier, in the Greek East, the 4th century was dominated by the controversy over the position of Arius, an Alexandrian presbyter (c. 250–336), that the incarnate Lord—who was born, wept, suffered, and died—could not be

THE ARIAN CONTROVERSY

The basic concern of Arius was and remained disputing the oneness of essence of the Son and the Holy Spirit with God the Father, in order to preserve the oneness of God. The Son, thus, became a "second God, under God the Father"—i.e., he is a divine figure begotten by God. The Son is not himself God, a creature that was willed by God, made like God by divine grace, and sent as a mediator between God and humankind. Arius's teaching was intended to defend the idea of the oneness of the Christian concept of God against all reproaches that Christianity introduces a new, more sublime form of polytheism.

This attempt to save the oneness of God led, however, to an awkward consequence. For Jesus Christ, as the divine Logos become human, moves thereby to the side of the creatures— i.e., to the side of the created world that needs redemption. How, then, should such a Christ, himself a part of the creation, be able to achieve the redemption of the world? On the whole, the Christian Church rejected, as an unhappy attack upon the reality of redemption, such a formal attempt at saving the oneness of God as was undertaken by Arius.

Arius's main rival was Athanasius of Alexandria, for whom the point of departure was not a philosophical-speculative principle but rather the reality of redemption, the certainty of salvation. The redemption of humanity from sin and death is only then guaranteed if Christ is total God and total human being, if the complete essence of God penetrates human nature right into the deepest layer of its carnal corporeality. Only if God in the full meaning of divine essence became human in Jesus Christ is deification of man in terms of overcoming sin and death guaranteed as the resurrection of the flesh. The Athanasian view was accepted at the Council of Nicaea (325) and became orthodox Christian doctrine.

one with the transcendent first cause of creation—who is beyond all suffering. The Council of Nicaea (325) condemned Arianism and affirmed the Son of God to be identical in essence with the Father. Because this formula included no safeguard against a complicated heresy called Monarchianism, a long controversy followed, especially after Constantine's death (337). Athanasius, bishop of Alexandria (reigned 328–373), fought zealously against Arianism in the East and owed much to Rome's support, which only added to the tensions between East and West.

These tensions survived the settlement of the Arian dispute in 381, when the Council of Constantinople (381) proclaimed Catholic Christianity the official religion of the empire, thus eliminating Arianism in the East, but also asserted Constantinople, as the new Rome, to be the second see of Christendom. This assertion was unwelcome to Alexandria, traditionally the second city of the empire, and to Rome, because it implied that the dignity of a bishop depended on the secular standing of his city. Rivalry between Alexandria and Constantinople led to the fall of John Chrysostom, patriarch of Constantinople (reigned 398–404), when he appeared to support Egyptian monks who admired the controversial theology of Origen. It became a major feature of the emerging Christological debate (the controversy over the nature of Christ).

The Christological controversy—that is, the controversy over the nature and doctrines of Christ—stemmed from the rival doctrines of Apollinaris of Laodicea

(flourished 360–380) and Theodore of Mopsuestia (c. 350–428), representatives of the rival schools of Alexandria and Antioch, respectively. At the Council of Ephesus (431), led by Cyril, patriarch of Alexandria (reigned 412–444), an extreme Antiochene Christology—taught by Nestorius, patriarch of Constantinople—was condemned for saying that the man Jesus is an independent person beside the divine Word and that therefore Mary, the mother of Jesus, may not properly be called mother of God (Greek *theotokos*, or "God-bearer"). Cyril's formula was "one nature of the Word incarnate." A reaction led by Pope Leo I (reigned 440–461) against this alleged one-nature, or monophysite, doctrine culminated in the Council of Chalcedon (451), which affirmed a position called dyophysitism. According to this view, Christ has two natures in one person (hypostasis). Thus, the Council of Chalcedon alienated believers in Egypt, Ethiopia, Armenia, and Syria who rejected the council's Christological statement, and they were branded as monophysite heretics.

During the next 250 years the Byzantine emperors and patriarchs desperately sought to reconcile the non-Chalcedonian Christians. Three successive attempts failed. First, under the emperor Zeno (482) the *Henotikon* (union formula) offended Rome by suggesting that criticism of Chalcedon might be justified. Second, under the emperor Justinian the Chalcedonian definition was glossed by condemning the "Three Chapters," which includes

COUNCIL OF CHALCEDON

The fourth ecumenical council of the Christian Church was held in Chalcedon (modern Kadiköy, Tur.) in 451. Convoked by the emperor Marcian, it was attended by about 520 bishops or their representatives and was the largest and best-documented of the early councils. It approved the creed of Nicaea (325), the creed of Constantinople (381; subsequently known as the Nicene Creed), two letters of Cyril against Nestorius that insisted on the unity of divine and human persons in Christ, and the Tome of Pope Leo I confirming two distinct natures in Christ and rejecting the so-called monophysite doctrine that Christ had only one divine nature. The council then explained these doctrines in its own confession of faith. Besides reinforcing canons of earlier church councils as well as declarations of some local synods, the council issued disciplinary decrees affecting monks and clergy and declared Jerusalem and Constantinople patriarchates.

the writings of Theodore of Mopsuestia, Theodoret, and Ibas, all strong critics of Cyril of Alexandria's theology and of monophysitism. The Syrian Jacob Baradaeus responded to this by helping to create a rival episcopate in Syria. During the third attempt, which came under the emperor Heraclius (reigned 610–641), the Chalcedonians invited the non-Chalcedonians to reunite under the formula that Christ had two natures but only one will (Monothelitism). This approach, however, had the dual effect of reconciling almost none of the churches who denounced Chalcedon while creating divisions among the Chalcedonians themselves. Chalcedon's "two natures" continues to be rejected by the churches of the Oriental Orthodox communion: the Armenian Apostolic Church, the Coptic Orthodox Church of Alexandria, the Ethiopian Orthodox Tewahedo Church, the Malankara (Indian) Orthodox Church, the Eritrean Orthodox Tewahedo Church, and the Syriac Orthodox Patriarchate of Antioch and All the East (commonly and erroneously called the "Syrian Jacobites" by many Western and Eastern Orthodox Christians).

LITURGY AND THE ARTS AFTER CONSTANTINE

Along with these developments in higher theology, various forms of religious devotion emerged.

NEW FORMS OF WORSHIP

One of the more important was the "cult of the saints," the public veneration of saints and its related shrines and rituals. Shrines were erected in honour of local holy men and women and those who had suffered for the faith. The saints were recognized as the special representatives of God and were thought to be vehicles for his miraculous power. The shrines became the focus of religious pilgrimage, and the relics of the saints were highly valued.

The veneration of martyrs and the growth of pilgrimages stimulated liturgical elaboration. Great centres (Jerusalem and Rome, in particular) became models for others, which encouraged regional standardization and cross-fertilization. Though the pattern of the eucharistic liturgy was settled by the 4th century, there were many variant forms, especially of the central prayer called by the Greeks *anaphora* ("offering") and by the Latins *canon* ("prescribed form"). Liturgical prayers of Basil of Caesarea became widely influential in the East. Later, liturgies were ascribed to local saints: Jerusalem's to St. James, Alexandria's to St. Mark, and Constantinople's to John Chrysostom. The spirit of Greek liturgies encouraged rich and imaginative prose. Latin style was restrained, with epigrammatic antitheses; and the Roman Church changed from Greek to Latin about AD 370. The Canon of the Latin mass as used in the 6th century was already close to the form it has since retained.

Music also became elaborate, with antiphonal psalm chanting. Some reaction came from those who believed that the music was obscuring the words. Both Athanasius of Alexandria and Augustine defended music on the condition that the sense of the words remained primary in importance. The Latin theologians Ambrose of Milan, Prudentius, and Venantius Fortunatus provided Latin hymns of distinction. The ascription of the Roman chants (Gregorian) to Pope Gregory I the Great was first made in the 9th century. In the Greek East in the time of Justinian, Romanos Melodos created the kontakion, a long poetic homily.

The development of church architecture was stimulated by Constantine's great buildings at Jerusalem and Rome, and his example as a church-builder was emulated by his successors, most notably by Justinian in the 6th century. The exteriors of these churches remained simple, but inside they were richly ornamented with marble and mosaic, the decoration being arranged on a coherent plan to represent the angels and saints in heaven with whom the church on earth was joining for worship. An enormous number of churches built in and after the 4th century have been excavated. The outstanding buildings that survive largely intact, Hagia Sophia at Constantinople (now Istanbul) and San Vitale at Ravenna in Italy, belong to the age of Justinian.

The veneration of saints led to the production of a specific category of literature known as hagiography, which told the story of a saint's life. Hagiography was not a biography in the modern sense but was a work of religious devotion that portrayed the saint as a model of Christian virtue. If available, authentic tradition would be used, but hagiographers also drew from a stock of conventional tales about earlier saints that were generally intended to convey a moral lesson. Saints' lives also contained accounts of the miracles performed by the saints in their lifetimes and at their shrines after their deaths. The lives of saints belong to the poetry of the Middle Ages but are important to the historian as documents of social and religious history.

POLITICAL RELATIONS BETWEEN EAST AND WEST

The old tensions between East and West were sharpened by the quarrels about Chalcedon. In Rome every concession made by Constantinople toward the non-Chalcedonians increased the distrust. Justinian's condemnation of the Three Chapters (Fifth Council, Constantinople, 553) was forced on a reluctant West, parts of which had been brought back under imperial control by Justinian's conquests. From the time of Pope Gregory I the papacy—encouraged by the successful mission to the Anglo-Saxons—was looking as much to the Western kingdoms as to Byzantium.

The growing division between East and West was reinforced by developments outside the church itself. In the 7th century the Eastern Empire fought for its life, first against the Persians and then the Arabs, and the Balkans were occupied by the Slavs. The rise of Islam had an especially profound impact on the church. The Arab military conquest broke upon the Byzantine Empire in 634, just as it was exhausted after defeating Persia. In 678 and again in 718, the Arabs were at the walls of Constantinople. The non-Chalcedonians in Egypt and in Syria soon found that they enjoyed greater toleration under Muslim Arabs than under Chalcedonian Byzantines. Christian territory from the Holy Land to Spain was conquered by the forces of Islam, and many of the inhabitants of this region eventually converted to the new faith.

The submergence of Alexandria, Antioch, and Jerusalem under Muslim rule left the patriarch of Constantinople with enhanced authority, which altered the internal dynamic of the Christian community. The divisions between East and West were heightened by developments in both the Latin and the Greek churches. In 726, the emperor Leo III the Isaurian, after his successful defense against the Islamic advance, introduced a policy of iconoclasm (destruction of images) to the Byzantine church that was continued and expanded by his son Constantine V. For much of the rest of the century, the empire was absorbed in the Iconoclastic Controversy, which became a struggle not only to keep icons, a traditional focus of religious veneration, but also to combat the subjection of the church to the will of the emperor. The greatest champion of icons was John of Damascus, a monk in Muslim Palestine. Within the empire, Theodore Studites, abbot of the Studium (monastery) near Constantinople, vigorously attacked iconoclasm; he also led a revival of monasticism and stressed the importance of copying manuscripts.

The imperial attack on images was severely criticized in the West. The Frankish king Charlemagne, who was not invited to Nicaea, censured the decision at the synod of Frankfurt in Germany (794). The hostility between the iconoclast emperors and the popes encouraged the 8th-century popes to seek a protector. Charlemagne was made emperor at Rome on Christmas Day, 800—laying the foundation for the Holy Roman Empire, which lasted until 1806. Charlemagne exercised immense authority over the Western Church. In the 10th century, however, the Ottonian dynasty in Germany established a new imperial line and became the preeminent power in Latin Europe.

LITERATURE AND ART OF THE "DARK AGES"

The Monothelite and iconoclastic controversies produced herculean theological endeavours: the criticism of Monothelitism by the monk Maximus the Confessor (580–662) was based upon subtle and very careful considerations of the implications of Chalcedon. The great opponents of iconoclasm, John of Damascus and Theodore Studites, also composed hymns and other theological treatises. Greek mystical theology had an outstanding representative in Symeon the New Theologian (949–1022), abbot of St. Mamas at Constantinople, whose doctrines about light visions anticipated the hesychasm (quietistic prayer methods) of Gregory Palamas in the 14th century.

Iconoclasm was not an anti-intellectual, anti-art movement. The iconoclasts everywhere replaced figures with the cross or with exquisite patterns. The ending of iconoclasm in 843 (the restoration of orthodoxy), however, liberated the artists adept in mosaic and fresco to portray figures once again, spurring a new revival of decoration. Music also became more elaborate; the kontakion was replaced by the kanon, a cycle of nine odes, each of six to nine stanzas and with a different melody. The kanon gave more scope to the musicians by providing greater variety. Byzantine hymns were classified according to their mode, and the mode changed each week. Besides John of Damascus and Theodore Studites, the great hymn writers of this period were Cosmas of Jerusalem and Joseph of Studium.

The so-called Dark Ages in the West produced virtually no sculpture or painting—with the notable exception of illuminated manuscripts, of which marvelous specimens were made (e.g., the Book of Kells and the Lindisfarne Gospels). The Irish and Anglo-Saxon monks did not construct noble buildings but knew how to write and to illustrate a book.

In the age of Charlemagne exquisite calligraphy was continued (e.g., the Utrecht Psalter), as was the composition of illuminated manuscripts (e.g. the Coronation Gospels and the Codex aureus). Manuscripts during the Carolingian period were often bound with covers of intricate ivory and metalwork of superb finesse. Great buildings, notably the palace complex at Aachen, also began to emerge, partly based on Byzantine models, such as the churches at Ravenna. The Ottonian renaissance in Germany encouraged even more

A page from the Book of Kells, *thought to have been created by Irish monks from on the Scottish island of Iona between the 7th and 9th centuries AD.* Hulton Archive/Getty Images

confidently the erection of church buildings, producing such masterpieces as the surviving cathedrals at Hildesheim and Spires and setting out a characteristically German style of architecture; it also continued the Carolingian tradition of manuscript illumination.

The barbarian kingdoms soon produced their own Christian literature: Gregory of Tours wrote the history of the Franks, Isidore of Sevilla that of the Visigoths, and Cassiodorus that of the Ostrogoths. Isidore, utilizing his vast

reading, compiled encyclopaedias on everything from liturgical ceremonies to the natural sciences. The outstanding figure of this incipient "nationalist" movement was the English monk Bede, whose *Ecclesiastical History of the English People* was completed in 731 and whose exegetical works came to stand beside Augustine and Gregory I as indispensable for the medieval student. Carolingian authors compiled a broad range of literary works, including sermons, biblical commentaries, works on the liturgy and canon law, and theological treatises on the Eucharist, predestination, and other topics.

MISSIONS AND MONASTICISM

The Arian barbarians became Catholics, including, by 700, even the Lombards in northern Italy. There remained immense areas of Europe, however, to which the Gospel had not yet been brought. Gregory I evangelized the Anglo-Saxons, who in turn sent missionaries to northwestern Europe—Wilfrid and Willibrord to what is now the Netherlands, and Boniface to Hesse, Thuringia, and Bavaria. In consequence of Boniface's work in Germany in the 8th century, a mission to Scandinavia was initiated by Ansgar (801–865), and the mission reached Iceland by 996. In the 10th century the mission from Germany moved eastward to Bohemia, to the Magyars, and (from 966) to the Poles. By 1050 most of Europe was under Christian influence with the exception of Muslim Spain.

In the Byzantine sphere, early missions went to the Hunnish tribesmen north of the Caucasus. The Nestorians, entrenched in Persia, carried the Gospel to the Turkmen and across Central Asia to China. In the 9th century the mission to the Slavs began with the work of Cyril and Methodius, who created a Slavonic alphabet and translated the Bible into the Slavonic language. Although their labours in Moravia were

undermined by Frankish clergy, it was their achievement that made possible the faith and medieval culture of both Russia and Serbia.

The Benedictine Rule—initiated by Benedict of Nursia—succeeded in the West because of its simplicity and restraint; more formidable alternatives were available in the 6th century. By 800, abbeys existed throughout western Europe, and the observance of Benedict's Rule was fostered by Charlemagne and, especially, his son Louis the Pious. These houses, such as Bede's monastery at Jarrow (England) or the foundations of Columban (c. 543–615) at Luxeuil (France) and Bobbio (Italy), which followed Columban's Rule and not Benedict's, became centres of study and made possible the Carolingian renaissance of learning. In this renaissance the 8th-century English scholar Alcuin, an heir to the tradition of Bede, and his monastery at Tours occupy the chief place. Around monasteries and cathedrals, schools were created to teach acceptable Latin, to write careful manuscripts, and to study not only the Bible and writings of the Church Fathers but also science. Scribes developed the beautiful script that was known as Carolingian minuscule. Although the Carolingian renaissance was short-lived, it laid the foundation for later cultural and intellectual growth.

Monasticism in 9th-century Byzantium was centred upon the Studites, who came to be a faction against the court. A remoter and other-worldly asceticism developed with the foundation of monasteries on Mount Athos (Greece) from 963 onward. A distinctive feature of Athonite monasticism was that nothing female was to be allowed on the peninsula.

THE PHOTIAN SCHISM

The end of iconoclasm in 843 left a legacy of faction. Ignatius, patriarch of Constantinople intermittently from 847 to 877, was exiled by the government in 858 and replaced by Photius, a scholarly layman who was head of the imperial chancery—he was elected patriarch and ordained within six days. Ignatius's supporters dissuaded Pope Nicholas I (reigned 858–867) from recognizing Photius. Nicholas was angered by Byzantine missions among the Bulgars, whom he regarded as belonging to his sphere. When Nicholas wrote to the Bulgars attacking Greek practices, Photius replied by accusing the West of heretically altering the creed in saying that the Holy Spirit proceeds from the Father and from the Son (*Filioque*). He declared Pope Nicholas deposed (867), but his position was not strong enough for such imprudence.

A new emperor, Basil the Macedonian, reinstated Ignatius as patriarch; and in 869 Nicholas's successor, Adrian II (reigned 867–872), condemned Photius and sent legates to Constantinople to extort submission to papal supremacy from the Greeks. The Greeks resented the papal demands, and

when Ignatius died in 877 Photius quietly became patriarch again. Rome (at that moment needing Byzantine military support against Muslims in Sicily and southern Italy) reluctantly agreed to recognize Photius, but on the condition of an apology and of the withdrawal of Greek missions to the Bulgars. Photius acknowledged Rome as the first see of Christendom, discreetly said nothing explicitly against the *Filioque* clause, and agreed to the provision that the Bulgars could be put under Roman jurisdiction providing that Greek missions were allowed to continue.

The main issue in the Photian schism was whether Rome possessed monarchical power of jurisdiction over all churches (as Nicholas and Adrian held), or whether Rome was the senior of five semi-independent patriarchates (as Photius and the Greeks thought) and therefore could not canonically interfere with the internal affairs of another patriarchate.

THE GREAT EAST-WEST SCHISM

The mutual distrust shown in the time of Photius erupted again in the middle of the 11th century after papal enforcement of Latin customs upon Greeks in southern Italy. The patriarch of Constantinople, Michael Cerularius, closed Latin churches in Constantinople as a reprisal. Cardinal Humbert came from Italy to protest, was accorded an icy reception, and on July

People visit the Hagia Sofia church November 26, 2006, in Istanbul, Turkey. The church began construction by Constantine I in 325 and was finished by his son Constantine II in 360. Carsten Koall/Getty Images

16, 1054, left a bull of excommunication on the altar of the great church of Hagia Sophia. The bull anathematized (condemned) Michael Cerularius, the Greek doctrine of the Holy Spirit, the marriage of Greek priests, and the Greek use of leavened bread for the Eucharist.

At the time, the breach was treated as a minor storm in which both sides had behaved with some arrogance. As Greeks and Latins became more estranged, however, people looked back on the events of 1054 as the moment of the final breach between East and West. Not until Dec. 7, 1965, were the mutual excommunications of 1054 abolished by Pope Paul VI and the ecumenical patriarch Athenagoras I.

FROM THE SCHISM TO THE PRESENT

A major factor in the consolidation and expansion of Christianity in the West was the growth in the prestige and power of the bishop of Rome. Pope Leo I the Great made the primacy of the Roman bishop explicit both in theory and in practice and must be counted as one of the most important figures in the history of the centralization of authority in the church. The next such figure was Gregory I the Great, whose work shaped the worship, the thought, and the structure of the church as well as its temporal wealth and power. Although some of Gregory's successors advocated papal primacy, it was the popes of the 11th century and thereafter who sought to exploit claims of papal authority over the church hierarchy and over all Christians.

Even while still a part of the universal church, Byzantine Christianity had become increasingly isolated from the West by difference of language, culture, politics, and religion and followed its own course in shaping its heritage. The Eastern churches never had so centralized a polity as did the church in the West but developed the principle of the administrative independence or "autocephaly" of each national church. All these differences between the Eastern and Western parts of the church, both the religious differences and those that were largely cultural or political, came together to cause the schism between the two. The break in 1054 was followed by further evidences of alienation—in the 13th century, in the sack of Constantinople by Western Christians in 1204 and the establishment of the Latin patriarchate there; and in the 15th century, after the failure of the union of Florence and after the fall of Constantinople to the Turks in 1453.

PAPACY AND EMPIRE

Conflict with the East was both a cause and an effect of the distinctive development of Western Christianity during the Middle Ages. Pope Gregory VII (reigned 1073–85) reformed both the church and the papacy from within, establishing the canonical and moral authority of the papal office; in the pontificate of Innocent III (reigned 1198–1216) the papal claims to universality reached their zenith at all levels of the life of the church. Significantly, both these popes were obliged to defend the papacy against the Holy Roman emperor and other temporal rulers. The battle between the church and the empire is a persistent theme in the history of medieval Christianity.

MEDIEVAL THOUGHT

No product of medieval Christianity has been more influential in the centuries since the Middle Ages than medieval thought, particularly the philosophy and theology of Scholasticism, whose outstanding exponent was Thomas Aquinas (1224/25–1274). Scholastic theology was an effort to harmonize the doctrinal traditions inherited from the Fathers of the early church with the intellectual achievements of classical antiquity—in other words, to create a synthesis of faith and reason. Scholasticism is a landmark both in the history of Christianity and in the history of Western culture and a symbol of the Christianization of society and culture.

REFORMATION

Initially the Protestant Reformers maintained the hope that they could accomplish the reformation of the doctrine and life of the church from within, but this proved impossible because of the intransigence of the church, the polemic of the Protestant movements, or the political and cultural situation—or because of all of these factors. The several parties of the Reformation may be conveniently classified according to the extent of their protest against medieval theology, piety, and polity. The Anglican Reformers, as well as Martin Luther and his movement, were, in general, the most conservative in their treatment of the Roman Catholic tradition; John Calvin and his followers were less conservative; the Anabaptists and related groups were least conservative of all. Despite their deep differences, almost all the various Reformation movements were characterized by an emphasis upon the Bible, as distinguished from the church or its tradition, as the authority in religion; by an insistence upon the sovereignty of free grace in the forgiveness of sins; by a stress upon faith alone, without works, as the preconditions of acceptance with God; and by the demand that the laity assume a more significant place in both the work and the worship of the church.

The Reformation envisaged neither schism within the church nor the dissolution of the Christian culture that had developed for more than a millennium. But when the Reformation was over, both the church and the culture had been radically transformed. The voyages of discovery, the beginnings of a capitalist economy, the rise of modern nationalism, the dawn of the scientific age, the culture of the Renaissance—all these factors, and others besides, helped to break up the "medieval synthesis." Among these factors, however, the Reformation was one of the most important. For the consequences of the Reformation, not in intention but in fact, were a divided Christendom and a secularized West. Roman Catholicism, no less than Protestantism, has developed historically in the modern world as an effort to adapt historic forms to the implications of these consequences. Established Christianity, as it had been known in the West since the 4th century, ended after the Reformation, though not everywhere at once.

CHRISTIANITY FROM THE 16TH TO THE 20TH CENTURY

Paradoxically, the end of "established Christianity" in the old sense resulted in the most rapid and most widespread expansion in the history of Christianity. The Christianization of the Americas and the evangelization of Asia, Africa, and Australasia gave geographic substance to the Christian title "ecumenical." Growth in areas and in numbers, however, need not be equivalent to growth in influence. Despite its continuing strength throughout the modern period, Christianity retreated on many fronts and lost much of its prestige and authority both politically and intellectually.

During the formative period of modern Western history, roughly from the beginning of the 16th to the middle of the 18th century, Christianity participated in many of the movements of cultural and political expansion. The explorers of the New World were followed closely by missionaries—that is, when the two were not in fact identical. Protestant and Roman Catholic clergymen were prominent in politics, letters, and science. Although the rationalism of the Enlightenment alienated many people from the Christian faith, especially among the intellectuals of the 17th and 18th centuries, those who were alienated often kept a loyalty to the figure of Jesus or to the teachings of the Bible even when they broke with traditional forms of Christian doctrine and life. Citing the theological conflicts of the Reformation and the political conflicts that followed upon these as evidence of the dangers of religious intolerance, representatives of the Enlightenment gradually introduced disestablishment, toleration, and religious liberty into most Western countries.

The state of Christian faith and life within the churches during the 17th and 18th centuries both reflected and resisted the spirit of the time. Even though the Protestant Reformation had absorbed some of the reform energy within Roman Catholicism, the theology and morals underwent serious revision in the Roman Catholic Counter-Reformation. Fighting off the attempts by various countries to establish national Catholic churches, the papacy sought to learn from the history of its encounter with the Reformation and to avoid the mistakes that had been made then. Protestantism in turn discovered that separation from Rome did not

necessarily inoculate it against many of the trends that it had denounced in Roman Catholicism. Orthodox theology of the 17th century both in Lutheranism and in the Reformed churches displayed many features of medieval Scholasticism, despite the attacks of the Reformers upon the latter. Partly as a compensation for the overemphasis of orthodoxy upon doctrine at the expense of morals, Pietism summoned Protestant believers to greater seriousness of personal faith and practical living.

In alliance with the spirit of the Enlightenment, the so-called "democratic" revolutions of the 18th, 19th, and 20th centuries aided this process of undermining Christianity. Roman Catholicism in France, Eastern Orthodoxy in Russia, and Protestantism in former European colonies in Africa and Asia were identified—by their enemies if not also by themselves—as part of the ancient régime and were nearly swept away with it. As the discoveries of science proceeded, they clashed with old and cherished notions about the doctrine of creation, many of which were passionately supported by various leaders of organized Christianity. The age of the revolutions—political, economic, technological, intellectual—was an age of crisis for Christianity. The 19th century was called the great century in the history of Christian missions, both Roman Catholic and Protestant. By the very force of their attacks upon Christianity, the critics of the church helped to arouse within the church new apologists for the faith, who creatively reinterpreted

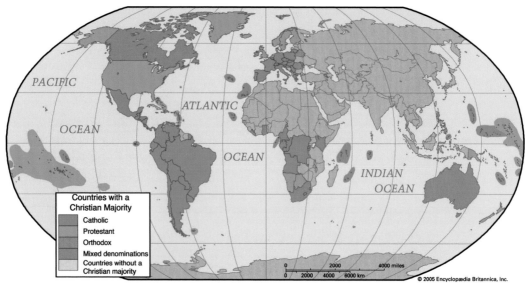

World distribution of Christianity, c. 2000.

it in relation to the new philosophy and science of the modern period. The 20th century saw additional challenges to the Christian cause in the form of totalitarianism, of resurgent world religions, and of indifference. Both the relation of church and state and the missionary program of the churches thus demanded reconsideration. But the 20th century also saw renewed efforts to heal the schisms within Christendom. The ecumenical movement began within Protestantism and Anglicanism, eventually included some of the Eastern Orthodox churches, and, especially since the Second Vatican Council (1962–65), has engaged the sympathetic attention of Roman Catholicism as well.

CONTEMPORARY CHRISTIANITY

By the late 20th century Christianity had become the most widely disseminated religion on earth. Virtually no nation remained unaffected by the activities of Christian missionaries, although in many countries Christians are only a small fraction of the total population. Most of the countries of Asia and of Africa have Christian minorities, some of which, as in India and in the People's Republic of China, number several million members. Massive increases in the size of such churches challenged the traditional dominance of Western Christianity.

CHRISTIAN DOCTRINE

I ndirectly or directly, Jesus and his Apostles left their principal—though perhaps not their only—records in the writings of the New Testament, the canonical texts that constitute the second part of the Christian Bible. The basic meaning of the term *doctrine* is "teaching." Christian doctrine, accordingly, is the attempt to state in intellectually responsible terms the message of the gospel and the content of the faith it elicits. The doctrine, therefore, encompasses both the substance of what is taught and the act of setting that substance forth. While a certain reticence is appropriate in the face of the transcendent mystery of God, Christians hold that God has revealed himself sufficiently to allow and require truthful speech about him and his ways. Thus, Christian talk of God claims to be a response to the divine initiative, not simply a record of humanly generated experience. As Hilary of Poitiers wrote in the mid-4th century in his *On the Trinity*, "God is to be believed when he speaks of himself, and whatever he grants us to think concerning himself is to be followed."

THE NATURE AND FUNCTIONS OF DOCTRINE

From the first, church teaching has occurred in several contexts and for several purposes: it happens when the gospel is newly preached to people who have not heard it before (evangelism), when those who accept the message are instructed

Communion of the Apostles, *panel by Justus of Ghent, c. 1473–74; in the Palazzo Ducale, Urbino, Italy.* SCALA/Art Resource, New York

in preparation for baptism (catechesis), when the believing and baptized communities gather for worship (liturgy), and when application is sought to daily life (ethics). Teaching may be specially required for the sake of clarification and consolidation, as when distortions threaten within (aversion of heresy), when the faith is under attack from outside (apologetics), when linguistic or epistemological shifts over time hinder intelligibility or change the terms of reference (restatement), or when geographical expansion prompts a more local expression (inculturation). The teaching may vary in the weight of the authority it claims and is granted, ranging from the most solemn definitions of supervisory bodies (dogma) through a broadly prevalent but internally somewhat differentiated "common mind" (consensus) to the works of individual thinkers (theology).

The most stable and widely recognized teaching is that preserved in the ancient creeds—the Apostles' Creed and the Nicene Creed—that are transmitted in the worship of the churches and expounded in their confessions (symbolics). The agreed doctrine may sometimes have been achieved only through a period of maturing reflection and debate, and the continuation of these processes within the established parameters is not excluded (development). In the course of history, however, differences concerning accepted teaching sometimes became so serious that communities divided over them (schism). The divided communities may continue their conversation in tones that range from the persuasive to the polemical (controversy). In the 20th century, determined efforts on the part of several Christian communions were made to overcome the doctrinal differences between them with the aim of restoring ecclesiastical unity (ecumenism).

Thus there are many aspects to the question of Christian doctrine, and in what follows they will be treated in the sequence just outlined: the permanent basis, the perennial functions, the levels of authority, the stable pattern, and the institutional vicissitudes.

SCRIPTURE AND TRADITION

In his First Letter to the Corinthians, the apostle Paul summarized the gospel he himself had received and then preached to them, in which they now stood for their salvation: "that Christ died for our sins in accordance with the [Hebrew] scriptures, and that he was buried, and that he was raised on the third day in accordance with the scriptures, and that he appeared to Cephas [Peter], then to the twelve..." (15:1–8). The speeches in the Acts of the Apostles are the basis of the following synthesis, by the biblical scholar C.H. Dodd, of the early apostolic preaching, or *kerygma* (from the Greek term for a herald's proclamation); in Dodd's synthesis, the story of Jesus is located a little more fully in God's history with Israel and with the entire human race:

The Kingdom of God had made its appearance with the coming of the Messiah; His works of power and His 'new teaching with authority' had provided evidence of the presence of God among men; His death 'according to the determinate counsel and foreknowledge of God' had marked the end of the old order, and his resurrection and exaltation had definitely inaugurated the new age, characterized, as the prophets had foretold, by the outpouring of the Holy Spirit upon the people of God. It remained only for the new order to be consummated by the return of

Christ in glory to judge the quick and the dead and to save His own from the wrath to come.

Moreover, according to Dodd, "the kerygma always closes with an appeal for repentance, the offer of forgiveness and of the Holy Spirit, and the promise of 'salvation,' that is, of 'the life of the Age to come,' to those who enter the elect community."

Embedded in the New Testament also are certain short formulas used by believers to confess their faith (*homologein*): "Jesus is Lord" (Romans 10:9; 1 Corinthians 12:3), "Jesus is the Son of God" (1 John 4:15), and Peter's "You are the Christ" (Mark 8:29) and Thomas's "My Lord and my God" (John 20:28). Confessions of faith were sometimes sung when the Christians assembled for worship (Ephesians 5:19; Colossians 3:16); Paul seems to use quotations from such hymns in arguments in his letters to the Philippians (2:5–11) and Colossians (1:15–20). The earthly worship of the church is probably the immediate source for the heavenly songs of the Apocalypse (Revelation 4:8–11; 5:9–10, 13–14; 7:9–12; 11:16–18; 19:1–8).

The fullest apostolic record of the teachings of Jesus is found in narrative form in the Gospels, where his life and sayings are set amid faithful conclusions about who he was and is and what he will still accomplish. The most discursive reflections of the apostolic faith are found in the New Testament epistles, where salvation is at stake in the matter of right belief and right practice. Thus in the Letter to the Romans, the apostle Paul first shows how worshipping creatures rather than the Creator leads to destruction. He then expounds the redemptive work of God in Christ and shows how those who believe are renewed by the Holy Spirit for life as God means it to be.

By the late 2nd century there was widespread agreement among the local churches about which writings were to be reckoned apostolic by virtue of their origin and content, but it was not until the 4th century that the list became settled into what is now known as the "New Testament." About 400, St. Augustine wrote the highly influential *De doctrina christiana* (*On Christian Doctrine*), which provides practical guidance for interpreting the faith. In medieval terms, sacred doctrine (*sacra doctrina*) is to be read as directly as possible from the sacred page (*sacra pagina*). Moreover, it is a commonplace—from Thomas à Kempis (*The Imitation of Christ*, I.5) in the 15th century through John Calvin (*Institutes* I.7.1–5) in the 16th century to the 1992 *Catechism of the Catholic Church* (§ 111)—that Scripture must be read in the same (Holy) Spirit as that in which it was written. In other words, the reading of Scripture, whether corporate or individual, is properly done prayerfully by people who have pure hearts and live holy lives. It is such use that permits Scripture to function authoritatively in Christian teaching.

While the New Testament, which sets the terms also for the reading of the Hebrew Scriptures as the promissory and prophetic Old Testament, is consistently held to be the primary witness to the apostolic preaching and a permanent statement of "the faith once delivered to the saints" (Jude 3), there are other possible legacies from the Apostles.

EVANGELISM

When the gospel is preached to people for the first time, the hearers usually have some idea of "the divine" in their minds. This idea provides an initial point of contact for the evangelist. According to the Acts of the Apostles, Paul, in addressing the Athenians, noted that their altars included one "to an unknown god." Whether that designated a supreme deity or simply one who might have been left out, Paul took the opportunity to teach them about "the God who made the world and everything in it, the Lord of heaven and earth." The Greek poets Epimenides and Aratus, he said, had hinted at such a God, "in whom we live and move and have our being" (Epimenides), for "we are indeed his offspring" (Aratus). As such, Paul confirmed, "He is not far from each of us." The crucial point, however, is that God now "commands all men everywhere to repent, because he has fixed a day on which he will judge the world in righteousness by a man whom he has appointed, and of this he has given assurance to all men by raising him from the dead." In this way Paul appealed to what he could in his hearers' conceptions but brought radical news

concerning the will and actions of God in history. The responses of his audience are reported as ranging from scorn through mild curiosity to belief.

Christian evangelists must often decide which name of the divine they will employ among those used by their hearers. Jesuit missionaries to China in the 16th and 17th centuries could use *tian* (simply "heaven," a Confucian usage), *shangdi* ("sovereign on high"), and *tianzhu* or *tiandi* ("lord of heaven"). Matteo Ricci (1552–1610) favoured using all three interchangeably. He rejected other terms—e.g., *taiji* ("supreme ultimate") and *li* ("principle")—from Neo-Confucian philosophy.

In Vietnam, Alexandre de Rhodes (1591–1660) rejected the terms *but* and *phat* because they were used for the Buddha, whom he regarded as an idol. Instead he chose the vernacular compound *Duc Chua Troi Dat* ("noble ruler of heaven and earth"), thus coming close to Acts 17:24 and Luke 10:21. Some missionaries to East Asia resorted to transliterating the Latin *Deus* ("God"), which had either the advantage or the disadvantage of being an empty container waiting to be filled.

A modern missionary to India, Lesslie Newbigin (1909–98), recounted how, in preaching to villagers in the south, he would tell stories about Jesus that could not be told about the Hindu gods Shiva, Vishnu, or Ganesha, until gradually their conceptions of the Divine would be changed. Newbigin saw a radical contrast between the nature of God

An illustration from a Chinese manuscript of the Jesuit missionary to China, Matteo Ricci, and his first convert, circa 1667. Hulton Archive/Getty Images

implied in "the higher Hinduism"—when atman and brahman are identified and the material world is considered an illusion (maya)—and in the Bible—when the universal Creator is presented as one who personally engages with humankind in concrete history.

Christian theological opinions may vary concerning the degree to which an existing idea of the divine needs to be "completed" and the degree to which it needs to be "corrected" through the preaching of the God of Jesus Christ. Features of the previous religion that are affirmed may then be viewed as having constituted a "preparation for the gospel" (*praeparatio evangelica*), while elements that are rejected as incompatible with Christianity will at least have served as a negative point of contrast. Ultimately, Christians expect that the Holy Trinity— Father, Son, and Spirit—will be recognized as the sole true God.

CATECHESIS

By the 3rd century at the latest, it was normal for two to three years to elapse before an initial inquirer into the gospel might eventually be admitted to the church by baptism. During this period, the catechumens received instruction in faith and morals and their manner of life was observed. As the time for their baptism drew closer, they were enrolled as "applicants" (*competentes*), "chosen" (*electi*), or "destined for illumination" (*photizomenoi*). There is considerable evidence from the 4th and 5th centuries that those preparing for baptism underwent intensive preparation during the final weeks of their catechumenate. This final period usually coincided with the season that became known as Lent, and baptism was administered on Easter. Toward the end of the period of instruction, a dual ceremony took place, in which the words of the creed were orally "handed over" to the candidates (the *traditio symboli*; "hand over the Creed") and then, a day or two before Easter, "given back" (the *redditio symboli*; "give back the Creed"). Thus the candidates had to learn the creed—which the bishop expounded to them—and then be able to repeat it.

As the rite is described in an early church order—which most 20th-century scholarship identified with the treatise *Apostolic Tradition* (c. 215) by Hippolytus of Rome—the baptism itself took the form of a threefold immersion in water. At each immersion the candidates replied "I believe" to the questions put by the minister: "Do you believe in God the Father almighty? Do you believe in Christ Jesus, the Son of God, who was born of the Holy Spirit and the Virgin Mary, was crucified under Pontius Pilate, and died, and rose the third day alive from the dead, and ascended into the heavens, and sits at the right hand of the Father, and will come to judge the living and the dead? Do you believe in the Holy Spirit and the holy church and the resurrection of the flesh?" Following baptism, the new believers participated in the sacrament of the Eucharist for the first time.

In the days immediately after Easter, the bishop would give more detailed teaching to the neophytes on the meaning and effect of the sacraments they had just received. Lectures attributed to Cyril of Jerusalem and to Ambrose of Milan

are still extant. In other places—such as Antioch, where John Chrysostom taught—these "mystagogical catecheses" were delivered before the initiatory rites were undertaken.

As infant baptism gradually became the preponderant practice, verbal instruction around baptism fell out of use, although some of the old ceremonies of the catechumenate continued to be administered in compressed form. Instead, children were taught the faith when they reached the age of reason. In the medieval West, this instruction came to be associated with confirmation, that part of the initiation process which

Father Sean Charles Rene (right) delivers communion in front of St. Gerard Church during Easter services April 4, 2010, in Port-au-Prince, Haiti. Services have often been held outside since the January 12, 2010, earthquake destroyed many churches in Haiti. Lee Celano/Getty Images

remained for the bishop to do. The parish priest was expected to teach the local children at least the Apostles' Creed, the Lord's Prayer, the Hail Mary, the sacraments, the Ten Commandments, and the Seven Beatitudes or some other lessons on the vices and virtues. In the 16th century, Protestant reformers adapted this practice by providing official printed catechisms for use with children, each more or less marked with the doctrinal emphasis brought by the particular reformer. After the Council of Trent, the Roman Catholic Church produced the *Catechismus AD Parochos* (1566), intended for parish priests rather than immediately for their wards. Simpler, shorter catechisms were also composed locally.

Modern educational theory discountenanced rote learning, especially in the form of cut-and-dried questions and answers, and the genre of the catechism became unpopular. Many churches in the West, however, have sought to retrieve the loss of informed faith that has occurred over several generations. In the second half of the 20th century, "adult catechisms" of various literary types were produced for study by individuals or groups; and some churches have tried to introduce a kind of remedial catechumenate on more ancient models.

LITURGY

Christians gather regularly for worship, particularly on Sundays and on the great annual festivals. In these assemblies, their faith is directed to God in praise and prayer; it is also exposed to God for strengthening, deepening, and enriching. In the living encounter with God, the content and verbal formulations of faith are shaped, while in turn the tried and accepted teaching of the community provides the basis for each new celebration.

Worship contributed to the evolution of doctrine from the earliest days of Christianity. In the first decade of the 2nd century, the Roman investigator Pliny reports that the Christians meet "on a fixed day" and "recite a hymn to Christ as to a god." The experienced presence of the risen and exalted Christ as living Lord is reflected even earlier in such New Testament texts as Matthew 18:20 (gathering "in his name" for prayer), Matthew 28:16–20 (Christ's accompaniment of his Apostles in teaching and baptizing), 1 Corinthians 16:22 (the invocation *Maranatha* as "The Lord has come" or "Our Lord, come"), Philippians 2:9–11 (the bowing of the knee to Jesus and the confession from the tongue that he is Lord), and Revelation 1:4–18 (John's vision, when he was "in the Spirit on the Lord's Day," of Christ standing among seven golden lamp stands and holding seven stars). The practice of worshipping Christ as the Lord, as early Christian and non-Christian sources indicate, was an important part of early Christian ritual, which played a central role in establishing the doctrine of his divine status. In the fierce debates of the 4th century, Athanasius maintained that the church's worship of Christ established that he is fully God, for otherwise Christians would commit an unthinkable idolatry.

Influence also traveled in the other direction. From the beginning of the faith, doctrine contributed to the development of patterns of worship and has continued to do so. Theological reflection on Christ's sovereignty in the present most likely led to belief also in his preexistence as the agent of the Father's creative work from the very beginning. This belief then found expression in the hymns or other liturgical forms that are echoed at several places in the New Testament: 1 Corinthians 8:6; Colossians 1:15–20; and Hebrews 1:1–2, for example.

Church authorities have been keen to ensure that the language used in worship is doctrinally orthodox. The *Apostolic Tradition*, an early church order, sets out a sample prayer for a newly ordained bishop to use at the Eucharist, saying that it is not necessary that he use exactly these words, "only let his prayer be correct and orthodox." A similar concern led some North African councils around the year 400 to discourage new compositions. In the Middle Ages, the great metropolitan bishoprics—and even, in the case of Charlemagne, the imperial court—sought to standardize liturgical forms in their areas. The advent of printing made this easier, and the Protestant reformers issued books for the purpose, either laying down verbally the entire content of the service (as in the Church of England's *Book of Common Prayer*) or publishing "directories" that set out in some detail the principles according to which the minister should conduct the service (as sometimes in the Reformed or Presbyterian case). Following the Council of Trent, the Roman see produced a series of books that regulated the words and gestures of the rites down to the last detail (*Breviary*, 1568; *Missal*, 1570; *Pontifical*, 1596; and *Ritual*, 1614). Less bookish churches have relied more on individual ministers, assuming the fundamental doctrinal soundness of the ministers or their recurrent inspiration by the truth of God or both.

Wherever sermons are preached to the congregation, a special responsibility rests on the preacher to build the local community up in the Christian faith. The theological assumption is that the entire liturgy is both a school and the feast of faith: in the same act, believers both learn and celebrate the transgenerational faith of the Church into which they grow. This assumption was the motivation of the liturgical revisions and renewals attempted in many Western churches in the second half of the 20th century. An outstanding example is provided by Eucharistic Prayer IV in the Roman Missal of 1969–70, which has been borrowed and adapted by several other churches. Here the words and the ritual actions allow a reappropriation of the entire story of salvation:

> *Father in heaven, it is right that we should give you thanks and glory: you alone are God, living and true. Through all eternity you live in unapproachable light.*

Source of life and goodness, you have created all things, to fill your creatures with every blessing and lead all men to the joyful vision of your light. Countless hosts of angels stand before you to do your will; they look upon your splendor and praise you night and day. United with them, and in the name of every creature under heaven, we too praise your glory as we say: Holy, holy, holy Lord, God of power and might, heaven and earth are full of your glory. Hosanna in the highest. Blessed is he who comes in the name of the Lord. Hosanna in the highest. Father, we acknowledge your greatness: all your actions show your wisdom and love. You formed man in your own likeness and set him over the whole world to serve you, his creator, and to rule over all creatures. Even when he disobeyed you and lost your friendship, you did not abandon him to the power of death, but helped all men to seek and find you. Again and again you offered a covenant to man, and through the prophets taught him to hope for salvation. Father, you so loved the world that in the fullness of time you sent your only Son to be our Savior. He was conceived through the power of the Holy Spirit, and born of the Virgin Mary, a man like us in all things but sin. To the poor he proclaimed the good news of salvation, to prisoners, freedom, and to those in sorrow, joy. In fulfillment of your will he gave himself up to death; but by rising from the dead, he destroyed death and restored life. And that we might live no longer for ourselves but for him, he sent the Holy Spirit from you, Father, as his first gift to those who believe, to complete his work on earth and bring us the fullness of grace. Father, may this Holy Spirit sanctify these offerings. Let them become the body and blood of Jesus Christ our Lord as we celebrate the great mystery which he left us as an everlasting covenant. He always loved those who were his own in the world. When the time came for him to be glorified by you, his heavenly Father, he showed the depth of his love. While they were at supper, he took bread, said the blessing, broke the bread, and gave it to his disciples, saying: Take this, all of you, and eat it: This is my body which will be given up for you. In the same way, he took the cup, filled with wine. He gave you thanks, and giving the cup to his disciples, said: Take this, all of you, and drink from it: this is the cup of my blood, the blood of the new and everlasting covenant. It will be shed for you and for all men, so that sins may be forgiven. Do this in memory of me. Let us proclaim the mystery of faith: Christ has died, Christ is risen, Christ will come again. Father, we now celebrate this memorial of our redemption. We recall Christ's death, his descent among the dead, his resurrection, and his ascension to your right hand; and, looking forward to his coming in glory, we offer you his body and blood, the acceptable sacrifice which brings salvation to the whole world. Lord, look upon this sacrifice which you have given to your church; and by your Holy Spirit, gather all who share this one bread and one cup into the one body of Christ, a living sacrifice of praise. Lord, remember those for whom we offer this sacrifice, especially N. our Pope, N. our bishop, and bishops and clergy everywhere. Remember those who take part in this offering, those here present and all your people, and all those who seek you with a sincere heart. Remember those who have died in the peace of Christ and all the dead whose faith is known to you alone. Father, in your mercy grant also to us, your children, to enter into our heavenly inheritance in the company of the Virgin Mary, the Mother of God, and your apostles and saints. Then, in your kingdom, freed from the corruption of sin and death, we shall sing your glory with every creature through Christ our Lord, through whom you give us everything that is good. Through him, with him, in him, in the unity of the Holy Spirit, all glory and honor is yours, almighty Father, for ever and ever. Amen.

So comprehensive was this prayer that the Catholic bishops of France made it the basis for a short popular catechism, *Il est grand, le mystère de la foi: Prière et foi de l'Église catholique* (1978; "It Is Great, the Mystery of the Faith: The Prayer and Faith of the Catholic Church").

Hymns have been significant vehicles of the Christian faith from the earliest days. They have been sung particularly in the daily offices of the Orthodox and Catholic churches, and they have figured prominently in the Sunday worship of many Protestant churches, especially the Lutheran and Methodist. Congregational singing is appropriate to the "bodily" character of Christianity in both the physical and the social senses of the word, as it permits the members of the Body of Christ to engage "with one heart and one voice" in the worship of God (Romans 5:5–6).

ETHICS

Christians acknowledge not only a duty to announce the gospel, profess the faith, and worship God but also to live their entire lives according to God's will. Being God's people means following God's law, which means walking in

Iraqi choir members sing during the Christmas Day mass at the Virgin Mary Church in the central Karrada neighbourhood in Baghdad on December 25, 2008. Sabah Arar/AFP/Getty Images

the way of truth (Psalm 25:4–5; 86:11) and obeying it (Romans 2:8; Galatians 5:7; 1 Peter 1:22; 3 John 3–4). The dual commandment holds good: to love God and to love neighbour (Matthew 22:37–39). To "dwell in love" is to dwell in God, who is both truth and love (1 John).

Historically, Christian ethical teaching has had two biblical foci, the Ten Commandments (Exodus 20:1–17; Deuteronomy 5:6–21) and the Sermon on the Mount (Matthew 5–7); the emphasis on one or the other has varied across time and space. The Decalogue, as the Ten Commandments are sometimes called, remains valid for Christians, although

the divine basis grounding the covenant between God and his elect people has been broadened, according to Christian belief, by the redemptive work of Jesus Christ—a move reflected in the shifting of the chief weekly "holy day" from the sabbath (Exodus 20:8–11; Deuteronomy 6:12–15) to Sunday, the day of the Lord's resurrection, when the Christian community gathers to celebrate the new covenant in his blood and the beginning of the new creation. The "second table" of the Law—honouring parents, and rejecting murder, adultery, theft, false witness, and coveting—has been held by Christians to apply universally, the core of a "natural law" extending beyond the community that has received God's "special revelation." In this regard, it functions at least to preserve society against the worst ravages of sin until the preaching of the gospel attains its full range and final goal.

In the Sermon on the Mount, Jesus radicalized the Law by, for instance, making anger murderous and lust adulterous (Matthew 5:21–22, 27–28) and calling for his disciples to be "perfect, as your heavenly Father is perfect" (Matthew 5:48). In the Beatitudes (Matthew 5:1–12), the blessings Jesus offered in the Sermon on the Mount, he declared that the qualities and powers of the impending Kingdom of God were available among his followers in such a way that they would bear a distinctive witness to God before the world (Matthew 5:14–16). Christians have believed that taking the "hard way" (Matthew 7:13–14) is possible by virtue of the divine gift of the Holy Spirit (Luke 11:9–13; cf. Matthew 7:7–12).

In the epistles of Paul, the indicatives of gospel and faith serve to ground the imperatives of attitude and behaviour. Following his exposition of God's saving actions in Christ in the first 11 chapters of the Letter to the Romans, Paul asserts, "I appeal to you therefore, brothers and sisters, by the mercies of God to present your bodies as a living sacrifice, holy and acceptable to God, which is your reasonable service. Do not be conformed to this world [or age] but be transformed by the renewal of your mind, that you may prove what is the will of God, what is good, and acceptable, and perfect" (Romans 12:1–2).

Christian ethical teaching and practice are intrinsic to the community of the faithful and its life. In the early centuries, certain occupations were considered incompatible with becoming a Christian. According to the *Apostolic Tradition*, brothel-keepers, prostitutes, sculptors, painters, keepers of idols, actors, charioteers, gladiators, soldiers, magicians, astrologers, and diviners could not become Christians. Moral instruction was provided throughout the catechumenate, and many patristic homilies reveal the ethical teaching and exhortation practiced by the preachers in the liturgical assemblies. Medieval catechesis included the Decalogue, the Beatitudes, and the lists of virtues and vices. The administration of sacramental penance on a regular basis served the formation of individual character and conduct.

Much material became codified in ecclesiastical regulations known as canon law. Whereas the earliest Christians could exercise little or no influence on civil rulers, the "conversion of the Empire" under the 4th-century emperors Constantine and Theodosius permitted bishops their say in the personal and political affairs of emperors and in the wider life of society. In Christendom, legal systems claimed foundations in Christian teaching.

Modernity brought a decline in the direct institutional role of the churches in society, but the rise of democracy encouraged church leaders to assume an advisory capacity in the shaping of public policy, seeking to guide not only the members of their own ecclesiastical communities but also the whole body politic. On the Roman Catholic part, this has occurred at the global level through the so-called "social encyclicals" of popes from Leo XIII (*Rerum Novarum*, 1891; "Of New Things") through John XXIII (*Pacem in Terris*, 1962; "Peace on Earth"), Paul VI (*Populorum Progressio*, 1968; "Progress of the Peoples"), and John Paul II (*Laborem Exercens*, 1981; "Through Work" and *Centesimus Annus*, 1991; "The 100th Year"). Protestant denominations have typically made pronouncements and initiated programs through their national or international assemblies and agencies. The World Council of Churches, a fellowship of Christian churches founded in 1948, has formulated what were sometimes called "middle axioms" (e.g., the notion of a "responsible society" or "justice, peace and the preservation of creation"), which were intended as common ground on which Christians and secular bodies could meet for thought and action.

A theological problem resides in the passage from the story of salvation in its broadest terms (the message of the gospel and the content of the faith, concisely and comprehensively formulated) to its enactment in particular questions and instances. For example, it is sometimes held that certain acts are simply contrary to God's will and purpose for humankind and therefore always morally wrong; yet there is also a view that circumstances can so greatly affect cases that the good

may be differently served in different situations. The difficulties that accompany the move from general principle to concrete discipline are illustrated in the report of the Anglican-Roman Catholic International Commission, *Life in Christ: Morals, Communion and the Church* (1994). It is there claimed that "Anglicans and Roman Catholics derive from the Scriptures and Tradition the same controlling vision of the nature and destiny of humanity and share the same fundamental moral values." Disagreements on such matters as "abortion and the exercise of homosexual relations" are relegated to the level of "practical and pastoral judgment," with no account offered of intermediate processes that might allow material differences to develop. Here are not only ecclesiastical but civilizational issues that the next generation may choose to revisit in the light of the moral teaching proposed to church and world in the encyclical letters of John Paul II, *Veritatis Splendor* (1993; "The Splendour of Truth") and *Evangelium Vitae* (1995; "The Gospel of Life").

DEFENDING THE FAITH

The First Letter of Peter tells its addressees that they must "always be prepared to make a defense (*apologia*) to anyone who calls you to account for the hope that is in you" (3:15). The defense of the faith has been required of Christians when they faced persecution, but "apologetics" have also been undertaken in the face of intellectual attacks.

In the 2nd century, several Christian writers—Aristides, Justin Martyr, Tatian, Theophilus, Athenagoras, Tertullian—defended Christianity against the popular and political charges brought against it by non-Christians. It was denounced as an unregistered and "secret" cult and was suspected of immorality (human flesh and blood were consumed at its love feasts) and disloyalty (Christians refused to participate in the civic religion). The Apologists also responded both to Jews who claimed the Hebrew Scriptures as their own and rejected the Christian interpretation of them as fulfilled in Jesus Christ and to the more philosophical criticisms addressed to the doctrine of the Incarnation.

These early apologetics came to a climax in the eight books of *Against Celsus*, a treatise written by Origen around 246–248 to answer the still troublesome work of a Platonist and critic of Christianity dating from about 70 years earlier and claiming to speak "the word of truth" (*alêthês logos*). Celsus was quite well informed about the Christian scriptures and doctrines, although he associated with them some gnostic beliefs that were disowned by the churches. He conducted his critique from the moving platform of his own eclectic Middle Platonism along with some Jewish objections to the story of Jesus. Celsus ridiculed the Christian worship of a man of recent appearance who had died a disgraceful death. In order to refute the tolerant and politically convenient polytheism of Celsus, which harmonized the notion of a supreme but distant Deity known under many names with belief in numerous subordinate local deities, Origen drew on arguments that had already been developed in Hellenistic Judaism in favour of monotheism. But Origen needed to defend specific doctrines concerning Christ. In defense of the Incarnation, he argued that the descent of Christ does not require spatial movement when "the Word out of great love for mankind brings down a Saviour to the human race," and in support of the Crucifixion he asserted that it was a "death willingly accepted for the human race," by analogy with "the fact that one righteous man dying voluntarily for the community may avert the activities of evil demons by expiation, since it is they who bring about plagues, or famines, or stormy seas, or anything similar." Origen insisted that his work was not written for convinced Christians but "either for those entirely without experience of faith in Christ, or for those whom the apostle calls 'weak in faith.'"

At the beginning of the 5th century, Augustine began his work *The City of God* as an answer to pagan complaints that the sack of Rome—supposedly "the eternal city"—by Alaric and his Goths in 410 was due to the abandonment of the old gods in favour of Christianity. Augustine showed the inconsistency of the critics in failing to blame the civic gods for previous setbacks and in failing to give credit for the divine benefits bestowed on Christian emperors. He asserted that the true God is the ruler of all nations, bestowing both success and calamity for his own purposes. Augustine developed an entire philosophy of history, which helped shape for a thousand years the Christian understanding of church and state. His vision embraced two "cities," the city of God and an earthly city, existing side by side through the course of history: "Two loves have created two cities: love of self, to the contempt of God, the earthly city; love of God, to the contempt of self, the heavenly" (XIV:28). The institutions of the earthly city are not without their divine rationale, for they ensure a relative justice amid the fallen condition of humankind. Yet the happiness the earthly city allows is only temporary, and its society is conflicted. Only the peace and eternity of the divine city match the Supreme Good. Nor is the pilgrim church quite to be equated with the city of God, for the latter already contains the angels and the saints, while the former will have tares mixed in with the wheat until the final judgment. Yet in the centuries of Christendom, Augustine's treatise was used to ground the doctrine of the superiority of the papacy over the empire and as the foundation for secular political theory and practice.

When, partly as a result of the European "wars of religion" in the 16th and 17th centuries, doubt took over from faith as a methodological principle in philosophy and the natural sciences, some tried a new apologetic tack. This approach is represented by the "Christian Deist," Matthew Tindal, who wrote *Christianity as Old as the Creation, or the Gospel as a Republication of the Religion of Nature* (1730). After a century's critique of the notion of divine revelation in the name of "Enlightenment," Immanuel Kant thought that Christianity could and should be fitted into "religion within the limits of reason alone," as the title of a treatise he published in 1793 suggested.

As the 18th century passed into the 19th, a different style of apologetic was conducted by the Berlin preacher Friedrich Schleiermacher (1768–1834). Belonging to a family of Reformed ministers and educated at Pietist institutions, Schleiermacher tapped into emergent Romanticism in his *On Religion: Speeches to Its Cultured Despisers* (1799). Refusing to identify religion with metaphysics or morals, Schleiermacher located its essence in intuition (*Anschauung*) and feeling (*Gefühl*), the "sense and taste for the infinite" (*Sinn und Geschmack fürs Unendliche*). The founder of Christianity, Schleiermacher noted in his *On Religion*, was remarkable as the best mediator yet of a clear consciousness of the divine being. Schleiermacher continued this apologetic theme in his comprehensive account of Christian doctrine, *The Christian Faith* (1821–22; 1831). In his wake, Protestant systematic theology in the 19th and 20th centuries generally sought to operate within the "plausibility structures" of "modernity." Sometimes it got no further than apologetically oriented considerations of method.

Among Roman Catholic writers, John Henry Newman's *An Essay in Aid of a Grammar of Assent* (1870) offered a major intellectual justification of the act of faith during what he viewed as a revolutionary, seismic period in the world of ideas. Modern Catholic scholars have made contemporary apologetics a component in the subdiscipline of "fundamental theology."

RESPECTING LANGUAGE AND KNOWLEDGE

Restatement of doctrine has been required whenever Christianity crossed a linguistic boundary. The extension from the largely Hebraic and Aramaic world of Jesus and his Apostles into the Hellenistic world had already occurred by the time of the New Testament writings, and Greek became the language of the texts that constitute the permanent basis of Christian doctrine. That was the beginning of what the German theologian Adolf von Harnack called the "Hellenization of Christianity," whose relation to "the historical Jesus"—the putative peasant from Nazareth—has been viewed as problematic by many modern scholars. The New Testament itself was later translated into Latin as the faith spread westward.

In some cases, however, a restatement may become necessary even within a single linguistic area. Thus the Council of Nicaea in 325 commandeered the non-scriptural term *homoousios* ("of one substance") in order to safeguard the essential relation of the Son to the Father that had been denied by Arius. During the 4th century the vocabulary in

HOMOOUSIOS

The key term of the Christological doctrine formulated at the first ecumenical council, at Nicaea in 325, to affirm that God the Son and God the Father are of the same substance was homoousios. *The Council of Nicaea, presided over by the emperor Constantine, was convened to resolve the controversy within the church over the relationship between the persons of the Trinity. The council condemned Arianism, which taught that Christ was more than human but not fully divine. The use of* homoousios *(Greek: "of one substance," or "of one essence") in the Nicene Creed was meant to put an end to the controversy, but Arianism revived within the church and was supported by Constantine and his family. In 381, Emperor Theodosius I, however, summoned the second ecumenical council (first Council of Constantinople), which produced a creed (also containing the word* homoousios*) that became the definitive statement of orthodox belief.*

which Christian belief in the Holy Trinity was stated was gradually stabilized and refined. A similar process took place in the Council of Chalcedon (451), which defined Christ as "one person, acknowledged in two natures, unconfusedly, unchangeably, indivisibly, inseparably."

Restatements internal to a linguistic tradition may go hand in glove with shifts in philosophical conceptions of knowledge (epistemology). A prime example is Thomas Aquinas's participation in the rediscovery of Aristotelian categories (e.g., substance, quantity, quality, and relation), even though he exceeded and transformed them in the service of theological, ethical, and sacramental teachings that in turn shaped doctrinal conceptions and formulations in the Catholic church of the West.

Although not always distinguishing between scientific knowledge and the wider philosophical claims sometimes made by particular scientists, many modern theologians have felt a need to restate the gospel and the faith in ways that do not infringe on the knowledge brought by the natural sciences (the very rise of which may have been fostered by the Christian doctrine of creation as both regular and contingent). A prominent attempt to restate the gospel and faith in this way was the program of "demythologization" proposed by the German biblical scholar and Lutheran theologian Rudolf Bultmann (1884–1976). Bultmann proposed to restate the message of and about Jesus in terms of the existentialist philosophy of Martin Heidegger: the word of the Cross summoned people to authentic existence by liberating them from the past and opening up to them a new future. In response to Bultmann's radical program, more traditional theologians argued that the Incarnation and the Resurrection cannot be fitted into any other world view than that of which they are the cornerstone.

In the 1960s, some theologians attempted to state "the secular meaning of the gospel" (the title of a book by P.M. Van Buren) by removing the last traces of transcendence from their accounts, leaving no room for communication or interaction between God and humankind ("revelation," "grace," "prayer") and no expectation of any destiny beyond this world. By the late 20th century, theologians had found hope in the explanatory inadequacy at the scientific level of a sheerly physicalist theory of efficient causality. The door was opened, at least slightly, to the notion of personal purpose, which can point by analogy from the level of human affairs to a view of God and the world that matches more easily the biblical story. This notion can also provide a framework for integrating—as most academic theologians have done—some kind of evolutionary theory into the elucidation of Christian doctrine concerning creation.

RESPECTING PLACES AND PEOPLES

As the gospel has spread into new regions of the world, there has proven to be need and opportunity for fresh conceptions and formulations of the faith. The process of inculturation begins when missionaries first arrive in a region in which Christianity does not exist and the instruction of converts (catechesis) takes place. Gradually, after perhaps experiencing more strongly an initial rupture with their previous culture, those who enter the Christian faith start to give it a more local expression.

Soteriology, the theological study of salvation, has often lent itself to inculturation. An early medieval example is found in the Saxon poem the *Heliand*, in which the gospel story is told with Christ as the warrior chieftain leading his companions into battle against Satan, the enemy of mankind. Anselm of Canterbury (1033/34–1109), in *Cur Deus homo* ("Why God Became Man"), presented the atoning work of Christ as the satisfaction of God's offended honour so that sinful men and women might be readmitted to his company.

In many parts of sub-Saharan Africa, Jesus has been received as the Healer from sickness and the Liberator from all other forces of evil. He has been looked to as the powerfully protective Ancestor or Elder Brother, as the Chief of Chiefs, and as the Initiation Master who introduces his pupils to the secrets of God.

The various dramatic accounts of the Saviour and salvation are stimulated by one or more of the presentations of Christ and his work in the New Testament. In turn, the gospel changes the vernacular language and culture. Liturgy and the arts are the milieux in which these transformative effects are most creatively achieved. By virtue of intercultural and interecclesiastical exchanges, some initially local contributions spread beyond their place of origin and become part of the cumulative tradition of Christianity.

DOGMA, OR AUTHORITATIVE TEACHING

Jesus "taught with authority" (Matthew 7:29), and the risen Lord gave his Apostles a share in his authority when he commissioned them to make disciples from all the nations by teaching what he had commanded them (Matthew 28:18–20). The apostolic church trusted that Christ had made provision for Christians to be kept by the Holy Spirit in the truth of the gospel (John 14–16). The apostle Paul charged Timothy to preserve the deposit of the faith among other appointed teachers (1 and 2 Timothy). By the 2nd century, bishops were regarded as the special guardians of apostolic teaching; and the practice grew of bishops meeting in council at various geographical levels to determine teaching as needed.

The very first ecclesiastical council, according to tradition, took place when, as narrated in Acts 15, the Apostles and elders met in Jerusalem to determine the conditions under which Gentiles were to be admitted to the church. They concluded that "it has seemed good to the Holy Spirit and to us to lay upon you no greater burden than these necessary things: that you abstain from what has been sacrificed to idols and from blood and from what is strangled and from unchastity" (Acts 15:28). The decisions of the council of Jerusalem were termed *dogmata* (Acts 16:4).

Dogma became the traditional term for truths believed to be indispensable to the Christian faith. The question of what precisely counts as dogma is bound up with questions of pronouncement and reception. The most widely recognized source of dogmatic formulations are ecumenical or general councils of the church, but Christian communities vary in the number of councils they recognize as ecumenical. Some ancient communities—now labeled Oriental Orthodox (Syrian, Coptic, Ethiopian, Armenian, Indian)—count only three such councils (Nicaea in 325, Constantinople in 381, and Ephesus in 431). The Byzantine or Eastern Orthodox churches also accept the decisions of the councils of Chalcedon (451), Constantinople II (553), Constantinople III (680–681), and Nicaea II (787). The Roman Catholic Church recognizes 21 such councils, the most recent of which are Trent (1545–63), Vatican I (1869–70), and Vatican II (1962–65). Most Protestant churches from the 16th century rely on the first four councils (Nicaea, Constantinople, Ephesus, Chalcedon). Not all councils claiming to be ecumenical have been recognized as such, and not all decisions taken by ecumenical councils are dogmatic in nature.

Conciliar decrees most generally accepted as dogma concern the identity of the Holy Trinity and of Jesus Christ as second person of the Trinity incarnate. The crucial councils of the 4th and 5th centuries clarified and reaffirmed—in the face of what were judged inadequate or deviant understandings—the core content of the confession "Jesus is Lord" and the names "Father, Son, and Holy Spirit," in which Christians were baptized. It is significant that the dogmatic affirmations of Nicaea and Constantinople took the form of precisions to extant creeds. Bishop Athanasius of Alexandria, the principal advocate and defender of Nicaea, insisted that salvation was at stake if the three persons confessed and invoked at baptism were not fully divine, for only God can save (*First Letter to Serapion*). Bishop Basil of Caesarea, in his treatise *On the Holy Spirit*, defended the same view and then deployed theological arguments to show that the three persons of the Trinity properly received equal praise and adoration in the church's liturgy. The council of Constantinople (381) could expand the creedal formulation to declare belief in the Holy Spirit, the "Lord and Life-giver,...who with the Father and the Son together is worshiped and glorified." Historically, what bishops declare in council, they teach in their churches. They expect to find adhesion from the faithful, since what they teach is "the faith once delivered to the saints," clarified and consolidated according to circumstances.

Since the First Vatican Council in 1869–70, the Roman Catholic Church has recognized in the office of the bishop of Rome a special charism, or spiritual gift, that allows him, under certain conditions, infallibly to define the Christian faith and morals in statements that are "irreformable" of themselves. The purpose of this charism is to provide the faithful the certainty of being taught the saving truth. The two dogmas that Catholics consider covered by this papal gift are those of the Immaculate Conception of Mary, promulgated by Pius IX in 1854, and Mary's assumption, body and soul, into heaven, promulgated by Pius XII in 1950.

Protestant churches have not claimed to hold general councils or to promulgate dogmas. Perhaps the closest attempt at the latter was the Lutheran Book of Concord, produced in Germany in 1580. Protestant churches have usually viewed their synods or assemblies as competent to "interpret" doctrine under the supreme norm of Scripture and with the guidelines provided by the earlier creeds and confessions that come from the general tradition of the "church universal" or their particular tradition. Since the 20th century, many Protestant synods have included not only pastors but also laypeople in their membership.

CONSENSUS

Short of dogma, considerable authority accrues to broad patterns of stating and practicing the Christian faith that have maintained themselves over time and space. They appear comprehensive and coherent, even though minor shades of difference are not excluded from their expression.

The Eastern Orthodox churches detect a "common mind of the fathers" (*consensus patrum*), which allows for some variety of contribution and emphasis among the Fathers. The most respected synthesis is that of John of Damascus (c. 675–749), whose defense of icon veneration also anticipated the decision of the seventh ecumenical council (Nicaea II, 787). In his "Exposition of

the Orthodox Faith," the Damascene first treats God, who is by nature incomprehensible. His existence and unity, however, can be inferred from the contingency and order of the created universe. He has, moreover, revealed himself adequately for our good in those things to which the Law, the Prophets, the Apostles, and the Evangelists bear testimony; humankind can thereby know that God is Trinity, though not the precise manner of the "mutual indwelling" (*perichôrêsis*) of the three hypostases. After his discussion of God, John treats creation, noting that the angels were created first and that the devil "was the first to depart from good and become evil." Concerning the wider material creation, he offers a theological perspective on astronomy, meteorology, geography, and zoology. Although human beings, John argues, were made "in God's image" (i.e., with mind and free will) and "after God's likeness" (i.e., to go forward in the path of goodness), they fell by pride and became slaves of passions and appetites; yet God continued to care for them. In the economy of salvation, John goes on, God has sought to win humankind back; God became human and acted from within in the person of the incarnate Son. Finally, he explains that since Christ was without sin, death could not hold him. Through faith and baptism humans are in him restored to communion with God, set upon the way of virtue, and renewed in a life that, nourished by the Eucharist, will be crowned by participation in the divine glory. John's work has remained influential in the Eastern church and was known to Peter Lombard (1100–60) and Thomas Aquinas (1225–74) in the medieval West.

Peter Lombard, master at the cathedral school of Notre Dame and archbishop of Paris, was author of the *Four Books of Sentences*. This seminal work treats God the Holy Trinity; creation, humankind, and sin; the Incarnation of the Word and the redemption of humanity; faith, hope, love, and the other virtues; the seven sacraments (baptism, confirmation, Eucharist, penance, unction of the sick and dying, ordination, marriage); and the last things (death, judgment, heaven, and hell). The Scriptures and the Fathers—notably Augustine, who is quoted more than 1,000 times—are its principal sources. Peter is not as rigorous as his own teacher, Peter Abelard, in discerning the apparent contradictions in his authorities, for which a dialectical resolution is to be sought (*Sic et non*; "Yes and No"). Lombard's "opinions" tend to harmonize with the chosen "sentences" of the Fathers. The *Sentences*, whose orthodoxy was established by the Lateran council of 1215, became the standard theological textbook in the medieval West and the subject of many commentaries; it thus helped to shape a nuanced consensus there too, from which disputes and disputations were not absent.

Of perhaps more delayed but certainly longer lasting effect was the *Summa theologiae* of Thomas Aquinas.

Called *Doctor Communis* ("Common Doctor") and *Doctor Angelicus* ("Angelic Doctor"), Aquinas was canonized by Pope John XXII in 1323 and declared a "Doctor of the Church" by Pius V in 1567. In 1879, Leo XIII enjoined the study of Aquinas on all Catholic theological students. A Neo-Thomist revival marked Roman Catholic theology at least until 1960, and the Angelic Doctor was again commended in Pope John Paul II's encyclical letter *Fides et Ratio* (1998; "Faith and Reason").

The *Summa theologiae* begins with the questions regarding human knowledge of God—what may be known by reason and what depends on faith, and the status of language used to refer to God. The first part of the *Summa* goes on to deal substantively with the Trinity, creation, and human nature. The second and longest part is modeled on Aristotle's *Nicomachean Ethics* and finds that much in Aristotle is congenial to Christian moral thinking. The third part—which was left unfinished—is concerned with the dogmatic topics of the Incarnation and the sacraments. Each major question is treated in several articles, which themselves begin with a subquestion, to which a plausible first answer is indicated (*Videtur quod*, "it seems that"). A different position is briefly stated (*Sed contra*, "But on the other hand"), usually in the name of a scriptural or patristic authority. Finally, Aquinas develops his own opinion (*Respondeo dicendum*, "I respond that"), which is basically the second

St. Thomas Aquinas Enthroned Between the Doctors of the Old and New Testaments, with Personifications of the Virtues, Sciences, and Liberal Arts, *fresco by Andrea da Firenze, c. 1365; in the Spanish Chapel of the church of Santa Maria Novella, Florence.* SCALA/Art Resource, New York

position (though it may integrate valid elements from the first answer) together with replies to remaining objections.

In Protestantism, the nearest approach to a broad consensus may be found in the respective traditions that stay within the vectors set by their chief reformers and their confessions and catechisms in the 16th century— so that at least a family resemblance remains among Lutherans or the Reformed. The individualism, however, that has characterized modernity—and

to which Protestantism itself has contributed—makes it harder to speak of an authoritative "common mind" in the Protestant communities at large. The difficulty is compounded insofar as Protestant theologians have tended to be more accommodating than Orthodox or Catholics to fast-moving shifts in the general culture. Nevertheless, Luther and, to a lesser degree, Calvin and Wesley are recurrently appealed to in various ways as doctrinal mentors in their respective traditions.

CREEDS AND CONFESSIONS

In the various communities that claim to be part of historic Christianity, the concise and comprehensive statement of Christian doctrine that is most widely recognized is the Nicene Creed. In 1982 the Faith and Order Commission of the World Council of Churches recognized that the Nicene Creed was the baptismal symbol (creed) used throughout the West but took the Nicene Creed as the "theological and methodological tool" to "identify the fundamentals of the apostolic faith which should be explicated." The commission recognized that the Nicene Creed has been universally accepted as containing the essential teachings of the faith and that the faith stated by the creed is shared by some "non-creedal churches" that are wary of "fixed" or "imposed" forms. The creed "thus serves to indicate whether the faith as set forth in modern situations is the same faith as the one the Church confessed through the centuries." It might also have been said, in reverse, that the creed summarizes the faith from which Christians start in preaching the gospel today.

NICENE CREED

The Nicene Creed is a Christian statement of faith. It is the only ecumenical creed because it is accepted as authoritative by the Roman Catholic, Eastern Orthodox, Oriental Orthodox, Anglican, and major Protestant churches.

Until the early 20th century, it was universally assumed that the Niceno-Constantinopolitan Creed (the more accurate term) was an enlarged version of the Creed of Nicaea, which was promulgated at the Council of Nicaea (325). It was further assumed that this enlargement had been carried out at the Council of Constantinople (381) with the object of bringing the Creed of Nicaea up to date in regard to heresies about the Incarnation and the Holy Spirit that had risen since the Council of Nicaea.

Additional discoveries of documents in the 20th century, however, indicated that the situation was more complex, and the actual development of the Niceno-Constantinopolitan Creed has been the subject of scholarly dispute. Most likely it was issued by the Council of Constantinople even though this fact was first explicitly stated at the Council of Chalcedon in 451. It was probably based on a baptismal creed already in existence, but it was an independent document and not an enlargement of the Creed of Nicaea.

The so-called Filioque clause (Latin "and from the son"), inserted after the words "the Holy Spirit...who proceedeth from the Father," was gradually introduced as part of the creed in the Western Church, beginning in the 6th century. It was probably finally accepted by the papacy in the 11th century. It has been retained by the Roman Catholic, Anglican, and Protestant churches. The Eastern churches have always rejected it because they consider it theological error and an unauthorized addition to a venerable document.

The Nicene Creed was originally written in Greek. Its principal liturgical use is in the Eucharist in the West and in both Baptism and the Eucharist in the East. A modern English version of the text without the Filioque is as follows:

We believe in one God,
the Father, the Almighty,
maker of heaven and earth,
of all that is seen and unseen.
We believe in one Lord, Jesus Christ, the only Son of God,
eternally begotten of the Father,
God from God, Light from Light, true God from true God,
begotten, not made, one in Being with the Father.
Through him all things were made.
For us men and for our salvation
he came down from heaven:
by the power of the Holy Spirit
he was born of the Virgin Mary, and became man.
For our sake he was crucified under Pontius Pilate;
he suffered, died, and was buried.
On the third day he rose again
in fulfillment of the Scriptures;
he ascended into heaven
and is seated on the right hand of the Father.
He will come again in glory
to judge the living and the dead,
and his kingdom will have no end.
We believe in the Holy Spirit, the Lord, the giver of life,
who proceeds from the Father.
With the Father and the Son he is worshipped and glorified.
He has spoken through the Prophets.
We believe in one holy catholic and apostolic Church.
We acknowledge one baptism for the forgiveness of sins.
We look for the resurrection of the dead,
and the life of the world to come. Amen.

Confessing the One Faith (1991), the document that the Faith and Order Commission placed before the member churches, works through each section and clause of the creed. The creed's phraseology is elucidated in terms of "its biblical witness" and, where necessary, in terms of the 4th-century controversies that prompted the introduction of certain technical formulations. The creed's affirmations are then explicated in the face of contemporary "challenges," which include the problem that the original language and philosophy in which the creeds were formulated are no longer those of the present day, the issue of the affirmation and appreciation of old and new religions in various cultures, and the fact that modern secular society questions many of the affirmations of Christianity.

In response to atheism and secularism, the Faith and Order document, which is much indebted in this section to Wolfhart Pannenberg, proclaims that "the world of finite things and the secular social system both lack ultimate meaning and purpose without a transcendent reality as their basis." The commission further asserts that the proper response to some Asian and African religious beliefs, which find the Christian doctrine of God too abstract and divorced from everyday life, is to be found in "the concreteness of the One God...in the work of the Father, the Son, and the Holy Spirit" as this occurs in "the history of salvation," which is the basis for faith in the eternal Trinity. Moreover, the doctrine of the Trinity offers a consistent monotheism because it incorporates the principle of plurality and diversity within the unity of God.

Regarding "the Father almighty," *Confessing the One Faith* argues that it is necessary to speak of the Father together with the Son in order to prevent the emergence of either a trivial or a sentimental view of divine fatherhood or of a view of

the Father's power as arbitrary. The term *Father* is to be retained because it is the name by which Jesus as the incarnate Son addressed him and because it defines the relationships within the Trinity as well as those between God and humankind. As an image, the divine fatherhood designates also the providential care and compassion of God, which may also contain motherly aspects. In relation to humankind, "God embraces, fulfils and transcends all that we know concerning human persons, both male and female, and human characteristics, whether masculine or feminine."

THE MATURATION OF UNDERSTANDING

It took some 350 years to get from the apostolic age to the doctrinal formulations of the Nicene Creed. The question thus arises whether a process of development was taking place. If so, what kinds of development were they? What was their significance, both for the substantive issues affected and for the way in which the formative period is viewed by subsequent generations of Christians? And is a principle of development allowed or established that may then be applied to other issues and at other times?

As the 2nd century turned into the 3rd, both Irenaeus, in *Against the Heresies*, and Tertullian, in *On the Prescription of Heretics*, in reference to the variability, innovations, and secretiveness of the teaching of the gnostics, pointed to the constant and public teaching given throughout the church, notably in the apostolic sees, and most particularly in Rome, where the church was founded by Peter and Paul. In setting out the "rule of faith," Irenaeus combines a recital of the mighty acts of God in creation and history with the threefold structure of the divine Name in which baptism is administered (Matthew 28:19, and the baptismal profession found in the *Apostolic Tradition*).

The rule of faith outlined by Irenaeus and Tertullian remains the formal pattern of the Nicene Creed. However, the evolution of doctrine between their time and the 4th-century councils of Nicaea and Constantinople is suggested by the insertions that the two councils made in the older texts concerning the essential being of the Son ("God from God, Light from Light, True God from True God, begotten not made, of one substance with the Father") and of the Holy Spirit ("the Lord, the Giver of Life, who proceeds from the Father, who with the Father and the Son together is worshiped and glorified"). These steps were taken in order to safeguard the established soteriological understandings and liturgical practices against rather blatant distortions of the apostolic message, and as a result of the exploration of previously unposed or unsettled questions and the intellectual and spiritual energy of successive generations in applying the inherited faith within their cultural circumstances.

This was the kind of process that John Henry Newman called "the development of an idea." As noted in his *Essay on the Development of Christian Doctrine*, a "great idea" takes a "longer time and deeper thought for [its] full elucidation," but this process of "germination and maturation" will be a "development" only if "the assemblage of aspects, which constitute its ultimate shape, really belongs to the idea from which they start." "Young birds do not grow into fishes," said Newman in that work.

Newman also thought that such a development would continue, and he left the Anglican church for the Roman Catholic Church in 1845 because he judged that the latter best embodied such a development. It would in fact be developmental grounds that provided a theological justification for the doctrines of Mary's Immaculate Conception (defined in 1854) and heavenly assumption (defined in 1950). The declaration of these teachings was held to make explicit things that were implicit in the apostolic witness but had required centuries of devotional practice and speculative reasoning to be brought out. Newman also considered that an infallible teaching office lay in the origins and logic of a developmental Christianity—indeed with a Roman focus, although he questioned the "opportunity" of its dogmatization in 1869–70, which in substance attributed that function to the pope without a general council.

The Eastern churches also accept a development of doctrine beyond Nicaea I and Constantinople I, embracing (in the case of the Byzantine churches) not only the Council of Ephesus in 431 (as the Oriental Orthodox do) but also the councils of Chalcedon, Constantinople II and III, and Nicaea II. The later councils are viewed as having clarified and explicated, but not altered, the teachings of the earlier councils. Thus Nicaea II, for instance, in deciding for the veneration of icons, was being true to the dogmas of the one person and two natures of Christ. The Eastern churches also hold to the infallibility of the church, thanks to its divine foundation and guidance by the Son and the Spirit and the pastoral oversight of its bishops in faithful succession. They do not, however, judge that the conditions have been met for the meeting of an ecumenical council after Nicaea II and the reception of its teaching by the whole body of the faithful. This has not stopped certain "doctrinal developments" from being widely regarded as legitimate and commendable. An example is the reception of the teaching of Gregory Palamas (14th century), who identified the "uncreated light" manifested at the Transfiguration of Christ on Mount Tabor with the "divine energies" by which Christian believers are savingly "deified" (an inner transformation mystically uniting God and the individual).

The Protestant reformers in the 16th century attempted to undo what they regarded as false developments ("corruptions," in Newman's terminology) in the Western church. They wished to go back—not so much historically as theologically—to Scripture, especially in matters of applied soteriology (though in matters of Christology and the Trinity they remained under the guidance of the councils of the 4th and 5th centuries).

CHAPTER 4

GOD

On the basis of their religious experiences, the mystics of Christianity of all eras have concurred in the belief that one can make no assertions about God, because God is beyond all concepts and images. Inasmuch as human beings are gifted with reason, however, the religious experience of transcendence demands historical clarification. Thus, in Christian theology two tendencies stand in constant tension with each other. On the one hand, there is the tendency to systematize the idea of God as far as possible. On the other, there is the tendency to eliminate the accumulated collection of current conceptions of God and to return to the understanding of his utter transcendence. Theologians, by and large, have had to acknowledge the limits of human reason and language to address the "character" of God, who is beyond normal human experience but who impinges on it. But because of the divine–human contact, it became necessary and possible for them to make some assertions about the experience, the disclosure, and the character of God.

All great epochs of the history of Christianity are defined by new forms of the experience of God and of Christ. Rudolf Otto, a 20th-century German theologian, attempted to describe to some extent the basic ways of experiencing the transcendence of the "holy." He called these the experience of the "numinous" (the spiritual dimension), the

Stained glass window depicting God the Father and angels. © Corbis

utterly ineffable, the holy, and the overwhelming. The "holy" is manifested in a double form: as the *mysterium tremendum* ("mystery that repels"), in which the dreadful, fearful, and overwhelming aspect of the numinous appears, and as the *mysterium fascinosum* ("mystery that attracts"), by which humans are irresistibly drawn to the glory, beauty, adorable quality, and the blessing, redeeming, and salvation-bringing power of transcendence. All of these features are present in the Christian concepts of God as explicated in the ever new experiences of the charismatic leaders.

CHARACTERISTIC FEATURES OF THE CHRISTIAN CONCEPT OF GOD

Within the Christian perception and experience of God, characteristic features stand out: (1) the personality of God, (2) God as the Creator, (3) God as the Lord of history, and (4) God as Judge. (1) God, as person, is the "I am who I am" designated in Exodus 3:14. The personal consciousness of human beings awakens in the encounter with God understood as a person: "The Lord used to speak to Moses face to face, as a man speaks to his friend" (Exodus 33:11). (2) God is also viewed as the Creator of heaven and Earth. The believer thus maintains, on the one hand, acknowledgement of divine omnipotence as the creative power of God, which also operates in the preservation of the world, and, on the other hand, trusts in the world, which—despite all its contradictions—is understood as one world created by God according to definite laws and principles and according to an inner plan. The decisive aspect of creation, however, is that God fashioned humans according to the divine image and made the creation subject to them. This special position of humans in the creation, which makes them coworkers of God in the preservation and consummation of the creation, brings a decisively new characteristic into the understanding of God. (3) This new characteristic is God as the Lord of history, which is the main feature of the understanding of God in the Hebrew Scriptures: God selects a special people and contracts a special covenant with them. Through the Law the divine agent binds this "people of God" in a special way. God sets before them a definite goal of salvation—the establishment of a divine dominion—and through the prophets admonishes the people by proclamations of salvation and calamity whenever they are unfaithful to the covenant and promise. (4) This God of history also is the God of judgment. The Israelite belief that the disclosure of God comes through the history of divinely led people leads, with an inner logic, to the proclamation of God as the Lord of world history and as the Judge of the world.

GOD THE FATHER

What is decisively new in the Christian, New Testament faith in God lies in the fact that this faith is so closely bound up with the person, teaching, and work of Jesus Christ that it is difficult to draw boundaries between theology (doctrines of God) and Christology (doctrines of Christ). The special relationship of Jesus to God is expressed through his designation of God as Father. In prayers Jesus used the Aramaic word *abba* ("father") for God, which is otherwise unusual in religious discourse in Judaism; it was usually employed by children for their earthly father. This father–son relationship became a prototype for the relationship of Christians to God. Appeal to the sonship of God played a crucial role in the development of Jesus's messianic self-understanding. According to the account of Jesus's baptism, Jesus understood his sonship when a voice from heaven said: "This is my beloved Son, with whom I am well pleased." In The Gospel According to John, this sonship constitutes the basis for the self-consciousness of Jesus: "I and the Father are one" (John 10:30).

THE BELIEF IN THE ONENESS OF THE FATHER AND THE SON

Faith in the Son also brought about a oneness with the Father. The Son became the mediator of the glory of the Father to those who believe in him. In Jesus's high priestly prayer (in John, chapter 17) he says: "The glory which thou hast given me I have given to them, that they may be one even as we are one, I in them and thou in me, that they may become perfectly one." In the Lord's Prayer Jesus taught his disciples to address God as "our Father."

The Father-God of Jesus after Jesus's death and Resurrection becomes—for his disciples—the God and Father of our Lord Jesus Christ (e.g., 2 Corinthians 1:3), who revealed his love through the sacrifice of his Son who was sent into the world. Faithful Christians can thus become the children of God, as noted in Revelation 21:7: "I will be his God and he shall be my son." For Christians, therefore, faith in God is not a doctrine to be detached from the person of Jesus Christ.

Medieval theologians often spoke of a "Beatific Vision," a blessed vision of God. In the history of Christian mysticism, this visionary experience of the transpersonal "Godhead" behind the personal "God" (as in the works of the medieval mystic Meister Eckhart)—also called an experience of the "trans-deity," the "divine ground," "groundlessness," the "abyss," and the divine "nothingness"—constantly breaks through and is renewed. Occasionally, this experience of transpersonal divine transcendence has directed itself against the development of a piety that has banalized the personal idea of God so much so that the glory and holiness of God have been trivialized.

The attempt of the 20th-century theologian Paul Tillich to reduce the Christian idea of God to the impersonal concept of "the Ground of Being," or "Being Itself," pointed toward an understanding of the pre-personal depths of the transcendence of Godhood.

Nevertheless, in the Christian understanding of Christ as being one with the Father, there is a possibility that faith in God will be absorbed in a "monochristism"—i.e., that the figure of the Son in the life of faith will overshadow the figure of the Father and thus cause it to disappear and that the figure of the Creator and Sustainer of the world will recede behind the figure of the Redeemer. Thus, the primacy of Christology and of the doctrine of justification in Reformation theology led to a depreciation of the creation doctrine and a Christian cosmology. This depreciation accelerated the estrangement between theology and the sciences during the period of the Enlightenment. This was subsequently distorted into a form of materialism. On the other hand, some 20th-century dialectical theologians, among them Karl Barth, in opposing materialism and humanism sometimes evoked a monochristic character that strongly accented the centrality of Christ at the expense of some cultural ties.

THE REVELATORY CHARACTER OF GOD

The God of the Bible is the God who presses toward revelation. The creation of the world is viewed as an expression of God's will toward self-revelation, for even the pagans "knew God." In a speech Paul gave in Athens, he said of God: "Yet he is not far from each one of us, for 'in him we live and move and have our being,'" in allusion to the words of the pagan writer Aratus: "For we are indeed his offspring" (Acts 17:27–28). This was the beginning of a knowledge of God that has manifested itself under the catchphrase of the "natural revelation" of God or God's revelation in the "book of nature." It has survived as one strand of theory throughout much of Christian history.

The self-revelation of God presupposes, however, a basic biblical understanding of the existing relationship between God and human beings. It cannot be separated from the view that God created humans according to the divine image and that in Jesus Christ, who "reflects the glory of God and bears the very stamp of his nature" (Hebrews 1:3), the heavenly man has appeared among humans as the "last Adam." The inner connection between the "natural" and the biblical revelation takes place through the view of Christ as the divine Logos become human.

Hellenistic thinkers had already been attracted by the emphasis in later Judaism on monotheism and transcendence. This tendency was sketched out earlier in Plato and later Stoicism, but it came to its mature development in Neoplatonism in the 3rd century AD. In the 1st century Philo of Alexandria interpreted the Hebrew Bible's concept of God in terms of the Logos idea of Hellenistic philosophy, but this Hellenization led to a tension that was to dominate the entire further history of Christian piety, as well as the Western history of ideas. The Greeks traced the idea of God to a "first cause" that stood behind all other causes and effects. Theologians under their influence used this understanding to contribute to a doctrine of God as "first cause" in Christian theology.

GOD AS CREATOR, SUSTAINER, AND JUDGE

The biblical understanding of God, however, was based on the idea of the freedom of the Creator, Sustainer, and Judge and included the concept that God could suspend the natural order or break the causal chain through miracles. This led theologians to two specific problems: (1) the attempt to prove the existence of God, and (2) the attempt to justify God in view of both the apparent shortcomings of the creation and the existence of evil in history. Both attempts have occupied the intellectual efforts of Western theologians and have inspired the highest of intellectual achievements. These attempts, however, often presumed that human reason could define the transcendent. Although theologians creatively addressed the issue, it was often simple Christian piety that served to guard the notion of transcendence, while concentrating on the historical revelation of God in the more accessible instrument of God's self-disclosure in Jesus Christ.

Efforts to explain the ways of God to humans, particularly in respect to the problem of the existence of evil, are called theodicy. This form of justification of God has addressed profound human impulses and has relied upon strenuous exercises of human reason, but it has also led to no finally satisfying conclusions. The problem, which was already posed by Augustine and treated in detail by Thomas Aquinas, became of pressing importance in the European Thirty Years' War (1618–48) and its aftermath. At that time Gottfried Wilhelm Leibniz, who did more than anyone to develop the concept of theodicy, endeavoured to defend the Christian notion of God against the obvious atheistic consequences that were evoked by the critical thinkers of his time. The result of such theological efforts, however, was either to declare God himself as the originator of evil, to excuse evil as a consequence of divine "permission," or instead—as with Hegel—to understand world history as the justification of God ("the true theodicy, the justification of God in history"). These answers did not always satisfy the Christian experience of faith. Many writers influenced by the Christian tradition have reacted against such justifications, most notably the Russian novelist Fyodor Dostoyevsky in his treatment of the suffering of children in *The Brothers Karamazov* (1879–80).

The German philosopher Immanuel Kant set the terms for much modern reflection on God's existence when he challenged the grounds of most previous efforts to prove it. Kant contended that it was finally impossible for the human intellect to achieve insights into the realm of the transcendent. Even as he was arguing this, modern science was shifting from grounds that presumed the nature of God and God's universe to autonomous views of nature that were grounded only in experiment, skepticism, and research. During the 19th century, philosophers in Kantian and scientific traditions despaired of the attempt to prove the existence of God.

During the same period some Western intellectuals turned against the very idea of God. One strand of Hegelian thinkers, typified by the German philosopher Ludwig Feuerbach, attempted to unmask the idea of religion as illusion. To Feuerbach, faith was an ideology designed to help humans delude themselves. The idea of dialectical materialism, in which the concept of "spirit" was dropped by thinkers such as Karl Marx, developed in this tradition. It also characterized religion as "bad faith" or "the opiate of the people," designed to seduce them from efforts to build a good society through the hope of rewards in a life to come.

At the same time, at first chiefly in Britain, scientific thinkers in the tradition of Charles Darwin hypothesized that evolutionary processes denied all biblical concepts of divine creation. Some dialectical materialists incorporated Darwinian theories in a frontal attack on the Christian worldview. Some Christians contended that this was a perversion of evolution, since certain

Christian teachings on divine creation, such as *creatio continua* ("continuing creation"), were both biblical and compatible with evolutionary theory. At the turn of the 20th century, some thinkers in both Britain and the United States optimistically reworked their doctrine of God in congruence with evolutionary thought.

THE VIEW THAT GOD IS NOT SOLITARY

The leaders of an 18th-century movement called Deism saw God as impersonal and unempathic—a principle of order and agent of responsibility not personal or addressable as the Christian God had been. Deism contributed to some intellectualizations of the idea of God, approaches that had sometimes appeared in the more sterile forms of medieval Scholasticism. God appeared to have been withdrawn from creation, which was pictured as a world machine; this God, at best, observed its running but never interfered.

According to the original Christian understanding of God of the early church, the Middle Ages, and the Reformation, God neither is solitary nor wishes to be alone. Instead, God is encircled with a boundless realm of angels, created in the divine image. They surround God in freely expressed love and devotion. They appear in a graduated, individuated hierarchy. These ranks of angels offer God their praise, and they appear active in the universe as messengers and executors of the divine will. From the beginning God appears as the ruler and centre in this divinely fashioned realm, and the first created of this realm are the angels. The church of the angels is the upper church; the earthly church joins with them in the "cherubic hymn," the Trisagion ("Holy, Holy, Holy"), at the epiphany of the Lord and with the angelic choirs surrounding him in the Eucharist. The earthly church is thus viewed as a participant—co-liturgist—in the angelic liturgy. Because the angels are created as free spiritual beings in accordance with the image of God, the first fall takes place in their midst—the first misuse of freedom was in the rebellion of the highest prince of the angels, Lucifer ("Light-bearer"), against God.

According to the view of Christian thinkers from the early Fathers to the reformers of the 16th century, humans are only the second-created. The creation of human beings serves to refill the Kingdom of God with new spiritual creatures who are capable of offering to God the free love that the rebellious angels have refused to continue. In the realm of the first-created creatures, there already commences the problem of evil, which appears immediately in freedom or the misuse of freedom.

CONTEMPORARY VIEWS OF GOD

If 18th- and 19th-century rationalism and scientific attacks on the idea of God were often called "the first Enlightenment" or "the first illumination," a set of trends began in the 20th century that represented, to a broader public, a "second illumination." This included a rescue of the idea of God, even if it was not always compatible with previous Christian interpretations. Some notable scientists of the 20th century, such as Albert Einstein, Max Planck, Max Born, and others, allowed—on occasion, and against the testimony of the majority of their colleagues—for an idea of God or religion in their concepts of life, the universe, and human beings.

When the German philosopher Friedrich Nietzsche prophesied what he called "the death of God," many Christian thinkers agreed that a certain set of culturally conditioned and dogmatic concepts of God were inaccessible, implausible, and dying out. Some of these apologists argued that such a "death of God" was salutary, because it made room for a "God beyond the gods" of argument, or a "greater God." The French Jesuit thinker Pierre Teilhard de Chardin for a time attracted a large following as he set out to graft the theory of evolution onto "greater God" proclamations. Likewise, advocates of process theology, which applies the philosophy of Alfred North Whitehead to theological matters, propose a conception of God as being both intimately connected with creation and the "divine lure" that helps to guide its development.

SATAN AND THE ORIGIN OF EVIL

In the Bible, especially the New Testament, Satan (the devil) comes to appear as the representative of evil.

Enlightenment thinkers endeavoured to push the figure of the devil out of Christian consciousness as being a product of the fantasy of the Middle Ages. It is precisely in this figure, however, that some aspects of the ways God deals with evil are especially evident. The devil first appears as an independent figure alongside God in the Hebrew Scriptures. There evil is still brought into a direct relationship with God; even evil, insofar as it has power and life, is effected by God: "I form light and create darkness, I make weal and create woe, I am the Lord, who do all these things" (Isaiah 45:7).

In the Book of Job, Satan appears as the partner of God, who on behalf of God puts the righteous one to the test. Only in postbiblical Judaism does the devil become the adversary of God, the prince of angels, who, created by God and placed at the head of the angelic hosts, entices some of the angels into revolt against God. In punishment for his rebellion he is cast from heaven together with his mutinous entourage, which were transformed into demons. As ruler over the fallen angels he continues the struggle against the Kingdom of God by seeking to seduce humans into sin, by trying to disrupt God's plan for salvation, and by appearing before God as a slanderer and accuser of saints, so as to reduce the number of those chosen for the Kingdom of God.

Thus, Satan is a creature of God, who has his being and essence from God; he is the partner of God in the drama of the history of salvation; and he is the rival

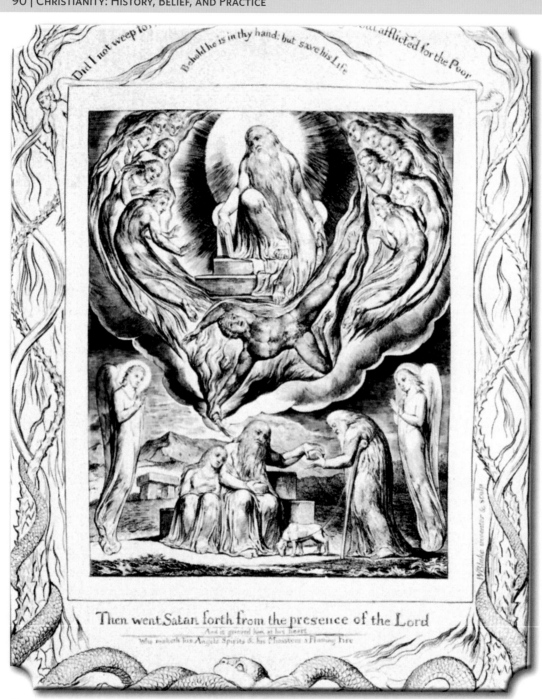

Satan leaves the presence of God to test God's faithful servant Job. Engraving by William Blake, 1825, for an illustration of The Book of Job. *Courtesy of the trustees of the British Museum; photograph, J.R. Freeman & Co. Ltd.*

of God, who fights against God's plan of salvation. Through the influence of the dualistic thinking of Zoroastrian religion during the Babylonian Exile (586–538 BC) in Persia, Satan took on features of a countergod in late Judaism. In the writings of the Qumran sects (who preserved the Dead Sea Scrolls), Belial, the "angel of darkness" and the "spirit of wickedness," appears as the adversary of the "prince of luminaries" and the "spirit of truth." The conclusion of the history of salvation is the eschatological (of or relating to the end of the world) battle of the prince of luminaries against Belial, which ends with judgment upon him, his angels, and people subject to him and ushers in the cessation of "worry, groaning, and wickedness" and the beginning of the rule of "truth."

In the New Testament the features of an anti-godly power are clearly prominent in the figures of the devil, Satan, Belial, and Beelzebub—the "enemy." He is the accuser, the evil one, the tempter, the old snake, the great dragon, the prince of this world, and the god of this world, who seeks to hinder the establishment of God's dominion through the life and suffering of Jesus Christ. Satan offers to give to Christ the riches of this world if Christ will acknowledge him as supreme lord. Thus, he is the real antagonist of the Messiah–Son of man, Christ, who is sent by God into the world to destroy the works of Satan.

He is lacking, however, the possibility of incarnation: he is left to rob others in order to procure for himself the appearance of personality and corporeality. As opposed to *philanthrōpia*, the love of man of Christ, who presents himself as an expiatory sacrifice for the sins of humankind out of love for it, Satan appears among early church teachers, such as Basil of Caesarea in the 4th century, as the *misanthrōpos*, the hater of humanity; vis-à-vis the bringer of heavenly beauty, he is the hater of beauty, the *misokalos*. With gnosticism, which postulated a transcendent god and a lesser, creator god, dualistic features also penetrated the Christian sphere of intuitive vision. In the *Letter of Barnabas* (early 2nd century), Satan appeared as "the Black One"; according to the 2nd-century apologist Athenagoras, he is "the one entrusted with the administration of matter and its forms of appearance," "the spirit hovering above matter." Under the influence of gnosticism and Manichaeism (a syncretistic religion founded by Mani, a 3rd-century Persian prophet), there also followed—based on their dualistic aspects—the demonization of the entire realm of the sexual. This appears as the special temptational sphere of the devil; in sexual activity, the role of the instrument of diabolic enticement devolves upon woman. Dualistic tendencies remained a permanent undercurrent in the church and determined, to a great extent, the understanding of sin and redemption. Satan remained the prototype of sin as the rebel who does not come to terms with fulfilling his godlikeness in love to his original image

MANICHAEISM

Manichaeism was a Dualistic religion founded by Mani in Persia in the 3rd century AD. Inspired by a vision of an angel, Mani viewed himself as the last in a line of prophets that included Adam, Buddha, Zoroaster, and Jesus. His writings, now mostly lost, formed the Manichaean scriptures. Manichaeism held that the world was a fusion of spirit and matter, the original principles of good and evil, and that the fallen soul was trapped in the evil, material world and could reach the transcendent world only by way of the spirit. Zealous missionaries spread its doctrine through the Roman Empire and the East. Vigorously attacked by both the Christian church and the Roman state, it disappeared almost entirely from Western Europe by the end of the 5th century but survived in Asia until the 18th century.

and Creator but instead desires equality with God and places love of self over love of God.

Among the early Church Fathers, the idea of Satan as the antagonist of Christ led to a mythical interpretation of the incarnation and disguise in the "form of a servant." Through this disguise the Son of God makes his heavenly origin unrecognizable to Satan. In some medieval depictions Christ appears as the "bait" cast before Satan, after which Satan grasps because he believes Christ to be an ordinary human being subject to his power. In the Middle Ages a further feature was added: the understanding of the devil as the "ape of God," who attempts to imitate God through spurious, malicious creations that he interpolates for, or opposes to, the divine creations.

In the Christian historical consciousness the figure of Satan plays an important role, not least of all through the influence of the Revelation to John. The history of salvation is understood as the history of the struggle between God and the demonic antagonist, who with constantly new means tries to thwart God's plan of salvation. The idea of the "stratagems of Satan," as developed by a 16th-century fortress engineer, Giacomo Aconcio, had its roots here. This altercation constitutes the religious background of the drama of world history. Characteristic here is the impetus of acceleration already indicated in Revelation: blow and counterblow in the struggle taking place between God and Satan follow in ever shorter intervals; for the devil "knows that his time is short" (Revelation 12:12), and his power in heaven has already been laid low. On Earth the possibility of his efficacy is likewise limited by the return of the Lord. Hence, his attacks upon the elect of the Kingdom so increase in the last times that God is moved to curtail the days of the final affliction, for "if those days had not been shortened, no human being would be saved" (Matthew 24:22). Many of these features were retained in the philosophy of religion of German idealism as well as in Russian philosophy of religion. According to the 20th-century Russian philosopher Nikolay Berdyayev, like the Germans Friedrich Schelling and Franz von Baader before him, the devil has no true personality and no genuine reality and, instead, is filled with an insatiable "hunger for reality," which he can attain by stealing reality from the people of whom he takes possession.

Since the Enlightenment, Christian theologians who found the mythical pictures of Satan to be irrelevant, distorting, or confusing in Christian thought and experience have set out to demythologize this figure. Apologists such as the British literary figure C.S. Lewis and the Russian philosopher Vladimir Solovyov, however, have written cautionary words against this trend. They conceive that it would represent the devil's most cunning attempt at self-camouflage to be demythologized and that camouflage would be a certain new proof of his existence.

GOD THE SON

Dogmatic teachings about the figure of Jesus Christ go back to the faith experiences of the original church. The faithful of the early church experienced and recognized the incarnate and resurrected Son of God in the person of Jesus. The disciples' testimony served as confirmation for them that Jesus really is the exalted Lord and Son of God, who sits at the right hand of the Father and will return in glory to consummate the Kingdom.

Transfiguration of Christ; mosaic icon, early 13th century; in the Louvre, Paris. Giraudon/Art Resource, New York

DIFFERENT INTERPRETATIONS OF THE PERSON OF JESUS

From the beginning of the church different interpretations of the person of Jesus have existed alongside one another. The Gospel According to Mark, for example, understands Jesus as the man upon whom the Holy Spirit descends at the baptism in the Jordan and about whom the voice of God declares from the heavens, "You are my beloved son" (Mark 1:11). The teaching in Mark's Gospel provided the foundation for one of two early schools of thought concerning the person of Christ. Approaches to Christology that derive from the theological school of Antioch have followed one line of interpretation: they proceed from the humanity of Jesus and view his divinity in his consciousness of God, founded in the divine mission that was imposed upon him by God through the infusion of the Holy Spirit.

Another view, adopted by the school of Alexandria, is expressed by The Gospel According to John, which regards the figure of Jesus Christ as the divine Logos become flesh. Here, the divinity of the person of Jesus is understood not as the endowment of the man Jesus with a divine power but rather as the result of the descent of the divine Logos taking on a human body of flesh so as to be realized in history. Thus it was that the struggle to understand the figure of Jesus Christ created a rivalry between the theologies of Antioch and Alexandria. Both schools had a wide sphere of influence, not only among the contemporary clergy but also among the monks and the laity.

THE CHRISTOLOGICAL CONTROVERSIES

As in the area of the doctrine of the Trinity, the general development of Christology has been characterized by a plurality of views and formulations. Solutions intermediate between the positions of Antioch and Alexandria were constantly proposed. During the 5th century the heresy of Nestorianism, with its strong emphasis upon the human aspects of Jesus Christ, arose from the Antiochene school, and the heresy of monophysitism, with its one-sided stress upon the divine nature of Christ, emerged from the Alexandrian school. After Constantine, the first Christian Roman emperor, the great ecumenical synods occupied themselves essentially with the task of creating uniform formulations binding upon the entire imperial church. The Council of Chalcedon (451) settled the dispute between Antioch and Alexandria by drawing from each, declaring: "We all unanimously teach... one and the same Son, our Lord Jesus Christ, perfect in deity and perfect in humanity...in two natures, without being mixed, transmuted, divided, or separated. The distinction between the natures is by no means done away with through the union, but rather the identity of each nature is preserved and concurs into one person and being."

Even the Christological formulas, however, do not claim to offer a rational, conceptual clarification; instead, they emphasize clearly three contentions in the mystery of the sonship of God. These are: first, that Jesus Christ, the Son of God, is completely God, that in reality "the whole fullness of deity dwells bodily" in him (Colossians 2:9); second, that he is completely human; and third, that these two "natures" do not exist beside one another in an unconnected way but, rather, are joined in him in a personal unity. Once again, the Neoplatonic metaphysics of substance offered the categories so as to settle conceptually these various theological concerns. Thus, the idea of the unity of essence (*homoousia*) of the divine Logos with God the Father assured the complete divinity of Jesus Christ, and the mystery of the person of Jesus Christ could be grasped in a complex but decisive formula: two natures in one person. The concept of person, taken from Roman law, served to join the fully divine and fully human natures of Christ into an individual unity.

Christology, however, is not the product of abstract, logical operations but instead originates in the liturgical and charismatic sphere wherein Christians engage in prayer, meditation, and asceticism. Not being derived primarily from abstract teaching, it rather changes within the liturgy in new forms and in countless hymns of worship—as in the words of the Easter liturgy:

> *The king of the heavens appeared on earth out of kindness to man and it was with men that he associated. For he took his flesh from a pure virgin and he came forth from her, in that he accepted it. One is the Son, two-fold in essence, but not in person. Therefore in announcing him as in truth perfect God and perfect man, we confess Christ our God.*

MESSIANIC VIEWS

Faith in Jesus Christ is related in the closest way to faith in the Kingdom of God, the coming of which he proclaimed and introduced. Christian eschatological expectations, for their part, were joined with the messianic promises, which underwent a decisive transformation and differentiation in late Judaism, especially in the two centuries just before the appearance of Jesus. Two basic types can be distinguished as influencing the messianic self-understanding of Jesus as well as the faith of his disciples.

The traditional Jewish view of the fulfillment of the history of salvation was guided by the idea that at the end of history the messiah will come from the house of David and establish the Kingdom of God—an earthly kingdom in which the Anointed of the Lord will gather the tribes of the chosen people and from Jerusalem will establish a world kingdom of peace. Accordingly, the expectation of the Kingdom had an explicitly inner-worldly character. The expectation of an earthly messiah as the founder of a Jewish kingdom became the strongest impulse for political revolutions, primarily against Hellenistic and Roman dominion. The period preceding the appearance of Jesus was filled with uprisings in which new messianic personalities appeared and claimed for themselves and their struggles for liberation the miraculous powers of the Kingdom of God. Especially in Galilee, guerrilla groups were formed in which hope for a better future blazed all the more fiercely because the present was so unpromising.

Jesus disappointed the political expectations of these popular circles; he did not let himself be made a political messiah. Conversely, it was his opponents who used the political misinterpretation of his person to destroy him. Jesus was condemned and executed by the Roman authorities as a Jewish rioter who rebelled against Roman sovereignty. The inscription on the cross, "Jesus of Nazareth, king of the Jews," cited the motif of political insurrection of a Jewish messianic king against the Roman government as the official reason for his condemnation and execution.

Alongside worldly or political messianism there was a second form of eschatological expectation. Its supporters were the pious groups in the country, the Essenes and the Qumran community on the Dead Sea. Their yearning was directed not toward an earthly messiah but toward a heavenly one, who would bring not an earthly but a heavenly kingdom. These pious ones wanted to know nothing of sword and struggle, uprising and rebellion. They believed that the wondrous power of God alone would create the new time. The birth of a new eon would be preceded by intense trials and tribulations and a frightful judgment upon the godless, the pagan peoples, and Satan with his demonic powers. The messiah would come not

as an earthly king from the house of David but as a heavenly figure, as the Son of God, a heavenly being, who would descend into the world of the Evil One and there gather his own to lead them back into the realm of light. He would take up dominion of the world and, after overcoming all earthly and supernatural demonic powers, lay the entire cosmos at the feet of God.

A second new feature, anticipation of the Resurrection, was coupled with this transcending of the old expectation. According to traditional Jewish eschatological expectation, the beneficiaries of the divine development of the world would be only the members of the last generation of humanity who were fortunate enough to experience the arrival of the messiah upon Earth; all earlier generations would be consumed with the longing for fulfillment but would die without experiencing it. Ancient Judaism knew no hope of resurrection. In connection with the transcending of the expectation of the Kingdom of God, however, even anticipations of resurrection voiced earlier by Zoroastrianism were achieved: the Kingdom of God was to include within itself in the state of resurrection all the faithful of every generation of humanity. Even the faithful of the earlier generations would find in resurrection the realization of their faith. In the new eon the Messiah–Son of man would rule over the resurrected faithful of all times and all peoples. A characteristic breaking free of the eschatological expectation was thereby presented. It no longer referred exclusively to Jews alone; with its transcendence a universalistic feature entered into it.

Jesus—in contrast to John the Baptist (a preacher of repentance who pointed to the coming bringer of the Kingdom)—knew himself to be the one who brought fulfillment of the Kingdom itself, because the wondrous powers of the Kingdom of God were already at work in him. He proclaimed the good news that the long promised Kingdom was already dawning, that the consummation was here. This is what was new: the promised Kingdom, supra-worldly, of the future, the coming new eon, already reached redeemingly into the this-worldly from its beyond-ness, as a charismatic reality that brought people together in a new community.

Jesus did not simply transfer to himself the promise of heavenly Son of man, as it was articulated in the apocryphal First Book of Enoch. Instead, he gave this expectation of the Son of man an entirely new interpretation. Pious Jewish circles, such as the Enoch community and other pietist groups, expected in the coming Son of man a figure of light from on high, a heavenly conquering hero, with all the marks of divine power and glory. Jesus, however, linked expectations of the Son of man with the figure of the suffering servant of God (as in Isaiah, chapter 53). He would return in glory as the consummator of the Kingdom.

THE DOCTRINE OF THE VIRGIN MARY AND HOLY WISDOM

The dogma of the Virgin Mary as the "mother of God" and "bearer of God" is connected in the closest way with the dogma of the incarnation of the divine Logos. The theoretical formation of doctrine did not bring the veneration of the mother of God along in its train; instead, the doctrine only reflected the unusually great role that this veneration already had taken on at an early date in the liturgy and in the church piety of orthodox faithful.

The expansion of the veneration of the Virgin Mary as the bearer of God (Theotokos) and the formation of the corresponding dogma comprise one of the most astonishing occurrences in the history of the early church. The New Testament offers only scanty points of departure for this development. Although she has a prominent place in the narratives of the Nativity and the Passion of Christ, Mary completely recedes behind the figure of Jesus, who stands in the centre of all four Gospels. From the Gospels themselves it can be recognized that Jesus's development into the preacher of the Kingdom of God took place in sharp opposition to his family, who were so little convinced of his mission that they held him to be insane (Mark 3:21); in a later passage Jesus refuses to recognize them (Mark 3:31). Accordingly, all the Gospels stress the fact that Jesus separated himself from his family. Even The Gospel According to John still preserved traces of Jesus's tense relationship with his mother. Mary appears twice without being called by name the mother of Jesus; and Jesus himself regularly withholds from her the designation of mother.

Nevertheless, with the conception of Jesus Christ as the Son of God, a tendency developed early in the church to grant to the mother of the Son of God a special place within the church. This development was sketched quite hesitantly in the New Testament. Only the Gospels of Matthew and Luke mention the virgin birth. On these scanty presuppositions the later veneration of the mother of God was developed. The view of the virgin birth entered into the creed of all Christianity and became one of the strongest religious impulses in the development of the dogma, liturgy, and ecclesiastical piety of the early church.

Veneration of the mother of God received its impetus when the Christian Church became the imperial church. Despite the lack of detail concerning Mary in the Gospels, cultic veneration of the divine virgin and mother found within the Christian Church a new possibility of expression in the worship of Mary as the virgin mother of God, in whom was achieved the mysterious union of the divine Logos with human nature. The spontaneous impulse of popular piety, which pushed in this direction, moved far in advance of the practice and doctrine of the church.

In Egypt, Mary was, at an early point, already worshiped under the title of Theotokos—an expression that Origen used in the 3rd century. The Council of Ephesus (431) raised this designation to a dogmatic standard. To the latter, the second Council of Constantinople (553) added the title "eternal Virgin." In the prayers and hymns of the Orthodox Church the name of the mother of God is invoked as often as is the name of Christ and the Holy Trinity.

The doctrine of the heavenly Wisdom (Sophia) represents an Eastern Church particularity. In late Judaism, speculations about the heavenly Wisdom—a figure beside God that presents itself to humanity as mediator in the work of creation as well as mediator of the knowledge of God—abounded. In Roman Catholic doctrine, Mary, the mother of God, was identified with the figure of the divine Wisdom. To borrow a term used in Christology to describe Jesus as being of the same substance (*hypostasis*) as the Father, Mary was seen as possessing a divine hypostasis.

This process of treating Mary and the heavenly Wisdom alike did not take place in the realm of the Eastern Orthodox Church. For all its veneration of the mother of God, the Eastern Orthodox Church never forgot that the root of this veneration lay in the incarnation of the divine Logos that took place through her. Accordingly, in the tradition of Orthodox theology, a specific doctrine of the heavenly Wisdom, Sophianism, is found alongside the doctrine of the mother of God. This distinction between the mother of God and the heavenly Sophia in 20th-century Russian philosophy of religion (in the works of Vladimir Solovyov, Pavel Florensky, W.N. Iljin, and Sergey Bulgakov) developed a special Sophianism. Sophianism did, however, evoke the opposition of Orthodox academic theology. The numerous great churches of Hagia Sophia, foremost among them the cathedral by that name in Constantinople (Istanbul), are consecrated to this figure of the heavenly Wisdom.

GOD THE HOLY SPIRIT

The Holy Spirit is one of the most elusive and difficult themes in Christian theology, because it refers to one of the three persons in the Godhead but does not evoke concrete images the way "Father" or "Creator" and "Son" or "Redeemer" do. A characteristic view of the Holy Spirit is sketched in The Gospel According to John: the outpouring of the Holy Spirit takes place only after the Ascension of Christ. It is the beginning of a new time of salvation, in which the Holy Spirit is sent as the Paraclete (Counsellor) to the church remaining behind in this world. The phenomena described in John, which are celebrated in the church at Pentecost, are understood as the fulfillment of this promise. With this event (Pentecost), the church entered into the period of the Holy Spirit.

CONTRADICTORY ASPECTS OF THE HOLY SPIRIT

The essence of the expression of the Holy Spirit is free spontaneity. The Spirit blows like the wind, "where it wills," but where it blows it establishes a firm norm by virtue of its divine authority. The spirit of prophecy and the spirit of knowledge (*gnōsis*) are not subject to the will of the prophet; revelation of the Spirit in the prophetic word or in the word of knowledge becomes Holy Scripture, which as "divinely breathed" "cannot be broken" and lays claim to a lasting validity for the church.

The Spirit, which is expressed in the various officeholders of the church, likewise founds the authority of ecclesiastical offices. The laying on of hands, as a sign of the transference of the Holy Spirit from one person to another, is a characteristic ritual that visibly represents and guarantees the continuity of the working of the Spirit in the officeholders chosen by the Apostles. It is, in other words, the sacramental sign of the succession of the full power of spiritual authority of bishops and priests. The Holy Spirit also creates the sacraments and guarantees the constancy of their action in the church. All the expressions of church life—doctrine, office, polity, sacraments, power to loosen and to bind, and prayer—are understood as endowed by the Spirit.

The Holy Spirit, however, is also the revolutionizing, freshly creating principle in church history. All the reformational movements in church history, which broke with old institutions, have appealed to the authority of the Holy Spirit. Opposition to the church—through appeal to the Holy Spirit—became noticeable for the first time in Montanism, in the mid-2nd century. Montanus, a Phrygian prophet and charismatic leader, understood himself and the prophetic movement sustained by him as the fulfillment of the promise of the coming of the Paraclete. In the 13th century a spiritualistic countermovement against the institutional church gained attention anew in Joachim of Fiore, who understood the history of salvation in terms of a continuing self-realization of the divine Trinity in the three times of salvation: (1) the time of the Father, (2) the time of the Son, and (3) the time of the Holy Spirit. He promised the speedy beginning of the period of the Holy Spirit, in which the institutional papal church, with its sacraments and its revelation hardened in the letter of scripture, would be replaced by a community of charismatic figures, filled with the Spirit, and by the time of "spiritual knowledge." This promise became the spiritual stimulus of a series of revolutionary movements within the medieval church—e.g., the reform movement of the radical Franciscan spirituals. Their effects extended to the Hussite reform movement led by Jan Hus in 15th-century Bohemia and to the 16th-century radical reformer, Thomas Müntzer, who substantiated his revolution against the princes and clerical hierarchs with a new outpouring of the Spirit. Quakerism represents the most radical mode of rejection—carried out in the name of the freedom of the Holy Spirit—of all institutional forms, which are regarded as shackles and prisons of the Holy Spirit. In the 20th century a revival of charismatic forms of Christianity, called Pentecostalism and the charismatic movement, centred on the recovery of the experience of the Holy Spirit and necessitated some fresh theological inquiry about the subject.

CONFLICT BETWEEN ORDER AND CHARISMATIC FREEDOM

As the uncontrollable principle of life in the church, the Holy Spirit considerably upset Christian congregations from the very outset. Paul struggled to restrict the anarchist elements, which are connected with the appearance of free *charismata* (spiritual phenomena), and, over against these, to achieve a firm order in the church. Paul at times attempted to control and even repress charismatic activities, which he seemed to regard as irrational or prerational and thus potentially disruptive of fellowship. Among these were *glossolalia*, or speaking in tongues, a form of unrepressed speech. Paul preferred rational discourse in sermons. He also felt that spontaneity threatened the focus of worship, even though he himself claimed to possess this gift in extraordinary measure and the Apostles spoke in tongues at Pentecost. This tendency led to an emphasis on ecclesiastical offices with their limited authority vis-à-vis the uncontrolled appearance of free charismatic figures.

The conflict between church leadership resident in the locality and the appearance of free charismatic figures in the form of itinerant preachers forms the main motif of the oldest efforts to establish church order. This difficulty became evident in the *Didachē*, the *Teaching of the Twelve Apostles* (early 2nd century). The authority of the Holy Spirit, in whose name the free charismatic figures claim to speak, does not allow its instructions and prophecies to be criticized in terms of contents; its evaluation had to be made dependent upon purely ethical qualifications. This tension ended, in practical terms, with the exclusion of the free charismatic figures from the leadership of the church. The charismatic continuation of the revelation, in the form of new scriptures of revelation, was also checked. In the long historical process during which the Christian biblical canon took shape, Bishop Athanasius of Alexandria, in his 39th Easter letter (367), selected the number of writings—of apostolic origin—that he considered "canonical." Revelation in the form of Holy Scriptures binding for the Christian faith was thereby considered definitively concluded and, therefore, could no longer be changed, abridged, or supplemented.

The church creeds reflect little of these struggles and suppress the revolutionary principle of the Holy Spirit. Neither the so-called Apostles' Creed nor the Nicene Creed goes beyond establishment of faith in the Holy Spirit and its participation in the incarnation. In the Nicene Creed, however, the Holy Spirit is also described as the life-creating power—i.e., the power both of creation and of rebirth—and is identified as having already spoken through the prophets.

The emergence of Trinitarian speculations in early church theology led to great difficulties in the article about the "person" of the Holy Spirit. In the New Testament the Holy Spirit appeared more as power than as person, though there was distinctive personal representation in the form of the dove at Jesus's baptism. But it was difficult to incorporate this graphic or symbolic representation into dogmatic theology. Nevertheless, the idea of the complete essence (*homoousia*) of the Holy Spirit with the Father and the Son was achieved through the writings of Athanasius. This was in opposition to all earlier attempts to subordinate the Holy Spirit to the Son and to the Father and to interpret the Spirit—similarly to anti-Trinitarian Christology—as a prince of the angels. According to Athanasius, the Holy Spirit alone guarantees the complete redemption of humanity: "through participation in the Holy Spirit we partake of the divine nature." In his work *De Trinitate* ("On the Trinity"), Augustine undertook to render the essence of the Trinity understandable in terms of the Trinitarian structure of the human person: the Holy Spirit appears as the Spirit of love, which joins Father and Son and draws people into this communion of love. In Eastern Orthodox thought, however, the Holy Spirit and the Son both proceed from the Father. In the West, the divine Trinity is determined more by the idea of the inner Trinitarian life in God; thus, the notion was carried through that the Holy Spirit goes forth from the Father and from the Son. Despite all the efforts of speculative theology, a graphic conception of the person of the Holy Spirit was not developed even later in the consciousness of the church.

THE OPERATIONS OF THE HOLY SPIRIT

For the Christian faith, the Holy Spirit is clearly recognizable in charismatic figures (the saints), in whom the gifts of grace (charismata) of the Holy Spirit are expressed in different forms: reformers and other charismatic figures. The prophet, for instance, belongs to these charismatic types. The history of the church knows a continuous series of prophetic types, beginning with New Testament prophets, such as Agabus (in Acts 11:28), and continuing with the 12th-century monk Bernard of Clairvaux and such reformers as Luther and Calvin. Christoph Kotter and Nicolaus Drabicius—prophets of the Thirty Years' War period—were highly praised by the 17th-century Moravian bishop John Amos Comenius. Other prophets have existed in Pietism, Puritanism, and the free churches.

Prophetic women are especially numerous. In church history they begin with Anna (in Luke 2:36) and the prophetic daughters of the apostle Philip. Others are: Hildegard of Bingen, Bridget of Sweden, Joan of Arc, and the prophetic women of the Reformation period. In the modern world numbers of pioneers in the "holiness" and Pentecostal traditions, such as Aimee Semple McPherson, were women, and women's gifts of prophecy have sometimes been cherished among Pentecostalists when they were overlooked or disdained by much of the rest of Christianity.

A further type of charismatic person is the healer, who functioned in the early church as an exorcist but who also emerged as a charismatic type in healing personalities of more recent church history (e.g., Vincent de Paul in the 17th century). Equally significant is the curer-of-souls type, who exercises the gift of "distinguishing between spirits" in daily association with people. This gift is believed to have been possessed by many of the great saints of all times. In the 19th century it stands out in Johann Christoph Blumhardt, in Protestantism, and in Jean-Baptiste Vianney, the curé of Ars, in Roman Catholicism.

The "holy fool" type conceals a radical Christianity under the mask of foolishness and holds the truth of the gospel, in the disguise of folly, before the eyes of highly placed personalities: the worldly and the princes of the church who do not brook unmasked truth. This type, which frequently appeared in the Byzantine

Church, has been represented especially in Western Christianity by Philip Neri, the founder of the religious order known as the Oratorians, in the 16th century.

The charismatic teacher (*didaskalos*), on the other hand, still appears. Filled with the spirit of intelligence or knowledge of the Holy Spirit, he carries out his teaching office, which does not necessarily need to be attached to an academic position. Many Free Church and ecclesiastical reform movements owe their genesis to such spirit-filled teachers, who are often decried as anomalous. The deacon likewise is originally the holder of a charismatic office of selfless service. Christian service, or *diakonia*, was not confined to Christian offices. Some of the energies that once went into it are now found in social service outside the church. Many of the agents of such service were originally or still may be inspired by Christian norms and examples in the care of the sick and the socially outcast or overlooked. Alongside such men as the Pietist August Hermann Francke, the Methodist John Wesley, Johann Wichern (the founder of the Inner Mission in Germany), and Friederich von Bodelschwingh (the founder of charitable institutions), important women have appeared as bearers of this charisma (e.g., the English nurse Florence Nightingale and the Salvation Army leader Catherine Booth).

The Holy Spirit that "blows where it wills" has often been recognized as the impulse behind an enlargement of roles for women in the church. However limited these have been, they enlarged upon those that Christians inherited from Judaism. Partitions had screened women in a special left-hand section of the synagogue. While the pace of innovation was irregular, in the ecstatic worship services of the Christian congregations women tended to participate in speaking in tongues, hymns, prayer calls, or even prophecies. Evidently, this innovation was held admissible on the basis of the authority of the Holy Spirit: "Do not quench the Spirit" (1 Thessalonians 5:19). Inasmuch as the appearance of charismatic women upset traditional concepts, however, Paul reverted to the synagogal principle and inhibited the speaking role of women: "the women should keep silence in the churches" (1 Corinthians 14:34).

Because expressions of free charisma were increasingly suppressed in the institutional churches, the emergence of Pentecostal movements outside the institutional churches and partly in open opposition to them arose. This movement led to the founding of various Pentecostal Free churches at the end of the 19th century and the beginning of the 20th; it is represented through numerous independent Pentecostal groups, such as the Church of God and the Assemblies of God. At first scorned by the established churches, the Pentecostal movement has grown to a world movement with strong missionary activity not only in Africa and South America but also Europe. In the United States, a strong influence of the Pentecostal movement—which has returned high esteem to the

This painting, "'The Holy Trinity, Seat of Mercy" shows God and Jesus seated together, while the third member of the Trinity, the Holy Spirit, is shown as a dove flying above them; in the National Museum of Warsaw. Joe Raedle/Getty Images

proto-Christian charismata of speaking in tongues, healing, and exorcism—is noticeable even in the Roman Catholic, Lutheran, and Anglican churches. This has occurred especially in liturgy and church music but also in preaching style and the return to faith healing.

THE HOLY TRINITY

The central Christian affirmations about God are condensed and focused in the classic doctrine of the Trinity, which has

its ultimate foundation in the special religious experience of the Christians in the first communities. This basis of experience is older than the doctrine of the Trinity. It consisted of the fact that God came to meet Christians in a three-fold figure: (1) as Creator, Lord of the history of salvation, Father, and Judge, as revealed in the Old Testament; (2) as the Lord who, in the figure of Jesus Christ, lived among human beings and was present in their midst as the "Resurrected One"; and (3) as the Holy Spirit, whom they experienced as the power of the new life, the miraculous potency of the Kingdom of God. The question as to how to reconcile the encounter with God in this three-fold figure with faith in the oneness of God, which was Jews' and Christians' characteristic mark of distinction from paganism, agitated the piety of ancient Christendom in the deepest way. In the course of history, it also provided the strongest impetus for a speculative theology, which inspired Western metaphysics for many centuries. In the first two centuries of the Christian Era, however, a series of different answers to this question developed.

THE BASIS FOR THE DOCTRINE OF THE TRINITY

The diversity in interpretation of the Trinity was conditioned especially through the understanding of the figure of Jesus Christ. According to the theology of The Gospel According to John, the divinity of Jesus Christ constituted the departure point for understanding his person and efficacy. The Gospel According to Mark, however, did not proceed from a theology of incarnation but instead understood the baptism of Jesus Christ as the adoption of the man Jesus Christ into the Sonship of God, accomplished through the descent of the Holy Spirit. The situation became further aggravated by the conceptions of the special personal character of the manifestation of God developed by way of the historical figure of Jesus Christ; the Holy Spirit was viewed not as a personal figure but rather as a power and appeared graphically only in the form of the dove and thus receded, to a large extent, in the Trinitarian speculation.

INTRODUCTION OF NEOPLATONIC THEMES

The Johannine literature in the Bible (i.e., the texts of John) provides the first traces of the concept of Christ as the Logos, the "word" or "principle" that issues from eternity. Under the influence of subsequent Neoplatonic philosophy, this tradition became central in speculative theology. There was interest in the relationship of the "oneness" of God to the "triplicity" of divine manifestations. This question was answered through the Neoplatonic metaphysics of being. The transcendent God, who is beyond all being, all rationality, and all conceptuality, is divested of divine transcendence. In a first act of becoming self-conscious the Logos recognizes itself as the divine mind (Greek: *nous*), or divine world reason, which was characterized by the Neoplatonic philosopher Plotinus as the "Son" who goes forth from the Father. The next step by which the transcendent God becomes self-conscious consists in the appearance in the divine *nous* of the divine world, the idea of the world in its individual forms as the content of the divine consciousness. In Neoplatonic philosophy both the *nous* and the idea of the world are designated the hypostases of the transcendent God. Christian theology took the Neoplatonic metaphysics of substance as well as its doctrine of hypostases as the departure point for interpreting the relationship of the "Father" to the "Son." This process stands in direct relationship with a speculative interpretation of Christology in connection with Neoplatonic Logos speculation.

In transferring the Neoplatonic hypostases doctrine to the Christian interpretation of the Trinity there existed the danger that the different manifestations of God—as known by the Christian experience of faith: Father, Son, Holy Spirit—would be transformed into a hierarchy of gods graduated among themselves and thus into a polytheism. Though this danger was consciously avoided and, proceeding from a Logos Christology, the complete sameness of essence of the three manifestations of God was emphasized, there arose the danger of a relapse into a triplicity of equally ranked gods, which would displace the idea of the oneness of God.

ATTEMPTS AT A DEFINITION

By the 3rd century it was already apparent that all attempts to systematize the mystery of the divine Trinity with the theories of Neoplatonic hypostases metaphysics were unsatisfying and led to a series of new conflicts. The high point of these conflicts was the Arian controversy. As has been mentioned previously, in his interpretation of the idea of God, Arius sought to maintain a formal understanding of the oneness of God. In defense of that oneness, he was obliged to dispute the sameness of essence of the Son and the Holy Spirit with God the Father, as stressed by other theologians of his day. From the outset, the controversy between both parties took place upon the common basis of the Neoplatonic concept of substance, which was foreign to the New Testament itself.

Augustine, of decisive importance for the development of the Trinitarian doctrine in Western theology and metaphysics, coupled the doctrine of the Trinity with anthropology. Proceeding from the idea that humans are created by God according to the divine image, he attempted to explain the mystery of the Trinity by uncovering traces of the Trinity in the human personality. He went from analysis of the Trinitarian structure of the simple act of cognition to ascertainment of the Trinitarian structure both of human self-consciousness and of the act of religious contemplation in which people recognize themselves as the image of God.

Another model of Trinitarian doctrine—suspected of heresy from the outset—which had effects not only in theology but also in the social metaphysics of the West as well, emanated from Joachim of Fiore. He understood the course of the history of salvation as the successive realization of the Father, the Son, and the Holy Spirit in three consecutive periods. This interpretation of the Trinity became effective as a "theology of revolution," inasmuch as it was regarded as the theological justification of the endeavour to accelerate the arrival of the third state of the Holy Spirit through revolutionary initiative.

The final dogmatic formulation of the Trinitarian doctrine in the so-called Athanasian Creed (c. 500), *una substantia—tres personae* ("one substance—three persons"), reached back to the formulation of Tertullian. In practical terms it meant a compromise in that it held fast to both basic ideas of Christian revelation—the oneness of God and divine self-revelation in the figures of the Father, the Son, and the Holy Spirit—without rationalizing the mystery itself. In the final analysis the point of view thereby remained definitive that the fundamental assumptions of the reality of salvation and redemption are to be retained and not sacrificed to the concern of a rational monotheism.

Characteristically, in all periods of the later history of Christianity, anti-Trinitarian currents emerged when a rationalistic philosophy questioned the role of the Trinity in the history of salvation. The ideas of Arius were revived by many critics, including the so-called anti-Trinitarians of the Italian Renaissance and the humanists of the 16th century. Researchers into the life of Jesus in the 18th century, such as Hermann Reimarus and Karl Bahrdt, who portrayed Jesus as the agent of a secret enlightenment order that had set itself the goal of spreading the religion of reason in the world, were at the same time anti-Trinitarians and pioneers of the radical rationalistic criticism of dogma. The Kantian critique of the proofs of God contributed further to a devaluation of Trinitarian doctrine. In German idealism, Hegel, in the framework of his attempt to raise Christian dogma into the sphere of the conceptual, took the Trinitarian doctrine as the basis for his system of philosophy and, above all, for his interpretation of history as the absolute spirit's becoming self-conscious. In subsequent theological work, at least in the accusations of some of its critics, the school of dialectical theology in Europe and the United States tended to reduce the doctrine of the Trinity and supplant it with a monochristism—the teaching that the figure of the Son in the life of faith will overshadow the figure of the Father and thus cause it to disappear and that the figure of the Creator and Sustainer of the world will recede behind the figure of the Redeemer.

In a brief but well-publicized episode in the mid-1960s in the United States, a number of celebrated Protestant theologians engaged in cultural criticism observed or announced "the death of God." The theology of the death of God downplayed any notion of divine transcendence and invested its whole claim to be Christian in its accent on Jesus of Nazareth. Christian dogma was reinterpreted and reduced to norms of human sociality and freedom. Before long, however, the majority of theologians confronted this small school with the demands of classic Christian dogma, which insisted on confronting divine transcendence in any assertions about Jesus Christ.

The transcendence of God has been rediscovered by science and sociology; theology in the closing decades of the 20th century endeavoured to overcome the purely anthropological interpretation of religion and once more to discover anew its transcendent ground. Theology has consequently been confronted with the problem of Trinity in a new form, which, in view of the Christian experience of God as an experience of the presence of the Father, Son, and Holy Spirit, cannot be eliminated.

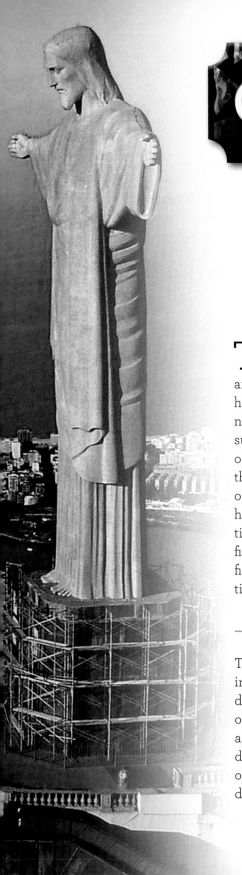

CHAPTER 5

THE CHRISTIAN CONCEPTION OF HUMAN NATURE

The starting point for the Christian understanding of what it is to be human is the recognition that humans are created in the image of God. This idea views God and humans joined with one another through a mysterious connection. God is thought of as incomprehensible and beyond substance; yet God desired to reflect the divine image in one set of creatures and chose humans for this. Man as the image of God belongs, therefore, to the self-revelation of God in quite a decisive way. God, being reflected in the human creature, makes this being a partner in the realization of the divine self; there is constant interaction. Humans find fulfillment in God, the divine prototype, but God also first comes to the fulfillment of the divine essence in relation, in this case, with the human.

THE HUMAN AS A CREATURE

The idea that human beings were created according to the image of God was already being interpreted in a twofold direction in the early church. For one thing, humans, like all other creatures of the universe, are the creation of God, and as creatures human beings stand in a relationship of utter dependency on God. They have nothing from themselves but owe everything, even their being, exclusively to the will of the divine Creator; they are joined with all other fellow creatures through a relationship of solidarity. The idea of the solidarity of all creatures was eventually eclipsed by the idea of the special position of humans and their special commission of dominion. The idea of solidarity with all creatures has been expressed and practiced by but few charismatic personalities in the history of Western piety, such as by Francis of Assisi in his "Canticle of the Sun": "Praised be Thou, my Lord, with all Thy creatures, especially with our sister sun."

The second aspect of the idea of the human being as a creature operated very much more emphatically: the superiority of humans over all other creatures. God placed humans in a special relationship to the divine. God created them in the divine image, thereby assigning to humans a special commission vis-à-vis all other creatures.

THE HUMAN AS THE IMAGE OF GOD

Influenced by Plato's philosophy, Christian theologians identified the image of God in human beings only in their intellectual capability and faculty of perception and not in their body. In his work *De Trinitate*, Augustine attempted to ascertain traces of divine Trinity in the human intellect. Christian mysticism confronted this dualistic view of humans, interpreting humans in their mind-body entirety as being in the image of God. The image of God is stamped all the way into the sphere of human corporeality. The idea of human creation according to the image of God

is already based upon the intention of the Incarnation, the self-representation of God in corporeality. Even according to their somatic (bodily) condition, humans are the universal form of being, in whom the powers and creative principles of the whole universe are combined in a personal unity of spirit, soul, and body.

The Christian understanding of evil is also linked with the idea of human creation according to the image of God. Evil cannot, in the Christian view, be derived from the dualistic assumption of the contrasts of spirit and body, reason and matter. According to the Christian understanding, the triumph of evil is not identical with the victory of matter, the "flesh," over the spirit. Nevertheless, a dualistic interpretation has been advocated, because for many centuries the Christian understanding of sin, even among many of the church's teachers, was influenced by the philosophical assumptions of Neoplatonic dualism. Moreover, in Augustine there are still the aftereffects of Manichaeism, which ultimately viewed the main motive force of sin in "concupiscence"—i.e., the sex drive.

The only genuine departure point for the Christian view of evil is the idea of freedom, which is based in the concept of the human being as the image of God. The human is person because God is person. It is apparent in Christian claims that the concept of the human as "being-as-person" is the real seal of that human as "being-as-the-image-of-God," and therein lies the true nobility that distinguishes human beings from all other creatures. If the Christian faith is differentiated from other religions through the fact that for the Christian God is person, then this faith takes effect in the thereby resulting consequence that the human being, too, is person.

God at the same time entered into a great risk in creating the human as person. The real sign of God as personal being is freedom. When God created humans according to his image, he also gave over to them this mark of nobility—i.e., freedom. This alone constitutes the presupposition of love. Only through this freedom can the human being as partner of God offer free love to God; only in this freedom can God's love be answered through free love in return. Love in its fulfilled form, according to the Christian understanding, is possible only between persons; conversely, the person can be realized only in the complete love to another person. Humans can use this freedom to offer God, their Creator, their freely given love.

Yet, in the gift of freedom itself there also lay enclosed the possibility for humans to decide against God and to raise themselves to the goal of divine love. The event that is portrayed in the story of the Fall (Genesis, chapter 3) is essentially the trying out of freedom, the free decision of humans against God. This rebellion consists of the fact that human beings improperly use their God-given freedom to set themselves against God and even to wish to be "like God."

HUMAN REDEMPTION

This special interpretation of sin likewise renders understandable the specifically Christian understanding of human redemption, namely, the view of Jesus Christ as the historical figure of the Redeemer—i.e., the specifically Christian view of the incarnation of God in Jesus Christ.

The Christian understanding of the incarnation is based upon an idea that is found in the simple saying of The Gospel According to John: "The Word became flesh" (chapter 1, verse 14). In Christianity, it is not a transcendent, divine being that takes on the appearance of an earthly corporeality, so as to be manifested through this semblance of a body; instead, God himself as human, as member of a definite people, a definite family, at a certain time—"suffered under Pontius Pilate"—enters into the corporeality, carnality, and materiality of the history of mankind. In the midst of history God creates the beginning of a thorough transformation of humans that in like manner embraces all spheres of human being—matter, soul, and mind. Incarnation so constituted did not have the character of veiling God in a human form, which would enable the divine being to reveal a new teaching with human words. The incarnation is not the special instance of a cyclic descent of God always occurring afresh in constantly new veils. Instead, it is the unique intervention of God in the history of the human world. Therein God took the figure of a single historical person into the divine being, suffered through the historical conditions of being, and overcame in this person, Jesus Christ, the root of human corruption—the misuse of freedom. God thereby established the dawn of a transformed, renewed, exalted form of human being and opened a realm in which love to God and to neighbour can be tranquilly fulfilled.

THE PROBLEM OF SUFFERING

The starting point for the Christian understanding of suffering is the messianic self-understanding of Jesus himself. A temptation to power and self-exaltation lay in the late Jewish promise of the coming of the Messiah–Son of man. The Gospel According to Matthew described the temptation of Jesus by Satan in the wilderness as a temptation to worldly power. Jesus himself deeply disappointed his disciples' notions aiming at power and exaltation, in that he taught them, in accordance with Isaiah, chapter 53: "The Son of man will suffer many things." In Jesus's announcements of suffering the Christian understanding of suffering is clearly expressed: suffering is not the final aim and end in itself in the realization of human destiny; it is the gateway to resurrection, to rebirth, to new creation. This idea receives its clarification from the Christian understanding of sin. Sin as the misuse of human freedom has led humans into total opposition against God. Turning to God can therefore take place only when the results of this rebellion are overcome in all levels of human being, all the way to physical corporeality.

In the early church the sign of the cross was not considered a glorification of suffering but a "sign of victory" (*tropaion*) in the sense of the ancient triumphal sign that was set up at the place where the victorious turning point of the battle took place. The cross was likewise considered the "dread of the demons," since as a victory sign it struck terror into the hitherto ruling demonic powers of the world. An ancient church hymn of the cross spoke of the "cross of the beauty of the Kingdom of God." The emperor Constantine, following his vision of a cross in the heavens, fastened to the standards of the imperial legions the cross, which was considered the victory sign for the community of Christians hitherto persecuted by the Roman Empire, and elevated it to a token of military triumph over the legions of his pagan foes that were assembled under the sign of the old gods.

In the Christian understanding, suffering also does not appear—as in Buddhism—as suffering simply under the general conditions of human existence in this world; it is instead coupled with the specifically Christian idea of the imitation of Christ. Individual Christians are called to follow the example of Christ; incorporation into the body of Christ is granted to those who are ready to carry out within themselves Christ's destiny of suffering, death, and resurrection. The early church's characterization of the Christian was that of *Christophoros*— "bearer of Christ." Suffering was an unalterable principle in the great drama of freedom, which was identical with the drama of redemption.

THE RESURRECTION OF THE BODY

Just as clear is the significance that lies in the Christian understanding of the resurrection. A dualistic understanding of what it is to be human, which assumes an essential difference between the spiritual and the material-bodily sides of human existence, necessarily leads to the idea of the immortality of the soul. The Christian hope, however, does not aim at the immortality of the soul but at the resurrection of the body. Corporeality is not a quality that is foreign to the spiritual. Everything spiritual presses toward corporealization; its eternal figure is a corporeal figure. This hope was expressed by Vladimir Solovyov:

> What help would the highest and greatest moral victory be for man, if the enemy, "death," which lurks in the ultimate depth of man's physical, somatic, material sphere, were not overcome?

The goal of redemption is not separation of the spirit from the body; it is rather the new human in the entirety of body, soul, and mind. It is appropriate to say that Christianity has contended for a "holistic" view of the human. The Christian image of the human being has an essentially corporeal aspect that is based in the idea of the incarnation and finds its most palpable expression in the idea of the resurrection.

PROGRESSIVE HUMAN PERFECTION

For a long time Christian anthropology maintained that the human was a complete being, placed in a finished world like a methodically provided-for tenant in a prefabricated, newly built residence ready for occupation. Redemption was understood just as statically: salvation appeared in the teachings of church dogma as restitution and restoration of the lost divine image and often in fact more a patching up of fragments through ecclesiastical remedies than as a real new creation.

Although their view is not uncontroversial, some theologians have found in the New Testament a progression of salvation in history. Indeed, there is a progress of both the individual human being and of mankind as a whole, what might be thought of under some terms and conditions as a potential for the progressive perfection of the human being. This characteristic stands out in the proclamation of Jesus when he promises his disciples: "Then the righteous will shine like the sun in the kingdom of their Father. He who has ears, let him hear" (Matthew 13:43). In The Gospel According to John, Jesus promises his disciples an increase of their divine powers that is to exceed even the spiritual powers at work in himself (John 14:12). Similar expectations are also expressed in the First Letter of John: "Beloved...it does not yet appear what we shall be, but we know that when he appears we shall be like him, for we shall see him as he is" (3:2).

The idea of the Christian "super-man," which was expressed by Montanus, is a result of this view. In connection with the breakthrough of the idea of evolution through Darwin in the areas of biology, zoology, and anthropology, the tendency asserted itself—above all in 19th-century American theology—of interpreting the Christian history of salvation in terms of the evolution and expectation of future human perfection in the form of reaching even higher charismatic levels and ever higher means of spiritual knowledge and communication.

THE HUMAN BEING IN THE LIGHT OF CHRIST

Probably no idea and no sentiment in the early church dominated the Christian feeling for life so thoroughly and comprehensively as the consciousness of the newness of the life into which persons viewed themselves transposed through participation in the life and body of Christ. The newness of the Christian message of salvation not only filled the hearts of the faithful but was also striking to the non-Christian milieu. The new humans experience the newness of life as the life of Christ that is beginning to mature in themselves, as the overwhelming experience of a new state already now commencing. In the New Testament statements about the new man, it was not a settled, complete new condition that was being spoken of, into which people are transposed through grace, but rather the beginning of a coming new state,

the consummation of which will first take place in the future. The new human is one who is engaged in the process of renewal; new life is a principle of growth of the Christian maturing toward "perfect manhood in Christ." The new situation of human beings, for their part, works anew as fermenting "leaven" within old humankind, as "fresh dough," and contributes to transforming the old form of humanity through its fermentation into the state of the Kingdom of God.

THE "REBORN" HUMAN

"Rebirth" has often been identified with a definite, temporally datable form of "conversion," especially in the pietistic and revival type of Christianity. In the history of Christian piety a line of prominent personalities, most notably Paul and Augustine, experienced their rebirth in the form of a temporally datable and also locally ascertainable conversion event. There is no single type of experience, however, that completes the mysterious event characterized with the expression rebirth. The mode of experience of rebirth itself is as manifold as the individuality of the person concerned. The different forms of rebirth experience are distinguished not only according to whether the event sets in suddenly with overwhelming surprise, as when one is "born again" or "sees the light," or as the result of a slow process, a "growing," a "maturing," and an "evolution." They are also distinguished according to the psychic capability predominant at the time that thereby takes charge (will, intellect), the endowment at hand, and the personal type of religious experience. With the voluntaristic type, rebirth is expressed in a new alignment of the will, in the liberation of new capabilities and powers that were hitherto undeveloped in the person concerned. With the intellectual type, it leads to an activation of the capabilities for understanding, to the breakthrough of a "vision." With others it leads to the discovery of an unexpected beauty in the order of nature or to the discovery of the mysterious meaning of history. With still others it leads to a new vision of the moral life and its orders, to a selfless realization of love of neighbour. In the experience of Christian rebirth, the hitherto existing old condition of humanity is not simply eliminated so far as the given personality structure is concerned—a structure dependent upon heredity, education, and earlier life experiences. Instead, each person affected perceives his life in Christ at any given time as "newness of life."

HUMAN LIBERATION

The condition of "fallen" humanity is frequently characterized in the New Testament as "slavery." It is the slavery of human willfulness that wants to have and enjoy all things for itself: the slavery of alienated love, which is no longer turned toward God but toward one's own self and the things of this world and which also degrades one's fellows into the means for egoism and exploitation. The servitude of people fallen away from God is much more oppressive than mere slavery of the senses and of greed for life. It is the enslavement not only of their "flesh" but also of all levels of their being, even the "most spiritual."

In his commentary on the Letter of Paul to the Romans, Luther observed: "The entire man who is not reborn is flesh, even in his spirit; the entire man who is reborn is spirit, even when he eats and sleeps." Only from this perspective do Martin Luther's words about the "Freedom of a Christian Man"— the title of a work written in 1520—receive their true meaning. The freedom that Christians receive is the freedom that Christ, spoken of by Paul as the new Adam, gained for them. The freedom of Christians is the freedom reattained in Christ, in which the possibility of the misuse of freedom is addressed and overcome.

In the early centuries of the church special significance fell to the evangelical schema of liberation—and to the corresponding schema of ransom—in a society that, in its social structure, was constructed entirely upon the system of slavery. On the one hand, wide strata of the population lived in the permanent state of slavery; on the other hand, on the basis of the prevailing usage of war, even the free population could face the danger of passing into possession of the victor as a slave in case of a conquest. The schema of liberation could therefore count upon a spontaneous understanding.

Freedom alone also makes a perfect community possible. Such a community embraces God and the neighbour, in whom the image of God confronts human beings in the flesh. Community is fulfilled in the free service of love. Luther articulated the paradox of Christian freedom, which includes both love and service: "A Christian man is a free lord of all things and subordinate to no one. A Christian man is a submissive servant of all things and subject to everyone." Christian freedom is thus to be understood neither purely individually nor purely collectively. The motives of the personal and the social are indivisibly joined by the idea that each person is an image of God for himself alone, but in Christ he also recognizes the image of God in the neighbour and with the neighbour is a member in the one body of Christ. Here the evolutive principle of the idea of freedom is not to be mistaken; in it, for example, lay the spiritual impetus to the social and racial emancipation of slaves, as it was demanded by the great Christian champions of human rights in the 18th and 19th centuries and, through great efforts, pursued and achieved.

JOY IN HUMAN EXISTENCE

In the New Testament testimonials, joy appears as the characteristic mark of distinction of the Christian. It is the spontaneous result of being filled with the Holy Spirit and is among the main fruits of the Holy Spirit. Joy was the basic mood of congregational gatherings and was often expressed in an exuberant jubilation. It had its origin in the recognition that the dominion of evil had been broken through the power of Christ; that death, devil, and demons no longer possessed any claim upon believers; and that the forces of forgiveness, reconciliation, resurrection, and transfiguration were effective in humankind. This principle of the joy of the Christian is most strongly alive in the liturgy of the Eastern Orthodox Church.

The roots of a specifically Christian sense of humour also lie within this joy. Its peculiarity consists of the fact that in the midst of the conflicts of life the Christian is capable of regarding all sufferings and afflictions from the perspective of overcoming them in the future or from the perspective of victory over them already achieved in Christ.

THE CHARISMATIC BELIEVER

In the New Testament the Christian is depicted as the person who is filled with the powers of the Holy Spirit. The view of the gifts of the Spirit stands in a direct relationship with the understanding of the human as the image of God. For the believing Christian of the original period of the church, the Holy Spirit was the Spirit of the Lord Jesus Christ, who is already now made manifest in his body, the community of the faithful, as the miraculous principle of life of the new eon. Throughout the centuries the

Holy Spirit has remained the ferment of church history—all great reformations and the founding of new churches and sects have occurred as the result of new charismatic breakthroughs.

CHRISTIAN PERFECTION

The demand for perfection is frequently repeated in the New Testament and has played a significant role in the history of the faith. In The Gospel According to Matthew, Jesus says to his disciples: "You, therefore, must be perfect, as your heavenly Father is perfect" (5:48). Although this demand may exceed the measure of reasonableness for humans, it is meant literally and is repeated in other parts of the New Testament. The meaning of this claim is recognizable only from the understanding of the human as the image of God and from the apprehension of Christ as the "new Adam." The perfection of believers is the perfection with which they reflect the image of God. This image has been disfigured through willful alienation from the original, but in Christ believers can recover the perfection of the image of God.

The idea of the deification of man, which captures the Greek notion of "partaking" of the divine character, also points in the direction of perfection. Post-Reformation theology, out of anxiety about "mysticism," struck this concept almost entirely from its vocabulary. In the first one and a half millennia of the Christian church, however, the idea of deification—of partaking in God's being—was a central concept of Christian anthropology. Athanasius created the fundamental formula for the theology of deification: "God became man in order that we become God." In the teachings of the early church these words became the basis of theological anthropology. Only the idea of perfection makes understandable a final enhancement of the Christian image of the human—the intensification from "child of God" to "friend of God." This appears as the highest form of communion reached between God and human beings.

FELLOW HUMANS AS THE PRESENT CHRIST

For the Christian, the fellow human is the present Christ himself; in the eye of Christian faith, Christ is present in everyone, even in the most debased, a belief that constitutes the basis of Christian ethics. According to Matthew (chapter 25, verses 40 and 45), the Judge of the world says to the redeemed: "Truly, I say to you, as you did it to one of the least of these my brethren, you did it to me," and to the damned: "As you did it not to one of the least of these, you did it not to me." Tertullian cites another saying of the Lord: "If you have seen your brother, you have seen your Lord." In other humans, Christians see, under the wrapping of misery, degeneration, and suffering, the image of the present Lord, who became human, who suffered, died, and was resurrected in order to lead all humanity back into the Kingdom of God.

In the self-understanding of the Christian community two tendencies have battled with one another from the beginning of church history. They lead to completely different consequences in the basic orientation of Christians toward fellow Christians and fellow human beings.

One attitude concerns the governing idea of election. God chooses some out of the human race, which exists in opposition to all that is divine, and includes the elect in his Kingdom. This idea underlines the aristocratic character of the Kingdom of God; it consists of an elite of elect. In the Revelation to John, the 144,000 "...who have not defiled themselves with women" (Revelation 14:4) constituted those chosen for entry into the Kingdom of God. For Augustine and his theological successors up to Calvin, the community of the elect is numerically restricted; their number corresponds to the number of fallen angels, who must be replaced through the matching number of redeemed men and women so that the Kingdom of God would be restored numerically. The church is here understood as a selection of a few out of the masses of perdition who constitute the jetsam of the history of salvation. This orientation, it has been argued, conceals a grave endangering of the consciousness of community, for self-righteousness, which is the root of self-love and thereby the death of love of neighbour, easily enters as a result of the consciousness of exclusive election.

The other attitude proceeds from the opposite idea that the goal of the salvation inaugurated through Jesus Christ is the redemption of all humanity. According to this view, God's love of humans (*philanthrōpia*), as the drama of divine self-surrender for human salvation shows, is greater than the righteousness that craves the eternal damnation of the guilty. Since the time of Origen, this second attitude has been found not only among the great mystics of the Eastern Church but among some mystics of Western Christianity. The teaching of universal reconciliation (*apokatastasis pantōn*) has struck against opposition in all Christian confessions. This is connected with the fact that such a universalistic view easily leads to a disposition that regards redemption as a kind of natural process that no one can evade. Such an orientation can lead to a weakening or loss of a consciousness of moral responsibility before God and neighbour; it contains the temptation to spiritual security and moral indolence.

ESCHATOLOGY ("LAST THINGS")

The "last things" were the first things, in terms of urgency, for the faithful of the early church. The central content of their faith and their hope was the coming Kingdom of God. They believed that

ESCHATOLOGY

In the history of religion, the term eschatology *refers to conceptions of the last things: immortality of the soul, rebirth, resurrection, migration of the soul, and the end of time. These concepts also have secular parallels—for example, in the turning points of one's life and in one's understanding of death. Often these notions are contrasted with the experience of suffering in the world. Eschatological themes thrive during crises, serving as consolation for those who hope for a better world or as motivation for a revolutionary transformation of society.*

Shaped by the extent and nature of the believer's involvement in the world, eschatological expectations assume either an individual or a collective form, embracing individual souls, a people or group, humanity, or the whole cosmos. The social implications of the two forms of eschatology are significant. Individual forms tend to foster either apolitical or politically conservative attitudes—predicated on the belief that each person experiences God's judgment upon death and that there is therefore little purpose to changing the world. Some forms of collective eschatology, however, involve political activism and the expectation of the public manifestation of God's justice. Not only do they hope for collective corporeal salvation and a transformation of the world, but they actively prepare for it.

the promises of the Old Testament about the coming bringer of salvation had been fulfilled in Jesus Christ, but that the fulfillment was not yet complete. Thus, they awaited Christ's Second Coming, which they believed was imminent.

EXPECTATIONS OF THE KINGDOM OF GOD IN EARLY CHRISTIANITY

In early Christianity's expectation of the Kingdom of God, two types were inherited from Judaism. The first was the expectation of a messianic Kingdom in this world, with its centre in Jerusalem, which was to be established by an earthly Messiah from the house of David. The second expectation was that of a heavenly Kingdom, which was to be inaugurated by the heavenly Messiah, Son of man,

and in which the elected comrades of the Kingdom from all times would share in the state of the resurrection.

The two types of eschatological expectation did not remain neatly separated in the early church but rather intersected in manifold ways. Under the influence of the persecutions, a combination of the end-time expectations was established. In Paul's letters and in the Revelation to John, the notion emerged that faithful Christians will first reign together with their returning Lord for some time in this world. Those Christians who are still alive at his return will take part in the reign without dying (1 Thessalonians 4:17). Christians who have already died will rise again and, as resurrected ones, share in the Kingdom upon Earth. Only after completion of this first act of the events of the end time will there then follow the general resurrection of all the dead and the Last Judgment, in which the elect will participate as co-judges (1 Corinthians 6:2).

In the Revelation to John this expectation is condensed into the concept of the 1,000-year (millennial) kingdom. The dragon (Satan) is to be chained up and thrown into the abyss, where he will remain for 1,000 years. In John's vision, Christians, the first resurrected, "came to life and reigned with Christ a thousand years" (Revelation 20:4). Only later does the resurrection of all the dead take place, as well as the general judgment, creation of the new heaven and the new Earth, and the descent of the new Jerusalem. According to the Revelation to John, this 1,000-year Kingdom is composed of the saints and martyrs and all who stood the test in times of persecution; it is a Kingdom of the privileged elect.

This promise has exerted revolutionary effects in the course of church history. In the early church the expectation of the millennium was viewed as a social and political utopia, a state in which the chosen Christians would rule and judge with their Lord in this world. Such *chiliastic* (or millennial) expectations provided the impetus for ecclesiastical, political, and social reformations and revolutions in the course of church history. The establishment of a 1,000-year kingdom in which the elect, with Christ, will reign has fascinated religious expectations as well as political and social imagination far more than

the second part of the eschatological expectation, the "Last Judgment."

The delay of the Parousia resulted in a weakening of the imminent expectation in the early church. In this process of "de-eschatologizing," the institutional church increasingly replaced the expected Kingdom of God. The formation of the church as a hierarchical institution is directly connected with the declining of the imminent expectation. The theology of Augustine constitutes the conclusion of this development in the West. He de-emphasized the original imminent expectation by declaring that the Kingdom of God has already begun in this world with the institution of the church, which is the historical representative of the Kingdom of God on Earth. The first resurrection, according to Augustine, occurs constantly within the church in the sacrament of baptism, through which the faithful are introduced into the Kingdom of God. The expectation of the coming Kingdom of God, the resurrection of the faithful, and the Last Judgment have become a doctrine of the "last things" because the gifts of salvation of the coming Kingdom of God are interpreted as being already present in the sacraments of the church.

EXPECTATIONS OF THE KINGDOM OF GOD IN THE MEDIEVAL AND REFORMATION PERIODS

Despite Augustine's teachings to the contrary, the original imminent expectation has spontaneously and constantly reemerged in the history of Christianity. It was a powerful undercurrent throughout much of the Middle Ages, shaping numerous movements in that period. Charlemagne and his advisors may have been motivated by eschatological concerns, including those associated with the legend of the "Last Emperor," to accept imperial coronation on Christmas Day, 800. Indeed, several medieval rulers, including Otto III, were inspired by the legend in which the Last Emperor struggles against the Antichrist in preparation for the Second Coming. About the year 1000, eschatological expectations influenced the Peace of God movement (a social and religious reform movement that emerged in southern and central France), and numerous apparent signs and miracles suggested the imminence of Christ's return. The knights of the First Crusade (1095–99), especially those involved in massacres of Jews in Germany, were most likely influenced by apocalyptic expectations. Joachim of Fiore developed a millennialist theology and philosophy of history that influenced the Spiritual Franciscans in the 13th century. In the 14th century peasant revolts in France and England were shaped by eschatological as well as economic concerns, and the Taborites, extremist followers of Jan Hus, sought to bring about the Kingdom of God by force. In the medieval church new outbreaks of an imminent expectation also occurred in connection with great historical catastrophes, such as epidemics of the plague, Islamic invasions, schisms, and wars.

Luther's Reformation also was sustained by an imminent expectation. For the Reformers, the starting point for their eschatological interpretation of contemporary history was that the "internal Antichrist," the pope, had established himself in the temple at the Holy Place and that through persecution by the "external Antichrist," the Turk, the church had entered into the travails of the end time. The Reformation churches, however, soon became institutional territorial churches, which in turn repressed the end-time expectation, and thus doctrine of the "last things" became an appendix to dogmatics.

Although heightened apocalyptic fervour was quickly drained from the movements of the magisterial reformers (who received support from the civil powers or magistrates and who stressed the authority of teachers [Latin: *magister*]), the so-called radical reformers were often intensely eschatological, and some even advocated violence to usher in the Second Coming. Thomas Müntzer, inspired as much by the apocalyptic books of the Bible as by Luther, identified the poor as God's special elect who were charged with overthrowing their earthly rulers to bring about God's kingdom. His preaching was one of the inspirations of the German Peasants' War of 1524–25. The sect led by Jan of Leiden at Munster was also radically and violently apocalyptic, and many Anabaptist groups expressed an imminent eschatology. In England, several groups were apocalyptic, even millenarian, in nature. The Fifth Monarchy Men believed that the fifth monarchy (i.e., the reign of Christ)—to follow the biblical Assyrian, Babylonian, Greek, and Roman kingdoms—was at hand. Independents, Diggers, and other groups expressed belief in the imminent Second Coming, but many of them were suppressed by Oliver Cromwell.

EXPECTATIONS OF THE KINGDOM OF GOD IN THE POST-REFORMATION PERIOD

In the post-Reformation period, the imminent expectation appeared in individual groups on the margin of the institutional Reformation churches; such groups generally made the imminent expectation itself the object of their sect formation. This has been the result of the fact that, since the Reformation, the Roman Catholic Church has been virtually immune to eschatological movements. The Lutheran Church has been less immune; a series of eschatological groups whose activity in the church was determined by their expectation of the imminent return of Christ appeared in Pietism. Among the congregational and evangelical churches of England and America, the formation of new eschatological groups has been a frequent occurrence, especially during revival movements, including that of William Miller, which laid the foundation for the Adventist church in the 19th century. Such groups shared significantly in the renewal and expansion of Christianity in domestic and foreign missions. Indeed, by late in the 20th century much of the Christian missionary

outreach had passed into the hands of millennial-minded groups.

THE ROLE OF IMMINENT EXPECTATION IN MISSIONS AND EMIGRATIONS

The great missionary activities of Christian history in most cases have been based upon a reawakened imminent expectation, which creates a characteristic tension. The tension between the universal mission of the church and the hitherto omitted missionary duties, as well as the idea that the colossal task must be accomplished in the shortest time possible, renders comprehensible the astonishing physical and spiritual achievements of the great Christian missionaries. After the inundation of Christian areas of Africa and Asia by Islam, Franciscan missionaries in the 13th and 14th centuries, enduring incredible hardships, went by land and by sea to India, China, and Mongolia to preach the gospel. In a similar way, the missionary movement of the 18th and 19th centuries also proceeded from such eschatological groups within Protestantism.

The expectation of the Kingdom of God, in the form of the imminent expectation, plays a strong role in emigration movements. Great masses of European Christians again and again set out for Palestine with a sense of finding there the land of their salvation and being present when Christ returns there to establish his Kingdom. Mass pilgrimages to Jerusalem took place in 1033

English evangelist John Wesley, the founder of Methodism, preaches to a group of Native Americans during his visit to Georgia in 1736. Hulton Archive/Getty Images

and again in 1064–65, and the Crusades can be seen as a form of pilgrimage whose participants held eschatological concerns. The peasants of the so-called "People's Crusade" and the knights of the First Crusade were clearly motivated by apocalyptic anxieties, and Count Emicho of Flonheim, who led the massacres of Jews in Germany, may have seen himself in the role of the Last Emperor. The eschatological strain of the Crusades can also be noted in the Crusade sermons of Bernard of Clairvaux in 1147, who kindled enthusiasm to liberate Jerusalem with reference to the pressing terminal dates of the end time.

A great number of the attempts undertaken to found radical Christian communities in North America may be viewed as anticipations of the coming Jerusalem. The emigration movement toward America was influenced by beliefs in eschatologically fixed dates (e.g., Columbus). Puritans who traveled to America in the 17th century and Quakers, Baptists, and Methodists in the 18th century believed that America was the "wilderness" promised in the Revelation to John.

William Penn gave the name "Philadelphia" to the capital of the woodland areas ceded to him (1681) because he took up the idea of establishing the true church of the end time, represented by the Philadelphia community of the Revelation to John. The same influence holds true for the emigration of German revivalists of the 18th and early 19th centuries to Russia and Palestine. The "Friends of the Temple"—Swabians who went with Christoph Hoffmann to Palestine in 1866—and the Swabians, Franks, Hessians, and Bavarians, who after the Napoleonic Wars followed the call of Tsar Alexander I to Bessarabia, were all dominated by the idea of living in the end time and preparing themselves for the coming Kingdom of God. In Tsar Alexander I they saw the "eagle... as it flew in midheaven" (Revelation 8:13), which prepared the "recovery spot" for them in the East upon which Christ will descend.

ESCHATOLOGICAL EXPECTATIONS AND SECULARIZATION

In the eyes of some theologians, the very process of secularization, which progressively rules out transcendent explanations of natural and historical conditions, has been a working out of a form of eschatological expectation. Of course, the substance is quite different in the cases where people work in expectation of the Kingdom of God and in the other cases where they become "futurologists." But the impulse to prepare oneself for such futures has analogues and origins, it is contended, in old Christian ideas of penance and preparation for the coming Kingdom.

In the Gospels the attitude toward the coming Kingdom of God led, over and beyond the expectation of nullifying sin and death, to certain worldly conclusions of an organizational kind. The disciples of Jesus knew that there will be "first ones" in the Kingdom of Heaven; they pressed for the administrative posts in the coming Kingdom of God (e.g., the apostles James and John). The promise, too, that they are to take part as judges at the Last Judgment (Luke 22:30) sparked definite conceptions of rank. Jesus castigated them in their disputes over rank with the words, "If any one would be first, he must be last of all and servant of all" (Mark 9:35).

Despite this warning, the imminent expectation of the coming Kingdom of God awakened concrete, substantial ideas that led ever closer to social utopias. With the 18th-century German Lutheran mystic and Pietist F.C. Oetinger, the end-time expectation generated definite social and political demands—e.g., dissolution of the state, abolition of property, and elimination of class differences. Some of the aspects of the end-time expectation of Pietism were revived in the French Revolution's political and social programs. The transition from the end-time expectation to the social utopia, however, had already been achieved in writings from the 16th and early 17th centuries—e.g., the English humanist and saint Thomas More's... *de optimo reipublicae statu deque nova Insula Utopia* (1516; "On the Highest State of a Republic and on the New Island Utopia"), the German theologian

Johann Valentin Andrea's *Reipublicae Christianopolitanae Descriptio* (1619; "A Description of the Christian Republic"), the English philosopher Francis Bacon's *New Atlantis* (1627), and the English bishop Francis Godwin's *Man in the Moone* (1638). It is also found in early socialism of the 19th century—e.g., the French social reformer Henri de Saint-Simon's *Nouveau Christianisme* (1825; "The New Christianity") and the French Socialist Étienne Cabet's *Voyage en Icarie* (1840; "Voyage to Icaria").

What distinguishes the Christian social utopia from the earlier kind of eschatology is the stronger emphasis upon social responsibility for the preparation of the Kingdom of God and a considerable preponderance of various techniques in the establishment of the utopian society. (In general, the end-time expectation has also inspired technical fantasy and science fiction.) Also characteristic is the basic attitude that people themselves must prepare the future perfect society in a formative and organizing manner and that "hoping" and "awaiting" are replaced by human initiative. A graduated transition from a social utopia still consciously Christian to a purely Socialist one can be observed in the writings and activities of the French Socialists Charles Fourier, Saint-Simon, and Pierre-Joseph Proudhon, the English Socialist Robert Owen, and the German Socialist Wilhelm Weitling. Secularized remnants of a glowing Christian end-time expectation were still found even in the Marxist view of the social utopia.

Contemporary planning and projection of alternative futures is a secularization of the end-time expectations previously envisioned in Christian terms. The future is thus manipulated through planning (i.e., "horizontal eschatology") in place of eschatological "hoping" and "waiting for" fulfillment. "Horizontal eschatology" is thus taken out of the sphere of the unexpected and numinous (spiritual); it is made the subject not only of a detailed prognosis based upon statistics but also of a detailed programming undertaken on the basis of this prognosis. An eschatological remainder is found only in an ideological image of man, upon which programming and planning are based.

CONCEPTS OF LIFE AFTER DEATH

The Christian end-time expectation is directed not only at the future of the church but also at the future of the individual believer. It includes definite conceptions of the personal continuance of life after death. Many baptized early Christians were convinced they would not die at all but would still experience the advent of Christ in their lifetimes and would go directly into the Kingdom of God without death. Others were convinced they would go through the air to meet Christ returning upon the clouds of the sky: "Then we who are alive, who are left, shall be caught up together with them in the clouds to meet the Lord in the air; and so we shall always be with the Lord" (1 Thessalonians 4:17). In the early imminent expectation, the period between death and the coming of the Kingdom still constituted no object of concern. An expectation that one enters into bliss or perdition immediately after death is also found in the words of Jesus on the cross: "Today you will be with me in Paradise" (Luke 23:43).

In the Nicene Creed the life of the Christian is characterized as "eternal life." In the Gospels and in the apostolic letters, "eternal" is first of all a temporal designation: in contrast to life of this world, eternal life has a deathless duration. In its essence, however, it is life according to God's kind of eternity—i.e., perfect, sharing in his glory and bliss (Romans 2:7, 10). "Eternal life" in the Christian sense is thus not identical with "immortality of the soul"; rather, it is only to be understood in connection with the expectation of the resurrection. "Continuance" is neutral vis-à-vis the opposition of salvation and disaster, but the raising from the dead leads to judgment, and its decision can also mean eternal punishment (Matthew 25:46). The antithesis to eternal life is not earthly life but eternal death.

Eternal life is personal life, and precisely therein is fulfilled the essence of man who is created according to the image of God. Within eternal life there are differences. In the present life there are variations in talent, duty, responsibility, and breadth and height of life, just as there are also distinctions in "wages" according to the measure of the occupation, the sacrifice of suffering, and the trial (1 Corinthians 3:8). Correspondingly,

the resurrected are also distinguished in eternal life according to their "glory":

There is one glory of the sun, and another glory of the moon, and another glory of the stars; for star differs from star in glory. So it is with the resurrection of the dead (1 Corinthians 15:41-42).

This expectation has had a great influence upon the Christian conception of marriage and friendship. The idea of a continuation of marriage and friendship after death has contributed very much to the deepening of the view of marriage, as is shown by the strong influence of the 17th–18th-century Swedish mystic, philosopher, and scientist Emanuel Swedenborg's ideas upon the romantic philosophy of religion and its interpretation of marriage and friendship in the thought of the German scholars Friedrich Schelling and Friedrich Schleiermacher. The Western concept of personality was thus deepened through the Christian view of its eternal value.

The delay of the imminent expectation brought about the question of the fate of the dead person in the period between the death of the individual Christian and the resurrection. Two basic views were developed. One view is that of an individual judgment, which takes place immediately after death and brings the individual to an interim state, from which he enters into the realm of bliss or that of perdition. The idea of an individual judgment, however, cannot be readily harmonized with the concept of the general Last Judgment on the day of the general resurrection of the dead. It anticipates the decision of the general judgment and thus deprives of its significance the notion of the Last Judgment. A second view, therefore, also prevailed: the sleep of the soul—i.e., the soul of the dead person enters into a sleeping state that continues until the Last Judgment, which will occur after the general resurrection. At the Last Judgment the resurrected will be assigned either to eternal life or eternal damnation. This conception, accepted in many churches, contains many discrepancies, especially the abandonment of the fundamental idea of the continuity of personal life.

Both views contain an inhuman consequence. The first leaves to people no further opportunity to improve the mistakes of their lives and to expiate their guilt. The second preserves the personality in an intermediate state for an indefinite period so as to later punish it for sins or reward it for good deeds from a time prior to entrance into the sleep of the soul. The belief in purgatory (an interim state in which a correction of a dead person's evil condition is still possible) of the Roman Catholic Church gives the deceased opportunities for repentance and penance to ameliorate their situation.

The presupposition of the doctrine of purgatory is that there is a special judgment for each individual at once after death. Hence, the logical conclusion is that purgatory ceases with the Last Judgment. The stay in purgatory can be shortened through intercession, alms, indulgences, and benefits of the sacrifice of the mass. The Eastern Orthodox Church has no doctrine of purgatory but does practice an intercession for the dead. It assumes that, on the basis of the connection between the church of the living and that of the dead, an exertion of influence upon the fate of the dead through intercession is possible before the time of the Last Judgment.

The idea of the Last Judgment has often become incomprehensible to the modern world. At the most, people apparently are still open to the concept of judgment of the guilt and innocence of the individual. The idea decisive for the early church's expectation of the Judgment, however, was that the Last Judgment will be a public one. This corresponds to the fundamental Christian idea that human beings—both the living and the dead—are bound together in an indissoluble communion; it presupposes the conception of the church as the body of Christ. All of humanity is as one person. Humans sin with one another, and their evil is connected together in the "realm of sin" in a manifold way, unrecognizable in the individual. Each person is responsible for the other and is guilty with the other. The judgment upon each person, therefore, concerns all. Judgment upon the individual is thus at the same time judgment upon the whole, and vice versa. The Judgment is also public in regard to the positive side—the praise and reward of God for that which is done rightly and practiced in the common life, often without knowing it.

CHAPTER 6

THE CHURCH

The Christian view of the church was influenced by the Old Testament concept of the *qahal*, the elected people of God of the end time, and by the expectation of the coming of the Messiah in Judaism. The Greek secular word *ekklēsia*, the term used for the church, means an assembly of people coming together for a meeting.

In Christianity the concept of the church received a new meaning through its relationship to Jesus Christ as the messianic inaugurator of the Kingdom of God: (1) with Christ the elected community of the end time has appeared; (2) the church is the eschatological gift of the Holy Spirit, which already flows through the life of the church (Acts 2:33); (3) the community of the end time consists of those who believe in Jesus Christ—the idea of the elected covenant people (i.e., the Jews) is transferred to the "new Israel"; (4) the church forms the body of its Lord; and (5) the church consists of "living stones," from which its house is "built" (1 Peter 2:5).

Jesus himself created no firm organization for his community; the expectation of the immediate imminence of the Kingdom of God provided no occasion for this. Nevertheless, the selection of Apostles and the special position of individual Apostles within this circle pointed to the beginnings of a structuralization of his community. After the community was constituted anew because of the impressions made by the appearances of the resurrected Christ, the trend toward structuralization continued.

The unity of the church, which was dispersed geographically, was understood from the viewpoint of the Diaspora (the dispersion of Jews outside Palestine after the Babylonian Captivity). In the Letter of James, the scattered churches of the new Israel are identified as "the twelve tribes in the Dispersion" (1:1). The *Didachē*, or the *Teaching of the Twelve Apostles* (2nd century), viewed the church in terms of the bread of the Eucharist, whose wheat grains "are gathered from the mountains." The idea of the preexistent divine Logos became the concept of the preexistence of the church, which included the view that the world was created for the sake of the church. The earthly church is thus the representative of the heavenly church.

NORMATIVE DEFENSES IN THE EARLY CHURCH

Establishment of norms for the church was necessary because diverse interpretations of the Christian message were conceived under the influence of the religions of late antiquity, especially gnosticism. In gnostic interpretations, mixed Christian and pagan ideas appealed to divine inspiration or claimed to be revelations of Christ. The church erected three defenses against the prophetic and visionary efficacy of pneumatic (spiritual) figures as well as against pagan syncretism: (1) the New Testament canon, (2) the apostolic "rules of faith," or "creeds," and (3) the apostolic succession of bishops. The common basis of these three defenses is the idea of "apostolicity."

The early church never forgot that it had created and fixed the canon of the New Testament, primarily in response to the threat of gnostic writings. This is one of the primary distinctions between the Orthodox Church and the Reformation churches, which view the Scriptures as the final norm and rule for the church and church teaching. The Orthodox Church, like the Roman Catholic Church, teaches that the Christian Church existed prior to the formation of the canon of Scripture—that it is indeed the source and origin of the Scripture itself. Thus, tradition plays a significant role alongside the Holy Scriptures in the Orthodox and Roman churches.

The apostolic rule of faith—i.e., the creed—issued from the apostolic tradition of the church as a second, shorter form of its solidification, at first oral and then written. It also served as a defense against gnosticism and syncretistic heretical interpretations of the Christian faith.

The third defense that the church used against the gnostics and syncretistic and charismatic movements within the church was the office of bishop, which became legitimized through the concept of apostolic succession. The mandate for missions, the defense against prophecy, the polemics with gnosticism and other alternative versions of Christianity, the persecution of the church, and, not least of all, management of church discipline

CANON LAW

Canon law is the body of laws established within Roman Catholicism, Eastern Orthodoxy, the Oriental Orthodox churches, and the Anglican Communion for church governance. Canon law concerns the constitution of the church, relations between it and other bodies, and matters of internal discipline. The monk Gratian, an ecclesiastical lawyer and teacher, published the first definitive collection of Roman Catholic canon law c. 1140; the Decretum Gratiani *drew on older local collections, councils, Roman law, and the Church Fathers. The enlarged* Corpus juris canonici *("Body of Canon Law") was published in 1500. A commission of cardinals issued the new* Codex juris canonici *("Code of Canon Law") in 1917, and a revised version was commissioned after the Second Vatican Council and published in 1983. Following the Schism of 1054, the Eastern Orthodox Church developed its own canon law under the patriarch of Constantinople.*

allowed the monarchical episcopacy to emerge in the early centuries. The bishop, as leader of the eucharistic worship service, as teacher, and as curer of souls, became the chief shepherd of the church and was considered its representative.

EVOLUTION OF THE EPISCOPAL OFFICE

The evolution of the episcopal office followed a different development in the East and in the West. The Orthodox Church accepts the monarchical episcopacy insofar as it involves the entire church, both the visible earthly and the invisible heavenly churches bound together inseparably. The monarchical principle in the Orthodox Church, however, is based on democratic principles that are grounded in the polity of the early church. Just as all Apostles without exception were of equal authority and none of them held a

paramount position over the others, so too their successors, the bishops, are of equal authority without exception.

Thus, the politics of the Eastern Orthodox churches have a decidedly synodal character. The ecumenical council, an assembly of the bishops of the whole church, constitutes the highest authority of Orthodox synodal polity. The bishops gathered at an ecumenical council resolve all questions of faith as well as of worship and canon law according to the principle of majority rule. Not only the priesthood but also the laity have been able to participate in Orthodox synods. Election to ecclesiastical offices (i.e., pastor, bishop, or patriarch) involves participation by both clergy and laity. The individual polities of modern Orthodox churches (e.g., Greek or Russian) are distinguished according to the amount of state participation in the settlement of ecclesiastical questions.

Orthodoxy was divided into various old and new types of churches. Some of these were "patriarchal," which meant that they were directly responsible to a patriarch. Others were "autocephalous" (Greek: *autokephalos*, "self-headed"), which has come to mean in the modern world that as national churches they are in communion with Constantinople but are responsible for authority to their own national synods. This division, and the fact that Orthodoxy has so often been the victim of revolutionary change and political onslaught, have served as a hindrance against any new ecumenical council, even though many Orthodox have asked for one.

In the Roman Catholic Church the papacy evolved out of the monarchical episcopate. The city of Rome occupied a special position in the early church because, as the capital of the Roman Empire, it contained a numerically significant Christian community already in the 1st century. A leading role devolved upon the bishop of Rome in questions of discipline, doctrine, and ecclesiastical and worship order. This occurred in the Latin provinces of the church in the West (Italy, Gaul, Spain, Africa), whose organization followed the provincial organization of the Roman Empire. After the collapse of the Western Roman Empire in the late 5th century, the status of the Roman bishop increased. The theological underpinning of this special position was emphasized by Petrine theology, which saw in the words of Jesus,

"You are Peter, and on this rock I will build my church" (Matthew 16:18), a spiritual-legal instituting of the papacy by Jesus Christ himself; in the Greek Church of the East (e.g., Origen) and also for Augustine in the West, however, these words were referred to Peter's confession of faith. Since the time of popes Gelasius I (reigned 492–496), Symmachus (reigned 498–514), and Gregory I (reigned 590–604), these words have served as the foundation for the claim of papal primacy over the entire Christian Church.

AUTHORITY AND DISSENT

Christianity, from its beginning, tended toward an intolerance that was rooted in the understanding of itself as revelation of the divine truth that became human in Jesus Christ himself. "I am the way, and the truth, and the life; no one comes to the Father, but by me" (John 14:6). To be a Christian is to "follow the truth" (3 John); the Christian proclamation is "the way of truth" (2 Peter 2:2). Those who do not acknowledge the truth are enemies "of the cross of Christ" (Philippians 3:18) who have "exchanged the truth about God for a lie" (Romans 1:25) and made themselves the advocates and confederates of the "adversary, the devil," who "prowls around like a roaring lion" (1 Peter 5:8). Thus, one cannot make a deal with the devil and his party—and in this lies the basis for intolerance in Christianity.

Christianity developed an intolerant attitude toward Judaism early in its history, especially after the destruction of the Temple in Jerusalem in AD 70. This intolerance was rooted in the competition for religious converts and for possession of the Hebrew Scripture and its legacy. In order to proclaim itself as the "new Israel," Christianity had to repudiate the claims of Israel's traditional children. From the time of the composition of the Gospels, therefore, Jews were identified as the killers of Christ, and subsequent Christian theologians developed an elaborate picture of Jews as the enemy of the faith, though some argued that the Jews must survive until the end of time as witness to the truth of Christian revelation. Such hostile and irrational views laid the foundation for centuries of anti-Semitism among Christians. Not until the 20th century was the negative depiction of Jews in official teachings overturned in some churches.

Early Christianity, especially following the conversion of the emperor Constantine, aimed at the elimination of paganism—the destruction of its institutions, temples, tradition, and the order of life based upon it. After Christianity's victory over Greco-Roman religions, it left only the ruins of paganism still remaining. Christian missions of later centuries constantly aimed at the destruction of indigenous religions, including their cultic places and traditions (as in missions to the Anglo-Saxons, Germans, and Slavs). This objective was not realized in mission areas in which Christian political powers did not succeed in conquests—e.g.,

China and Japan; but in Indian Goa, for example, the temples and customs of all indigenous religions were eliminated by the Portuguese conquerors.

The attitude of intolerance was further reinforced when Islam confronted Christianity from the 7th century on. Islam understood itself as the conclusion and fulfillment of the Old and New Testament revelation. Christianity, however, understood Islam either as a new heresy (Muhammad, it was believed, was taught by a heretical or apostate monk) or eschatologically as the religion of the "false prophets" or of the Antichrist. The aggression of Christianity against Islam—on the Iberian Peninsula, in Palestine, and in the entire eastern Mediterranean area during the Crusades—was carried out under this fundamental attitude of intolerance. Intolerance of indigenous religions was also manifested in Roman Catholic missions in the New World; in the Western Hemisphere, these missions resulted in the wholesale destruction of Native American cults and cultic places.

When the Reformation churches asserted the exclusive claim of possessing the Christian truth, they tried to carry it out with the help of the political and military power at their disposal. In the religious wars of the 16th and 17th centuries, Christian intolerance developed into an internal fratricidal struggle in which each side sought to annihilate the other party in the name of truth. The fact that such attempts did not succeed led to new reflections upon the justification of claims to exclusive possession of absolute truth.

The intolerance of the Reformation territorial churches found its counterpart in the intolerance of the revolutionary groups of the Reformation period, such as that of the German radical Reformer Thomas Müntzer, which wanted to force the coming of the Kingdom of God through the dominion of the "elect" over the "godless." In the intolerance of the ideology and techniques of many modern political revolutions and authoritarian regimes some see either a legacy or a mimicking of old Christian patterns and methods.

Although calls for tolerance had been made earlier in church history, among the first to speak up consistently for tolerance were the Baptists and Spiritualists of the Reformation period. Their defense of tolerance contributed especially to the recognition of the evident contradiction between the theological self-conception of Christianity as a religion of love of God and neighbour and the inhumanity practiced by the churches in the persecution of dissenters. This recognition even provoked criticism of the Christian truths of faith themselves.

The Roman Catholic Church in the past has consistently opposed the development of religious toleration and as late as the 20th century in some countries ensured that legal restrictions against Protestant minorities were established. With Pope John XXIII and the Second Vatican Council (1962–65), however, the church adopted a much more accommodating stance, which has been appropriate both to the ecumenical situation of Christendom since the late 20th century and to the personal character of the Christian faith.

ORGANIZATION

In the early church, discipline concerned four areas in which there arose violations of the demand for holiness: (1) the relationship to the pagan social milieu and the forms of life and culture connected with it (e.g., idolatry, the emperor's cult, the theatre, and the circus); (2) the relationship of the sexes within the Christian community (e.g., rejection of polygamy, prostitution, pederasty, sodomy, and obscene literature and art); (3) other offenses against the community, especially murder and property crimes of all kinds; and (4) the relationship to teachers of false doctrine, false prophets, and heretics.

Employment of church discipline at an early date led at first to the simple distinction between "mortal" and "not mortal" sins (1 John 5:15 ff.)—i.e., between sins that through their gravity resulted in loss of eternal life and those that did not. In earliest Christianity, the relapse of a baptized Christian into paganism (i.e., apostasy) was believed to be the most serious offense. In the Letter to the Hebrews one who is baptized irrevocably forfeits salvation through a relapse into grievous sin. The difficulties in substantiating the theory and practice of a second repentance were solved by Pope Calixtus (reigned 217?–222). This question was especially important in Rome because of the great number of offenses against the idea of holiness. Calixtus granted bishops the right to decide about definitive exclusion from the congregation or readmission as well as the right to evaluate church punishments. Although it did not occur without fierce opposition (e.g., Montanism), the concentration of penitential discipline in the bishops' hands probably contributed more to the strengthening of episcopal power and to the achievement of the monarchical episcopate in the church than any other single factor.

Attainment of the church's demand of holiness was made more difficult in the large cities, especially in reference to sexual purity. The period of persecution by the emperors and the demand that subjects of the empire sacrifice before the altars of the emperor's images brought countless new instances of apostasy. The so-called Lapsi (Lapsedones), who had performed sacrifices before the emperor's image but, after persecution, moved back into the churches again, became a serious problem for the church, sometimes causing schisms (e.g., the Donatists).

The execution of church discipline by the clergy was subordinated to the regulations of canon law provided for priests. A genuine practice of church discipline was maintained in the monasteries in connection with the public confession of guilt, which was made by every monk before the entire assembly in the weekly gatherings of the chapter. A strong revival of church discipline among the laity also resulted from the church discipline pursued within monasticism.

On the whole, the casuistic regulation of church discipline led to its externalization and devaluation. The medieval sects, therefore, always stressed in their critique of the worldly church the lack of spiritual discipline and endeavoured to realize a voluntary church discipline in terms of a renewed radical demand of holiness based on early Christianity. The radical sects that emerged in the Reformation reproached the territorial churches by claiming that they had restricted themselves to a renovation of doctrine and not to a renewal of the Christian life and a restoration of the "communion of saints." Different groups of Anabaptists (e.g., Swiss Brethren, Mennonites, and Hutterites), especially, attempted to realize the ideal of the purity and holiness of the church through the reintroduction of a strict church discipline.

The Reformed churches in particular endeavoured to make church discipline a valid concern of the community. In Geneva, church discipline was expressed, at the instigation of Calvin, in the establishment of special overseers, who were assigned to watch over the moral behaviour of church members. Calvin's reforms in Geneva also led to the creation of such social arrangements as ecclesiastically controlled inns and taverns, in which not only the consumption of food and drink but even the topics of conversation were subject to stern regulation. The cooperation of ecclesiastical discipline and state legislation found its characteristic expression in the United States in the Prohibition amendment to the Constitution. Its introduction came most strongly from congregational churches, above all those characterized by Evangelical, Fundamentalist, or Pentecostal outlooks. They united forces with more moderate or liberal churches that were experienced in trying to affect the social order through legislation. Together they battled against the misuse of alcohol as part of their ideal to extend Christian norms and influence to the whole of society.

In the early 21st century, church discipline, in the original spiritual sense of voluntary self-control, is practiced only in smaller communities of evangelical Christians, in which the ideal of holiness of the community is still maintained and in which the mutual, personal bond of the congregational members in the spirit of Christian fellowship still allows a meaningful realization of a church discipline. It is also practiced in churches in developing nations where the practice of church discipline still appears as a vitally necessary centre of the credible self-representation of the Christian community. Characteristically, therefore, these churches' main criticism of the old institutional churches has been directed against the cessation of church discipline among their members.

CHURCH POLITY

The Orthodox and Roman Catholic churches are organized around the office of the bishop. This section will examine the organization of the Reformation churches.

Occupying a special position among these churches is the episcopal polity of the Anglican Communion. Despite the embittered opposition of Puritan and independent groups in England during the 16th and 17th centuries, this polity has maintained the theory and practice of the episcopal office of apostolic succession. The Low Church tradition of the Anglican Communion views the episcopal office as a form of ecclesiastical polity that has been tested through the centuries and is therefore commendable for pragmatic reasons; the Broad Church tradition, however, emphatically adheres to the traditional worth of the episcopal office without allowing the faithful to be excessively dependent upon its acknowledgement. The High Church tradition, on the other hand, values episcopal polity as an essential element of the Christian Church that belongs to the church's statements of faith. The episcopal branch of the Methodist Church has also retained the bishop's office in the sense of the Low Church and Broad Church view.

In the Reformation churches an episcopal tradition has been maintained in the Swedish state church (Lutheran), whose Reformation was introduced through a resolution of the imperial Diet of Västerås in 1527, with the cooperation of the Swedish bishops. In the German Evangelical (Lutheran and Reformed) territories, the bishops' line of apostolic succession was ruptured by the Reformation. As imperial princes, the Roman Catholic German bishops of the 16th century were rulers of their territories; they did not join the Reformation in order to avoid renouncing the exercise of their sovereign (temporal) rights as demanded by Luther's Reformation. On the basis of a legal construction originally intended as a right of emergency, the Evangelical rulers functioned as the bishops of their territorial churches but only in questions concerning external church order. This development was promoted through the older conception of the divine right of kings and princes, which was especially operative in Germanic lands.

In matters of church polity, controversial tendencies that began in the Reformation remained as divisive forces within the ecumenical movement that started in the 20th century. For Luther and Lutheranism, the polity of the church has no divine–legal characteristics; it is of subordinate significance for the essence of the church, falls under human ordinances, and is therefore alterable. In Calvinism, on the other hand (e.g., in the *Ecclesiastical Ordinances* of 1541 and in Calvin's *Institutes of the Christian Religion* [1536]), the Holy Scriptures appear as a codex from which the polity of the congregation can be inferred or derived as a divine law. Thus, on the basis of its spiritual–legal character, church polity would be a component of the essence of the church itself. Both tendencies stand in a constant inner tension with one another in the main branches of the Reformation and within the individual confessions as well.

Even in Lutheranism, however, there has been a demand for a stronger emphasis upon the independent episcopal character of the superintendent's or president's office. Paradoxically, in the Lutheran Church, which came forth with the demand of the universal priesthood of believers, there arose the development of ecclesiastical authorities but not the development of self-contained congregational polities. When a merger of three Lutheran bodies produced a new Evangelical Lutheran Church in America in 1988, it established the bishop as leader of the synodal jurisdictions. In Lutheranism these bishops replaced presidents. Bishops were regarded there, as in Methodism, as part of the well-being—but not the being or essence—of the church. Reformed churches developed more or less self-contained congregational polities because the Reformed church congregation granted greater participation in the life of the congregation to the laity as presbyters and elders.

Presbyterian polity appeals to the model of the original church. The polity of the Scottish Presbyterian Church and the Presbyterian churches of North America is primarily based upon this appeal, which was also found among many English Puritan groups and other spiritual descendants of John Calvin. It proceeds from the basic view that the absolute power of Christ in his church postulates the equality of rights of all members and can find expression only in a single office, that of the presbyter. Holders of this office are elected by church members, formally analogous to the democratic, republican political mode, and, accordingly, in contrast with the monarchy of the papal and the aristocracy of the episcopal church polity. In Presbyterian churches the differences between clergy and laity have been abolished in theory and, to a great extent, in practice. A superstructure of consistories and presbyteries is superposed one upon the other, with increasing disciplinary power and graduated possibilities of appeal. Through their emphases upon the divine–legal character of Presbyterian polity, the Presbyterian churches have represented a Protestant polity that counters the Roman Catholic concept of the church in the area of ecclesiastical polity. In ecumenical discussions held since the 20th century, the divine–legal character of this polity has been occasionally noticeable in its thesis of an apostolic succession of presbyters as a counter-thesis to that of the apostolic succession of bishops.

Congregationalism stresses the autonomous right of the individual congregation to order its own life in the areas of teaching, worship, polity, and administration. This demand had been raised and practiced by the medieval sects and led to differentiated polities and congregational orders among the Hussites and the Bohemian Brethren. Congregationalism was advanced during the Reformation period by the most diverse parties in a renewed way not only by "Enthusiasts" (or, in German, *Schwärmer*) and Anabaptists, who claimed the right to shape their congregational life according to the model of the original church, but also by individual representatives of Reformation sovereigns, such as Franz Lambert (François Lambert d'Avignon), whose resolutions at the Homberg Synod of 1526 were not carried out because of a veto by Luther. The beginnings of modern Congregationalism, however, probably lie among the English refugee communities on the European mainland, in which the principle of the established church was replaced by the concept of a covenant sealed between God or Jesus Christ and the individual or the individual congregation.

The basic concepts of Congregationalism are: the understanding of the congregation as the "holy people" under Jesus Christ; the spiritual priesthood, kingship, and prophethood of every believer and the exchange of spiritual experiences between them, as well as the introduction of a strict church discipline exercised by the congregation itself; the equal rank of all clergy; the

The Landing of the Pilgrims at Plymouth, Mass., Dec. 22, 1620, *lithograph by Currier & Ives, c. 1876*. Library of Congress, Washington D.C.

freedom of proclamation of the gospel from every episcopal or official permission; and performance of the sacraments according to the institution of Jesus. By virtue of the freedom of self-determination fundamentally granted every congregation, no dogmatic or constitutional union but rather only county union of the Congregationalist churches developed in England. North America, however, became the classic land of Congregationalism as a result of the great Puritan immigration to New England, beginning with the Pilgrims on the *Mayflower* (1620). By the 20th century, acknowledgement of the full authority of the individual congregation had become a feature of almost all Protestant denominations in the United States and was even found among the Lutherans.

Numerous other forms of congregational polity have arisen in the history of Christendom, such as the association idea in the Society of Friends. Even Pentecostal communities have not been able to maintain themselves in a state of unrestrained and constant charismatic impulses but instead have had to develop a legally regulated polity. This was what happened in the early church, which likewise was compelled to restrain the freedom of charisma in a system of rulers and laws. Pentecostal communities either have been constituted in the area of a biblical fundamentalism theologically and on the basis of a congregationalist church polity constitutionally or they have ritualized the outpouring of the Spirit itself. Thus, the characteristic dialectic of the Holy Spirit is confirmed: the Spirit creates law and the Spirit breaks law even in the most recent manifestations of its working.

LITURGY

The central focus of the liturgy of the early church was the Eucharist, which was interpreted as a fellowship meal with the resurrected Christ. Most expressions of Judaism at the time of Christ were dominated by an intense expectation, appropriated by the early Christian church, of the Kingdom of God, which would be inaugurated by the Messiah–Son of man. At the centre of Jesus's preaching on the Kingdom of God is the promise that the blessed would "eat bread" with the exalted Messiah–Son of man (Luke 13:29). The Lord himself would serve the community of the Kingdom at the messianic meal (Luke 12:37 ff.), which bears the features of a wedding banquet. The basic mood in the community gathered about him is thus one of nuptial joy over the inauguration of the promised end time. The supper that Jesus celebrated with his disciples "on the night when he was betrayed" (1 Corinthians 11:23) inaugurated the heavenly meal that will be continued in the Kingdom of God, as Jesus indicated

when he declared, "I shall not drink again of this fruit of the vine until that day when I drink it new with you in my Father's kingdom" (Matthew 26:29).

The death of Jesus at first bewildered his community in the face of his promise, but the appearances of the risen Christ confirmed their expectations about the messianic Kingdom. These appearances influenced the expectations about the messianic meal and the continuation of fellowship with the Son of man in the meal. Faith in the Resurrection and an expectation of the continuation of the fellowship meal with the exalted Son of man are two basic elements of the Eucharist that have been a part of the liturgy from the beginnings of the church. In meeting the risen Christ in the eucharistic meal the community sees all the glowing expectations of salvation confirmed.

The Christian community experiences a continuation of the appearances of the Resurrected One in the eucharistic meal. Thus, many liturgical forms developed, all of which served to enhance the meal's mystery. In the liturgical creations of the 1st to the 6th century, diversity rather than uniformity was a commanding feature of the development of worship forms. This diversity is preserved in the Clementine liturgy (Antioch), the Liturgy of St. James of the church of Jerusalem, the liturgy of St. Mark in Egypt, the Roman mass, and others. The eucharistic mystery developed from a simple form, as depicted in the 2nd-century *Didachē*, to the fully developed liturgies of the 5th and 6th centuries in both the East and the West.

In the 6th century two types of liturgies were fixed by canon law in the Eastern Orthodox Church: the Liturgy of St. John Chrysostom (originally the liturgy of Constantinople) and the Liturgy of St. Basil (originally the liturgy of the Cappadocian monasteries). The Liturgy of St. Basil, however, is celebrated only 10 times during the year, whereas the Liturgy of St. John Chrysostom is celebrated most other times. In addition to these liturgies is the so-called Liturgy of the Preconsecrated Offerings, attributed to Pope Gregory I. In this liturgy no consecration of the eucharistic offering occurs—because the eucharistic offerings used have been consecrated on the previous Sunday—and it is celebrated on weekday mornings during Lent as well as from Monday to Wednesday during Holy Week.

The period of liturgical improvisation apparently was concluded earlier in the Latin West than in the East. The liturgy of the ancient Latin Church is textually available only since the 6th century. Though the Gallic liturgies are essentially closer to the Eastern liturgies, the liturgy of Rome followed a special development. From the middle of the 4th century, the Roman mass was celebrated in Latin rather than in Greek, which had been the earlier practice. The fixing of the Roman mass by canon law is congruent with the historical impulse of the Roman Catholic Church to follow the ancient Roman pattern of rendering sacred observance in legal forms and with stipulated regularities.

NEW LITURGICAL FORMS AND ANTILITURGICAL ATTITUDES

In the 16th century, new liturgical forms emerged in association with the Protestant Reformation. Luther in Germany restricted himself to revising the Roman Catholic liturgy of the mass and translating it into German, whereas Huldrych Zwingli in Switzerland attempted to create a completely new liturgy based solely on his reading of the New Testament. The free churches also showed a strong liturgical productivity; in the Herrnhut Brethren (Moravian) community, Graf von Zinzendorf ushered in the singing worship services. Methodism, influenced by the spiritual songs and melodies of the Moravian church, also produced new liturgical impulses, especially through its creation of new hymns and songs and its joyousness in singing.

Churches that arose in the 19th and 20th centuries have been especially productive in liturgical reform. The Church of Jesus Christ of Latter-Day Saints, whose members are commonly called Mormons, developed not only a new type of church song but also a new style of church music in the context of their liturgical ·creation (e.g., "sealing"). The Baptist churches of African Americans, whose spirituals are the most impressive sign of a free and spontaneous liturgy, have introduced a charismatic mood in their liturgical innovations. The

Pentecostal churches of the 20th century quite consciously attempted to protect themselves against liturgical formalism. The often spontaneously improvised liturgy of the Pentecostal tent missions was transformed into patterns that became familiar to a wider audience through televised evangelism.

Though definite and obligatory liturgies have been established as normative, the forms of the liturgy continue to develop and change. The impulse toward variations in worship services was especially noticeable in the latter part of the 20th century. In the Eastern Orthodox liturgy, in the Roman Catholic mass and breviary, and in Anglican and Lutheran liturgies, there are both fixed and changing sections. The fixed parts represent the basic structure of the worship service concerned, and the alternating parts emphasize the individual character of a particular service for a certain day or period of the church year. The changing parts consist of special Old and New Testament readings that are appropriate for a particular church festival, as well as of special prayers and particular hymns.

The eucharistic liturgy consists of two parts: the Liturgy of the Catechumens and the Liturgy of the Faithful. This basic structure goes back to a time in which the church was a missionary church that grew for the most part through conversion of adults who were first introduced to the Christian mysteries as catechumens. They received permission to take part in the first part of the worship service (which was instructional) but had to leave the service before the eucharistic mystery was celebrated. The first part of the Orthodox worship service still ends with a threefold exclamation, reminiscent of pre-Christian, Hellenistic mystery formulas: "You catechumens, go forth! None of the catechumens (may remain here)!"

The eucharistic liturgy of the Orthodox Church is a kind of mystery drama in which the advent of the Lord is mystically consummated and the entire history of salvation—the Incarnation, death, and Resurrection of Christ the Logos, up to the outpouring of the Holy Spirit—is recapitulated. The Orthodox Church also attaches the greatest value to the fact that the transformation of the elements in bread and wine takes place during the eucharistic mystery. This is not the same as the Roman Catholic dogma of transubstantiation, which teaches that the substance of the bread and wine is changed into the body and blood of Christ, though the properties of the elements remain the same, when the priest consecrates the bread and wine. According to some Orthodox authorities, the Orthodox view is similar to the Lutheran doctrine of the real presence. The essential and central happening in the Orthodox liturgy, however, is the descent of the resurrected Lord himself, who enters the community as "the King of the universe, borne along invisibly above spears by the angelic hosts." The transformation of the elements is, therefore, the immediate emanation of this personal presence. Thus, the

Orthodox Church does not preserve and display the consecrated host after and outside the eucharistic liturgy, as in the Roman Catholic Church, because the consecrated offerings are mystically apprehended and actualized only during the eucharistic meal.

In the Roman Catholic mass, the sacrificial character of the Eucharist is strongly emphasized, but it is less so in the Orthodox liturgy because in the Orthodox liturgy the Eucharist is not only a representation of the crucifixion sacrifice (as in the Roman mass) but also of the entire history of salvation, in which the entire congregation, priest and laity, participates. Thus, the Orthodox Church has also held fast to the original form of Holy Communion in both kinds and preserves the liturgical gestures of the early church. The Orthodox worshiper prays while standing (because he stands throughout the service), with arms hanging down, crossing himself at the beginning and ending of the prayer.

The prayerful gesture of folded hands among Protestant churches derives from an old Germanic tradition of holding the sword hand with the left hand, which symbolizes one's giving himself over to the protection of God because he is now defenseless. The prayerful gesture of hands pressed flat against one another with the fingertips pointed upward—the symbol of the flame—is practiced among Roman Catholics. Other liturgical gestures found in many Christian churches are crossing oneself, genuflecting, beating oneself on the chest, and kneeling during prayer or when receiving the eucharistic elements. Among some Holiness or Pentecostal churches spontaneous handclapping and rhythmic movements of the body have been stylized gestures in the worship services. These gestures are often familiar features of worship in churches in Africa, Asia, and Latin America. Liturgical dancing, widely spread in pagan cults, was not practiced in the early church, but in the latter part of the 20th century, liturgical dances were reintroduced in some churches in a limited fashion. Among the many other gestures of devotion and veneration practiced in the liturgically oriented churches such as the Roman Catholic Church, the High Church Anglican churches, and the Orthodox Church, are kissing the altar, the Gospel, the cross, and the holy icons.

Liturgical vestments have developed in a variety of fashions, some of which have become very ornate. The liturgical vestments all have symbolic meaning (see church year: liturgical colours). In the Orthodox Church the liturgical vestments symbolize the wedding garments that enable the liturgists to share in the heavenly wedding feast, the Eucharist. The *epitrachēlion*, which is worn around the neck and corresponds to the Roman stole, represents the flowing downward of the Holy Spirit.

CHURCH TRADITION

Christianity has exhibited a characteristic tension toward tradition from its very beginnings. This tension, which is grounded in its essence, has been continued throughout its entire history. It began with rejecting the pious traditions of piety of the Hebrew Scriptures and synagogue practices. In the Sermon on the Mount, Jesus set forth his message as a renunciation of the Old Testament tradition of the Law. Yet he created a new tradition, a "new law," that has been carried on in the church. The dogmatic controversies of the Reformation period give the impression that the tradition of the church has to do primarily, if not exclusively, with ecclesiastical doctrinal tradition. Tradition, however, includes all areas of life of the Christian community and its piety, not just the teachings but also the forms of worship service, bodily gestures of prayer and the liturgy, oral and written tradition and the characteristic process of transition of the oral into written tradition, a new church tradition of rules for eating and fasting, and other aspects of the Christian life.

The break with the tradition of Judaism was not total. The Scriptures were adopted from Jewish tradition, but their interpretation was based upon the concepts of salvation that emerged around the figure of Jesus Christ. The book of Psalms, including its musical form, was taken over in Christian worship as the foundation of the liturgy. The new revelation became tradition in the oral transmission of the words of the Lord (the logia) and the reports (kerygma) concerning the events of his life that were important for the early church's faith in

him; his baptism, the story of his Passion, his Resurrection, and his Ascension. The celebration of the Lord's Supper as anticipation of the heavenly meal with the Messiah-Son of man in the coming Kingdom of God, even to the point of preserving in the liturgy the Aramaic exclamation *maranatha* ("O Lord, Come") and its Greek parallel *erche kyrie* ("Come, Lord!") as the supplicant calling for the Parousia (Second Coming)—all this became tradition.

Of special significance is the unique tradition of the oral transmission of teachings developed in Judaism. According to rabbinic doctrine, orally transmitted tradition coexisted on an equal basis with the written Law. Both text and tradition were believed to have been entrusted to Moses on Mount Sinai. The doctrinal contents of the tradition were initially passed on orally and memorized by the students. Because of the possibilities of error in a purely oral transmission, however, the extensive and growing body of tradition was, by necessity, fixed in written form. The rabbinic tradition of the Pharisees (a Jewish sect that sanctioned the reinterpretation of the Mosaic Law) was established in the Mishna (commentaries) and later in the Palestinian and Babylonian Talmuds (compendiums of Jewish Law, lore, and commentary). Because the essence of tradition is never concluded—i.e., by its very nature is never completely fixed in writing—the learned discussion of tradition by necessity continued in constant exegetical debate with the

Holy Scriptures. The written record of tradition, however, never claimed to be equal to the Holy Scriptures in Judaism. A similar process of written fixation also occurred among the sectarians of the community at Qumran, which in its *Manual of Discipline* and in the *Damascus Document* recorded its interpretation of the Law, developed first orally in the tradition.

In the Christian church a tradition proceeding from Jesus himself was formed. The oral transmission of the tradition was written down between the end of the 1st and the first half of the 2nd century in the form of various gospels, histories of the Apostles, letters, sermonic literature, and apocalypses. Among Christian gnostics the tradition also included what was believed to be secret communications of the risen Christ to his disciples.

A new element, however, inhered in the Christian in relation to the Jewish tradition. For Jewish piety, revelation encompassed two forms of divine expression: the Law and the Prophets. This revelation is considered concluded with the last Prophets, and its actualization further ensues through interpretation. In the Christian church the tradition is joined not only to the teachings of Jesus and the story of his life as prophet and teacher but also to the central event of the history of salvation, which his life, Passion, death, and Resurrection represent—namely, to the resurrected Christ who is henceforth present as the living Lord of the church

and guides and increases it through his Holy Spirit. This led to the literary form of church tradition—the Holy Scripture. As the "New Testament," it takes its place next to the Holy Scripture of Judaism, henceforth reinterpreted as the "Old Testament." The tradition of the church itself thereby entered into the characteristic Christian tension between spirit and letter. The spirit creates tradition but also breaks tradition as soon as the latter is solidified into an external written form and thus impedes charismatic life.

Throughout church history, however, the core of this field of tension has been formed by the transmission of the Christ event—the kerygma—itself. On the one hand, the kerygma is the bearer and starting point for tradition; on the other hand, it molds the impetus for ever-new impulses toward charismatic, fresh interpretations and, under certain circumstances, suggests or even enforces elimination of accumulated traditions. Decisive in this respect is the self-understanding of the church. According to the self-understanding of the Roman Catholic and the Eastern Orthodox churches, the church, as the institution of Jesus Christ, is the bearer of the oral and the written tradition and the creator of the New Testament canon. The church's selection of canonical writings presupposes a dogmatic distinction between "ecclesiastical" teachings—which, in the opinion of its responsible leaders, are "apostolic"—and "heretical" teachings. It thereby already presupposes a far-reaching intellectualization of the tradition and its identification with "doctrine." The oral tradition thus became formalized in fixed creedal formulas.

Accordingly, in the history of the Christian church a specific, characteristic dialectic has been evidenced between periods of excessive growth and formalistic hardening of tradition that hindered and smothered the charismatic life of the church and periods of a reduction of tradition that follow new reformational movements. The latter occurred, in part, within the church itself, such as in the reforms of Cluny, the Franciscans, and the Dominicans; they also took on the form of revolutionary movements. The Reformation of the 16th century broke with the institution of monasticism, the liturgical and sacramental tradition of the Roman Catholic Church, and certain elements of doctrinal tradition. Luther, however, was more conservative in his attitude toward the Roman Catholic Church than were Zwingli and Calvin. The Anabaptists and other Enthusiasts (*Schwärmer*) went even further, demanding and practicing a revolutionary break with the entire Roman Catholic tradition. The churches that arose from the Reformation, however, soon created their own traditions, which emerged from the confessional writings and doctrines of the reformers. The rejection of the tradition of the Roman Catholic Church had practical as well as dogmatic effects—e.g., the eating of sausage on fast days in Zürich at the start of Zwingli's reformation or the provocative marriages of monks and nuns.

In the 19th century, a period of progressive political revolutions and anti-Catholic movements such as the Kulturkampf, the Roman Catholic Church sought to safeguard its tradition—threatened on all sides—through an emphatic program of "antimodernism." It endeavoured to protect tradition both by law and through theology (e.g., in returning to neo-Thomism). The representatives of this development were the popes from Pius IX (reigned 1846–78) to Pius XII (reigned 1939–58). With Pope John XXIII (reigned 1958–63), a dismantling (*aggiornamento*) of antimodernism and a more critical attitude toward "tradition" set in; this extended to traditional dogmatic views as well as to the liturgy and church structure. The Second Vatican Council (1962–65) guided this development into moderate channels. On the other hand, an opposite development took place in the Soviet Union and the eastern European countries. In these nations the remains of the Orthodox Church, which survived extermination campaigns of the Leninist and Stalinist eras from the 1920s to the 1950s, preserved themselves in a political environment hostile to the church precisely through a retreat to their church tradition and religious functioning in the realm of the liturgy. From the late 1980s the Orthodox Church experienced greater religious freedom and new growth, as the openly hostile governments in the Soviet Union and eastern Europe dissolved with the fall of communism. In the World Council of Churches, the Orthodox Church in the latter part of the 20th century viewed its task as the bearer of Christian tradition against the predominant social-ethical tendencies of certain Protestant member churches that disregarded or de-emphasized the tradition of the church in a wave of anti-historical sentiment.

THE SACRAMENTS

The interpretation and number of the sacraments vary among the Christian churches of the world. The number of sacraments also varied in the early church, sometimes including as many as 10 or 12. In his *Book of Sentences* (1148–51), Peter Lombard asserted that there were seven sacraments, a position adopted by contemporary theologians. At the Council of Trent (1545–63), the Roman Catholic Church formally fixed the number of sacraments at seven: baptism, confirmation, the Eucharist, penance, holy orders, matrimony, and anointing of the sick. The theology of the Eastern Orthodox Church also fixed the number of sacraments at seven. The classical Protestant churches (i.e., Lutheran, Anglican, and Reformed) have accepted only two sacraments, baptism and the Eucharist, though Luther allowed that penance was a valid part of sacramental theology.

The New Testament mentions a series of "holy acts" that are not, strictly speaking, sacraments. Though the Roman Catholic Church recognizes a difference between such "holy acts," which are called sacramentals, and sacraments, the Orthodox Church does not, in principle, make such strict distinctions. Baptism and the Eucharist, therefore, have been established as sacraments of the church, but foot washing, which replaces the Lord's Supper in The Gospel According to John, was not maintained as a sacrament. It is still practiced on special occasions, such as on Holy Thursday (the Thursday preceding Easter Sunday) in the Roman Catholic Church and as a rite prior to the observance of the Lord's Supper, as in the Church of the Brethren. The "holy acts" of the Orthodox Church are symbolically connected to its most important mysteries. Hence, baptism consists of a triple immersion that is connected with a triple renunciation of Satan that the candidates say and act out symbolically prior to the immersions. Candidates first face west, which is the symbolic direction of the Antichrist, spit three times to symbolize their renunciation of Satan, and then face east, the symbolic direction of Christ, the sun of righteousness. Immediately following baptism, chrismation (anointing with consecrated oil) takes place, and the baptized believers receive the "seal of the gift of the Holy Spirit."

VENERATION OF PLACES, OBJECTS, AND PEOPLE

In addition to the tradition of the Holy Scriptures and its interpretation, traditions centring on holy places also developed. The veneration of holy places is the oldest expression of Christian popular piety. From Judaism Christianity adopted the idea and practice of venerating holy places. In post-exilic Judaism (i.e., after the 5th century BC), Jerusalem was the sanctuary and the centre of Jews in Palestine and the destination of the pilgrimages of Jews of the Diaspora. After the destruction in AD 70 of Jerusalem, which had become the holy city for the early church, it remained for Christians—as the site of the suffering and Resurrection of Jesus Christ and as the place of his return in glory—a holy city and a goal of pilgrimages. Early bishops such as Melito of Sardis and Alexander of Jerusalem and theologians, including Origen, made pilgrimages to Jerusalem. When Christianity became the state church in the 4th century, pilgrimages to the holy places in Palestine became increasingly popular.

The journey of the empress mother Helena to the Holy Land before AD 330 stimulated the growth of the "cult" (in the sense of a general system of religious belief and practice) of relics through the alleged discovery of the holy cross. Her son, the emperor Constantine, built the Church of the Holy Sepulchre in Jerusalem (335) and the Church of the Nativity over the Grotto of the Nativity in Bethlehem. Shrines commemorating numerous other places identified in the Old and New Testaments soon followed.

The cult of martyrs and saints led to the establishment of shrines outside Palestine that became pilgrimage sites. The idea that the martyrs are present at the places of their martyrdom (e.g., Peter's tomb at the Vatican) secured a prominent position for holy places connected with the cult of saints and martyrs. The cult of the martyrs was developed especially in the Roman catacombs, and it contributed to the formation of the Petrine doctrine and the teaching of the primacy of the Roman bishop. After the 4th century it spread further and created an abundance of new holy places in the West, including Santiago de Compostela in Spain, the site of the tomb of the apostle St. James and one of the great pilgrimage centres of Christendom; Trier in Germany, with the tomb of the apostle Matthias, which exerted a special power of attraction through the relic of the holy robe; and Marburg in Germany, with the shrine of St. Elizabeth of Hungary, a 13th-century princess known for her devotion to the poor. In the Middle Ages, holy places became places of grace, the visitation of which was considered a work of penance.

The original historical consciousness of the Christian Church is also alive in the cult of relics, which began as a result of veneration of a martyr at his or her tomb, over which later was erected an altar of the church built to honour the saint. From the 4th century on in the East, and later also in the West, the remains of the martyrs were distributed in order that as many as possible could share in their miraculous power. Fragments of relics, in which the saint is believed to be present, were sewn into a silken cloth (antimension), a practice still used in some churches, and the Eucharist could be celebrated only upon an altar that was covered with such an antimension. In times of persecution the Eucharist could be celebrated upon any table, as long as it was covered with the antimension and consecrated through the presence of the martyr. In the Latin Church relics are enclosed in a cavity (*sepulcrum*) in the altar top. During the deconsecration of a church, the relic is again removed from the *sepulcrum*.

In the late Middle Ages the character of the pilgrimage, just like the veneration of relics, suffered degeneration in connection with the degeneration of the sacrament of penance because of the abuse of the indulgence. Luther's critique of the indulgence began with a criticism of the display of the elector of Saxony Frederick III the Wise's imposing collection of relics in the Schlosskirche (Castle Church) of Wittenberg on All Saints' Day (1516). In response to the attacks of Luther, the Council of Trent declared that

> the holy bodies of the holy martyrs and others living with Christ, whose bodies were living members of Christ and temples of the Holy Spirit, and will be by him raised to eternal life and glorified, are to be venerated by the faithful, since by them God bestows many benefits upon men.

In order to avoid the development of a holy place at his grave and a reliquary and saintly cult around his person, Calvin arranged by will that his body be buried at an unknown spot. The erection of the giant monument to the reformer at the supposed place of his burial shows the futility of his effort and the strength of the Christian consciousness of tradition.

MONASTICISM

The origins of and inspiration for monasticism, an institution based on the Christian ideal of perfection, have traditionally been traced to the first apostolic community in Jerusalem—which is described in the Acts of the Apostles—and to Jesus's sojourn in the wilderness. In the early church, monasticism was based on the identification of perfection with world-denying asceticism and on the view that the perfect Christian life would be centred on maximum love of God and neighbour.

Monasticism emerged in the late 3rd century and had become an established institution in the Christian church by the 4th century. The first Christian monks, who had developed an enthusiasm for asceticism, appeared in Egypt and Syria. Notably including St. Anthony, the founder of Christian monasticism, they appeared as solitary figures who, out of a desire for further and more advanced isolation, established themselves in tombs, in abandoned or half-deteriorated human settlements, in caves, and, finally, in the wilderness of the desert to do battle against the desires of the flesh and the wiles of the devil. Soon there were great numbers of desert anchorites, living solitary lives of devotion to God and coming together for weekly prayer services.

The pious lifestyle of these earliest holy men attracted numerous imitators and admirers.

Certain writings that captured the spirit of monasticism were essential for the development of this way of life in the church. Athanasius of Alexandria, the 4th century's most significant bishop spiritually and in terms of ecclesiastical politics, wrote the *Life of St. Antony*, which described the eremitic (hermit) life in the desert and the awesome struggle of ascetics with demons as the model of the life of Christian perfection. The *Life* had a profound impact on its many readers and was one of the first great testimonials praising the emerging monastic tradition.

A former Roman soldier of the 4th century, Pachomius, created the first cenobitic, or communal, monastery. He united the monks under one roof and one abbot (father, or leader). In 323 he founded the first true monastic cloister in Tabennisi, north of Thebes, in Egypt, and joined together houses of 30 to 40 monks, each with its own superior. Pachomius also created a monastic rule, though it served more as a regulation of external monastic life than as spiritual guidance. During the remainder of the 4th century, monasticism soon developed in areas outside Egypt. Athanasius brought the monastic rule of Pachomius to the West during his banishment (340–346) to Trier, Germany—as a result of his opposition to the imperially sanctioned heretical doctrines of Arianism. Mar Awgin, a Syrian monk, introduced the monastic rule in Mesopotamia, and Jerome established a monastic cloister in Bethlehem.

Basil the Great, one of the three Cappadocian Fathers of the 4th century, definitively shaped monastic community life in the Byzantine Church. His ascetic writings furnished the theological and instructional foundation for the "common life" (cenobitism) of monks. He was the creator of a monastic rule that, through constant variations and modifications, became authoritative for later Orthodox monasticism. The Rule of Basil has preserved the Orthodox combination of asceticism and mysticism into the 21st century.

Western monasticism, which has been shaped by the rule of Benedict of Nursia, has been characterized by two distinct developments. The first consists of its clericalization. In modern Roman Catholic cloisters, monks are, except for the serving brothers (*fratres*), ordained priests and are thereby drawn in a direct way into the ecclesiastical tasks of the Roman Church. Originally, however, monks were laymen. Pachomius had explicitly forbidden monks to become priests on the ground that "it is good not to covet power and glory." Basil the Great, however, by means of a special vow and a special ceremony, enabled monks to cease being just laymen and to attain a position between clergy and laity. Even in the 21st century, monks of the Orthodox Church are, for the most part, from the laity; only a few fathers (abbots) of each cloister are ordained priests (*hieromonachoi*), who are thus allowed to administer the sacraments.

SAINT PACHOMIUS

(born c. 290, probably in Upper Egypt, died 346, feast day May 9)

Pachomius was founder of Christian cenobitic (communal) monasticism, whose rule (book of observances) for monks is the earliest extant.

Of Egyptian origin, Pachomius encountered Coptic (Egyptian) Christianity among his cohorts in the Roman emperor Constantine's North African army and, on leaving the military about 314, withdrew alone into the wilderness at Chenoboskion, near his Theban home. Soon after, he joined the hermit Palemon and a colony of solitaries (anchorites) in the same area at Tabennisi, on the east bank of the Nile River. With a talent for administration, Pachomius built the first monastic enclosure, replacing the scattered hermits' shelters, and he drew up a common daily program providing for proportioned periods of work and prayer patterned about a cooperative economic and disciplinary regimen.

This rule was the first instance in Christian monastic history of the use of a cenobitic, or uniform communal, existence as the norm, the first departure from the individualistic, exclusively contemplative nature that had previously characterized religious life. Pachomius, moreover, instituted a monarchic monastic structure that viewed the relationship of the religious superior's centralized authority over the community as the symbolic image of God evoking obedient response from man striving to overcome his egocentrism by self-denial and charity. By the time he died, Pachomius had founded 11 monasteries, numbering more than 7,000 monks and nuns.

The second special development in Roman Catholicism consists of the functional characteristics of its many orders. The individual orders aid the church in its various areas of activity—e.g., missions, education, care for the sick and needy, and combating heresy. Developing a wide-ranging diversification in its structure and sociological interests, Roman Catholic monasticism has extended all the way from the knightly orders to orders of mendicant friars, and it has included orders of decided feudal and aristocratic characteristics alongside orders of purely bourgeois characteristics. To the degree that special missionary, pedagogical, scholarly-theological, and ecclesiastically political tasks of the orders increased in the West, the character of ancient monasticism—originally focused completely on prayer, meditation, and contemplation—receded more and more in importance. Few monastic orders—the Benedictines and the Carmelites are notable exceptions—still attempt to preserve the ancient character and purposes of monasticism in Roman Catholicism.

THE SAINTLY LIFE

The term *saint* was originally a self-designation of all Christians. "The saints," according to the First Letter of Paul to the Corinthians (1:31), are "sanctified through the name of the Lord Jesus Christ and through the Spirit of our God." Saints were also understood as Christians who endeavoured to fulfill the binding demand of holiness in obedience to God and in love of their neighbours (2 Corinthians 7:1; 1 Thessalonians 4:3) or as charismatic figures in whom the gifts of the Holy Spirit operated according to their personal and temporal circumstances. Because of certain views on being "called to holiness," members of many sects have designated themselves as "the saints"—from Oliver Cromwell's "saints" in 17th-century England to the Mormon "latter-day saints" from the 19th to the 21st century.

The general meaning of *saint* was transformed during the period of the persecutions of Christians in the Roman Empire. The martyr, the witness in blood to Christ and follower in his suffering, became the prototypical saint. Veneration of the saints began because of a belief that martyrs were received directly into heaven after their martyrdoms and that their intercession with God was especially effective—in the Revelation to John the martyrs occupy a special position in heaven, immediately under the altar of God (Revelation 6:9). The veneration of confessors (i.e., those who had not denied their belief in Christ but had not been martyred), bishops, popes, early Church Fathers, and ascetics who had led a godlike life was established soon after cessation of the persecutions.

In the Greek church the saints were regarded as charismatic figures in whom the prototype of Christ is reflected in multifarious images. Veneration of the saints in the Orthodox churches was thus based more upon the idea that the saints provided instructional examples of the Christian life of sanctification. In the West, however, cultic veneration of the saints, the concept of patron saints, and the view that saints are helpers for those in need became predominant. During the 12th and 13th centuries, the veneration of saints came under the control of the papacy, which established a process of canonization strictly defined by canon law. The saints thus dominated the church calendar, which notes the names of the ecclesiastically recognized saints of each day of the year. They are venerated on a particular day in the prayer of intercession, and references are made to their deeds, sufferings, and miracles in the liturgy.

Under Pope Paul VI, the Roman Catholic Church attempted to reduce the significance of the veneration of saints—and thereby emphasize the idea of their historical exemplariness—by deleting some legendary figures from the calendar of saints, most notably St. Christopher. The deletion, however, has had little influence on popular piety. Pope John Paul II, fully respectful of the directions of the Second Vatican Council, nonetheless paid renewed respect to some of the pre-council forms of devotion which the reformers had tended to displace. His respect for the traditional veneration of saints was further demonstrated by the fact that he performed far more canonizations than had any previous pope.

In the early church the veneration of saints at first was restricted to celebrations at their tombs, but the cult of saintly relics soon spread the devotion to particular saints to many areas. The *Martyrdom of Polycarp*, for example, called the remains of the bishop Polycarp of Smyrna, martyred in 155, "more precious than costly stones and more excellent than gold." A belief in the need of special protection by saints is the basis of the system of patron saints. Saints became patrons of cities, regions, vocational groups, or classes, and most Roman Catholic churches have a saint as their patron, whose presence in the church is represented by a particular relic. Saints also won a special significance as patrons of names: in the Roman Catholic and Eastern Orthodox churches a Christian generally received the name of the saint on whose holiday (day of death) he is baptized. The believer was thus joined for life with the patron of his name through the name and the name day, which, as the day of rebirth (i.e., baptism), is of much greater significance than the natural birthday.

Although the Reformation did not in theory deny the significance of the saints as historical witnesses to the power and grace of God, it did eliminate their veneration and remove their images and relics from churches and homes. Luther's view that all believers are saints contributed to this development. At the same time, the experience of martyrdom in the persecutions of the Reformation and Counter-Reformation encouraged the development of a new saintly ideal in the radical Protestant sects. In the 20th century, the Swedish archbishop Nathan Söderblom's attempt to develop a new understanding of the notion of the saint led to a rediscovery of saints in the Protestant realm. In modern Roman Catholicism, emphasis is increasingly being placed upon the charismatic aspects of the saints and their significance as models of a spiritual, holy Christian life.

ART AND ICONOGRAPHY

Christian art constitutes an essential element of the religion. Until the 17th century the history of Western art was largely identical with the history of Western ecclesiastical and religious art. During the early history of the Christian Church, however, there was very little Christian art, and the church generally resisted it with all its might. Clement of Alexandria, for example, criticized religious (pagan) art for encouraging people to worship that which is created rather than the Creator. There was also little need for Christian art, because monumental churches had yet to be built and there were few wealthy patrons to commission it. By the late 2nd century an incipient pictorial art had appeared in the Christian Church, and by the mid-3rd century art inspired by pagan models as well as Christian themes began to be produced. Pictures began to be used in the

The Annunciation, tempera on wood by Simone Martini, 1333 (saints on either side of the central panel by Lippo Memmi); in the Uffizi Gallery, Florence. SCALA/Art Resource-EB, Inc.

churches when Christianity was legalized and supported by the Roman emperor Constantine in the early 4th century, and they soon struck roots in Christian popular religiosity.

A number of factors explain the slow development of Christian art in the early centuries of the church. Christianity received from its Jewish origins a prohibition against the use of images to depict the sacred or holy, including humans, who were created in "the image of God." The early church was also deeply involved in a struggle against paganism—which, to the Christian observer, was idolatry in that its many gods were represented in various pictorial and statuary forms. In early Christian missionary preaching, the attacks within the Hebrew Scriptures upon pagan veneration of images were transferred directly to pagan image veneration of the first three centuries AD. The struggle against images was conducted as a battle against "idols" with all the intensity of faith in the oneness and exclusiveness of the imageless biblical God. The abhorrence of images was strengthened further by the emperor's cult, which Christians so despised. Christians were compelled to venerate the imperial images by offering sacrifices to them; refusal to make sacrifice was the chief cause of martyrdom. Characteristically, then, the church's reaction to its public recognition was expressed in the riotous destruction of pagan divine images.

In spite of these very strong religious and emotional restraints, the church developed a form of art peculiar to its needs. From late antiquity to the time of the Counter-Reformation, Western art was essentially the art of the church; both lay and secular patrons commissioned works of art that illustrated important Christian themes and stood as testimony to their own faith. Assuming many forms, Christian art could be found in private homes, churches, and public spaces. Churches, themselves artistic triumphs, were adorned with a broad range of art, including statuary, paintings, and stained glass. Another important form was illumination; illuminated manuscripts were prized possessions and often displayed on high holy days. The attitude reflected in these practices was expressed in the famous dictum of Pope Gregory I, that art is the book of the illiterate; art was thus conceived as having a didactic function.

The starting point for the development of Christian pictorial art lies in the basic teaching of the Christian revelation itself—namely, the incarnation, the point at which the Christian proclamation is differentiated from Judaism. The incarnation of the Son of man, the Messiah, in the form of a human being—who was created in the "image of God"—granted theological approval of a sort to the use of images that symbolized Christian truths. Clement of Alexandria, at one point, called God "the Great Artist," who formed humans according to the image of the Logos, the archetypal light of light. The great theological struggles over the use of images within the church, particularly in the Byzantine Empire, during the period of the so-called Iconoclastic Controversy in the 8th and 9th centuries indicate how a new understanding of images emerged on the basis of Christian doctrine. This new understanding was developed into a theology of icons that still prevails in the Eastern Orthodox Church in the 21st century.

The great significance of images of the saints for the Orthodox faithful is primarily expressed in the cultic veneration of the images within the worship service. Second, it is expressed in the dogmatic fixation of the figures, gestures, and colours in Eastern Church iconic art. In the West, the creative achievement of the individual artist is admired, but Orthodox painting dispenses with the predominance of the individual painter's freely creative imagination. Throughout the centuries the Eastern Church has been content with reproducing certain types of holy images, and only seldom does an individual artist play a predominant role within the history of Orthodox Church painting. Most Orthodox ecclesiastical artists have remained anonymous. Icon painting is viewed as a holy skill that is practiced in cloisters in which definite schools of painting have developed. In the schools, traditional principles prevail so much that different artist-monks generally perform only certain functions in the production of a single icon. Style motifs—e.g., composition, impartation of colour, hair and beard fashions, and gestures of the figures—are fixed in painting books that contain the canons of the different monastic schools of icon painters.

The significance of the image of the saint in the theology, piety, and liturgy of the Eastern Orthodox Church can be judged historically from the fact that the struggle over holy images within Orthodox Church history brought about a movement whose scope and meaning can be compared only with the Reformation of Luther and Calvin. In the 7th century a tendency hostile to images and fostered by both theological and political figures gained ground within the Byzantine Church and upset Orthodox Christendom to its very depths; the Iconoclastic Controversy was supported by some reform-minded emperors. Although opponents of icons had all the political means of power at their disposal, they were not able to succeed in overthrowing the use of icons. The conclusion of this struggle with the victory of the supporters of the use of icons is celebrated in the entire Orthodox Church on the first Sunday of Lent as the Feast of Orthodoxy.

Orthodox icon painting is not to be separated from its ecclesiastical and liturgical function. The painting of the image is, in fact, a liturgical act in which the artist-monks prepare themselves by fasting, doing penance, and consecrating the materials necessary for the painting. Before the finished icon is used, it likewise is consecrated. Not viewed as a human work, an icon (according to 8th- and 9th-century literature) was understood instead as a manifestation of a heavenly archetype. A golden background is used on icons to indicate a heavenly perspective. The icon is always painted two-dimensionally because it is viewed as a window through which worshipers can view the heavenly archetype from their earthly position. A figure in the three-dimensionality of the plastic arts, such as sculpture, would thus be an abandonment of the character of epiphany (appearance).

Ideas of the iconic liturgy dominate the manuals of the Orthodox icon painters. The model of the Christ figure for icon painters was found in an apocryphal writing of the early church—the *Letter of Lentulus*, supposedly written by a certain Lentulus, who was named consul in the 12th year of the emperor Tiberius. As the superior of Pontius Pilate, the procurator of Judaea, he by chance was staying in Palestine at the time of the trial of Jesus. In an official report to the emperor about the trial of Jesus, Lentulus included an official warrant for Jesus with a description of the Christ. This apocryphal description furnished the basic model for the Byzantine Christ type.

The Trinity also may not be represented, except in those forms in which, according to the view of Orthodox church doctrine, the Trinity showed itself in the divine Word of the Old and New Testaments. Early church theology interpreted an Old Testament passage (Genesis 18:1 ff.) as an appearance of the divine Trinity—namely, the visit of the three men with the patriarch Abraham at Mamre in Palestine. Also included in icons of the Trinity are the appearance of the three divine persons—symbolized as a hand, a man, and a dove—at the baptism of Jesus (Matthew 3:16 ff.) and the Pentecostal scene, in which the Lord, ascended to heaven, sits at the right hand of God and the Comforter (the Holy Spirit) is sent down to the Apostles in the form of fiery tongues (Acts 2). Another Trinitarian iconic scene is the Transfiguration of Jesus at Mount Tabor (Matthew 17:2).

Icons of Mary were probably first created because of the development of Marian doctrines in the 3rd and 4th centuries. The lack of New Testament descriptions of Mary was compensated by numerous legends of Mary that concerned themselves especially with wondrous appearances of miraculous icons of the mother of God. In Russian and many other Orthodox churches, including the monasteries at Mount Athos, such miraculous mother of God icons, "not made by hands," have been placed where the appearances of the mother of God took place.

The consecration liturgy of the icons of saints expresses the fact that the saints themselves, for their part, are viewed as likenesses of Christ. In them, the image of God has been renewed again through the working of salvation of the incarnate Son of God.

THEOLOGY OF ICONS

The foes of images explicitly deny that the New Testament contains any new attitude toward images. Their basic theological outlook is that the divine is beyond all earthly form in its transcendence and spirituality; representation in earthly substances and forms of the divine already indicate its profanation. The relationship to God, who is Spirit, can only be a purely spiritual one; the worship of the individual as well as the community can happen only "in spirit and in truth" (John 4:24). Similarly, the divine archetype can also be realized only spiritually and morally in life. The religious path of the action of God upon humans is not the path of external influence upon the senses but rather that of spiritual action upon the mind and the will. Such an effect does not come about through the art of painting. Opponents of icons thus claim that the only way to reach an understanding of the truth is by studying the writings of the Old and New Testaments, which are filled with the Spirit of God.

The decisive contrast between the iconodules (image lovers) and the iconoclasts (image destroyers) is found in their understanding of Christology. The iconodules based their theology upon the view of Athanasius—who reflected Alexandrian Christology—that Christ, the God become human, is the visible, earthly, and corporeal icon of the heavenly Father, created by God himself. The iconoclasts, on the other hand, explain, in terms of ancient Antiochene Christology, that the image conflicts with the ecclesiastical dogma of the Person of the Redeemer. It is unseemly, according to their views, to desire to portray a personality such as Christ, who is himself divine, because that would mean pulling the divine down into the materialistic realm.

The history of iconoclasm began in the early church with an emphatic (and, from the viewpoint of lovers of Greek and Roman culture, catastrophic) iconoclastic movement that led to the annihilation of nearly all of the sacred art of the pagan religions of the Roman Empire. In Western Christendom, an iconoclastic attitude was again expressed in various medieval lay movements and sects. Iconoclasm underwent a revolutionary outbreak in the 16th-century Reformation in Germany, France, and England. Despite the different historical types of iconoclasm, a surprising uniformity in regard to their affective structure and theological argumentation exists. The Iconoclastic Controversy of the 8th and 9th centuries also became a point of contention in the Western Church. To be sure, the latter had recognized the seventh ecumenical council at Nicaea (787), in which iconoclasm was condemned. Nevertheless, an entirely different situation existed in the West. The Frankish–Germanic Church was a young church in which images were much more infrequent than in the old Byzantine Church, in which holy icons had accumulated over the centuries. In the West there was still no Christian pictorial art as highly developed as in the East. Also, Christianity there did not have to struggle against a highly developed pagan pictorial art. Donar, a Germanic god, reputedly whispered in a holy oak, and Boniface merely had to fell the Donar oak in order to demonstrate the superiority of Christ over the pagan god. Among the Germanic tribes in the West, there was no guild of sculptors or goldsmiths, as in Ephesus (Acts 19:24 ff.), who would have been able to protest in the name of their gods against the Christian iconoclasts.

The Western viewpoint is revealed most clearly in the formulations of the synodal decisions on the question of images, as they were promulgated in the Frankish kingdom in the *Libri Carolini*, a theological treatise composed primarily by Theodulf of Orléans at Charlemagne's request. In this work it is emphasized that images have only a representative

Orthodox pilgrims carry an icon of the Virgin Mary during an annual religious march marking the second day of Easter at the Bachkovo monastery near Plavdiv, Bulgaria, on April 5, 2010. Dimitar Dilkoff/AFP/Getty Images

character. Thus, they are understood not as an appearance of the saint but only as a visualization of the holy persons for the support of recollecting spiritual meanings that have been expounded intellectually through sermons. Hence, this led to an essentially instructional and aesthetic concept of images. The Western Church also viewed images as the Holy Scriptures' substitute for the illiterate—i.e., for the overwhelming majority of church people in this period. Images thus became the Bible for the laity. Pope Adrian I, who encouraged Western recognition of the iconodulic Council of Nicaea, also referred to the perspicuity of the icons. This idea

of perspicuity—i.e., the appeal to one's imagination to picture the biblical persons and events to oneself—enabled him to recognize the Greek high esteem for the image without completely accepting the complicated theological foundation for icon veneration. The ideas articulated in the *Libri Carolini* remained decisive for the Western tradition. According to Thomas Aquinas, one of the greatest medieval theologians of the West, images in the church serve a threefold purpose: (1) for the instruction of the uneducated in place of books; (2) for illustrating and remembering the mystery of the incarnation; and (3) for awakening the passion of devotion, which is kindled more effectively on the basis of viewing than through hearing.

In the Western theology of icons, the omnipotence of the two-dimensionality of church art also was abandoned. Alongside church pictorial painting, ecclesiastical plastic arts developed; even painting in the three-dimensional form was introduced through the means of perspective. Art, furthermore, became embedded in the entire life of personal religiosity. The holy image became the devotional image; the worshiper placed himself before an image and became engrossed in his meditation of the mysteries of the Christian revelation. As devotional images, the images became the focal points for contemplation and mystical representation. Conversely, the mystical vision itself worked its way back again into pictorial art, in that what was beheld in the vision was reproduced in church art. The burden of ecclesiastical tradition, which weighs heavily upon Byzantine art, has been gradually abolished in the Western Church. In the Eastern Church the art form is just as fixed as ecclesiastical dogma; nothing may be changed in the heavenly prototypes. This idea plays little or no role in the West. There, religious art adjusts itself at any given time to the total religious disposition of the church, to the general religious mental posture, and also to religious needs. Religious art in the West also has been shaped by the imaginative fantasy of the individual artist. Thus, from the outset, a much more individual church art developed in the West. Thus, it became possible to dissociate sacred history from its dogmatic milieu and to transpose it from the past into the actual present, thereby allowing for an adaptable development of ecclesiastical art.

CHAPTER 7

CHRISTIAN PHILOSOPHY

It has been debated whether there is anything that is properly called Christian philosophy. Christianity is not a system of ideas but a religion, a way of salvation. But as a religion becomes a distinguishable strand of human history, it absorbs philosophical assumptions from its environment and generates new philosophical constructions and arguments both in the formation of doctrines and in their defense against philosophical objections. Moreover, philosophical criticism from both within and without the Christian community has influenced the development of its beliefs.

INFLUENCE OF GREEK PHILOSOPHY

As the Christian movement expanded beyond its original Jewish nucleus into the Greco-Roman world, it had to understand, explain, and defend itself in terms that were intelligible in an intellectual milieu largely structured by Greek philosophical thought. By the 2nd century AD several competing streams of Greek and Roman philosophy—Middle Platonism, Neoplatonism, Epicureanism, Stoicism—had merged into a common worldview that was basically Neoplatonic, though enriched by the ethical outlook of the Stoics. This constituted the broad intellectual background for most educated people throughout the Roman Empire, functioning in a way comparable to the pervasive contemporary Western secular view of the universe as an autonomous system within which everything can in principle be understood scientifically.

NEOPLATONISM: ITS NATURE AND HISTORY

Neoplatonism is the modern name given to the form of Platonism developed by Plotinus in the 3rd century AD and modified by his successors. It represents the final form of pagan Greek philosophy. It incorporated important Aristotelian and Stoic elements as well.

Neoplatonism began as a complex (and in some ways ambiguous) philosophy and grew vigorously in a variety of forms over a long period; it is therefore not easy to generalize about it. But the leading ideas in the thought of philosophers who can properly be described as Neoplatonists seem always to have included the following:

1. There is a plurality of levels of being, arranged in hierarchical descending order, the last and lowest comprising the physical universe, which exists in time and space and is perceptible to the senses.
2. Each level of being is derived from its superior, a derivation that is not a process in time or space.
3. Each derived being is established in its own reality by turning back toward its superior in a movement of contemplative desire, which is implicit in the original creative impulse of outgoing that it receives from its superior; thus the Neoplatonic universe is characterized by a double movement of outgoing and return.
4. Each level of being is an image or expression on a lower level of the one above it. The relation of archetype and image runs through all Neoplatonic schemes.
5. Degrees of being are also degrees of unity; as one goes down the scale of being there is greater multiplicity, more separateness, and increasing limitation—until the atomic individualization of the spatiotemporal world is reached.
6. The highest level of being, and through it all of what in any sense exists, derives from the ultimate principle, which is absolutely free from determinations and limitations and utterly transcends any conceivable reality, so that it may be said to be "beyond being." Because it has no limitations, it may be called "the One" to designate its complete simplicity. It may also be called "the Good" as the source of all perfections and the ultimate goal of return, for the impulse of outgoing and return that constitutes the hierarchy of derived reality comes from and leads back to the Good.

7. Since this supreme principle is absolutely simple and undetermined (or devoid of specific traits), man's knowledge of it must be radically different from any other kind of knowledge. It is not an object (a separate, determined, limited thing); hence it can be known only if it raises the mind to an immediate union with itself, which cannot be imagined or described.

PLOTINUS AND HIS PHILOSOPHY

As far as is known, the originator of this distinctive kind of Platonism was Plotinus (AD 205–270). He had been the pupil at Alexandria of a self-taught philosopher called Ammonius, who also taught the Christian Origen.

Plotinus, like most ancient philosophers from Socrates on, was a religious and moral teacher as well as a professional philosopher. He was an acute critic and arguer, with an exceptional degree of intellectual honesty. Philosophy for him was not only a matter of abstract speculation but also a way of life in which, through an exacting intellectual and moral self-discipline and purification, those who are capable of the ascent can return to the source from which they came. His written works explain how from the eternal creative act—at once spontaneous and necessary—of that transcendent source, the One, or Good, proceeds the world of living reality, constituted by repeated double movements of outgoing and return in contemplation; and this account, showing the way for the human self—which can experience and be active on every level of being—to return to the One, is at the same time an exhortation to follow that way.

Plotinus always insisted that the One, or Good, is beyond the reach of thought or language; what he said about this supreme principle was intended only to point the mind along the way to it, not to describe or define it.

The original creative or expressive act of the One is the first great derived reality, *nous* (which can be only rather inadequately translated as "Intellect" or "Spirit"); from this again comes Soul, which forms, orders, and maintains in being the material universe. It must be remembered that, to Plotinus, the whole process of generation is timeless; Nous and Soul are eternal, while time is the life of Soul as active in the physical world, and there never was a time when the material universe did not exist. The "levels of being," then, though distinct, are not separate but are all intimately present everywhere and in everyone. To ascend from Soul through Intellect to the One is not to travel in space but to awake to a new kind of awareness.

Intellect for Plotinus is at one and the same time thinker, thought, and object of thought; it is a mind that is perfectly one with its object. As object, it is the world of Forms, or Ideas, the totality of real being in the Platonic sense. These Forms, being one with Intellect and therefore with each other, are not merely objects but are living, thinking subjects, each not only itself but, in its contemplation, the whole. They are the archetypes and causes of the necessarily imperfect realities on lower levels, souls and the patterns or structures that make bodies what they are. Men at their highest are intellects, or souls perfectly conformed to Intellect.

Soul for Plotinus is very much what it was for Plato, the intermediary between the worlds of Intellect and Sense and the representative of the former in the latter. It is produced by Intellect, as Intellect is by the One, by a double movement of outgoing and return in contemplation, but the relationship between the two is more intimate and the frontier less clearly defined. For Plotinus, as for Plato, the characteristic of the life of the Soul is movement, which is the cause of all other movements. The life of the Soul in this movement is time, and on it all physical movement depends. Soul both forms and rules the material universe from above; and in its lower, immanent phase, which Plotinus often calls nature, it acts as an indwelling principle of life and growth and produces the lowest forms, those of bodies. Below these lies the darkness of matter, the final absence of being, the absolute limit at which the expansion of the universe—from the One through diminishing degrees of reality and increasing degrees of multiplicity—comes to an end.

INFLUENCE OF NEOPLATONISM ON CHRISTIANITY

Neoplatonic themes that provided intellectual material for Christian and non-Christian thinkers alike in the early centuries of the Common Era included a hierarchical conception of the universe, with the spiritual on a higher level than the physical; the eternal reality of such values as goodness, truth, and beauty and of the various universals that give specific form to matter; and the tendency of everything to return to its origin in the divine reality. The Christian Apologists, Christian writers of the 2nd century who provided a defense of the faith against prevailing Greco-Roman culture, were at home in this thought-world, and many of them used its ideas and assumptions both in propagating the Gospel and in defending it as a coherent and intellectually tenable system of belief. They accepted the prevailing Neoplatonic worldview and presented Christianity as its fulfillment, correcting and completing rather than replacing it. Philosophy, they thought, was to the Greeks what the Law was to the Jews—a preparation for the Gospel; and several Apologists agreed with the Jewish writer Philo that Greek philosophy must have received much of its wisdom from Moses. Tertullian (c. 155/160–after 220)—who once asked, "What has Athens to do with Jerusalem?"—and Tatian (c. 120–173), on the other hand, rejected pagan learning and philosophy as inimical to the Gospel; and the question has been intermittently discussed by theologians ever since whether the Gospel completes and fulfills the findings of human reason or whether reason is itself so distorted by sin as to be incapable of leading toward the truth.

Greek philosophy, then, provided the organizing principles by which the central Christian doctrines were formulated. It is possible to distinguish between, on the one hand, first-order religious expressions, directly reflecting primary religious experience, and, on the other, the interpretations of these in philosophically formulated doctrines whose articulation both contributes to and is reciprocally conditioned by a comprehensive belief-system. Thus the primitive Christian confession of faith, "Jesus is Lord," expressed the Disciples' perception of Jesus as the one through whom God was transformingly present to them and to whom their lives were accordingly oriented in complete trust and commitment. The interpretive process whereby the original experience developed a comprehensive doctrinal superstructure began with the application to Jesus of the two distinctively Jewish concepts of the expected messiah and the Son of man who was to come on the last day and also of the son of God metaphor, which was commonly applied in the ancient world to individuals, whether kings or holy men, who were believed to be close to God. It continued on a more philosophical level with the use, in The Gospel According to John, of the idea of the Logos, drawn both from the Hebraic notions of the Wisdom and the Word of God and from the Greek notion of the Logos as the universal principle of rationality and self-expression. As Jesus, son of God, became Christ, God the Son, the second Person of the Trinity, he was identified with the Logos.

EMERGENCE OF OFFICIAL DOCTRINE

During the first several generations of Christian history there was great variety and experimentation in Christian thinking. But as the faith was legally recognized under Constantine in 313 and then became the sole official religion of the Roman Empire under Theodosius, its doctrines had to be formalized throughout the church. This pressure for uniformity provoked intense debates. The orthodox versions of the doctrine of Christ and the Trinity were finally established at the great ecumenical councils (principally Nicaea in 325; Constantinople in 381; and Chalcedon in 451). The key ideas of these Christological and Trinitarian debates and their conclusions were based upon the Greek concepts of ousia (nature or essence) and hypostasis (entity, used as virtually equivalent to prosōpon, person). (In Latin these terms became substantia and persona.) Christ was said to have two natures, one of

J. B. Corneille pinxit

J. Mariette excud.

Stus Augustinus Hipponensis Episcopus Ecclesiæ Doctor
St. Augustine, bishop of the Church of Hippo in Africa.
Paris chez J. Mariette rue St Jacques aux Colomnes d'Hercules

which was of the same nature (*homoousios*) as the Father, whereas the other was of the same nature as humanity; and the Trinity was said to consist of one ousia in three hypostases. The Platonic origin of this conceptuality is clear in the explanation of the Cappadocian Fathers that the Father, Son, and Holy Spirit share the same divine ousia in the way Peter, James, and John shared the same humanity.

The influence of Neoplatonism on Christian thought also appears in the response of the greatest of the early Christian thinkers, St. Augustine (354–430), to the perennially challenging question of how it is that evil exists in a world created by an all-good and all-powerful God. Augustine's answer (which, as refined by later thinkers, remained the standard Christian answer until modern times) includes both theological aspects (the ideas of the fall of angels and then of humans, of the redemption of some by the cross of Christ, and of the ultimate disposal of souls in eternities of bliss and torment) and philosophical aspects. The basic philosophical theme, drawn directly from Neoplatonism, is the idea that the best possible universe does not consist only of the highest kind of creature, the archangels, but contains a maximum richness of variety of modes of being, thus realizing every possible kind of existence from the highest to the lowest.

The result is a hierarchy of degrees both of being and of goodness, for the identity of being and goodness was another fundamental idea Augustine inherited from Neoplatonism and in particular from Plotinus (205–270). God, as absolute being and goodness, stands at the summit, with the great chain of being descending through the many forms of spiritual, animal, and plant life down to lifeless matter. Each embodies being and is therefore good on its own level; and together they constitute a universe whose rich variety is beautiful in the sight of God. Evil occurs only when creatures at any level forfeit the distinctive goodness with which the Creator had endowed them. Evil is thus negative or privative, a lack of proper good rather than anything having substance in its own right. This, too, was a theme that had been taken over from Neoplatonism by a number of earlier Christian writers. And if evil is not an entity, or substance, it follows that it was not a part of God's original creation. It consists instead in the going wrong of something that is in itself good, though also mutable. Augustine locates the origin of this going-wrong in the sinful misuse of freedom by some of the angels and then by the first humans. His theodicy is thus a blend of Neoplatonic and biblical themes and shows clearly the immense influence of Neoplatonism upon Christian thought during its early formative period.

Saint Augustine. Hulton Archive/Getty Images

Augustine and Christian thinkers in general departed from Neoplatonism at one crucial point. Neoplatonism maintained that the world was continuous in being with the ultimate divine reality, the One. The One, in its limitless plenitude of being, overflows into the surrounding void, and the descending and attenuating degrees of being constitute the many-leveled universe. In contrast to this emanationist conception Augustine held that the universe is a created realm, brought into existence by God out of nothing (*ex nihilo*). It has no independent power of being, or aseity, but is contingent, absolutely dependent upon the creative divine power. Further, Augustine emphasized that God did not create the universe out of preexistent matter or chaos, but that "out of nothing" simply means "not out of anything" (*De natura boni*). This understanding of creation, entailing the universe's total emptiness of independent self-existence and yet its ultimate goodness as the free expression of God's creative love, is perhaps the most distinctively Christian contribution to metaphysical thought. It goes beyond the earlier Hebraic understanding in making explicit the *ex nihilo* character of creation in contrast to the emanationism of the Neoplatonic thought-world. This basic Christian idea entails the value of creaturely life and of the material world itself, its dependence upon God, and the meaningfulness of the whole temporal process as fulfilling an ultimate divine purpose.

Modern Christian treatments of the idea of creation *ex nihilo* have detached it from a literal use of the Genesis creation myth. The idea of the total dependence of the universe upon God does not preclude the development of the universe in its present phase from the "big bang" onward, including the evolution of the forms of life on Earth. Although creation *ex nihilo* (a term apparently first introduced into Christian discourse by Irenaeus in the 2nd century) remains the general Christian conception of the relation between God and the physical universe, some Christian thinkers of the 20th century and early 21st century promoted a view derived from process philosophy. Drawing from the work of Alfred North Whitehead and, later, Charles Hartshorne, such thinkers posited that God, instead of being its transcendent Creator, is an aspect of the universe itself, being either the inherent creativity in virtue of which it is a living process or a deity of finite power who seeks to lure the world into ever more valuable forms.

ARISTOTLE AND AQUINAS

Although Neoplatonism was the major philosophical influence on Christian thought in its early period and has never ceased to be an important element within it, Aristotelianism also shaped Christian teachings. At first known for his works on logic, Aristotle gained fuller appreciation in the 12th and 13th centuries when his works on physics, metaphysics, and ethics became available in Latin, translated either from the Greek or from Arabic sources. Aristotle's thought had a profound impact on generations of medieval scholars and was crucial for the greatest of the medieval Christian thinkers, St. Thomas Aquinas (c. 1225–74).

One of Aristotle's ideas that particularly influenced Thomas was that knowledge is not innate but is gained from the reports of the senses and from logical inference from self-evident truths. (Thomas, however, in distinction from Aristotle, added divinely revealed propositions to self-evident truths in forming his basis for inference.) Thomas also adopted Aristotle's conception of metaphysics as the science of being. His doctrine of analogy, according to which statements about God are true analogically rather than univocally, was likewise inspired by Aristotle, as were his distinctions between act and potency, essence and existence, substance and accidents, and the active and passive intellect and his view of the soul as the "form" of the body.

Thomas Aquinas's system, however, was by no means simply Aristotle Christianized. He did not hesitate to differ from "the Philosopher," as he called him, when the Christian tradition required this; for whereas Aristotle had been concerned to understand how the world functions, Thomas was also concerned, more fundamentally, to explain why it exists.

With the gradual breakdown of the medieval worldview, the nature of

the philosophical enterprise began to change. The French thinker René Descartes (1596–1650) is generally regarded as the father of modern philosophy, and in the new movements of thought that began with him philosophy became less a matter of building and defending comprehensive metaphysical systems, or imagined pictures of the universe, and more a critical probing of presuppositions, categories of thought, and modes of reasoning, as well as an inquiry into what it is to know, how knowledge and belief are arrived at in different areas of life, how well various kinds of beliefs are grounded, and how thought is related to language.

There has long ceased to be a generally accepted philosophical framework, comparable with Neoplatonism, in terms of which Christianity can appropriately be expressed and defended. There is instead a plurality of philosophical perspectives and methods—analytic, phenomenological, idealist, pragmatist, and existentialist. Thus modern Christianity, having inherited a body of doctrines developed in the framework of ancient worldviews that are now virtually defunct, lacks any philosophy of comparable status in terms of which to rethink its beliefs.

In this situation some theologians turned to existentialism, which is not so much a philosophical system as a hard-to-define point of view and style of thinking. Indeed, the earlier existentialists, such as the Danish philosopher Søren Kierkegaard (1813–55), vehemently rejected the idea of a metaphysical system—in particular, for 19th-century existentialists, the Hegelian system—though some later ones, such as the German philosopher Martin Heidegger (1889–1976), developed their own systems. Existentialists are identified by the appearance in their writings of one or more of a number of loosely related themes. These include the significance of the concrete individual in contrast to abstractions and general principles; a stress upon human freedom and choice and the centrality of decision, and hence a view of religion as ultimate commitment; a preference for paradox rather than rational explanation; and the highlighting of certain special modes of experience that cut across ordinary consciousness, particularly a generalized anxiety or dread and the haunting awareness of mortality. Some existentialists have been atheists (e.g., Jean-Paul Sartre); others have been Christians (e.g., the Protestant Rudolf Bultmann, and the Roman Catholic Gabriel Marcel). Existentialist themes have also been incorporated into systematic Christian theologies by such theologians as John Macquarrie.

OTHER INFLUENCES

Others have sought to construct theologies in the mold of 19th-century German idealism (e.g., Paul Tillich); some, as process theologians, in that of the early 20th-century British mathematician and metaphysician Alfred North Whitehead (e.g., Charles Hartshorne on the doctrine of God, John Cobb on Christology); some, the liberation theologians, in highly pragmatic and political terms (e.g., Juan Luis Segundo, Gustavo Gutiérrez); and some, as feminist theologians, in terms of the self-consciousness of women and the awareness of a distorting patriarchal influence on all past forms of Christian thought (e.g., Rosemary Ruether, Elizabeth Fiorenza). Most theologians, however, have continued to accept the traditional structure of Christian beliefs. The more liberal among them have sought to detach these from the older traditions and reformulate them so as to connect with modern consciousness (e.g., Friedrich Schleiermacher, Albrecht Ritschl, Adolf von Harnack, Karl Rahner, Gordon Kaufman); while the more conservative have sought to defend the traditional formulations within an increasingly alien intellectual environment (e.g., B.B. Warfield, Charles Hodge, Karl Barth, Cornelis Berkouwer).

Of the factors forming the intellectual environment of Christian thought in the modern period, perhaps the most powerful have been the physical and human sciences. The former have compelled the rethinking of certain Christian doctrines, as astronomy undermined the assumption of the centrality of the Earth in the universe, as geologic evidence concerning its age rendered implausible the biblical chronology, and as biology located humanity within the larger evolution of the forms of life on Earth. The human sciences of anthropology, psychology, sociology, and history have suggested possible naturalistic explanations of religion itself based, for example, upon the projection of desire for a cosmic father figure, the need for socially cohesive symbols, or the power of royal and priestly classes. Such naturalistic interpretations of religion, together with the ever-widening scientific understanding of the physical universe, have prompted some Christian philosophers to think of the religious ambiguity of the universe as a totality that can, from the human standpoint within it, be interpreted in both naturalistic and religious ways, thus providing scope for the exercise of faith as a free response to the mystery of existence.

FAITH AND REASON

Different conceptions of faith cohere with different views of its relation to reason or rationality. The classic medieval understanding of faith, set forth by Thomas Aquinas, saw it as the belief in revealed truths on the authority of God as their ultimate source and guarantor. Thus, though the ultimate object of faith is God, its immediate object is the body of propositions articulating the basic Christian dogmas. Such faith is to be distinguished from knowledge. Whereas the propositions that are the objects of scientia, or knowledge, compel belief by their self-evidence or their demonstrability from self-evident premises, the propositions accepted by faith do not thus compel assent but require a voluntary act of trusting acceptance. As unforced belief, faith is "an act of the intellect assenting to the truth at the command of the will"; and it is because this is a free and responsible act that faith is one of the virtues. It follows that one cannot have knowledge and faith at the same time in relation to the same proposition; faith can only arise in the absence of knowledge. Faith also differs from mere opinion, which is inherently changeable. Opinions are not matters of absolute commitment but allow in principle for the possibility of doubt and change. Faith, as the wholehearted acceptance of revealed truth, excludes doubt.

In the wider context of his philosophy, Aquinas held that human reason, without supernatural aid, can establish the existence of God and the immortality of the soul; for those who cannot or do not engage in such strenuous intellectual activity, however, these matters are also revealed and can be known by faith. Faith, though, extends beyond the findings of reason in accepting further truths such as the triune nature of God and the divinity of Christ. Aquinas thus supported the general (though not universal) Christian view that revelation supplements, rather than cancels or replaces, the findings of sound philosophy.

From a skeptical point of view, which does not acknowledge divine revelation, this Thomist conception amounts to faith—belief that is without evidence or that is stronger than the evidence warrants, the gap being filled by the believer's own will to believe. As such it attracts the charge that belief upon insufficient evidence is always irrational.

In response to this kind of attack the French philosopher Blaise Pascal (1623–62) proposed a voluntarist defense of faith as a rational wager. Pascal assumed, in disagreement with Thomas Aquinas but in agreement with much modern thinking, that divine existence can neither be proved nor disproved. He reasoned, therefore, that if one decides to believe in God and to act on this basis, one gains eternal life if right but loses little if wrong, whereas if one decides not to believe, one gains little if right but may lose eternal life if wrong, concluding that the rational course is to believe. The argument has been criticized theologically for presupposing an unacceptable image of God as rewarding such calculating worship and also on the philosophical ground that it is too permissive in that it could justify belief in the claims, however fantastic, of any person or group who threatened nonbelievers with damnation or other dangerous consequences.

The American philosopher William James (1842–1910) refined this approach by limiting it, among matters that cannot be proved, to belief-options that one has some real inclination or desire to accept, carry momentous implications, and are such that a failure to choose constitutes a negative choice. Theistic belief is for many people such an option, and James claimed that they have the right to make the positive decision to believe and to proceed in their lives on that basis. Either choice involves unavoidable risks: on the one hand the risk of being importantly deluded and on the other the risk of missing a limitlessly valuable truth. In this situation each individual is entitled to decide which risk to run. This argument has also been criticized as being too permissive and as constituting in effect a license for wishful believing, but its basic principle can perhaps be validly used in the context of basing beliefs upon one's religious experience.

The element of risk in faith as a free cognitive choice was emphasized, to the exclusion of all else, by Kierkegaard in his idea of the leap of faith. He believed that without risk there is no faith, and that the greater the risk the greater the faith. Faith is thus a passionate commitment, not based upon reason but inwardly necessitated, to that which can be grasped in no other way.

The epistemological character of faith as assent to propositions, basic to the Thomist account, is less pronounced in the conceptions of Pascal and James in that these accept not a system of doctrines but only the thought of God as existing, which itself has conceptual and implicitly propositional content. Kierkegaard's self-constituting leap of faith likewise only implicitly involves conceptual and propositional thought, as does the account of faith based upon Ludwig Wittgenstein's concept of seeing-as (*Philosophical Investigations*, 1953). Wittgenstein pointed to the epistemological significance of puzzle pictures, such as the ambiguous "duck-rabbit" that can be seen either as a duck's head facing one way or a rabbit's head facing another way. The enlarged concept of experiencing-as (developed by the British philosopher John Hick) refers to the way in which an object, event, or situation is experienced as having a particular character or meaning such that to experience it in this manner involves being in a dispositional state to behave in relation to the object or event, or within the situation, in ways that are appropriate to its having that particular character. All conscious experience is in this sense experiencing-as. The application of this idea to religion suggests that the total environment is religiously ambiguous, capable of being experienced in both religious and naturalistic ways. Religious faith is the element of uncompelled interpretation within the distinctively religious ways of experiencing—for theism, experiencing the world or events in history or in one's own life as mediating the presence and activity of God. In ancient Hebrew history, for example, events that are described by secular historians as the effects of political and economic forces were experienced by the prophets as occasions in which God was saving or punishing, rewarding or testing, the Israelites. In such cases, religious experiencing-as does not replace secular experiencing-as but supervenes upon it, revealing a further order of meaning in the events of the world. And the often unconscious cognitive choice whereby someone experiences religiously constitutes, on this view, faith in its most epistemologically basic sense.

For these voluntarist, existentialist, and experiential conceptions of faith the place of reason in religion, although important, is secondary. Reason cannot directly establish the truth of religious propositions, but it can defend the propriety of trusting one's deeper intuitions or one's religious experience and basing one's beliefs and life upon them. These schools of thought assume that the philosophical arguments for and against the existence of God are inconclusive, and that the universe is capable of being consistently thought of and experienced in both religious and naturalistic ways. This assumption, however, runs counter to the long tradition of natural theology.

CHRISTIAN PHILOSOPHY AS NATURAL THEOLOGY

Natural theology is generally characterized as the attempt to establish religious truths by rational argument and without reliance upon alleged revelations. It has focused traditionally on the topics of the existence of God and the immortality of the soul.

ARGUMENTS FOR THE EXISTENCE OF GOD

The most fundamental task of natural theology is to provide an argument for God's existence.

THE ARGUMENT FROM DESIGN

The most popular, because it is the most accessible, of the theistic arguments is that which infers a divine designer from perceived evidence of design in nature.

The argument, propounded by medieval Christian thinkers, was developed in great detail in 17th- and 18th-century Europe by writers such as Robert Boyle, John Ray, Samuel Clarke, and William Derham and at the beginning of the 19th century by William Paley. They asked: Is not the eye as manifestly designed for seeing, and the ear for hearing, as a pen for writing or a clock for telling the time; and does not such design imply a designer? The belief that the universe is a coherent and efficiently functioning system likewise, in this view, indicates a divine intelligence behind it.

The argument from design was criticized by the Scottish philosopher David Hume in his *Dialogues Concerning Natural Religion* (1779). Hume conceded that the world constitutes a more or less smoothly functioning system; indeed, he points out, it could not exist otherwise. He suggests, however, that this may have come about as a result of the chance permutations of particles falling into a temporary or permanent self-sustaining order, which thus has the appearance of design. A century later the idea of order without design was rendered more plausible by Charles Darwin's discovery that the adaptations of the forms of life are a result of the natural selection of inherited characteristics having positive, and the elimination of those having negative, survival value within a changing environment. Hume also pointed out that, even if one could infer an intelligent designer of the world, one would not thereby be entitled to claim that such a designer is the infinitely good and powerful Creator who is the object of Christian faith. For the world is apparently imperfect, containing many inbuilt occasions of pain and suffering, and one cannot legitimately infer a greater perfection in the cause than is observed in the effect.

In the 20th century, however, the design argument was reformulated in more comprehensive ways, particularly by the British philosophers Frederick R. Tennant (*Philosophical Theology*, 1928–30) and Richard Swinburne (using Thomas Bayes's probability theorem in *The Existence of God*, 1979), taking account not only of the order and functioning of nature but also of the "fit" between human intelligence and the universe, whereby humans can understand its workings, as well as human aesthetic, moral, and religious experience. There were also attempts to show that the evolution of the universe, from the "big bang" of 13.8 billion years ago to the present state that includes conscious life, required the conjunction of so many individually improbable factors as to be inexplicable except as the result of a deliberate coordinating control. If, for example, the initial heat of the expanding universe, or its total mass, or the strength of the force of gravity, or the mass of neutrinos, or the strength of the strong nuclear force, had been different by a small margin, there would have been no galaxies, no stars, no planets, and hence no life. Surely, it was argued, all this must be the work of God creating the conditions for human existence.

These probability arguments were, however, strongly criticized. A basic consideration relevant to them all is that there is by definition only one universe, and it is difficult to see how its existence, either with or without God, can be assessed as having a specific degree of probability in any objective sense. It can of course be said that any form in which the universe might be is statistically enormously improbable, as it is only one of a virtual infinity of possible forms. But its actual form is no more improbable, in this sense, than innumerable others. It is only the fact that humans are part of it that makes it seem so special, requiring a transcendent explanation. Debate about the design argument continued through the late 20th and early 21st centuries, particularly in the United States.

THE COSMOLOGICAL ARGUMENT

Aquinas gave the first-cause argument and the argument from contingency—both forms of cosmological reasoning—a central place for many centuries in the Christian enterprise of natural theology. (Similar arguments also appeared in parallel strands of Islamic philosophy.) Thomas's formulations (*Summa theologiae*, I, Q. 2, art. 3) were refined in modern neo-Thomist discussions and remained topics of Christian philosophical reflection during the 20th century.

The first-cause argument begins with the assumption that there is change in the world. Change is always the effect of some cause or causes. Each cause is itself the effect of a further cause or set of causes; this chain moves in a series that either never ends or is completed by a first cause, which must be of a radically different nature in that it is not itself caused. Such a first cause is an important aspect, though not the entirety, of what Christianity means by God.

Although taking a different route, the argument from contingency follows the same basic movement of thought from the nature of the world to its ultimate ground. It starts with the premise that everything in the world is contingent for its existence upon other factors. Its presence is thus not self-explanatory but can only be understood by reference beyond itself to prior or wider circumstances that have brought it about. These other circumstances are also contingent, pointing beyond themselves for the ground of their intelligibility. If this explanatory regress is unending, explanation is perpetually postponed and nothing is finally explained. The existence of anything and everything thus remains ultimately unintelligible. But rational beings are committed to the search for intelligibility and cannot rest content until it is found. The universe can only finally be intelligible as the creation of an ontologically necessary being who is eternal and whose existence is not contingent upon anything else. This is also part of what Christianity has meant by God.

Criticism of these arguments points to the possibility that there is no first cause because the universe had no beginning, having existed throughout time, and is itself the necessary being that has existed eternally and without dependence upon anything else. Proponents of the cosmological argument reply that the existence of such a universe, as a procession of contingent events without beginning, would still be ultimately unintelligible. On the other hand, a personal consciousness and will, constituting a self-existent Creator of the universe, would be intrinsically intelligible; for human beings have experience in themselves of intelligence and free will as creative. Critics respond that insofar as the argument is sound it leaves one with the choice between believing that the universe is ultimately intelligible, because created by a self-existent personal will, or accepting that it is finally unintelligible, simply the ultimate given brute fact. The cosmological argument does not, however, compel one to choose the first alternative; logically, the second remains equally possible.

THE ONTOLOGICAL ARGUMENT

The ontological argument, which proceeds not from the world to its Creator but from the idea of God to the reality of God, was first clearly formulated by St. Anselm (1033/34–1109) in his *Proslogion* (1077–78). Anselm began with the concept of God as that than which nothing greater can be conceived (*aliquid quo*

The inauguration ceremony for a monument of Immanuel Kant in Kaliningrad, Russia, on June 27, 1992. Kant was born in Kaliningrad (formerly, Königsberg, Prussia) in 1724. AFP/Getty Images

nihil majus cogitari possit). To think of such a being as existing only in thought and not also in reality involves a contradiction. For an X that lacks real existence is not that than which no greater can be conceived. A yet greater being would be X with the further attribute of existence. Thus the unsurpassably perfect being must exist—otherwise it would not be unsurpassably perfect.

This argument has intrigued philosophers ever since. After some discussion in the 13th century it was reformulated by Descartes in his *Meditations* (1641). Descartes made explicit the assumption, implicit in Anselm's reasoning, that existence is an attribute that a given X can have or fail to have. It follows from this—together with the assumption that existence is an attribute that is better to have than to lack—that God, as unsurpassably perfect, cannot lack the attribute of existence.

It was the assumption that existence is a predicate that has, in the view of most subsequent philosophers, proved fatal to the argument. The criticism was first made by Descartes's contemporary Pierre Gassendi and later and more prominently by the German philosopher Immanuel Kant (1724–1804) in his *Critique of Pure Reason* (1781).

Bertrand Russell and others in the 20th century further clarified this objection. According to Russell, to say that something with stated properties—whether it be a triangle, defined as a three-sided plane figure, or God, defined as an unsurpassably perfect being—exists is not to attribute to it a further property, namely existence, but to assert that the concept is instantiated—that there actually are instances of that concept. But whether or not a given concept is instantiated is a question of fact. It cannot be determined a priori but only by whatever is the appropriate method for discovering a fact of that kind. This need for observation cannot be circumvented by writing existence into the definition of the concept ("an existing three-sided plane figure," "an existing unsurpassably perfect being"), for the need arises again as the question of whether this enlarged concept is instantiated.

In the 20th century several Christian philosophers (notably Charles Hartshorne, Norman Malcolm, and Alvin Plantinga) asserted the validity of a second form of Anselm's argument. This hinges upon "necessary existence," a property with even higher value than "existence." A being that necessarily exists cannot coherently be thought not to exist. And so God, as the unsurpassably perfect being, must have necessary existence—and therefore must exist. This argument, however, has been criticized as failing to observe the distinction between logical and ontological, or factual, necessity. Logically necessary existence, it is said, is an incoherent idea, for logical necessity applies to the relations between concepts, not to their instantiation. God's necessity, then, must be an ontologically, or factually, rather than a logically, necessary existence: God exists as the ultimate fact, without beginning or end and without depending upon anything else for existence. But whether this concept of an ontologically necessary being is instantiated cannot be determined a priori. It cannot be validly inferred from the idea of an eternal and independent being that there actually is such a being.

MORAL ARGUMENTS

Moral theistic argument belongs primarily to the modern world and perhaps reflects the modern lack of confidence in metaphysical constructions. Kant, having rejected the cosmological, ontological, and design proofs, argued in the *Critique of Practical Reason* (1788) that the existence of God, though not directly provable, is a necessary postulate of the moral life. To take seriously the awareness of a categorical imperative to act rightly is to commit oneself to work for an ideal state of affairs in which perfect goodness and happiness coincide. But as this universal apportioning of happiness to virtue is beyond human power, a divine agent capable of bringing it about must be assumed.

Other Christian thinkers, particularly during the 19th and early 20th centuries, argued that to accept the absolute demands of ethical obligation is to presuppose a morally structured universe, which implies a personal God whose commands are reflected in the human conscience. It cannot be proved that this is such a universe, but it is inevitably assumed in acknowledging the claims of morality.

Attempts to trace ethical obligation to a transcendent divine source have been criticized on the grounds that it is possible to account for morality without going beyond the human realm. It has been argued that the exigencies of communal life require agreed codes of behaviour, which become internalized in the process of socialization as moral laws; and the natural affection that develops among humans produces the more occasional sense of a call to heroic self-sacrifice on behalf of others.

ARGUMENTS FROM RELIGIOUS EXPERIENCE AND MIRACLES

Religious experience is used in Christian apologetics in two ways—in the argument from religious experiences to God as their cause and in the claim that it is (in the absence of contrary indications) as reasonable to trust religious as it is to trust nonreligious experience in forming beliefs about the total environment.

The argument maintains that special episodes, such as seeing visions of Christ or Mary or hearing the voice of God, as well as the more pervasive experience of "living in God's presence" or of "absolute dependence upon a higher power," constitute evidence of God as their source. Although such experiences may be accepted as having occurred, their cause, as critics have noted, might be purely natural. To establish that the experiences are real, as experiences, is not to establish that they are caused by an infinite, omnipotent, omniscient, divine being. As Thomas Hobbes succinctly put it, when someone says that God has spoken to him in a dream, this "is no more than to say he dreamed that God spake to him."

The analogous argument, from miracles to God as their cause, is more complex and involves two sets of problems. The argument may assert that the children of Israel were miraculously rescued from Egypt or Jesus was miraculously raised from the dead and therefore that God must exist as the agent of these miracles. The first problem concerns the reports. Whereas in the case of private religious experiences the skeptic (to whom the argument is addressed) may well be willing to grant that such experiences occurred, in the case of public miracles the skeptic will require adequate evidence for the described event; and this is not forthcoming for the classic miracle stories referring to alleged extraordinary events of many centuries ago. There are, however, well-evidenced contemporary and recent accounts of "miraculous" healings and other remarkable happenings. On the assumption that some of these, and also some of the classic miracle stories, are historically accurate, the second problem arises. How can it be established that these events were caused by divine intervention rather than by the operation of natural phenomena?

Once again, strict proof seems to be lacking. These arguments, however, display aspects of the explanatory power of the idea of God. Divine activity is not the only possible way of understanding the character of the universe, its contingent existence, the unconditional claims of morality, or the occurrence of religious experiences and "miracles." Nevertheless, the concept of deity offers a possible, satisfying answer to the fundamental questions to which these various factors point. These questions may thus be said to open the door to rational theistic belief—while still leaving the nonbeliever waiting for a positive impetus to go through that door. The work of some contemporary Christian philosophers can be characterized as a search for such a positive impetus.

THE IMMORTALITY OF THE SOUL

Human beings seem always to have had some notion of a shadowy double that survives the death of the body. But the idea of the soul as a mental entity, with intellectual and moral qualities, interacting with a physical organism but capable of continuing after its dissolution, derives in Western thought from Plato and entered into Judaism during approximately the last century before the Common Era and thence into Christianity. In Jewish and Christian thinking it has existed in tension with the idea of the resurrection of the person conceived as an indissoluble psychophysical unity. Christian thought gradually settled into a pattern that required both of these apparently divergent ideas. At death the soul is separated from the body and exists in a conscious or unconscious disembodied state. But on the future Day of Judgment souls will be re-embodied (whether in their former but now transfigured earthly bodies or in new resurrection bodies) and will live eternally in the heavenly kingdom.

Within this framework, philosophical discussion has centred mainly on the idea of the immaterial soul and its capacity to survive the death of the body. Plato, in the *Phaedo*, argued that the soul is inherently indestructible. To destroy something, including the body, is to disintegrate it into its constituent elements; but the soul, as a mental entity, is not composed of parts and is thus an indissoluble unity. Although Aquinas's concept of the soul, as the "form" of the body, was derived from Aristotle rather than Plato, Aquinas too argued for its indestructibility. The French philosopher Jacques Maritain (1882–1973), a modern Thomist, summarized the conclusion as follows: "A spiritual soul cannot be corrupted, since it possesses no matter; it cannot be disintegrated, since it has no substantial parts; it cannot lose its individual unity, since it is self-subsisting, nor its internal energy since it contains within itself all the sources of its energies." But though it is possible to define the soul in such a way that it is incorruptible, indissoluble, and self-subsisting, critics have asked whether there is any good reason to think that souls as thus defined exist. If, on the other hand, the soul means the conscious mind or personality—something whose immortality would be of great interest to human beings—this does not seem to be an indissoluble unity. On the contrary, it seems to have a kind of organic unity that can vary in degree but that is also capable of fragmentation and dissolution.

Much modern philosophical analysis of the concept of mind is inhospitable to the idea of immortality, for it equates mental life with the functioning of the physical brain. Impressed by evidence of the dependence of mind on brain, some Christian thinkers have been willing to accept the view—corresponding to the ancient Hebrew understanding—of the human being as an indissoluble psycho-physical unity, but these thinkers have still maintained a belief in immortality, not as the mind surviving the body, but as a divine resurrection or re-creation of the living body-mind totality. Such resurrection persons would presumably be located in a space different from that which they now inhabit and would presumably undergo a development from the condition of a dying person to that of a viable inhabitant of the resurrection world. But all theories in this area have their own difficulties, and alternative theories emerged.

Kant offered a different kind of argument for immortality—as a postulate of the moral life. The claim of the moral law demands that human beings become perfect. This is something that can never be finally achieved but only asymptotically approached, and such an unending approach requires the unending existence of the soul. This argument also is open to criticism. Are humans indeed subject to a strict obligation to attain moral perfection? Might not their obligation, as finite creatures, be to do the best they can? But this does not seem to entail immortality.

It should be noted that the debate concerning arguments about the immortality of the soul and the existence of God has been as much among Christian philosophers as between them and non-Christian thinkers. It is by no means the case that Christian thinkers have all regarded the project of natural theology as viable. There have indeed been, and are, many who hold that divine existence can be definitively proved or shown to be objectively probable. But many others not only hold that the attempted proofs all require premises that a disbeliever is under no rational obligation to accept but also question the evidentialist assumption that the only route to rational theistic belief is by inference from previously accepted evidence-stating premises.

CHAPTER 8

CHRISTIAN MYSTICISM

Mysticism is the sense of some form of contact with the divine or transcendent, frequently understood in its higher forms as involving union with God. Mysticism played an important role in the history of Christian religion and emerged as a living influence in modern times.

Scholars have studied mysticism from many perspectives, including the psychological, comparativist, philosophical, and theological. Hermeneutical (the study of the methodological principles of interpretation, as of the Bible) and deconstructionist (a critical method which asserts that meanings are always rendered unstable by their dependence on arbitrary signifiers) philosophies in the 20th century brought increasing attention to the mystical text.

Among the theoretical questions that have been much debated are issues such as whether mysticism constitutes the core or essence of personal religion or whether it is better viewed as one element interacting with others in the formation of concrete religions. Those who emphasize a strong distinction between mystical experience and subsequent interpretation generally seek out a common core of all mysticism; others insist that experience and interpretation cannot be so easily sundered and that mysticism is in most cases tied to a specific religion and contingent upon its teachings. Both those who search for the common core, such as the British philosopher Walter T. Stace, and those who emphasize the differences among forms of mysticism, such as the British historian of religion Robert C. Zaehner, have employed typologies of mysticism, often based on the contrast between introvertive and extrovertive mysticism developed by the comparativist Rudolf Otto.

The cognitive status of mystical knowing and its clash with the mystics' claims about the ineffability of their experiences have also been topics of interest for modern students of mysticism. Among the most important investigations of mystical knowing are those of the Belgian Jesuit Joseph Maréchal and the French philosophers Henri Bergson and Jacques Maritain.

The relation between mysticism and morality has been a topic of scholarly debate since the time of William James, but certain questions have concerned Christian mystics for centuries. Does mystical experience always confirm traditional religious ideas about right and wrong, or is mysticism independent of moral issues? Although the problems regarding mysticism are fairly easy to identify, their solutions seem far off.

The role of mysticism in Christianity has been variously evaluated by modern theologians. Many Protestant thinkers, from Albrecht Ritschl and Adolf von Harnack through Karl Barth and Rudolf Bultmann, have denied mysticism an integral role in Christianity, claiming that mystical union was an import from Greek thought that is incompatible with saving faith in the Gospel word. Other Protestant theologians, such as Ernst Troeltsch in *The Social Teaching of the Christian Churches* (trans. 1931) and Albert Schweitzer in *The Mysticism of Paul the Apostle* (trans. 1931), were more sympathetic. Anglican thinkers, especially William R. Inge, Evelyn Underhill, and Kenneth E. Kirk, championed the importance of mysticism in Christian history. Orthodox Christianity has given mysticism so central a role in Christian life that all theology in the Christian East by definition is mystical theology, as the Russian emigré thinker Vladimir Lossky showed in *The Mystical Theology of the Eastern Church* (trans. 1957).

The most extensive theological discussions of mysticism in Christianity have been found in modern Roman Catholicism. In the first half of the 20th century Neoscholastic authors—invoking the authority of Thomas Aquinas and the Spanish mystics Teresa of Ávila and John of the Cross—debated whether mystical contemplation was the goal of all Christians or a special grace offered only to a few.

The discrimination of the various forms of prayer and the distinction between acquired contemplation, for which the believer could strive with the help of grace, and infused contemplation, which was a pure and unmerited gift, framed much of this discussion. Other Roman Catholic theologians, such as Cuthbert Butler in *Western Mysticism* (1922) and Anselm Stolz in *Theologie der Mystik* (1936), broke with Neoscholasticism to consider the wider scriptural and patristic tradition. In the second half of the century Roman

Saint Teresa of Avila. Archive Photos/Getty Images

Catholic theologians including Karl Rahner and Hans Urs von Balthasar addressed key theological issues in mysticism, such as the relation of mystical experience to the universal offer of grace and the status of non-Christian mysticism, and Pope John Paul II, whose devotion to the Virgin Mary was mystical, expressed profound admiration for the works of John of the Cross.

HISTORY OF CHRISTIAN MYSTICISM

Although the essence of mysticism is the sense of contact with the transcendent, mysticism in the history of Christianity should not be understood merely in terms of special ecstatic experiences but as part of a religious process lived out within the Christian community.

EARLY CHURCH

From this perspective mysticism played a vital part in the early church. Early Christianity was a religion of the spirit that expressed itself in the heightening and enlargement of human consciousness. It is clear from the Synoptic Gospels (e.g., Matthew 11:25–27) that Jesus was thought to have enjoyed a sense of special contact with God. In the primitive church an active part was played by prophets, who were believed to be recipients of a revelation coming directly from the Holy Spirit.

The mystical aspect of early Christianity finds its fullest expression, however, in the letters of Paul and The Gospel According to John. For Paul and John, mystical experience and aspiration are always for union with Christ. It was Paul's supreme desire to know Christ and to be united with him. The recurring phrase, "in Christ," implies personal union, a participation in Christ's death and Resurrection. The Christ with whom Paul is united is not the man Jesus who is known "after the flesh." He has been exalted and glorified so that he is one with the Spirit.

Christ-mysticism appears again in The Gospel According to John, particularly in the farewell discourse (chapters 14–16), where Jesus speaks of his impending death and of his return in the Spirit to unite himself with his followers. In the prayer of Jesus in chapter 17 there is a vision of an interpenetrating union of souls in which all who are one with Christ share his perfect union with the Father.

In the early Christian centuries the mystical trend found expression not only in the traditions of Pauline and Johannine Christianity (as in the writings of Ignatius of Antioch and Irenaeus of Lyon) but also in the gnostics—particularly in the way that the latter viewed matter as evil and the spirit as good. Scholars still debate the origins of gnosticism, but most gnostics thought of themselves as followers of Christ, albeit a Christ who was pure spirit. The religion of Valentinus, who was excommunicated in about AD 150, is a notable example of the mysticism of the gnostics. He believed that human beings are alienated from God because of their spiritual ignorance; Christ brings them into the gnosis (esoteric revelatory knowledge) that is union with God. Valentinus held that all human beings come from God and that all will in the end return to God. Other gnostic groups held that there were three types of people—"spiritual," "psychic," and "material"—and that only the first two can be saved. The *Pistis Sophia* (3rd century) is preoccupied with the question of who finally will be saved. Those who are saved must renounce the world completely and follow the pure ethic of love and compassion so that they can be identified with Jesus and become rays of the divine Light.

Eastern Christianity

The classic forms of Eastern Christian mysticism appeared toward the end of the 2nd century, when the mysticism of the early church began to be expressed in categories of thought explicitly dependent on the Greek philosophical tradition of Plato and his followers. This intermingling of primitive Christian themes with Greek speculative thought has been variously judged by later Christians, but contemporaries had no difficulty in seeing it as proof of the new religion's ability to adapt and transform all that was good in the world. The philosophical emphasis on the unknowability of God found an echo in many biblical texts, affirming that the God of Abraham and the Father of Jesus could never be fully known. The

understanding of the role of the preexistent Logos of The Gospel According to John in the creation and restoration of the universe was clarified by locating the Platonic conception of Ideas in the Logos. Greek emphasis on the vision or contemplation (*theōria*) of God as the goal of human blessedness found a scriptural warrant in the sixth Beatitude: "Blessed are the pure in heart, for they shall see God" (Matthew 5:8). The notion of deification (*theiosis*) fit with the New Testament emphasis on becoming sons of God and texts such as 2 Peter 1:4, which talked about sharing in the divine nature. These adaptations later provided an entry for the language of union with God, especially after the notion of union became more explicit in Neoplatonism. Many of these themes are already present in germ in the works of Clement of Alexandria, written in about 200. They are richly developed in the thought of Origen, the greatest Christian writer of the pre-Constantinian period and the earliest major speculative mystic in Christian history.

Origen's mystical theology, which made the union of God and man in Christ the pattern for the union of Christ and the believer, required a social matrix in which it could take on life as formative and expressive of Christian ideals. This was the achievement of early Christian monasticism, the movement into the desert that began to transform ideals of Christian perfection at the beginning of the 4th century. The combination of the religious experience of the desert

Christians and the generally Origenist theology that helped shape their views created the first great strand of Christian mysticism, one that remains central to the East and that was to dominate in the West until the end of the 12th century. Though not all Eastern Christian mystical texts were deeply imbued with Platonism, all were marked by the monastic experience.

The first great mystical writer of the desert was Evagrius Ponticus (346–399), whose works were influenced by Origen. His writings show a clear distinction between the ascetic, or "practical," life and the contemplative, or "theoretical," life, a distinction that was to become classic in Christian history. His disciple, John Cassian, conveyed Evagrian mysticism to the monks of western Europe, especially in the exposition of the "degrees of prayer" in his *Collations of the Fathers*, or *Conferences*. Gregory of Nyssa, the younger brother of St. Basil the Great, sketched out a model for progress in the mystical path in his *Life of Moses* and, following the example of Origen, devoted a number of homilies to a mystical interpretation of the Song of Solomon, showing how the book speaks both of Christ's love for the church and of the love between the soul and the Divine Bridegroom.

Perhaps the most influential of all Eastern Christian mystics is Pseudo-Dionysius, who was probably a Syrian monk of the 5th or 6th century and who wrote in the name of Dionysius the Areopagite, Paul's convert at Athens. In the chief works of Pseudo-Dionysius, *Mystical Theology* and *On the Divine Names*, the main emphasis was on the ineffability of God ("the Divine Dark") and hence on the "apophatic" or "negative" approach to God. Through a gradual process of ascension from material things to spiritual realities and an eventual stripping away of all created beings in "unknowing," the soul arrives at "union with Him who transcends all being and all knowledge" (*Mystical Theology*, chapter 1). The writings of the Pseudo-Dionysius also popularized the threefold division of the mystical life into purgative, illuminative, and unitive stages. Later Eastern mystical theologians, especially Maximus the Confessor in the 7th century, adopted much of this thought but imbued it with greater Christological emphasis, showing that union with God is possible only through the action of the God-man, Jesus Christ.

Eastern mystics distinguish between the essence of God and divine attributes, which they regard as energies that penetrate the universe. Creation is a process of emanation, whereby the divine Being is "transported outside of Himself...to dwell within the heart of all things..." (Pseudo-Dionysius the Areopagite, *On the Divine Names*, iv. 13). The divinization of humanity is fundamental to Eastern mysticism.

Divinization comes through contemplative prayer, and especially through the method of hesychasm (from *hesychia*, "stillness"), which was adopted widely by the Eastern monks. The method consisted in the concentration of the mind on the divine Presence, induced by the

PSEUDO-DIONYSIS THE AREOPAGITE

Pseudo-Dionysius (flourished c. 500) was probably a Syrian monk who, known only by his pseudonym, wrote a series of Greek treatises and letters for the purpose of uniting Neoplatonic philosophy with Christian theology and mystical experience. These writings established a definite Neoplatonic trend in a large segment of medieval Christian doctrine and spirituality—especially in the Western Latin Church—that has determined facets of its religious and devotional character to the present time. Historical research has been unable to identify the author, who, having assumed the name of the New Testament convert of St. Paul (Acts 17:34), could have been one of several Christian writers familiar with the Neoplatonic system of the 5th-century Athenian Proclus. In the 9th century Dionysius was confused with St. Denis of France; but this was disproved in the 12th century by Peter Abalard.

The treatises "On the Divine Names," "On Mystical Theology," "On the Celestial Hierarchy," and "On the Ecclesiastical Hierarchy" comprise the bulk of the Dionysian corpus of writings, supplemented with 10 letters affecting a 1st-century primitive Christian atmosphere. Their doctrinal content forms a complete theology, covering the Trinity and angelic world, the incarnation and redemption, and the last things, and provides a symbolic and mystical explanation of all that is. The system is essentially dialectical, or "crisis" (from the Greek word meaning "crossroads, decision"), theology—i.e., the simultaneous affirmation and denial of paradox in any statement or concept relative to God. God's transcendence above all rational comprehension and categorical knowledge ultimately reduces any expression of the divinity to polar pairs of contraries: grace and judgment, freedom and necessity, being and nonbeing, time and eternity. The incarnation of the Word, or Son of God, in Christ, consequently, was the expression in the universe of the inexpressible, whereby the One enters into the world of multiplicity. Still, the human intellect can apply to God positive, analogous terms or names such as The Good, Unity, Trinity, Beauty, Love, Being, Life, Wisdom, or Intelligence, assuming that these are limited forms of communicating the incommunicable.

The "Divine Names" and "Mystical Theology" treat the nature and effects of contemplative prayer—the disciplined abandonment of senses and intelligible forms to prepare for the immediate experience of "light from the divine darkness" and ecstatic union—in a manner and scope that make them indispensable to the history of Christian theology and piety. His treatises on the hierarchies, wherein he theorized that all that exists—the form of Christian society, the stages of prayer, and the angelic world—is structured as triads that are the images of the eternal Trinity, introduced a new meaning for the term hierarchy.

repetition of the "Jesus-prayer" (later formalized as "Lord Jesus Christ, Son of God, have mercy on me a sinner"). This culminated in the ecstatic vision of the divine Light and was held to divinize the soul through the divine energy implicit in the name of Jesus. Although much of this program appears in the writings of Symeon the New Theologian (c. 949–1022), a monk of Constantinople, it reached its most developed form in the works of Gregory Palamas (1296–1359), who defended the hesychast tradition against its opponents. This rich form of Christian mysticism found a new centre in the Slavic lands after the conquest of the Greek East by the Turks. It experienced a flowering in Russia, beginning with the *Philokalia*, an anthology of ascetical and mystical texts first published in 1782, and continuing to the Revolution of 1917. Eastern Christian mysticism is best known in the West through translations of the anonymous 19th-century Russian text *The Way of the Pilgrim*, but noted Russian mystics, such as Seraphim of Sarov (1759–1833) and John of Kronshtadt (1829–1909), also became known in the West during the 20th century. Among mystic sects native to Russia, the Dukhobors, who originated in the 18th century among the peasants, resembled the Quakers in their indifference to outer forms and their insistence on the final authority of the Inner Light. They were severely persecuted and migrated to Canada early in the 20th century.

In the Eastern as in the Western Church mystical religion was at times declared heretical. The earliest of the mystics to be denounced as heretics were the Messalians (Syriac for "praying people") of the 4th century. They were accused of neglecting the sacraments for ceaseless prayer and of teaching a materialistic vision of God. Later mystics, both orthodox and suspect, have been accused of Messalianism.

WESTERN CATHOLIC CHRISTIANITY

The founder of Latin Christian mysticism is Augustine, bishop of Hippo (354–430). In his *Confessions* Augustine mentions two experiences of "touching" or "attaining" God. Later, in the *Literal Commentary on Genesis*, he introduced a triple classification of visions—corporeal, spiritual (i.e., imaginative), and intellectual—that influenced later mystics for centuries. Although he was influenced by Neoplatonist philosophers such as Plotinus, Augustine did not speak of personal union with God in this life. His teaching, like that of the Eastern Fathers, emphasized the ecclesial context of Christian mysticism and the role of Christ as mediator in attaining deification, or the restoration of the image of the Trinity in the depths of the soul. The basic elements of Augustine's teaching on the vision of God, the relation of the active and contemplative lives, and the sacramental dimension of Christian mysticism were summarized by Pope Gregory I the Great in the 6th century and conveyed to the medieval West by many monastic authors.

Two factors were important in the development of this classic Augustinian form of Western mysticism. The first was the translation of the writings of Pseudo-Dionysius the Areopagite and other Eastern mystics by the 9th-century thinker Johannes Scotus Erigena. In combining the Eastern and Western mystical traditions, Erigena created the earliest version of a highly speculative negative mysticism that was later often revived. The other new moment began in the 12th century when new forms of religious life burst on the scene, especially among monks and those priests who endeavoured to live like monks (the canons). The major schools of 12th-century mysticism were inspired by new trends in monastic piety, especially those introduced by Anselm of Canterbury, but they developed these in a systematic fashion unknown to previous centuries. The great figures of the era, especially Bernard of Clairvaux among the Cistercians and Richard of Saint-Victor among the canons, have remained the supreme teachers of mystical theology in Catholic Christianity, along with the Spanish mystics of the 16th century.

Cistercian and Victorine authors made two significant contributions to the development of Catholic mysticism: first, a detailed study of the stages of the ascent of the soul to God on the basis of a profound understanding of the human being as the image and likeness of God (Genesis 1:26) and, second, a new emphasis on the role of love as the power that unites the soul to God. Building on both Origen and Augustine, Bernard and his contemporaries made affective, or marital, union with God in oneness of spirit (1 Corinthians 6:17) a central theme in Western mysticism, though along with Gregory the Great they insisted that "love itself is a form of knowing," that is, of vision or contemplation of God.

The great mystics of the 12th century contributed to an important expansion of mysticism in the following century. For the first time mysticism passed beyond the confines of the monastic life, male writers, and the Latin language. This major shift is evident not only in the life of Francis of Assisi, who emphasized the practical following of Jesus and came to be identified with him in a new form of Christ-mysticism, manifested in his reception of the stigmata, or wounds of the crucified Christ, but also in the remarkable proliferation of new forms of religious life and mystical writing in the vernacular on the part of women. Although female mystics such as Hildegard of Bingen and Elizabeth of Schönau were an important influence on mysticism and spirituality in the 12th century, the 13th century witnessed a flowering of interest in mysticism among women, evident in the Flemish Hadewijch of Brabant, the German Mechthild von Magdeburg, the French Marguerite Porete, and the Italians Clare of Assisi and Àngela da Foligno.

Among the important themes of the new mysticism of the 13th century was a form of Dionysian theology in which the stage of divine darkness surpassing all understanding was given a strong affective emphasis, as well as the emergence of an understanding of union with God that insisted upon a union of indistinction in which God and the soul become one without any medium. The first of these tendencies is evident in the writings of Bonaventure, the supreme master

Sculptures of St. Bernadin and St. Clare of Assisi at Crivelli, Italy, c. 1500. Hulton Archive/Getty Images

of Franciscan mysticism; the second is present in some of the women mystics, but its greatest proponent was the Dominican Meister Eckhart.

Eckhart taught that "God's ground and the soul's ground is one ground," and the way to the realization of the soul's identity with God lay less in the customary practices of the religious life than in a new state of awareness achieved through radical detachment from all created things and a breakthrough to the God beyond God. Though Eckhart's thought remained Christological in its emphasis on the necessity for the "birth of Son in the soul," his expressions of the identity between the soul that had undergone this birth and the Son of God seemed heretical to many. Without denying the importance of the basic structures of the Christian religion, and while insisting that his radical preaching to the laity was capable of an orthodox interpretation, Eckhart and the new mystics of the 13th century were a real challenge to traditional Western ideas of mysticism. Their teaching seemed to imply an autotheism in which the soul became identical with God, and many feared that this might lead to a disregard of the structures and sacraments of the church as the means to salvation and even to an antinomianism that would view the mystic as exempt from the moral law. In 1329, therefore, Pope John XXII condemned 28 of Eckhart's propositions as heretical or open to evil interpretation. Eckhart, however, seems to have retracted these errors before his death in 1327 or 1328.

Even before Eckhart's posthumous condemnation, the church struck out against the mystics. The Council of Vienne condemned their errors in 1311, shortly after Marguerite Porete was burned as a heretic for continuing to disseminate her book, *The Mirror of Simple Souls*. Marguerite's work was a highly popular treatise and handbook that described the seven stages of the ascent to God and maintained that the soul could achieve union with God while still on earth. The council associated these views with the Beguines, groups of religious women who did not live in cloister or follow a recognized rule of life. The council also denounced the Beghards, a group of heretical mystics who were the male counterparts of the Beguines and were often associated with them, for their antinomian and libertine views. In the centuries that followed, some mystics were condemned and others executed, though evidence for a widespread "mystical heresy" is lacking.

The great mystical writers of the late Middle Ages, however, took pains to prove their orthodoxy. Eckhart's followers among the Rhineland mystics, especially Heinrich Suso and Johann Tauler, defended his memory but qualified his daring language. Texts such as the anonymous *Theologia Germanica* of the late 14th century, which reflects the ideas of the loose groups of mystics who called themselves the Friends of God, conveyed this German mysticism to the Reformers. The rich mystical literature that developed in the Low Countries reached its culmination in writings of Jan van Ruysbroeck (1293–1381). In Italy two remarkable women, Catherine of Siena in the 14th century and Catherine of Genoa in the 15th, made important contributions to the theory and practice of mysticism. The 14th century also was the "Golden Age" of English mysticism, as conveyed in the writings of the hermit Richard Rolle; the canon Walter Hilton, who wrote *The Scale* (or *Ladder*) *of Perfection*; the anonymous author of *The Cloud of Unknowing*; and his contemporary, the visionary recluse Julian of Norwich, whose *Revelations of Divine Love* is unsurpassed in English mystical literature. Julian's meditations on the inner meaning of her revelations of the crucified Christ express the mystical solidarity of all humanity in the Redeemer, who is conceived of as a nurturing mother.

In the 16th century the centre of Roman Catholic mysticism shifted to Spain, the great Roman Catholic power at the time of the Reformation. Important mystics came both from the traditional religious orders, such as Francis de Osuna among the Franciscans, Luis de León among the Augustinians, and Luis de Grenada among the Dominicans, and from the new orders, as with Ignatius of Loyola, the founder of the Jesuits. The two pillars of Spanish mysticism, however, were Teresa of Ávila (1515–82) and her friend John of the Cross (1542–91), both members of the reform movement in the Carmelite order. Teresa's *Life* is one of the richest and most convincing accounts of visionary and unitive

experiences in Christian mystical literature; her subsequent synthesis of the seven stages on the mystical path, *The Interior Castle*, has been used for centuries as a basic handbook. John of the Cross was perhaps the most profound and systematic of all Roman Catholic mystical thinkers. His four major works, *The Dark Night of the Soul*, *The Ascent of Mount Carmel*, *The Spiritual Canticle*, and *The Living Flame of Love*, constitute a full theological treatment of the active and passive purgations of the sense and the spirit, the role of illumination, and the unification of the soul with God in spiritual marriage.

In the 17th century France took the lead with figures such as Francis of Sales, Pierre de Bérulle, Brother Lawrence (the author of *The Practice of the Presence of God*), and Marie Guyard. At this time concentration on the personal experience of the mystic as the source for "mystical theology" (as against the common scriptural faith and sacramental life of the church) led to the creation of mysticism as a category and the description of its adherents as mystics. At the same time, the rise of the Quietist controversy brought about renewed conflict over mysticism. A Spaniard resident in Rome, Miguel de Molinos, author of the popular *Spiritual Guide* (1675), was condemned for his doctrine of the "One Act," that is, the teaching that the will, once fixed on God in contemplative prayer, cannot lose its union with the divine. In France Mme Guyon and her adviser, François Fénelon, archbishop of Cambrai, were also condemned for Quietist tendencies emphasizing the role of pure love to the detriment of ecclesiastical practice. These debates cast a pall over the role of mysticism in Roman Catholicism into the 20th century, though important mystics continued to be found, most notably Thomas Merton and Pope John Paul II.

PROTESTANT CHRISTIANITY

The chief representatives of Protestant mysticism are the continental "Spirituals," among whom Sebastian Franck (c. 1499–c. 1542), Valentin Weigel (1533–88), and Jakob Böhme (1575–1624) are especially noteworthy. Among traditional Lutherans Johann Arndt (1555–1621) in his *Four Books on True Christianity* took up many of the themes of medieval mysticism in the context of Reformation theology and prepared the way for the spiritual revival known as Pietism, within which mystics such as Count von Zinzendorf flourished. The important mystics in England included the Cambridge Platonists (a group of Anglican divines), the Quakers, and William Law (1686–1761). In Holland a mystical group known as Collegiants, similar to the Quakers, broke away from the Remonstrant (Calvinist) Church. Other groups of mystics were the Schwenckfeldians, founded by Kaspar Schwenckfeld, and the Family of Love, founded in Holland by Hendrik Niclaes in about 1540. He later made two trips to England, where his group had its largest following and survived into the

17th century. The religion of the Ranters and other radical Puritans in 17th-century England also had mystical aspects.

Protestant mysticism emphasized the divine element in humanity, which was called the "spark" or "ground" of the soul, the "divine image" or "holy self," the "Inner Light," or the "Christ within." This was one of the essential elements of Rhineland mysticism and shows the connection between medieval and Reformation mysticism. For Böhme and the Spirituals, essential reality lies in the ideal world, which Böhme described as "the uncreated Heaven." Böhme adopted the Gnostic belief that the physical world arose from a primeval fall, renewed with the Fall of Adam. His teaching was the main formative influence on the developed outlook of William Law and William Blake (1757–1827).

For Protestant as well as for Roman Catholic mystics, sin is the assertion of the self in its separation from God. The divine life is embodied in "the true holy self that lies within the other" (Böhme, *First Epistle*). When that self is manifested, there is a birth of God (or of Christ) in the soul. Protestant mystics rejected the Lutheran and Calvinist doctrine of the total corruption of human nature. William Law remarked, "The eternal Word of God lies hid in thee, as a spark of the divine nature" (*The Spirit of Prayer*, I.2). "The eternal Word of God" is the inner Christ, incarnate whenever people rise into union with God. The Spirituals also viewed Christ as the ideal humanity born in God from all eternity. This conception received its greatest emphasis from Schwenckfeld, who, unlike Protestant mystics generally, taught that humans as created beings are totally corrupt; salvation means deliverance from the creaturely nature and union with the heavenly Christ.

Protestant mystics explicitly recognize that the divine Light or Spark is a universal principle. Hans Denck in the early 16th century spoke of the witness of the Spirit in "heathens and Jews." Sebastian Franck, like the Cambridge Platonists, found divine revelation in the work of the sages of Greece and Rome.

George Fox cited the conscience of the Native Americans as proof of the universality of the Inner Light.

William Law described non-Christian saints as "apostles of a Christ within." Protestant mystics stated plainly that, for the mystic, supreme authority lies of necessity not in the written word of Scripture but in the Word of God in the self. Fox said, "I saw, in that Light and Spirit that was before the Scriptures were given forth" (*Journal*, chapter 2). It was especially on this ground that the mystics came into conflict with the established church, whether Roman Catholic or Protestant.

George Fox, founder of the Society of Friends, preaching in a tavern, circa 1650. Followers of the movement later became known as Quakers. Hulton Archive/Getty Images

The Ranters provide a good example of the conflict between mysticism and established religion. They held, with Fox and Hendrik Niclaes, that perfection is possible in this life. Puritan leaders under the Commonwealth denounced them for their "blasphemous and execrable opinions," and there was, no doubt, an antinomian tendency among them that rejected the principle of moral law. Some rejected the very notion of sin and believed in the universal restoration of all things in God.

STAGES OF CHRISTIAN MYSTICISM

Christian mystics have described the stages of the return of the soul to God in a variety of ways. According to the Belgian Jesuit Joseph Maréchal, Christian mysticism includes three broadly defined stages: (1) the gradual integration of the ego under the mastery of the idea of a personal God and according to a program of prayer and asceticism, (2) a transcendent revelation of God to the soul experienced as ecstatic contact or union, frequently with a suspension of the faculties, and (3) "a kind of readjustment of the soul's faculties" by which it regains contact with creatures "under the immediate and perceptible influence of God present and acting in the soul" (Maréchal, *Studies in the Psychology of the Mystics*). This final stage, which almost all of the greatest Christian mystics have insisted upon, belies the usual claim that mysticism is a selfish flight from the world and an avoidance of moral responsibility.

THE DYING TO SELF

The mystics agree on the necessity of dying to the false self dominated by forgetfulness of God. To attain the goal, the soul must be purified of all those feelings, desires, and attitudes that separate it from God. This dying to the self implies the "dark night of the soul" in which God gradually and sometimes painfully purifies the soul to ready it for the divine manifestation.

Christian mystics have always taken Christ, especially the crucified Christ, as the model for this process. According to the *Theologia Germanica*, "Christ's human nature was so utterly bereft of self, and apart from all creatures, as no man's ever was, and was nothing but a 'house and habitation of God'" (chapter 15). Following Christ involves a dying to self, a giving up of oneself wholly to God, so that one may be possessed by divine Love. Such detachment and purgation were frequently expressed in extreme terms that imply the renunciation of all human ties. Paradoxically, those who insist upon the most absolute detachment also emphasize that purifying the self is more a matter of internal attitude than of flight from the world and external penance. In the words of William Law: "The one true way of dying to self wants no cells, monasteries or pilgrimages. It is the way of patience, humility and resignation to God" (*The Spirit of Love*, Part 1).

The practice of meditation and contemplative prayer, leading to ecstasy, is typical of Christian and other varieties of theistic mysticism. This usually involves a process of introversion in which all images and memories of outer things must be set aside so that the inner eye may be opened and readied for the appearance of God. Introversion leads to ecstasy in which "the mind is ravished into the abyss of divine Light" (Richard of Saint-Victor, *The Four Grades of Violent Love*). Illumination may express itself in actual radiance. Symeon the New Theologian speaks of himself as a young man who saw "a brilliant divine Radiance" filling the room. Many Christian mystics experienced unusual and extraordinary psychic phenomena—visions, locutions, and other altered states of consciousness. The majority of mystics, however, have insisted that such phenomena are secondary to the true essence of mysticism and can even be dangerous. "We must never rely on them or accept them," as John of the Cross said in *The Ascent of Mount Carmel*, 2.11.

THE UNION WITH GOD

Christian mystics claim that the soul may be lifted into a union with God so close and so complete that it is merged in the being of God and loses the sense of any separate existence. Jan van Ruysbroeck wrote that in the experience of union "we can nevermore find any distinction between ourselves and God" (*The Sparkling Stone*, chapter 10); and Eckhart speaks of the birth of the Son in the soul in which God "makes me his only-begotten Son without any difference" (German *Sermons*, 6). These expressions of a unity of indistinction have seemed dangerous to many, but Eckhart and Ruysbroeck insisted that, properly understood, they were quite orthodox. Bernard of Clairvaux, who insisted that in becoming one spirit with God the human "substance remains though under another form" (*On Loving God*, chapter 10), and John of the Cross, who wrote "the soul seems to be God rather than a soul, and is indeed God by participation" (*The Ascent of Mount Carmel* ii, 5:7), express the more traditional view of loving union.

THE READJUSTMENT

The goal of the mystic is not simply a transient ecstasy; it is a permanent state of being in which the person's nature is transformed or deified. This state is frequently spoken of as a spiritual marriage involving God and the soul. This unitive life has two main aspects. First, while the consciousness of self and the world remains, that consciousness is accompanied by a continuous sense of union with God, as Teresa of Ávila clearly shows in discussing the seventh mansion in *The Interior Castle*. Brother Lawrence wrote that while he was at work in his kitchen he possessed God "in as great tranquillity as if I were upon my knees at the Blessed Sacrament" (*The Practice of the Presence of God*, chapter 4). Second, the spiritual marriage is a theopathic state: the soul is felt to be in all things the organ or instrument of God. In the unitive life Mme Guyon says that the soul "no longer lives or works of herself, but God lives, acts and works in her." In this state the mystic is able to engage in manifold activities without losing the grace of union. In the words of Ignatius of Loyola, the mystic is "contemplative in action."

FORMS OF CHRISTIAN MYSTICISM

The many forms that Christian mysticism has taken during the last two millennia can be divided into three broad types. These types, however, should not be seen as mutually exclusive, since some mystics make use of all of them.

CHRIST-MYSTICISM

The earliest form of Christian mysticism was the Christ-mysticism of Paul and John. Although Christian mysticism in its traditional expression has centred on the desire for union with God, Christ-mysticism has always been present in the church. The Eastern Church emphasized the divine Light that appeared to the disciples at the Transfiguration, and mystics sought to identify with this light of Christ in his divine glory. Symeon says of a certain mystic that "he possessed Christ wholly…. He was in fact entirely Christ." As a result of the influence of Augustine, in the Catholic West it is in and through the one Christ, the union of Head and body that is the church, that humans come to experience God. For Augustine the mystical life is Christ "transforming us into himself" (*Homily on Psalm*, 32.2.2). During the Middle Ages some of the most profound expressions of Christ-mysticism were voiced by women mystics, such as Catherine of Siena and Julian of Norwich. Luis de León spoke of the theopathic life in terms of Christ-mysticism: "The very Spirit of Christ comes and is united with the soul—nay, is infused throughout its being, as though he were soul of its soul indeed."

The Protestant attempt to return to primitive Christianity has led to strong affirmations of Christ-mysticism. The early Quaker George Keith wrote that Christ is born spiritually in humanity when "his life and spirit are united unto the soul." The chief representative of Christ-mysticism among the early Protestants, Kaspar Schwenckfeld, held that Christ was from all eternity the God-man, and as such he possessed a body of spiritual flesh in which he lived on Earth and which he now possesses in heaven. In his exalted life Christ unites himself inwardly with human souls and imparts to them his own divinity.

TRINITARIAN MYSTICISM

Pure God-mysticism is rare in Christianity, though not unknown, as Catherine of Genoa shows. Christ as God incarnate is the Word, the second Person of the Trinity, and Christian mysticism has, from an early era, exhibited a strong Trinitarian dimension, though this has been understood in different ways. What ties the diverse forms of Trinitarian mysticism together is the insistence that through Christ the Christian comes to partake of the inner life of the Trinity. The mysticism of Origen, for example, emphasizes the marriage of the Word and the soul within the union of Christ and the church but holds out the promise that through this action souls will be made capable of receiving the Father (*First Principles*, 3.6.9). The mystical thought of Augustine and his medieval followers, such as Richard of Saint-Victor, William of Saint-Thierry, and Bonaventure, is deeply Trinitarian. Meister Eckhart taught that the soul's indistinction from God meant that it was to be identified with the inner life of the Trinity—that is, with the Father giving birth to the Son, the Son being born, and the Holy Spirit proceeding from both. A similar teaching is found in Ruysbroeck. John of the Cross wrote of mystical union that "it would not be a true and total transformation if the soul were not transformed into the three Persons of the Most Holy Trinity" (*Spiritual Canticle*, stanza 39.3). Such strong Trinitarian emphasis is rarer, but not absent from Protestant mysticism.

St. John of the Cross. Hulton Archive/Getty Images

NEGATIVE MYSTICISM: GOD AND THE GODHEAD

The most daring forms of Christian mysticism have emphasized the absolute unknowability of God. They suggest that true contact with the transcendent involves going beyond all that we speak of as God—even the Trinity—to an inner "God beyond God," a divine Darkness or Desert in which all distinction is lost. This form of "mystical atheism" has seemed suspicious to established religion; its adherents have usually tried to calm the suspicions of the orthodox by an insistence on the necessity, though incompleteness, of the affirmative ways to God. One of the earliest and most important exponents of this teaching was the Pseudo-Dionysius, who distinguished "the super-essential Godhead" from all positive terms ascribed to God, even the Trinity (*The Divine Names*, chapter 13). In the West this tradition emerged later; it is first found in Erigena in the 9th century and is especially evident in the

Rhineland school in the 13th and 14th centuries. According to Eckhart, even being and goodness are "garments" or "veils" under which God is hidden. In inviting his hearers to "break through" to the hidden Godhead, he exclaimed, "Let us pray to God that we may be free of 'God,' and that we may apprehend and rejoice in that everlasting truth in which the highest angel and the fly and the soul are equal" (German *Sermons*, 52). The notion of the hidden Godhead was renewed in the teaching of Jakob Böhme, who spoke of it as the *Ungrund*—"the great Mystery," "the Abyss," "the eternal Stillness." He stressed the fact of divine becoming (in a nontemporal sense): God is eternally the dark mystery of which nothing can be said but ever puts on the nature of light, love, and goodness wherein the divine is revealed to human beings.

SIGNIFICANCE OF CHRISTIAN MYSTICISM

The study of Christian mysticism reveals both the unity of mysticism as an aspect of religion and the diversity of expression that it has received in the history of Christian faith. The mystic claims contact with an order of reality transcending the world of the senses and the ordinary forms of discursive intellectual knowing. Christian mystics affirm that this contact is with God the Trinity and can take place only through the mediation of Christ and the church. The claim is all the more significant in that Eastern Orthodox Christians, Roman Catholics, and Protestants are here in agreement.

Without suggesting that all mysticism is everywhere one and the same, it can be said that the Christian mystics take their stand with the mystics of other traditions in pointing to "the Beyond that is within." If Christianity is to embark upon truly cooperative relations with other religions, it must be deeply imbued with the insight and experience of the mystics. Even if it is to attempt to plumb the depths of its own history, it cannot neglect its mystical dimensions.

CHAPTER 9

CHRISTIANITY'S RELATIONSHIP WITH THE WORLD

From the perspectives of history and sociology, the Christian community has been related to the world in diverse and even paradoxical ways. This is reflected not only in changes in this relationship over time but also in simultaneously expressed alternatives ranging from withdrawal from and rejection of the world to theocratic triumphalism. For example, early Christians so consistently rejected imperial deities that they were known as atheists, while later Christians so embraced European monarchies that they were known as reactionary theists. Franciscans, especially the Spiritual Franciscans, proclaimed that true Christians should divest themselves of money at the same time that the Catholic church erected magnificent churches and the clergy dressed in elaborate finery. Another classic example of this paradoxical relationship is provided by the monks, who withdrew from the world but also preserved and transmitted classical culture and learning to medieval Europe. In the modern period some Christian communities regard secularization as a fall from true Christianity; others view it as a legitimate consequence of a desacralization of the world initiated by Christ.

The Christian community has always been part of the world in which it exists. It has served the typical religious function of legitimating social systems and values and of creating structures of meaning, plausibility, and compensation for society as it faces loss and death. The Christian community has sometimes exercised this religious function in collusion with tribalistic nationalisms (e.g., the "German Christians" and Nazism) by disregarding traditional church tenets. When the Christian community has held to its teachings, however, it has opposed such social systems and values. Given the inherent fragility of human culture and society, religion in general and the Christian community in particular frequently are conservative forces.

However, the Christian community has not always been a conservative force. Liberation theology, which originally arose in Latin America in the 1970s, arose from the conviction that God takes the side of the oppressed against the world's injustices. Other similar movements—e.g., black theology, Dalit theology, feminist and womanist theologies, queer theology, and even environmental or ecotheology—arose in the late 20th and early 21st centuries; they were rooted within the particular context of an oppressed group and sought to counteract the sinful structures that constituted the agent of oppression. From the perspective of theology or faith, the criticism of the world of which the Christian community itself is a part is the exercise

Rev. Katharine Jefferts Schori at her investiture as the 26th Presiding Bishop of the Episcopal Church at the National Cathedral in Washington in 2006. She became its first woman primate. NICHOLAS KAMM/AFP/Getty Images

of its commitment to Jesus Christ. For the Christian community, the death and Resurrection of Jesus call into question all structures, systems, and values of the world that claim ultimacy.

The relationship of the Christian community to the world may be seen differently depending upon one's historical, sociological, and theological perspectives because the Christian community is both a creation in the world and an influence upon it. This complexity led the American theologian H. Richard Niebuhr to comment in *Christ and Culture* (1956) that "the many-sided debate about the relations of Christianity and civilization... is as confused as it is many-sided."

CHURCH AND STATE

The relationship of Christians and Christian institutions to forms of the political order has shown an extraordinary diversity throughout church history. There have been, for example, theocratically founded monarchies, democracies, and communist communities. In various periods, however, political revolution, based on theological foundations, has also belonged to this diversity.

In certain eras of church history the desire to establish the Kingdom of God stimulated political and social strivings. The political power of the Christian proclamation of the coming sovereignty of God resided in its promise of both the establishment of a kingdom of peace and the execution of judgment.

The church, like the state, has been exposed to the temptation of power, which resulted in the transformation of the church into an ecclesiastical state. This took place in the development of the Papal States and, to a lesser degree, in several theocratic churches, as well as in Calvin's ecclesiastical state in Geneva in the 16th century. At times, too, the secular state declared itself Christian and the executor of the spiritual, political, and social commission of the church; it understood itself to be the representative of the Kingdom of God. This development took place in both the Byzantine and the Carolingian empires as well as in the medieval Holy Roman Empire.

The struggle between the church, understanding itself as state, and the state, understanding itself as representative of the church, not only dominated the Middle Ages but also continued into the Reformation period. The wars of religion in the era of the Reformation and Counter-Reformation discredited in the eyes of many the theological and metaphysical rationales for a Christian state. The Anabaptists in the 16th century and some Puritans in the 17th century contributed to this skepticism by advocating religious liberty and rejecting the involvement of the state in religious matters. The Enlightenment idea of grounding the relationship between church and state on natural law, as advanced by Friedrich Schleiermacher among others, led to the advocacy of the legal separation of church and state.

THE CHURCH AND THE ROMAN EMPIRE

The attitude of the first generations of Christians toward the existing political order was determined by the imminent expectation of the Kingdom of God, whose miraculous power had begun to be visibly realized in the figure of Jesus Christ. The importance of the political order was, thus, negligible, as Jesus himself asserted when he said, "My kingship is not of this world." Orientation toward the coming kingdom of peace placed Christians in tension with the state, which made demands upon them that were in direct conflict with their faith.

This contrast was developed most pointedly in the rejection of the emperor cult and of certain state offices—above all, that of judge—to which the power over life and death was professionally entrusted. Although opposition to fundamental orderings of the ruling state was not based upon any conscious revolutionary program, contemporaries blamed the expansion of the Christian church in the Roman Empire for an internal weakening of the empire on the basis of this conscious avoidance of many aspects of public life, including military service.

Despite the early Christian longing for the coming Kingdom of God, even the Christians of the early generations acknowledged the pagan state as the bearer of order in the world. Two contrary views thus faced one another within the Christian communities. On the one hand, under the influence of Pauline missions, was the idea that the "ruling body"—i.e., the existing political order of the Roman Empire—was "from God…for your good" (Romans 13:1–4) and that Christians should be "subject to the governing authorities." Another similar idea held by Paul (in 2 Thessalonians) was that the Roman state, through its legal order, "restrains" the downfall of the world that the Antichrist is attempting to bring about. On the other hand, and existing at the same time, was the apocalyptic identification of the imperial city of Rome with the great whore of Babylon (Revelation 17:3–7). The first attitude, formulated by Paul, was decisive in the development of a Christian political consciousness. The second was noticeable especially in the history of radical Christianity and in radical Christian pacifism, which rejects cooperation as much in military service as in public judgeship.

THE CHURCH AND THE BYZANTINE EMPIRE

In the 4th century, the emperor Constantine granted himself, as "bishop of foreign affairs," certain rights to church leadership. These rights concerned not only the "outward" activity of the church but also encroached upon the inner life of the church—as was shown by the role of the emperor in summoning and leading imperial councils to formulate fundamental Christian doctrine and to ratify their decisions.

In the Byzantine Empire, the secular ruler was called "priest and emperor" and exercised authority as head of the church. Although never ordained, the emperor held jurisdiction over ecclesiastical affairs. The belief that his authority came directly from God was symbolically expressed in the ceremony of both crowning and anointing him. This tradition was continued in the Russian realms, where the tsardom claimed a growing authority for itself even in the area of the church.

THE CHURCH AND WESTERN STATES

In the political vacuum that arose in the West because of the invasion by the German tribes, the Roman church was the single institution that preserved in its episcopal dioceses the Roman provincial arrangement. In its administration of justice the church largely depended upon the old imperial law and—in a period of legal and administrative chaos—was viewed as the only guarantor of order. The Roman popes, most notably Gregory I the Great (reigned 590–604), assumed many of the duties of the decadent imperial bureaucracy. His administrative skill helped lay the foundation for the Papal States, which emerged in the 8th century.

Although he considered himself part of a Christian commonwealth headed by the emperor in Constantinople, Gregory sought to improve the religious life of the peoples of the West. Under him the church in Spain, Gaul, and northern Italy was strengthened, and England was converted to Roman Christianity.

Later popes forged an alliance with the rulers of the Frankish (Germanic) kingdom in the 8th century and succeeded in winning them as protectors of the Papal States when the Byzantine emperor was no longer able to protect Rome. The relationship created a new area of tension, as religious and secular leaders sought to define the exact nature of the relationship between them. The emperor Charlemagne claimed for himself the right to appoint the bishops of his empire, who were thus increasingly involved in political affairs.

Emperors in the 10th century, building on Carolingian precedent, continued to involve themselves in church affairs. As a result, bishops in the empire were sometimes also the reigning princes of their dioceses, and they were occasionally guilty of being more interested in the political than in the spiritual affairs of their dominions.

These conflicting perspectives were the cause of a series of struggles between popes and secular rulers that began in the 11th century, when lay and religious leaders sought to reform society and the church. Already in the 10th century, monastic reform movements attempted to improve the religious life of the monks and establish a new understanding of ecclesiastical liberty. Although the empire was reconstituted in the 12th century on the basis of Roman law and the understanding of the empire as a distinct sacred institution (*sacrum imperium*), it broke down during the 13th century as the result of a new struggle between the emperors and several successive popes. Papal fortunes declined even further during the subsequent Babylonian Captivity of the church, when the papacy resided in Avignon (1309–77) and was perceived as being dominated by the French monarchy.

Secular control of the church increased during the Great Schism (1378–1417). The schism was partly the result of growing demands for the papacy's return to Rome. Pope Urban VI settled in Rome and alienated a number of cardinals, who returned to Avignon and elected a rival pope, Clement VII. Popes and antipopes reigning simultaneously excommunicated each other, thus demeaning the papacy. The schism spread great uncertainty throughout Europe about the validity of the consecration of bishops and the sacraments as administered by the priests they ordained. It was perpetuated in part by European politics, as rival rulers supported either the pope in Rome or the pope in Avignon to assert ever greater authority over the church in their realms.

The changes brought by the Reformation and the growth of state power recast the nature of the debate between the temporal and spiritual powers. Under King Henry VIII of England a revolutionary dissociation of the English church from papal supremacy took place. In the German territories the reigning princes became, in effect, the legal guardians of the Protestant churches—a movement already in the process of consolidation in the late Middle Ages.

The ideas of the freedom and equality of Christians and their representation in a communion of saints by virtue of voluntary membership had been disseminated in various medieval sects such as the Cathari, Waldenses, Hussites, and the Bohemian Brethren and were reinforced during the Reformation by groups such as the Hutterites, Mennonites, and Schwenckfelders. These groups also renounced involvement with the state in certain respects, such as through military service and the holding of state offices; some of these groups attempted to structure their own form of common life in Christian, communist communities. Many of their political ideas—at first bloodily suppressed by the Reformation and Counter-Reformation states and churches—were later prominent in the Dutch wars of independence and in the English Revolution.

In the Thirty Years' War (1618–48) confessional antitheses were intermingled with politics, and the credibility of the feuding ecclesiastical parties was thereby called into question. Subsequently, from the 17th century on, the tendency toward a new, natural-law conception of the relationship between state and church began to develop. Henceforth, in the Protestant countries, state sovereignty was increasingly emphasized vis-à-vis the churches. The state established the right to regulate educational and marriage concerns as well as all administrative affairs of the church. A similar development also occurred in Roman Catholic areas.

SEPARATION OF CHURCH AND STATE

The separation of church and state was one of the legacies of the American and French revolutions at the end of the 18th century. It was achieved as a result of ideas arising from opposition to the English episcopal system and the English throne as well as from the ideals of the Enlightenment. It was implemented in France because of the social-revolutionary criticism of the wealthy ecclesiastical hierarchy but also because of the desire to guarantee the freedom of the church. The French state took over education and other functions of a civic nature that had been traditionally exercised by the church.

Beginning in the late 18th century, two fundamental attitudes developed in matters related to the separation of church and state. The first, as implied in the Constitution of the United States, was supported by a tendency to leave to the church, set free from state supervision, a maximum freedom in the realization of its spiritual, moral, and educational tasks. In the United States, for example, a comprehensive church school and educational system has been created by the churches on the basis of this freedom, and numerous colleges and universities have been founded by churches. The separation of church and state by the French Revolution and later in the Soviet Union and the countries under the Soviet Union's sphere of influence was based upon an opposite tendency. The attempt was not only to restrict the public role of the church but also to work toward its gradual disappearance. The church was to be replaced with a secular ideology.

In contrast to this, the attitude of National Socialism in Germany under Hitler was contradictory. On the one hand, Nazi ideology allowed no public role for the church and its teaching. On the other hand, Hitler was concerned not to trigger an outright confrontation with the church. The concordat concluded in 1933 between Germany and the Roman Catholic Church illustrates this policy of official neutrality.

In Germany state-church traditions had been largely eliminated in 1918 with the establishment of the Weimar Republic; the abolition of the monarchical system of government also deprived the territorial churches of their supreme Protestant episcopal heads. The Weimar Constitution sanctioned the separation of church and state. State-church traditions were maintained in various forms in Germany, not only during the Weimar Republic but also during the Hitler regime and afterward in the Federal Republic of Germany. Thus, through state agreements, definite special rights, primarily in the areas of taxes and education, were granted to both the Roman Catholic Church and the Evangelical (Lutheran-Reformed) churches of the individual states.

Even in the United States, however, the old state-church system, overcome during the American Revolution, still produces aftereffects in the form of tax privileges of the church (exemption from most taxation), the exemption of the clergy from military service, and the financial furtherance of confessional school and educational systems through the state. These privileges have been questioned and even attacked by certain segments of the American public.

Church and State in Eastern and Western Theology

The two main forms of the relationship between church and state that have been predominant and decisive through the centuries and in which the structural difference between the Roman Catholic Church and Eastern Orthodoxy becomes most evident can best be explained by comparing the views of two great theologians: Eusebius of Caesarea and Augustine.

Eusebius

Eusebius (c. 260–339), the bishop of Caesarea, was a historian and exegete who formed the Orthodox understanding of the relationship between church and state. He saw the empire and the imperial church as sharing a close bond with each other; in the centre of the Christian empire stood the figure of the Christian emperor rather than that of the spiritual head of the church.

In Eusebian political theology, the Christian emperor appears as God's representative on Earth in whom God himself "lets shine forth the image of his absolute power." He is the "Godloved, three times blessed" servant of the highest ruler, who, "armed with divine armor cleans the world from the horde of the godless, the strong-voiced heralds of undeceiving fear of God," the rays of which "penetrate the world." Through the possession of these characteristics the Christian emperor is the archetype not only of justice but also of the love of humankind. When it is said about Constantine, "God himself has chosen him to be the lord and leader so that no man can praise himself to have raised him up," the rule of the Orthodox emperor has been based on the immediate grace of God.

To a certain extent this understanding of the emperor was the Christian reinterpretation of the ancient Roman view of the emperor as the representative of God or the gods. Some of Eusebius's remarks echo the cult of the Unconquered Sun, Sol Invictus, who was represented by the emperor according to pagan understanding. The emperor—in this respect he also played the role of the *pontifex maximus* (high priest) in the state cult—took the central position within the church as well. He summoned the synods of bishops, "as though he had been appointed bishop by God," presided over the synods, and granted judicial power for the empire to their decisions. He was the protector of the church who stood up for the preservation of unity and truth of the Christian faith and who fought not only as a warrior but also as an intercessor, as a second Moses during the battle against God's enemies, "holy and purely praying to God, sending his prayers up to him." The Christian emperor entered not only the political but also the sacred succession of the divinely appointed Roman emperor. Next to such a figure, an independent leadership of the church could hardly develop.

Orthodox theologians have understood the coexistence of the Christian emperor and the head of the Christian church as *symphōnia*, or "harmony." The church recognized the powers of the emperor as protector of the church and preserver of the unity of the faith and asserted its own authority over the spiritual domain of preserving Orthodox doctrine and order in the church. The emperor, on the other hand, was subject to the church's spiritual leadership as far as he was a son of the church.

The special position of the emperor and the function of the Byzantine patriarch as the spiritual head of the church were defined in the 9th century in the *Epanagoge*, the judicial ruling establishing this relationship of church and state. The church-judicial affirmation of this relationship in the 6th and 7th centuries made the development of a judicial independence of the Byzantine patriarch in the style of the Roman papacy impossible from the beginning.

The *Epanagoge*, however, did not completely subject the patriarch to the supervision of the emperor but rather directed him expressly "to support the truth and to undertake the defense of the holy teachings without fear of the emperor." Therefore, the tension between the imperial reign that misused its absolutism against the spiritual freedom of the church and a church that claimed its spiritual freedom against an absolutist emperor or tsar was characteristic of Byzantine and Slavic political history but not the same as the political tension between the imperial power and the papacy that occurred in the West, especially during the period from 1050 to 1300.

AUGUSTINE

Augustine's *City of God* attempted to answer questions arising from the most painful event of his day: the sack of the city of Rome by the Visigoths in 410. Augustine responded to the shock and dismay his contemporaries experienced with the collapse of their world by delivering a literary demolition of paganism. From Augustine's perspective the "splendid vices" of the pagans had led inexorably to the fall of an idolatrous world. In sharp contrast to this "earthly city," epitomized by Rome but everywhere energized by the same human desires for praise and glory, Augustine projected the "most glorious city" of praise and thanks to God, the heavenly Jerusalem. However, Augustine did not simply identify the state with the earthly city and the church with the city of God. He perceived that the state existed not simply in opposition to God but as a divine instrument for the welfare of humankind. The *civitas dei* ("city of God") and the *civitas terrena* ("earthly city") finally correspond neither to church and state nor to heaven and earth. They are rather two opposed societies with antagonistic orders of value that intersect both state and church and in each case show the radical incompatibility of the love of God with the values of worldly society.

LATER DEVELOPMENTS

The historical development of the church in the Latin West took a different course from that of the Byzantine imperial church. In the West a new power gradually emerged—the Roman church, the church of the bishop of Rome. This church assumed many of the administrative, political, and social-welfare functions of the ancient Roman state in the West following the invasion of the Germans.

It was in this context that the judicial pretense of the "Gift of the emperor Constantine"—the Donation of Constantine—became possible, to which the later development of the papacy was connected. The Donation is the account of Constantine's purported conferring upon Pope Sylvester I (reigned 314–335) of the primacy of the West, including the imperial symbols of rulership. The pope returned the crown to Constantine, who in gratitude moved the capital to Byzantium (Constantinople). The Donation thereby explained and legitimated a number of important political developments and papal claims, including the transfer of the capital to Byzantium, the displacement of old Rome by the new Rome of the church, papal secular authority, and

the papacy's separation from allegiance to the Byzantine empire and association with the rising power of the Latin West. The Donation, which was based on traditions dating to the 5th century, was compiled in the mid-8th century and is associated with the political transformation that took place in Italy at that time.

This was the point from which the developments in the East and in the West led in two different directions. The growing independence of the West was markedly illustrated by the Donation of Pippin (Pippin, father of Charlemagne, was anointed king of the Franks by Pope Stephen III in 754), which laid the foundation of the Papal States as independent of any temporal power and gave the pope the Byzantine exarchate of Ravenna.

The idea of the church as a state also appeared in a democratic form and in strict contrast to its absolutist Roman model in some Reformation church and sect developments and in free churches of the post-Reformation period. The sects of the Reformation period renewed the old idea of the Christian congregation as God's people, wandering on this Earth—a people connected with God, like Israel, through a special covenant. This idea of God's people and the special covenant of God with a certain chosen group caused the influx of theocratic ideas, which were expressed in forms of theocratic communities similar to states and led to formations similar to an ecclesiastical state. Such tendencies were exhibited among various Reformation groups (e.g., the Münster prophets),

Puritans in Massachusetts, and groups of the American Western frontier. One of the rare exceptions to early modern theocratic theology was Luther's sharp distinction of political and ecclesial responsibilities by his dialectic of law and gospel. He commented that it is not necessary that an emperor be a Christian to rule, only that he possess reason.

The most recent attempt to form a church-state by a sect that understood itself as the chosen people distinguished by God through a special new revelation was undertaken by the Church of Jesus Christ of Latter-day Saints, or Mormons as they are commonly known. Based on the prophetic direction of their leaders, they attempted to found the state Deseret, after their entrance into the desert around the Great Salt Lake in Utah. The borders of the state were expected to include the largest part of the area of the present states of Utah, California, Arizona, Nevada, and Colorado. The Mormons, however, eventually had to recognize the fact that the comparatively small centre state, Utah, of the originally intended larger Mormon territory, could not exist as a theocracy (though structured as other secular models) under a government of Mormon Church leaders. Reports (some apparently spurious) by federal agents hostile to the church and widespread revulsion toward the Mormon practice of polygyny mitigated against federal sanction of the church leadership as the governmental heads of the proposed state. Utah eventually became a federal state of the United States.

CHURCH AND SOCIETY

The development of Christianity's influence on the character of society since the Reformation has been twofold. In the realm of state churches and territorial churches, Christianity contributed to the preservation of the status quo of society. In England, the Anglican Church remained an ally of the throne, as did the Protestant churches of the German states. In Russia the Orthodox Church continued to support a social order founded upon the monarchy, and even the monarch carried out a leading function within the church as protector.

Though the impulses for transformation of the social order according to the spirit of the Christian ethic came more strongly from the free churches and state and territorial churches made positive contributions in improving the status quo. In 17th- and 18th-century Germany, Lutheran clergy, such as August Francke (1663–1727), were active in establishing poorhouses, orphanages, schools, and hospitals. In England, Anglican clerics, such as Frederick Denison Maurice and Charles Kingsley in the 19th century, began a Christian social movement during the Industrial Revolution that brought Christian influence to the conditions of life and work in industry. Johann Hinrich Wichern proclaimed, "There is a Christian Socialism," at the Kirchentag Church Convention in Wittenberg [Germany] in 1848, the year of the publication of the *Communist Manifesto* and a wave of revolutions across Europe, and created the "Inner Mission" in order to address "works of saving love" to all suffering spiritual and physical distress. The diaconal movements of the Inner Mission were concerned with social issues, prison reform, and care of the mentally ill.

The Anglo-Saxon Free churches made great efforts to bring the social atmosphere and living conditions into line with a Christian understanding of human life. Methodists and Baptists addressed their message mainly to those segments of society that were neglected by the established church. They recognized that the distress of the newly formed working class, a consequence of industrialization, could not be removed by the traditional charitable means used by the state churches. In Germany, in particular, the spiritual leaders of the so-called revival movement, such as Friedrich Wilhelm Krummacher (1796–1868), denied the right of self-organization to the workers by claiming that all earthly social

injustices would receive compensation in heaven caused Karl Marx and Friedrich Engels to separate themselves completely from the church and its purely charitable attempts at a settlement of social conflicts and to declare religion with its promise of a better beyond as the "opiate of the people." This reproach, however, was as little in keeping with the social-ethical activities of the Inner Mission and of Methodists and Baptists as it was with the selfless courage of the Quakers, who fought against social demoralization, against the catastrophic situation in the prisons, against war, and, most of all, against slavery.

The Problem of Slavery and Persecution

Christian approaches to slavery have passed through many controversial phases. Paul recommended to Philemon that he accept back his runaway slave

Free Church

A free church is any Protestant religious body that exists in or originates in a land having a state church but that is itself free of governmental or external ecclesiastical control. Examples of such free churches are the Baptists in Scotland, where the established church is Presbyterian; the Presbyterians in England, where the Anglican Church is established; the Waldensian Church in Italy, where the Roman Catholic Church is established; and the Mission Covenant Church in Sweden, where the established church is Lutheran.

In the narrower sense, the term free churches *was first applied collectively to several non-episcopal Protestant evangelical communions in England that convened the first Congress in 1892 and combined in 1896 to form the National Council of the Evangelical Free Churches. In 1940 this group merged with the Federal Council of the Evangelical Churches to form the Free Church Federal Council.*

Onesimus "no longer as a slave but more than a slave, as a beloved brother...both in the flesh and in the Lord" (verse 16); the passage does not reject slavery but stresses that masters must treat their slaves humanely. Although the biblical writings made no direct attack upon the ancient world's institution of slavery, its proleptic abolition in community with Christ—"There is neither Jew nor Greek, there is neither slave nor free, there is neither male nor female; for you are all one in Christ Jesus" (Galatians 3:28)—has been a judgment upon the world's and the Christian community's failure to overcome slavery and all forms of oppression. Most scholars assume that the eschatological assumptions of the apostolic community—that the return of Jesus and thus the end of time were imminent—rendered social issues secondary. As it became evident that Jesus's return was not imminent and as the early church made its place in the world, the Church Fathers began to address social issues, and they identified slavery as the just punishment for sin. However, they also emphasized the need to treat slaves justly and maintained that Christians could not be enslaved. Medieval society made slow progress in the abolition of slavery, but by the year 1000 slavery had essentially disappeared in much of Western Europe, and by about 1100 it had been replaced by serfdom. One of the special tasks of the orders of knighthood was the liberation of Christian slaves who had fallen captive to the Muslims; and special knightly

orders were even founded for the ransom of Christian slaves.

With the discovery of the New World, the institution of slavery grew to proportions greater than had been previously conceived. The widespread conviction of the Spanish conquerors of the New World that its inhabitants were not fully human, and therefore could be enslaved, added to the problem. The importation of African slaves to North America was supported by various Christian churches, including the Anglican, which predominated in Virginia and other British colonies. Into the 18th century, African slaves were described as bearing the mark of Cain, and other scriptural passages were used to support slavery. When some churches began to champion abolition in the 19th century, churches in the American South continued to find support for the institution in the Bible.

The attempt of missionaries, such as Bartolomé de Las Casas in 16th-century Mexico, to counter the inhuman system of slavery in the colonial economic systems finally introduced the great basic debate concerning the question of human rights. A decisive part in the elaboration of the general principles of human rights was taken by the Spanish and Portuguese theologians of the 16th and 17th centuries, especially Francisco de Vitoria. In the 18th century Puritan leaders continued the struggle against slavery as an institution. In German Pietism, Nikolaus Ludwig, Graf von Zinzendorf, who became acquainted with slavery on the island of Saint Croix in the

Virgin Islands, used his influence on the king of Denmark for the human rights of the slaves. The Methodist and Baptist churches advocated abolition of slavery in the United States in the decisive years preceding the foundation of the New England Anti-Slavery Society in Boston in 1832 by William Lloyd Garrison. In England and in the Netherlands, the free churches were very active in the struggle against slavery, which was directed mainly against the participation of Christian trade and shipping companies in the profitable slave trade. The abolition of slavery did not end racial discrimination, of course. Martin Luther King, Jr., Baptist pastor and Nobel laureate, led the struggle for civil rights in the United States until his assassination in 1968.

Christian churches have engaged in similar struggles on behalf of other exploited or persecuted groups. In Germany in the 1930s some Christians fought against the Nazis' violent anti-Semitism and their attempts to euthanize the mentally ill and others they considered "unfit to live." For his leadership in the struggle against apartheid in South Africa, the Anglican Archbishop Desmond Tutu was awarded the Nobel Prize for Peace in 1984. He later served as head of the Truth and Reconciliation Committee, which investigated allegations of human rights abuses during the apartheid era. And Pope John Paul II used his enormous influence among Catholics and throughout the world to promote respect for human dignity and to deter the use of violence.

THEOLOGICAL AND HUMANITARIAN MOTIVATIONS

Decisive impulses for achieving social change based on Christian ethics have been and are initiated by men and women in the grasp of a deep personal Christian experience of faith, for whom the message of the coming Kingdom of God forms the foundation for faithful affirmation of social responsibility in the present world. Revival movements have viewed the Christian message as the call to work for the reorganization of society in the sense of a Kingdom of God ethic. Under the leadership of an American Baptist theologian, Walter Rauschenbusch (1861–1918), the Social Gospel movement spread in the United States. A corresponding movement was started with the Christian social conferences by German Protestant theologians, such as Paul Martin Rade (1857–1940) of Marburg. The basic idea of the Social Gospel— i.e., the emphasis on the social-ethical tasks of the church—gained widespread influence within the ecumenical movement and especially affected Christian world missions. In many respects modern economic and other forms of aid to developing countries—including significant ecumenical contributions from the World Council of Churches, the World Alliance of Reformed Churches, the Lutheran World Federation, and the Roman Catholic Church—replaced the Social Gospel.

Christians have sometimes argued that these developments reduce the

Christian message to a purely secular social program that is absorbed by political programs. Other Christians, however, have maintained that faithful responsibility in and to the world requires political, economic, and social assistance to oppressed peoples with the goal of their liberation to a full human life.

CHURCH AND EDUCATION

A positive approach to intellectual activities has made itself heard from the beginning of the Christian church; it was perhaps best expressed in the 11th century by Anselm of Canterbury in the formula *fides quaerens intellectum* ("faith seeking understanding"). But well before Anselm, Christians maintained that because people have been endowed with reason, they have an urge to express their experience of faith intellectually, to translate the contents of faith into concepts, and to formulate beliefs in a systematic understanding of the correlation between God, humankind, and creation.

INTELLECTUALISM VERSUS ANTI-INTELLECTUALISM

This desire was exemplified by Justin Martyr, a professional philosopher and Christian apologist of the 2nd century who saw Christian revelation as the fulfillment, not the elimination, of philosophical understanding. Even before Justin Martyr, the author of The Gospel According to John set the point of departure for the intellectual history of

salvation with his use of the term *Logos* to open the first chapter of the Gospel. The light of the Logos (the Greek word means "word" or "reason," in the sense of divine or universal reason permeating the intelligible world) had made itself manifest in a number of sparks and seeds in human history even before its incarnation in the person of Jesus Christ.

These contrasting opinions have stood in permanent tension with one another. In medieval thought the elevation of Christian belief to the status of scientific universal knowledge was dominant. Theology, the queen of the sciences, became the instructor of the different disciplines, organized according to the traditional classification of trivium (grammar, rhetoric, and dialectic) and quadrivium (music, arithmetic, geometry, and astronomy) and incorporated into the system of education as "servants of theology." This system of education became part of the structure of the universities that were founded in the 13th century.

With the Reformation there was widespread concern for education because the Reformers desired everyone to be able to read the Bible. Luther also argued that it was necessary for society that its youth be educated. He held that it was the duty of civil authorities to compel their subjects to keep their children in school so "that there will always be preachers, jurists, pastors, writers, physicians, schoolmasters, and the like, for we cannot do without them." This stress on education was made evident by the founding of many colleges in North America in the

Justus Sustermans, portrait of Galileo Galilei, date unknown, oil on canvas. In a private collection

17th and 18th centuries by Protestants and by members the Society of Jesus, or Jesuits, a Roman Catholic missionary and educational order.

Open conflict between science and theology occurred only when the traditional biblical view of the world was seriously questioned, as in the case of the Italian astronomer Galileo (1633). The principles of Galileo's scientific research, however, were themselves the result of a Christian idea of science and truth. The biblical faith in God as Creator and incarnate Redeemer is an explicit affirmation of the goodness, reality, and contingency of the created world—assumptions underlying scientific work. Positive tendencies concerning education and science have always been dominant in the history of Christianity, even though the opposite attitude arose occasionally during certain periods. Thus the German astronomer Johannes Kepler (1571–1630) spoke of celebrating God in science. In the 20th century, Pope John Paul II maintained that he saw no contradiction between the findings of modern science and biblical accounts of the Creation; he also declared the condemnation of Galileo to be an error and encouraged the scientific search for truth.

The attitude that had been hostile toward intellectual endeavours was heard less frequently after the Christian church had become the church of the Roman Empire. But the relationship between science and theology was attacked when the understanding of truth that had been developed within theology was turned critically against the dogma of the church itself. This occurred, for instance, after the natural sciences and theology had turned away from total dependence upon tradition and directed their attention toward experience—observation and experiment. A number of fundamental dogmatic principles and concepts were thus questioned and eventually abandoned. The struggle concerning the theory of evolution has been a conspicuous modern symptom of this trend.

The estrangement of theology and natural science in the modern period was a complex development related to confessional controversies and wars in the 16th and 17th centuries and philosophical perspectives in the 18th and 19th centuries. The epistemological foundation of faith was radically challenged by the Scottish philosopher David Hume. Building upon Hume's work, the German philosopher Immanuel Kant advocated freedom from any heteronomous authority, such as the church and dogmas, that could not be established by reason alone. Scholars withdrew from the decisions of church authorities and were willing to subject themselves only to critical reason and experience. The rationalism of the Enlightenment appeared to be the answer of science to the claim of true faith that had been made by the churches.

FORMS OF CHRISTIAN EDUCATION

The Christian church created the bases of the Western system of education.

From its beginning the Christian community faced external and internal challenges to its faith, which it met by developing and utilizing intellectual and educational resources. The response to the external challenge of rival religions and philosophical perspectives is termed *apologetics*—i.e., the intellectual defense of the faith. Apologetic theologians from Justin Martyr in the 2nd century to Paul Tillich in the 20th have promoted critical dialogue between the Christian community, the educated world, and other religions. This exchange was further encouraged by the Second Vatican Council, Pope John Paul II, and the ecumenical movement. The internal challenges to the Christian community were met not only by formulating the faith in creeds and dogmas but also by passing this faith on to the next generations through education.

By the 8th and 9th centuries, cathedral schools were established to provide basic education in Latin grammar and Christian doctrine to the clergy, and by the 11th century these schools emerged as centres of higher learning. The school at the court of Charlemagne (which was conducted by clergy), the medieval schools of the religious orders, cathedrals, monasteries, convents, and churches, the flourishing schools of the Brethren of the Common Life, and the Roman Catholic school systems that came into existence during the Counter-Reformation under the leadership of the Jesuits and other new teaching orders contributed much to the civilization of the West. Equally important were the schools started by the German Reformers Luther, Philipp Melanchthon, Johann Bugenhagen, John and August Hermann Francke, and the Moravian reformers John Amos Comenius and the graf von Zinzendorf. The church was responsible for overseeing schools even after the Reformation. Only in the 18th century did the school system start to separate itself from its Christian roots and fall more and more under state control.

With the separation of church and state, both institutions have entered into tensely manifold relationships. In some countries the state has taken over the school system and does not allow private church schools except in a few special cases. Other countries (e.g., France) maintain school systems basically free of religion and leave the religious instruction to the private undertakings of the different churches. In the American Revolution the concept of the separation of state and church was intended to free the church from all patronization by the state and to make possible a maximum of free activity, particularly in the area of education. The Soviet Union used its schools particularly for an anti-religious education based upon the state philosophy of dialectical materialism, practicing the constitutionally guaranteed freedom of anti-religious propaganda in schools, though the churches were forbidden to give any education outside their worship services.

A second issue that results from the separation of church and state is the question of state subsidies to private church schools. These are claimed in those countries in which the church schools in many places take over part of the functions of the state schools (e.g., in the United States). After the ideological positivism and the materialism of the 19th century faded away in many areas, it was realized that religious life had an important role in the cultural development of the West and the New World and that the exclusion of religious instruction from the curricula of the schools indicated a lack of balance in education. In the 20th century religion was adopted as a subject among the humanities. State universities in the United States, Canada, and Australia, which did not have theological faculties because of the separation of church and state, founded departments of religion of an interdenominational nature and included non-Christians as academic teachers of religion.

Another development in the history of Christian education was the founding of universities. The origins of the university can be traced to the 12th century, and by the 13th century the medieval university had reached its mature form. Universities were founded during the rest of the Middle Ages throughout Europe and spread from there to other continents after the 16th century. The earliest universities emerged as associations of masters or students (the Latin *universitas* means "guild" or "union") that were dedicated to the pursuit of higher learning. The universities, which superseded the cathedral schools as centres of advanced study, came to have a number of shared traits: the teaching methods of lecture and disputation, the extended communal living in colleges, the periodically changing leadership of an elected dean, the inner structure according to faculties or "nations," and the European recognition of academic degrees. Universities provided instruction in the liberal arts and advanced study in the disciplines of law, medicine, and, most importantly, theology. Many of the great theologians of the era, notably, Thomas Aquinas, were associated with the universities.

The advent of humanism and the Reformation, as well as the reforms initiated by some university faculty, created a new situation for all systems of education, especially the universities. Humanists demanded plans to provide designated places for free research in academies that were princely or private institutions and, as such, not controlled by the church. On the other hand, Protestant states and principalities founded new universities, such as Marburg in 1527, Königsberg in 1544, and Jena in 1558. As a counteraction, the Jesuits took over the leadership in the older universities that had remained Roman Catholic or else founded new ones in Europe and overseas.

In areas of missionary work, Christian education has had a twofold task. First, its function was to lay an educational foundation for evangelization of non-Christian peoples by forming a system of education for all levels from grammar school to university. Second, its function was to take care of the education of European settlers. To a large extent the European colonial powers had left the formation of an educational system in their colonies or dominions to the churches. In the Spanish colonial regions in America, Roman Catholic universities were founded very early (e.g., Santo Domingo in 1538, Mexico and Lima in 1551, Guatemala in 1562, and Bogotá in 1573). In China, Jesuit missionaries acted mainly as agents of European education and culture (e.g., astronomy, mathematics, and technology) in their positions as civil servants of the court.

Since the 18th century, the activities of competing Christian denominations in mission areas have led to an intensification of the Christian system of education in Asia and Africa. Even where the African and Asian states have their own system of schools and universities, Christian educational institutions have performed a significant function (St. Xavier University in Bombay and Sophia University in Tokyo are Jesuit foundations; Dōshisha University in Kyōto is a Japanese Presbyterian foundation).

In North America, Christian education took a different course. From the beginning, the churches took over the creation of general educational institutions, and various denominations did pioneer work in the field of education. In the English colonies, later the United States, the denominations founded theological colleges for the purpose of educating their ministers and established universities dealing with all major disciplines, including theology, often emphasizing a denominational slant. Harvard University was founded in 1636 and Yale University in 1701 as Congregational establishments,

and the College of William and Mary was established in 1693 as an Anglican institution. They were followed during the 19th century by other Protestant universities (e.g., Southern Methodist University, Dallas, Texas) and colleges (e.g., Augustana College, Rock Island, Illinois) and by Roman Catholic universities (e.g., the University of Notre Dame, Notre Dame, Indiana) and colleges (e.g., Boston College, Chestnut Hill, Massachusetts). In addition, many private universities were based upon a Christian idea of education according to the wishes of their founders.

Christian education has been undertaken in a variety of forms. The system of Sunday schools is nearly universal in all denominations. Confirmation instruction is more specialized, serving different tasks, such as preparation of the children for confirmation, their conscious acknowledgment of the Christian ethic, of the Christian confessions, of the meaning of the sacraments, and of the special forms of congregational life.

CHURCH AND SOCIAL WELFARE

The Christian church has responded to human illness and human suffering both by caring for and healing the sick and by expressing concern for the poor or the otherwise afflicted.

HEALING THE SICK

The practice of healing has retreated into the background in modern times, but healing played a decisive role in the success of the early church and was important in missionary apologetics. In the Gospels, Jesus appears as a healer of body and soul. The title "Christ the Physician" was the most popular name for the Lord in missionary preaching of the first centuries. Even the Apostles are characterized as healers. The Apologists of the 2nd to 4th century used numerous miraculous healings as arguments for the visible presence of the Holy Spirit in the church. The Fathers of the first centuries interpreted the entire sphere of charismatic life from the basic concepts that Christ is the physician, the church the hospital, the sacraments the medication, and orthodox theology the medicine chest against heresy. Ignatius of Antioch called the Eucharist the "medication that produces immortality." Healing within the church began to retreat only in connection with the transformation of the church into a state church under Constantine and with the replacement of free charismatics by ecclesiastical officials.

The early basis for healing was generally a demonological interpretation of sickness: healing was often carried out as an exorcism—that is, a ceremonial liturgical adjuration of the demon that was supposed to cause the illness and its expulsion from the sick person. The development of exorcism is characteristic in that the office of the exorcist eventually became one of the lower levels of ordination, which led to the priesthood. During the Enlightenment in the 18th century, the practice of exorcisms within the Roman Catholic Church was suppressed.

In the Protestant churches, exorcism never completely vanished; in Pietistic circles exorcists such as Johann Christoph Blumhardt the Elder (1805-80) have appeared. With the motto "Jesus is Conquerer," Blumhardt transformed his healing centre at Bad Boll in Germany into an influential resource for international missionary work. His son, Christoph Friedrich Blumhardt (1842-1919), continued his father's work and in sympathy with working-class needs entered politics as a member of the Württemberg Diet. Since the latter part of the 19th century, different groups of the Pentecostal and charismatic movements have revived the use of exorcistic rituals with great emphasis and—pointing to the power of the Holy Spirit—they claim the charisma of healing as one of the spiritual gifts granted the believing Christian. After the basic connection between healing of the body and healing of the soul and the psychogenic origin of many illnesses was acknowledged theologically and medically, different older churches, such as the Protestant Episcopal Church and even the Roman Catholic Church in the United States, have reinstituted healing services.

In terms of spiritual healing, one church has stood out in this respect. Mary Baker Eddy (1821–1910), the founder of Christian Science, referred particularly to healing through the Spirit as her special mission. Based on her experience of being healed from a serious illness by Phineas

Quimby, a pupil of the German hypnotist Franz Mesmer, she wrote *Science and Health with Key to the Scriptures* and founded the Church of Christ, Scientist. According to the instructions of its founder, Christian Science today carries out a practice of "spiritual healing" throughout the world.

CARE FOR THE SICK

In The Gospel According to Matthew, Jesus says to his Apostles, when the Son of Man comes in majesty to render final judgment on all of humankind, he will say to the chosen ones on his right hand: "I was sick and you visited me," and to the condemned on his left hand: "I was sick and you did not visit me." When the condemned ask the Lord when they saw him sick and did not visit him, they will receive the answer: "As you did it not to one of the least of these, you did it not to me."

In the early church, the care of the sick was carried out by the deacons and widows under the leadership of the bishop. This service was not limited to members of the Christian congregation but was directed toward the larger community, particularly in times of pestilence and plague. Eusebius noted in his *Ecclesiastical History* that while the heathen fled the plague at Alexandria, "most of our brother-Christians showed unbounded love and loyalty" in caring for and frequently dying with the victims.

Beginning in the 4th century, the monasteries created a new institution, the hospital, and continued to care for the sick throughout the Middle Ages. The growing number of pilgrims to the Holy Land and the necessity of care of their numerous sick, who had fallen victim to the unfamiliar conditions of climate and life, led to knightly hospital orders, the most important of which was the Order of the Hospital of St. John of Jerusalem (later called the Knights of Malta), founded in the 11th century. The service for the sick, which was carried out by the knights alongside their military service for the protection of the pilgrims, was not elaborate.

In connection with the orders of mendicant friars, especially the Franciscans, civil hospital orders were formed. Even the hospital in Marburg, which was founded by St. Elizabeth of Hungary (1207–31) on the territory of the Knights of the Teutonic Order, was influenced by the spirit of St. Francis. Other hospitals were founded as autonomous institutions under the leadership or supervision of a bishop. The centralization of the different existing institutions became necessary with the growth of cities and was most frequently undertaken by city councils. The laity began to take over, but the spiritual and pastoral care of the patients remained a major concern.

In Protestant lands during the Reformation, medieval nursing institutions were adapted to new conditions. The church constitutions in the different territories of the Reformation stressed the duty of caring for the sick and gave suggestions for its adequate realization. The office of the deacon was supplemented by that of the deaconess. The Counter-Reformation brought a new impulse for caring for the sick in the Roman Catholic Church, insofar as special orders for nursing service were founded—e.g., the Daughters of Charity, a non-enclosed congregation of women devoted to the care of the sick and the poor, founded by Vincent de Paul, a notable charismatic healer. A great number of new orders came into existence and spread the spirit and institutions of ecclesiastical nursing care throughout the world as part of Roman Catholic world missions.

The free churches led in the care of the sick in Protestant countries. Methodists, Baptists, and Quakers all had a great share in this development, founding numerous hospitals throughout the world and supplying them with willing male and female helpers. German Lutheranism was influenced by these developments. In 1823 Amalie Sieveking developed a sisterhood analogous to the Daughters of Charity and was active in caring for the cholera victims of the great Hamburg epidemic of 1831. She was an inspiration to Theodor Fliedner, who founded the first Protestant hospital in Kaiserswerth in 1836 and created at the same time the female diaconate, an order of nurses that soon found worldwide membership and recognition. Florence Nightingale received training at Kaiserswerth, which was an important model for modern nursing schools.

Church hospitals and ecclesiastical nursing care maintained a leading role in the 20th century, although along with the general political and social development of the 19th century the city or communal hospital was founded and overtook the church hospital.

The most impressive example of the universal spread of care for the sick was the founding of the Red Cross by the Swiss humanitarian Henri Dunant. The religious influence of Dunant's pious parental home in Geneva and the shocking impression he received on the battlefield of Solferino in June 1859 led him to work out suggestions that—after difficult negotiations with representatives of numerous states—led to the conclusion of the "Geneva convention regarding the care and treatment in wartime of the wounded military personnel." In the 20th century the activity of the Red Cross embraced not only the victims of military actions but also peace activity, which includes aid for the sick, for the handicapped, for the elderly and children, and for the victims of all types of disasters everywhere in the world.

CARE FOR WIDOWS AND ORPHANS

The Christian congregation has traditionally cared for the poor, the sick, widows, and orphans. The Letter of James says: "Religion that is pure and undefiled before God is this: to visit orphans and widows in their affliction." Widows formed a special group in the congregations and were asked to help with nursing care and other service obligations as long as they did not need help and care themselves.

The church had founded orphanages during the 4th century, and the monasteries took over this task during the Middle Ages. They also fought against the practice of abandoning unwanted children and established foundling hospitals. In this area, as in others, a secularization of church institutions took place in connection with the spreading autonomy of the cities. In Protestant churches the establishment of orphanages was furthered systematically. In Holland almost every congregation had its own orphanage, which was sustained through the gifts of the members.

Following the wars of religion of the 17th century, the orphanages were reorganized pedagogically, notably by August Hermann Francke, who connected the orphanage in Glaucha, Germany, which he had founded, with a modern system of secondary schools. Francke's orphanage became a model that was frequently imitated in England and also in North America. Another innovator was the Alsatian Lutheran pastor Johann Friedrich Oberlin (1740–1826), an exemplary proponent of comprehensive Christian caring and curing for the whole person and community. Responsible for a remote and barren area in the Vosges Mountains, Oberlin transformed the impoverished villages into prosperous communities. He led in establishing schools, roads, bridges, banks, stores, agricultural societies (with the introduction of potato cultivation), and industries. His nursery schools were imitated in many areas through "Oberlin Societies."

These efforts provided a significant contribution to the development of modern welfare, which in the 20th century was mainly the responsibility of state, communal, or humanitarian organizations but was still characterized strongly by its Christian roots.

PROPERTY, POVERTY, AND THE POOR

The Christian community's response to the questions of property, poverty, and the poor may be sketched in terms of four major perspectives, which have historically overlapped and sometimes coexisted in mutuality or contradiction. The first perspective, both chronologically and in continuing popularity, is personal charity. This was the predominant form of the church's relationship to the poor from the 1st to the 16th century. The second perspective supplements the remedial work of personal charity by efforts for preventive welfare through structural changes in society. This concern to remove causes of poverty was clearly expressed in the Reformation but was soon submerged in the profound sociopolitical and economic changes of the time. The third perspective is a retreat into the charity models of the earlier Christian community. Because of the overwhelming effects of the process of secularization and the human misery caused by industrialization, the key to social welfare was expressed in the Pietist maxim that social change depended upon the conversion of individuals. The fourth perspective, present in churches of the modern period, envisions systemic social change to facilitate redistribution of the world's wealth. Personal charity is not neglected, but the primary goal is to change the unjust structures of world society.

Augustine's doctrine of charity became the heart of Christian thought and practice. Augustine portrayed the Christian pilgrimage toward the heavenly city by analogy to a traveler's journey home. The city of God, humankind's true home, is characterized by the love of God even to the contempt of self, whereas the earthly city is characterized by the love of self even to the contempt of God. It is the goal—not the journey—that is important. The world and its goods may be used for the journey, but if they are enjoyed they direct the traveler away from God to the earth. This imagery incorporates into Christian theology the great themes of pilgrimage, renunciation, alienation, and asceticism; and the biblical and early Christian suspicion of riches receives systematic theological articulation. Pride and covetousness are the major vices; humility and almsgiving are the major virtues; and poverty is endorsed as the favoured status for the Christian life.

This view did not, however, lead to a rejection of property and its importance for society. Although Gregory of Nazianzus (c. 330–c. 389) linked private property to the Fall, he understood that the abolition of private property would not cure sin. Property and wealth should be shared, not relinquished. Yet the paradox of 2 Corinthians 6:10 remained: How could a Christian be poor yet make many rich,

have nothing yet possess everything? The answers given were communal property, charity to the needy, avoidance of avarice, and concentration upon heavenly treasure. The solutions of institutionalizing poverty in priesthood and monasticism, while rationalizing poverty as poverty of the spirit and material wealth as God's provision for ministry, formed the basis for medieval care of the poor.

The most influential medieval thinker on the problem of property was Thomas Aquinas, who saw community of goods as rooted in natural law because it makes no distinction of possessions. The natural law of common use protects every person's access to earthly goods and requires responsibility by everyone to provide for the needs of others. Private property, on the other hand, is rooted in positive law through human reason. Reason leads to the conclusion that the common good is served if everyone has disposition of his own property because there is more incentive to work, goods are more carefully used, and peace is better preserved when all are satisfied with what they have. Private property exists to serve the common good; thus, superfluous property is to be distributed as alms to the needy.

The other major effort to deal with property and poverty at this time was through rational direction and administration. As cities developed into political corporations, a new element entered welfare work: an organizing citizenry. Through their town councils, citizens claimed the authority to administer the ecclesiastical welfare work of hospitals and poor relief. The process was accelerated by the Reformers, whose theology undercut the medieval idealization of poverty. According to the Reformers, righteousness before God was by faith alone, and salvation was perceived as the foundation of life rather than its goal. Thus, the Reformation community found it difficult to rationalize the plight of the poor as a peculiar form of blessedness, and no salvific value either in being poor or in giving alms could be identified. When the Reformers turned to poor relief and social welfare, their new theological perspectives led them to raise questions of social justice and social structures. This was codified in Protestant church legislation in the "common chest," which spread throughout Europe from its origin in Wittenberg. The common chest—funded by church endowments, offerings, and taxes—was the community's financial resource for providing support to the poor, orphans, the aged, the unemployed, and the underemployed through subsidies, low-interest loans, and gifts.

In the 16th and 17th centuries Christian leaders, both Protestant and Roman Catholic, served the poor while ignoring the root causes of poverty. In the 18th and 19th centuries, however, the social institutions of Pietism, the Inner Mission, and European revival movements inspired social concern for the masses of people pauperized and proletarianized by industrialism. The Methodists in England undertook adult education, schooling, reform of prisons,

abolition of slavery, and aid to alcoholics. Famous missions arose in Basel, London, and Paris. The Young Men's Christian Association (YMCA; 1844), Young Women's Christian Association (YWCA; 1855), and the Salvation Army (1865) were only some of the numerous charitable institutions and organizations created to alleviate modern ills. In 1848 Johann Wichern, founder of the Inner Mission, proclaimed that "love no less than faith is the church's indispensable mark."

Yet this Christian social concern hardly was aware of and rarely attempted to expose the origins of the social ills it strove to remedy. Wichern himself was aware that poverty is social, not natural, but his orientation, like that of others, was toward renewing society through evangelization. This attitude—that society is changed by changing the hearts of individuals—is still prevalent.

In the second half of the 20th century, however, the Christian community, especially in its ecumenical organizations, began to analyze the social problems of property and poverty from the standpoint of justice and the perspectives of the poor and oppressed. In 1970 the World Council of Churches (WCC) established the Commission for the Churches' Participation in Development (CCPD). Initially involved in development programs and the provision of technical services, the CCPD focus shifted to the psychological and political character of the symbiosis of development and underdevelopment. This focus was endorsed at the 1975

WCC Assembly at Nairobi, Kenya, as "a liberating process aimed at justice, self-reliance and economic growth." Other church bodies, such as the Lutheran World Federation and the World Alliance of Reformed Churches, shared this perspective. There was also the sense that the biblical themes of justice and liberation entail the creation of social structures to enhance human life, economic structures for the just distribution of goods, and political structures to promote participation and minimize dependence. This attitude is well reflected in liberation theology, which was popular in segments of the Roman Catholic Church from the 1970s to the 1990s. Seeking to apply the faith by aiding the poor and oppressed, primarily in developing countries, advocates of liberation theology established local "base camps" to study the Bible and to address the economic needs and political interests of poor communities.

CHURCH AND FAMILY

The Christian understanding of sexuality, marriage, and family has been strongly influenced by the Old Testament view of marriage as an institution primarily concerned with the establishment of a family, rather than sustaining the individual happiness of the marriage partners. In spite of this, a transformation occurred from the early days of Christianity. This transformation is evident in the New Testament departure from the Hellenistic understanding of love. The classical understanding of love, expressed in the Platonic concept of eros, was opposed in the Christian community by the biblical understanding of love, agape. Although erotic love has frequently been understood primarily as sexual desire and passion, its classical religious and philosophical meaning was the idealistic desire to acquire the highest spiritual and intellectual good. The early Christian perception of eros as the most sublime form of egocentricity and self-assertion, the drive to acquire the divine itself, is reflected in the fact that the Greek New Testament does not use the word *erōs* but rather the relatively rare word *agapē*. *Agapē* was translated into Latin as *caritas* and thus appears in English as "charity" and "love." The Christian concept of love understood human mutuality and reciprocity within the context of God's self-giving love, which creates value in the person loved. "We love, because he first loved us. If any one says, 'I love God,' and hates his brother, he is a liar; for he who does not love his brother whom he has seen, cannot love God whom he has not seen. And this commandment we have from him, that he who loves God should love his brother also" (1 John 4:19–21). Love is presented as the greatest of the virtues (1 Corinthians 13:13) as well as a commandment. The Christian community understood faith active in love primarily in terms of voluntary obedience rather than emotion and applied this understanding to every aspect of life, including sexuality, marriage, and family.

CHURCH AND MARRIAGE

Christianity has contributed to a spiritualization of marriage and family life, to a deepening of the relations between marriage partners and between parents and children. During the first decades of the church, congregational meetings took place in the homes of Christian families. The family, indeed, became the archetype of the church. Paul called the members of his congregation in Ephesus "members of the household of God" (Ephesians 2:19). In the early church, children were included in this fellowship. They were baptized when their parents were baptized, took part in the worship life of the congregation, and received Holy Communion with their parents. The Eastern Orthodox Church still practices as part of the eucharistic rite Jesus's teaching, "Let the children come to me, and do not hinder them."

In the early church the Christian foundation of marriage—in the participation of Christians in the body of Christ—postulated a generous interpretation of the fellowship between a Christian and a pagan marriage partner: the pagan one is saved with the Christian one "for the unbelieving husband is consecrated through his wife, and the unbelieving wife is consecrated through her husband"; even the children from such a marriage in which at least one partner belongs to the body of Christ "are holy" (1 Corinthians 7:14). If the pagan partner, however, does not want to sustain the marriage relationship with a Christian partner under any circumstances, the Christian partner should grant the spouse a divorce.

Jesus himself based his parables of the Kingdom of God on the idea of love between a bride and groom and frequently used parables that describe the messianic meal as a wedding feast. In Revelation the glorious finale of salvation history is depicted as the wedding of the Lamb with the bride, as the beginning of the meal of the chosen ones with the Messiah–Son of Man (Revelation 19:9: "Blessed are those who are invited to the marriage supper of the Lamb"). The wedding character of the eucharistic meal is also expressed in the liturgy of the early church. It is deepened through the specifically Christian belief that understands the word of the creation story in Genesis "and they become one flesh" as indicative of the oneness of Christ, the head, with the congregation as his body. With this in mind the Christian demand of monogamy becomes understandable.

Christianity did not bring revolutionary social change to the position of women, but it made possible a new position in the family and congregation. In the ancient Mediterranean world, women were often held in low esteem, and this was the basis for divorce practices that put women practically at men's complete disposal. By preaching to women and prohibiting divorce, Jesus himself did away with this low estimation of women. The decisive turning point came in connection with the understanding of Christ and of the Holy Spirit. In fulfillment of the prophecy in Joel 2:28—according to

Peter in his sermon on Pentecost (Acts 2:17)—the Holy Spirit was poured out over the female disciples of Jesus as well.

This created a complete change in the position of women in the congregation: in the synagogue the women were inactive participants in the worship service and sat veiled on the women's side, usually separated from the rest by an opaque lattice. In the Christian congregation, however, women appeared as members with full rights, who used their charismatic gifts within the congregation. In the letters of Paul, women are mentioned as Christians of full value. Paul addresses Prisca (Priscilla) in Romans 16:3 as his fellow worker. The four daughters of Philip were active as prophets in the congregation. Pagan critics of the church, such as Porphyry (c. 234–c. 305), maintained that the church was ruled by women. During the periods of Christian persecution, women as well as men showed great courage in their suffering. The fact that they were honoured as martyrs demonstrates their well-known active roles in the congregations.

The attitude toward women in the early church, however, was ambivalent at best. Paul, on the one hand, included women in his instruction, "Do not quench the Spirit" (1 Thessalonians 5:19), but, on the other hand, carried over the rule of the synagogue into the Christian congregation that "women should keep silence in the churches" (1 Corinthians 14:34). Although women were respected for their piety and could hold the office of deaconess, they were excluded from the priesthood. In the early 21st century the Roman Catholic Church still refused to ordain women as priests.

THE TENDENCY TOWARD ASCETICISM

The proponents of an ascetic theology demanded exclusiveness of devotion by faithful Christians to Christ and deduced from it the demand of celibacy. This is found in arguments for the monastic life and in the Roman Catholic view of the priesthood. The radical-ascetic interpretation stands in constant tension with the positive understanding of Christian marriage. This tension has led to seemingly unsolvable conflicts and to numerous compromises in the history of Christianity.

In the light of the beginning Kingdom of God, marriage was understood as an order of the passing eon, which would not exist in the approaching new age. The risen ones will "neither marry nor are given in marriage, but are like angels in heaven" (Mark 12:25). Similarly, Paul understood marriage in the light of the coming Kingdom of God: "The appointed time has grown very short; from now on, let those who have wives live as though they had none...for the form of this world is passing away" (1 Corinthians 7:29–31). In view of the proximity of the Kingdom of God, it was considered not worthwhile to marry; and marriage was seen to involve unnecessary troubles: "I want you to be free from anxieties" (1 Corinthians 7:32). Therefore, the unmarried, the widowers, and widows "do better" if they do not marry, if they remain single. But according to this point of view marriage was recommended to those who "cannot exercise self-control...for it is better to marry than to be aflame with passion" (1 Corinthians 7:9). With the waning of the eschatological expectation that formed the original context for the Pauline views on marriage, his writings were interpreted ascetically. While these texts have been used alone in the course of church history, however, they do not stand alone in the New Testament, which also portrays marriage feasts as joyous occasions and sexual intercourse between spouses as good and holy (Ephesians 5:25–33).

By the 3rd century various gnostic groups and the Manichaeans (members of an Iranian dualistic religion) had come to reject sex. At the council of Elvira, in 300–303 or 309, the first decrees establishing clerical celibacy were pronounced, and in the 3rd and 4th centuries prominent Christians such as Anthony, Ambrose, and Jerome adopted chastity. The celibate lifestyle came to be regarded as a purer and more spiritual way of life. Gradually, celibacy came to be expected not only of ascetics and monks but also for all members of the clergy, as a function of their office.

The Reformation rejected clerical celibacy because it contravened the divine order of marriage and the family, and denied the goodness of sexuality. Luther viewed marriage as not merely the legitimation of sexual fulfillment but as above all the context for creating a new

awareness of human community through the mutuality and companionship of spouses and family. The demand that priests observe celibacy was not fully accepted in the East. The early church, and following it the Eastern Orthodox Church, decided on a compromise at the Council of Nicaea (325): the lower clergy, including the archimandrite, would be allowed to enter matrimony before receiving the higher degrees of ordination; of the higher clergy—i.e., bishops—celibacy would be demanded. This solution has saved the Eastern Orthodox from a permanent fight for the demand of celibacy for all clergymen, but it has resulted in a grave separation of the clergy into a white (celibate) and a black (married) clergy, which led to severe disagreements in times of crisis within Orthodoxy.

The early Christian community's attitude to birth control was formed partly in reaction against sexual exploitation and infanticide and partly against the Gnostic denigration of the material world and consequent hostility to procreation. In upholding its faith in the goodness of creation, sexuality, marriage, and family, the early church was also influenced by the prevalent Stoic philosophy, which emphasized procreation as the rational purpose in marriage.

In the 20th century the question of birth control entered a new phase with the invention and mass distribution of mechanical contraceptive devices on the one hand and through the appearance of a new attitude toward sexual questions on the other. The various Christian churches responded to this development in different ways: with a few exceptions—e.g., the Mormons—the Protestant churches accepted birth control in terms of a Christian social ethic. In contrast, the Roman Catholic Church, in the encyclical of Pius XI *Casti Connubii* (1930; "On Christian Marriage") and in the encyclical of Paul VI *Humanae Vitae* (1968; "On Human Life"), completely rejected any kind of contraception, a position confirmed by Paul's successors as pope in the late 20th and early 21st centuries. Modern economic and population concerns in connection with improved medical care and social and technological progress have once again confronted the Christian community with the issue of contraception.

CHURCH AND INDIVIDUAL

The Christian ethic understands the individual always as a neighbour in Christ. This understanding is based on an understanding and treatment of human beings as created in the image of God. Furthermore, the ethic does not deal with humanity in an abstract sense but with the actual neighbour. The innovative element of the Christian ethic, and its departure from the ethos of the Greco-Roman world in which it emerged, is the founding of the individual ethic in a corporate ethic, in the understanding of the fellowship of Christians as the body of Christ. The individual believer is understood not as a separate individual who has found a new spiritual and moral

relationship with God but as a "living stone" (1 Peter 2:4), as a living cell in the body of Christ in which the powers of the Kingdom of God are already working.

LOVE AS THE BASIS FOR CHRISTIAN ETHICS

The main commandment of the Christian ethic was derived from the Book of Leviticus: "You shall love your neighbour as yourself" (19:18), but Jesus filled this commandment with a new, twofold meaning. First, he closely connected the commandment "love your neighbour" with the commandment to love God. In the dispute with the scribes described in Matthew, chapter 22, he quoted Deuteronomy 6:5, "You shall love the Lord your God with all your heart, and with all your soul, and with all your might." He spoke of the commandment of love for neighbour, however, as being equal to it. With that he lifted it to the same level as the highest and greatest commandment, the commandment to love God. In The Gospel According to Luke, both commandments have grown together into one single pronouncement with the addition: "Do this, and you will live." Second, the commandment received a new content in view of God and in view of the neighbour through the relationship of the believer with Christ. Love of God and love of the neighbour is possible because the Son proclaims the Gospel of the Father and brings to it reality and credibility through his life, death, and Resurrection. Based on this

St. Luke, detail of St. Luke Drawing the Virgin, *oil on canvas by Rogier van der Weyden, 15th century; in the Hermitage, St. Petersburg, Russia.* © Photos.com/Jupiterimages

connection of the Christian commandment of love with the understanding of Christ's person and work, the demand of love for the neighbour appears as a new commandment: "A new commandment I give to you, that you love one another; even as I have loved you, that you also love one another" (John 13:34). The love for each other is supposed to characterize the disciples: "By this all men will know that you are my disciples, if you have love for one another" (John 13:35).

Christian love leads to the peculiar exchange of gifts and suffering, of exaltation and humiliations, of defeat and victory; the individual is able through personal sacrifice and suffering to contribute to the development of the whole. All forms of ecclesiastical, political, and social communities of Christianity are founded on this basic idea of the fellowship of believers as the body of Christ. It also has influenced numerous secularized forms of Christian society, even among those that have forgotten or denied their Christian origins.

From the beginning, the commandment contains a certain tension concerning the answer to the question: Does it refer only to fellow Christians or to "all"? The practice of love of neighbour within the inner circle of the disciples was a conspicuous characteristic of the young church. In Christian congregations and, above all, in small fellowships and sects throughout the centuries, love of the neighbour was highly developed in terms of personal pastoral care, social welfare, and help in all situations of life.

The Christian commandment of love, however, has never been limited to fellow Christians. On the contrary, the Christian ethic crossed all social and religious barriers and saw a neighbour in every suffering human being. Characteristically, Jesus himself explicated his understanding of the commandment of love in the parable of the Good Samaritan, who followed the commandment of love and helped a person in need whom a priest and a Levite had chosen to ignore (Luke 10:29–37). A demand in the Letter of James, that the "royal law" of neighbourly love has to be fulfilled without "partiality" (James 2:9), points to its universal validity.

The universalism of the Christian command to love is most strongly expressed in its demand to love one's enemies. Jesus himself emphasized this with these words: "Love your enemies and pray for those who persecute you, so that you may be sons of your Father who is in heaven; for he makes his sun rise on the evil and on the good, and sends rain on the just and on the unjust" (Matthew 5:44–45). According to this understanding, love of the enemy is the immediate emission of God's love, which includes God's friends and God's enemies

FREEDOM AND RESPONSIBILITY

The Reformation revitalized a personal sense of Christian responsibility by anchoring it in the free forgiveness of sins. Luther summarized this in "The Freedom of a Christian Man" (1520): "A Christian is a perfectly free lord of all, subject to none. A Christian is a perfectly dutiful servant of all, subject to all." The second sentence expressed the theme of Christian vocation developed by Luther and Calvin, which they applied to all Christians and to everyday responsibility for the neighbour and for the world. The Reformers emphasized that Christian service is not limited to a narrow religious sphere of life but extends to the everyday relationships of family, marriage, work, and politics.

Later Protestantism under the influence of Pietism and Romanticism restricted the social and communal orientation of the Reformers to a more individualistic orientation. This met, however, with an energetic counterattack from the circles of the free churches (e.g., Baptists and Methodists) who supported the social task of Christian ethic (mainly through the Social Gospel of the American theologian Walter Rauschenbusch, who attempted to change social institutions and bring about a Kingdom of God), which spread through the whole church, penetrating the area of Christian mission. Love rooted in faith played an important role in the 20th century in the struggle between Christianity and ideologies such as Fascism, Communism, and jingoistic nationalisms.

CHAPTER 10

CATHOLIC CHURCHES

The term *catholic* means "universal." Although many Christian churches include the term in their names, the largest and best-known of these is the Roman Catholic Church, which claims an unbroken line of succession from the Apostles. Yet even this claimed continuity and unity features great diversity of practice. The Roman Catholic Church itself is in full communion with several smaller, national churches that feature customs and liturgies that differ from the broader stream of Roman Catholic tradition. These Eastern rite churches maintain traditions that developed apart from Roman influence, though their primary bishops maintain allegiance to the pope as the supreme temporal head of the "one, holy, catholic, and apostolic church." Further, there are some churches that not only call themselves "Catholic" but also claim to be more faithful representatives of the Apostles than the Roman church is. Since the First Vatican Council (1869–1870), these "Old Catholic churches" have presented an alternative vision of what constitutes Catholicism.

ROMAN CATHOLICISM

At one level, the interpretation of Roman Catholicism is closely related to the interpretation of Christianity as such. By its own reading of history, Roman Catholicism originated with the very beginnings of Christianity. Its adherents hold that the church has maintained an unbroken continuity since the days of the Apostles, while all other denominations are deviations from it.

BELIEFS AND PRACTICES

Roman Catholicism is a living, vibrant tradition that counts one-sixth of the world's population as its adherents. Roman Catholics in the world outnumber all other Christians combined. In order to understand how the traditions shape the lives of Catholics worldwide, one needs a general knowledge of the beliefs that constitute the Roman Catholic faith and the practices that structure and enhance the spiritual experiences of believers.

CONCEPTS OF FAITH

Well before modern theologians considered the meaning of faith, Christian thinkers, beginning with Paul and the Evangelists, sought to explain faith. In the Synoptic Gospels, God was the object of faith, and faith itself was belief in Jesus as the Messiah and Son of God. The apostle Paul taught that faith meant belief in Christ and the preaching of Christ, which is the word of God, as well as obedience to Christ. Faith also was the key to salvation, and as such it offered confidence in the reconciliation with God. For John, faith was inspired by miracles and was knowledge of Jesus as the Messiah. The Apologists and other early writers commented on faith, but the most influential discussion of faith was that of Augustine, for whom faith was the acceptance of revelation and the freely given gift of God. This idea was developed and given official sanction at the second Council of Orange (529), which declared that the beginning and even the desire of faith was the result of the gift of grace. In the 13th century St. Thomas Aquinas defined faith as an intellectual assent to divine truth by the command of the will inspired by grace and the authority of God. Aquinas's definition was made canonical by the Council of Trent and Vatican I. The fathers at Vatican II confirmed this understanding of faith in the dogmatic constitution *Dei verbum* (Nov. 18, 1965; "The Word of God"), which declared that faith must be preceded and assisted by "the grace of God and the interior help of the Holy Spirit." Vatican II stressed that both the bestowal of grace and the human response to it are free acts.

PREAMBLES AND MOTIVATION OF FAITH

Two subjects are key to understanding Catholic faith: the preambles of faith and the motivation of faith. The preambles of faith include those rational steps through which the believer reaches the conclusion that belief in God is reasonable. The freedom of faith is respected by affirming that such a conclusion is as far as the preambles can take one. That is, the preambles show that there is good evidence for the existence of God and that belief in God is reasonable, but

SECOND VATICAN COUNCIL

The Second Vatican Council was the 21st ecumenical council of the Roman Catholic Church (1962–65). It was announced by Pope John XXIII on Jan. 25, 1959, as a means of spiritual renewal for the church and as an occasion for Christians separated from Rome to join in search for reunion. Preparatory commissions appointed by the Pope prepared an agenda and produced drafts (schemata) of decrees on various topics. In opening the council on Oct. 11, 1962, the Pope advised the council fathers to try to meet the pastoral needs of the church. Those summoned to the council included all Catholic bishops and certain other church dignitaries. Invited to the council sessions, but without the right to vote, were a number of observers from the major Christian churches and communities separated from Rome and a number of Catholics called auditors. The work of the council continued under Pope John's successor, Paul VI, and sessions were convened each autumn until the work of the council was completed on Dec. 8, 1965. Sixteen documents were enacted by the council fathers.

The "Dogmatic Constitution on the Church" reflects the attempt of the council fathers to utilize biblical terms rather than juridical categories to describe the church. The treatment of the hierarchical structure of the church counterbalances somewhat the monarchical emphasis of the First Vatican Council's teaching on the papacy by giving weight to the role of the bishops. The teaching of the constitution on the nature of the laity (those not in holy orders) was intended to provide the basis for the call of lay people to holiness and to share in the missionary vocation of the church. By describing the church as the people of God, a pilgrim people, the council fathers provided the theological justification for changing the defensive and inflexible stance that had characterized much of Catholic thought and practice since the Protestant Reformation.

The "Dogmatic Constitution on Divine Revelation" attempts to relate the role of Scripture and tradition (the postbiblical teaching of the church) to their common origin in the Word of God that has been committed to the church. The document affirms the value of Scripture for the salvation of men while maintaining an open attitude toward the scholarly study of the Bible.

The "Constitution on the Sacred Liturgy" establishes the principle of greater participation by the laity in the celebration of mass and authorizes significant changes in the texts, forms, and language used in the celebration of mass and the administration of the sacraments.

The "Pastoral Constitution on the Church in the World of Today" acknowledges the profound changes humanity is experiencing and attempts to relate the church's concept of itself and of revelation to the needs and values of contemporary culture.

The council also promulgated decrees (documents on practical questions) on the pastoral duties of bishops, ecumenism, the Eastern rite churches, the ministry and life of priests, the education for the priesthood, the religious life, the missionary activity of the church, the apostolate of the laity, and the media of social communication. Furthermore, declarations (documents on particular issues) on religious freedom, the church's attitude toward non-Christian religions, and on Christian education were produced. The impulse of the documents and the council deliberations in general had by the early 1970s been felt in nearly every area of church life and had set in motion many changes that may not have been foreseen by the council fathers.

they cannot establish God's existence with absolute certainty or beyond rational doubt. Thus, the preambles leave one free to accept faith or to reject it.

Traditional approaches to the preambles include the study of the scientific and historical difficulties raised against the Christian fact itself (i.e., the Incarnation, Resurrection, Ascension, and glorification of Jesus Christ), against the Roman Catholic interpretation and proclamation of the Christian fact, or against the Roman Catholic claim to be the exclusive custodian of revealed doctrine and the means of salvation. In their earlier forms, these studies attempted to show that faith is the necessary result of a purely rational process. But a faith that proceeds necessarily from reason alone can be neither free nor the result of grace.

The study of the motivation of faith attempted to meet this difficulty. Some analyses presented faith as resting solely on evidence and clumsily postulated a movement of grace necessary to assent to it. Normally, however, one "wills" to believe something only in cases where the evidence for the belief is less than rationally compelling. Ultimately, the Roman Catholic analysis must say that the evidence that belief is reasonable can never be so clear and convincing that it compels one to believe on rational grounds alone. At this point, the will inspired by grace chooses to accept revelation for reasons other than the evidence.

The motive of faith that has been presented by Catholic theologians is "the authority of God revealing." It is held that the preambles of faith show that it is reasonable to believe that God exists and that he has revealed himself. This evidence, together with an acceptance of the notion that, if God reveals himself, he does so authoritatively (i.e., through church authorities), motivates a person to make the act of faith. The problem with such an analysis has been to define how the authority of the revealer is manifest to the believer. It seems that the notion of the authority of God revealing must be an object of faith rather than a motive, because the believer cannot ever experience the conjunction of this authority together with the fact of revelation. This dilemma caused an increasing number of Catholic theologians to move closer to a view that emphasizes faith as a personal commitment to God rather than as an assent to revealed truth.

MAJOR DOGMAS AND DOCTRINES

The Roman Catholic Church in its formula of baptism still asks that the parents and godparents of infants to be baptized recite the Apostles' Creed as a sign that they accept the basic doctrines of the church and will help their children grow in the Catholic faith. The creed proclaims belief in the Holy Trinity; the Incarnation, Passion, and Resurrection of Christ; the coming judgment of Christ; the remission of sins; the church; and eternal life. The early Church Fathers made the creed the basis of the baptismal homilies given to catechumens, or those preparing for the rite. The homilies, like modern Roman Catholic doctrine, went considerably beyond the bare articles of the creed.

Roman Catholic faith incorporates into its structure the books of the Hebrew Bible, or Old Testament. From these books it derives its belief in original sin, conceived of as a hereditary and universal moral defect of human beings that makes them incapable of achieving their destiny and even incapable of basic decency. The importance of this doctrine lies in its explanation of the human condition as caused by human and not by divine failure (nor, in modern Roman Catholic theology, by diabolical influence). Humankind can be delivered from its debased condition only by a saving act of God—the death and Resurrection of Jesus. In Jesus, God is revealed as the Father who sends the Son on his saving mission, and through the Son the Spirit comes to dwell in the redeemed. Thus, the Trinity of persons is revealed, and the destiny of man is to share the divine life of the three persons of the Trinity. The saving act of Jesus introduces grace, which in Roman Catholic belief signifies both the love of God and the effect produced in human beings by his love. (The theological idea of grace has been hotly disputed.) The response of believers to the presence of grace is the three theological virtues of faith, hope, and charity; these enable them to live the Christian life. Human beings are introduced to grace and initiated into the church by baptism, and the life of grace is sustained in the church by the sacraments.

The life of grace reaches its fulfillment in eschatology. In this area of belief about the end of the world and "the last things," modern theology rejects the physical rewards and punishments that were central to earlier belief and so vividly depicted by Dante. Most theologians recognize the allegorical character of most of the traditional imagery of heaven, hell, and purgatory, and the church's catechism identifies separation from God as the greatest punishment of the "eternal fire" of hell. Judgment itself is both personal and general, according to the church. Every individual will be judged according to his faith and works immediately after death, but Christ will also

The Last Judgment, *fresco by Michelangelo, 1533–41; in the Sistine Chapel, Vatican City. 14.5 x 13.5 m. SCALA/Art Resource, New York*

come to judge the living and the dead at the end of time. Central to Catholic eschatology is belief in the resurrection of the body, which for Roman Catholics, as for all Christians, is confirmed by the bodily Resurrection of Jesus. Indeed, the importance of the Ascension of Christ in his flesh was noted in the Gospels and the letters of Paul the Apostle.

TRADITION AND SCRIPTURE

In Roman Catholic theology, tradition is understood both as channel and as content. As channel it is identical with the living teaching authority of the Catholic church. As content it is "the deposit of faith," the revealed truth concerning faith and morals. In Roman Catholic belief, revelation ends with the death of the Apostles; the deposit was transmitted to the college of bishops, which succeeded the Apostles.

The Roman Catholic Church recognizes that the Bible is the word of God and that tradition is the word of the church. In one sense, therefore, tradition yields to the Scriptures in dignity and authority. But against the Protestant slogan of *sola Scriptura* ("Scripture alone"), itself subject to misinterpretation, the Roman Catholic Church advanced the argument that the church existed before the New Testament. In fact, the church both produced and authenticated the New Testament as the word of God. For this belief, at least, tradition is the exclusive source. This belief also furnished a warrant for the Catholic affirmation of the body of truth that is

"St. Matthew," page from the Ada Codex, *c. 890; in the Stadtbibliothek Trier, Germany (MS. 22, fol. 15r).* Courtesy of the Stadtbibliothek Trier, Ger.

transmitted to the church through the college of bishops and preserved by oral tradition (meaning that it was not written in the Scriptures). The Roman church therefore affirmed its right to determine what it believed by consulting its own beliefs as well as the Scriptures. The Council of Trent affirmed that the deposit of faith was preserved in the Scriptures and in unwritten traditions and that the Catholic church accepts these two with equal reverence. The council studiously avoided the statement that they meant these "two" as two sources of the deposit, but most Catholic theologians after the council understood the statement as meaning two sources. Some Protestants thought it meant that the Roman Catholic Church had written a second Bible.

In contemporary Catholic theology this question has been raised again, and a number of theologians now believe that Scripture and tradition must be viewed as one source. They are, however, faced with the problem of nonbiblical articles of faith. To this problem several remarks are pertinent. The first is that no Protestant church preaches "pure" gospel; all of them have developed dogmatic traditions, concerning which they have differed vigorously. It is true, however, that they do not treat these traditions "with equal devotion and reverence" with the Bible. The second remark is that, through the first eight ecumenical councils (before the Schism of 1054), the Christian church arrived at nonbiblical formulas to profess its faith. Protestants respond that this is at least a matter of degree and that the consubstantiality of the Son (i.e., his being of the same substance as the Father), defined by the Council of Nicaea, is more faithful to the Scriptures than the Assumption of Mary, which was defined as dogma by Pius XII in 1950.

Roman Catholics and Protestants should be able to reach some consensus that tradition and Scripture mean the reading of the Bible in church. Protestants never claimed that a person and his Bible made a self-sufficient Christian church. The New Testament itself demands that the word be proclaimed and heard in a church, and the community is formed on a common understanding of the word "proclaimed." This suggests a way toward a Christian consensus on the necessity and function of tradition. No church pretends to treat its own history as nonexistent or unimportant. By reading the Scriptures in the light of its own beliefs, the church is able to address itself to new problems of faith and morals that did not exist or were not attended to in earlier times.

Catholic theologians of the 19th century dealt with this problem under the heading of the development of dogma. To a certain extent the question is an epistemological one: Is a new understanding of an ancient truth a "new" truth? It is important to note that the problem of the development of dogma does not arise out of faith. Thus, Sir Isaac Newton's observations of falling bodies consisted of nothing that people had not seen for thousands of years, yet his insights profoundly altered our understanding of the universe. The problem is important in theology because of the necessity of basing belief on the historical event of the revelation of God in Christ. Unless this link is maintained, the church is teaching philosophy and science, not dogma. Hence, Roman Catholic theology has tended to say that dogma develops through new understanding, not through new discoveries.

SACRAMENTS

In Roman Catholic theology a sacrament is an outward sign instituted by

Jesus Christ that is productive of inner grace. The number of sacraments varied throughout much of the first millennium of Christian history, as did the definition of the term *sacrament* itself. After extensive theological discussion during this period, church leaders in the 11th and 12th centuries decided upon seven as the exact number of sacraments. They are baptism, confirmation, the Eucharist, penance (reconciliation), anointing of the sick, marriage, and holy orders. This number was confirmed by the Council of Trent against the Protestant Reformers, who maintained that there were only two sacraments.

The sacrament in modern theology is frequently described as an encounter with mystery, the mystery being the saving act of God in Christ, and theological studies have explored the ideas of sign and significance. The traditional Roman Catholic view of the effectiveness of the sacraments (as defined by the Council of Trent) is described by the phrase *ex opere operato* ("from the work done"), which is best explained briefly by saying that the faith and virtue of the minister neither add to the sacrament by their presence nor detract from it by their absence. The minister is merely the agent of the church, and the effectiveness of the sacrament is based on the saving act of God in Christ, which is signified by the rite and applied to the recipient of the sacrament.

The theological explanation of the sign that effects by signifying is not easily communicated and has often been criticized by those outside the church.

Roman Catholic theologians remark, however, that the mystery of God's saving act is not capable of complete rational explanation, though there are analogies in common experience. Indeed, there is no society that does not employ effective signs. The inauguration of the president of the United States, for example, is an effective sign in the sense that the ceremony results in the oath taker becoming president. The sign of the coronation of a monarch is similarly effective.

Traditionally, the church attributes the institution of the sign to Jesus Christ (though this has been the subject of discussion among modern theologians), which removes the right of anyone to tamper with it. The Roman Catholic Church believes that, if God gives a sign, alteration of the sign might cause it to lose its significance or otherwise render it ineffective. Hence, the proper material and the traditional formula are treated as sacred. Since Aquinas, the material used is called "matter" and the words are called "form"; the terms are borrowed from Aristotelian metaphysics. The material becomes sacred and salutary only by its conjunction with the proper words. The effect produced has for centuries been called "grace."

The term *sacramental* is used to designate verbal formulas (such as blessings) or objects (such as holy water or medals) to which a religious significance has been attached. These are symbols of personal prayer and dedication, and their effectiveness is measured by the particular dispositions of the person who uses them.

BAPTISM

Baptism is the sacrament of regeneration and initiation into the church that was begun by Jesus, who accepted baptism from John the Baptist and also ordered the Apostles to baptize in the name of the Father, the Son, and the Holy Spirit (Matthew 28:19). According to the teaching of St. Paul, which draws an analogy with the death and Resurrection of Jesus, baptism is death to a former life and the emergence of a new person, which is signified by the outward sign of water (Catholic baptism involves pouring or sprinkling water over the candidate's head). Baptism is understood, therefore, as the total annulment of the sins of one's past and the emergence of a totally innocent person. The newly baptized person becomes a member of the church and is incorporated into the body of Christ, thus becoming empowered to lead the life of Christ. Nothing but pure natural water may be used, and baptism must be conferred, as Jesus taught, in the name of the Father, the Son, and the Holy Spirit. Baptism is normally conferred by a priest, but the Roman Catholic Church accepts baptism conferred in an emergency by anyone, Catholic or non-Catholic, having the use of reason "with the intention of doing what the church does." In the spirit of Vatican II, which acknowledged the validity of any baptism that is "duly administered as Our Lord instituted it" (*Unitatis redintegratio* ["The Restoration of Unity"]; Nov.

Baptism of Christ, page from the Benedictional of St. Aethelwold *(folio 25), Anglo-Saxon, Winchester School, c. 963–984; in the British Library.* Reproduced by permission of the British Library

21, 1964), the church has recognized as valid the baptisms of a wide range of non-Catholic churches.

As the sacrament of rebirth, in which the baptized person is made new and permanently sealed with the spiritual mark of belonging to Christ, baptism cannot be repeated. The Roman Catholic Church baptizes conditionally in cases of serious doubt of the fact of baptism or the use of the proper rite, but it no longer approves of the conditional baptism of miscarried or stillborn infants.

Two points of controversy still exist in modern times. One is baptism by pouring or sprinkling water on the head rather than by immersion of the entire body, even though immersion was probably the biblical and early Christian rite. The change almost certainly occurred during the spread of Christianity into Europe north of the Alps and the usual occurrence in early spring of the baptismal feasts, Easter and Pentecost. The Roman Catholic Church simply asserts that the symbolism of the bath is preserved by a ritual infusion of water.

The second point of controversy concerns the baptism of infants. There is no certain evidence of this practice earlier than the 2nd century, and the ancient baptismal liturgies are all intended for adults. There is, however, extensive testimony suggesting the introduction of infant baptism as early as the 1st century. The apostle Paul compares baptism with circumcision, the Jewish rite initiating male infants into the religious community. Other early Christian writers provide evidence of the practice: Tertullian rejected it, thus suggesting its widespread use, and Origen spoke of infant baptism as an established practice. It became the norm by the 4th century and remained so until the 16th century, when various Protestant groups rejected it. It remains the practice of the Roman Catholic Church and most mainline Protestant churches.

The long-standing liturgy of infant baptism, however, indicates the importance of an independent adult decision; without this decision the sacrament cannot be received. The Roman Catholic Church accepts this principle by introducing adults (sponsors, godparents), who make the decision for the infant at the commission of the parents and are given the responsibility of ensuring the child's Christian upbringing. The responsibilities of parents and godparents have received great emphasis in the church's rite of baptism for children, which was first promulgated in 1969 and subsequently revised. It is expected that, when they grow up, children who have been baptized will accept the decision made for them and will thus fulfill and validate the adult decision that was presumed.

Let the children come to me; do not prevent them, for the kingdom of God belongs to such as these. (Mark 10:14)

THE EUCHARIST

The Eucharist (from the Greek for "thanksgiving") is the central act of Christian worship; also known as Holy Communion and the Lord's Supper, it is practiced by most Christian churches in some form. Along with baptism it is one of the two sacraments most clearly found in the New Testament, and along with baptism and confirmation it is one of the sacraments of initiation. The Roman Catholic Church distinguishes the Eucharist as sacrifice (mass) and sacrament (communion).

The rite was instituted by Jesus and is recorded in the Synoptic Gospels (Matthew, Mark, and Luke) and in

Last Supper, *fresco by Domenico Ghirlandajo, 1480; in the Church of Ognissanti, Florence.* SCALA/Art Resource, New York

the letters of Paul. According to the Evangelists' account, Jesus established the practice at the Last Supper, a traditional Passover seder, when he blessed the bread, which he said was his body, and shared it with his disciples. He then shared a cup of wine with his disciples and told them "this is the blood of my covenant, which is poured out for many." According to the Evangelist Luke, Jesus called on his followers to repeat the ceremony in his memory, and it is clear that the earliest Christians regularly enacted it. Originally, the Eucharist was a repetition of the common meal of the local group of disciples with the addition of the bread and the cup signifying the presence of Jesus. During the 2nd century the meal became vestigial and was finally abandoned. The Eucharist was originally celebrated every Sunday; by the 4th century it was celebrated daily. The eucharistic formula was set in a framework of biblical readings, psalms, hymns, and prayers that depended in form somewhat on the synagogue service. This remained one basis of the various liturgies that arose, including the Roman rite.

The sacrificial character of the Eucharist is derived from the sacrament's relation to the death of Jesus. According to the Gospel accounts, Jesus spoke of himself as a sacrifice, possibly foreshadowing his imminent sacrifice on the cross. He used bread and wine to symbolize his body and blood, possibly reflecting contemporary Jewish usage of bread and wine as sacrificial elements, and gave them to his disciples so that they could share in his sacrifice. The theme is clearly elaborated on in Paul's Letter to the Hebrews, and the sacrificial character of the Eucharist was widely accepted by the early Christians. Roman Catholic theology preserves the early understanding of the Eucharist as a sacrifice in its teaching on the mass, and it has firmly insisted that the mass repeats the rite that Jesus told his disciples to repeat. The rite is the memorial of the original sacrifice of Christ. It is an effective commemoration of his death that also makes present the sacrifice on the cross; during the mass

the same Christ who offered himself once in a bloody manner on the altar of the cross is contained and offered in an unbloody manner. (Catechism of the Catholic Church; 1992)

Roman Catholics believe in the real presence, an issue that has dominated Catholic-Protestant controversies about Holy Communion. The celebrated term *transubstantiation* is defined as the change of the substance of bread and wine into the substance of the body and blood of Jesus Christ, even though the physical appearance of the offering remains unchanged. Roman Catholic teaching, which was developed during the Middle Ages and supported by later councils and popes such as Paul VI, applies Aristotelian categories to explain the mystery of Christ's literal presence in the sacramental bread and wine. This teaching of the real presence is intended to emphasize the intimate relationship

between Jesus and the communicant. Although Catholic theologians developed new ways to interpret the mystery of the sacrament of the Eucharist in the period after Vatican II, the doctrine of transubstantiation remains the fundamental understanding of all Catholics.

As a result of Vatican II, the church sought to restore to the Eucharist the symbolism of Christian unity that the sacrament clearly has in the New Testament. Originally, the symbolism was that of a community meal, an accepted symbol of community throughout the whole of human culture. Roman Catholic efforts to restore this symbolism have included the use of the vernacular and the active participation of the laity. As a means of symbolizing unity, the ancient rite of concelebration—i.e., several priests or bishops jointly celebrating a single eucharistic liturgy—was restored by Vatican II, which also emphasized the corporate nature of communion as well as the important role of the laity in eucharistic celebrations. The practice of celebrating the Eucharist in an informal setting—i.e., in private homes or classrooms—was instituted in some places as a way of drawing the laity more intimately into the rite.

Church law obliges Roman Catholics to receive Holy Communion at least once a year (during the Lent-Easter season) but encourages them to take it at mass every Sunday, on feast days, and even every day. In this way the faithful can receive the many benefits of the Eucharist. In addition to strengthening community, frequent communion also strengthens contact with Jesus Christ and allows the faithful to participate in Jesus's sacrificial work. Finally, the Eucharist focuses attention on the ultimate goal, the return of Jesus Christ. Communion is the anticipation of the coming glory of heaven.

CONFIRMATION

A sacrament that is conferred through the anointing with oil and the imposition of hands, confirmation is believed to strengthen or confirm the grace bestowed by the Holy Spirit at baptism. Apostolic precedent for the sacrament has been found in the Acts of the Apostles, chapters 8 and 19, in which Peter and Paul on separate occasions put their hands on already-baptized Christians to confer on them the gifts of the Holy Spirit. The sacrament was originally administered as part of baptism, as it still is in Orthodox churches, but gradually evolved into a distinct sacrament. As a result of its detachment from baptism, confirmation came to be delayed until later in life, so that in the modern church the minimum age for receiving it is seven; many dioceses, however, have established an older minimum age. The postponement of confirmation has led many Roman Catholic theologians to interpret it as a rite of passage from childhood, like the Jewish bar mitzvah ceremony. It is also understood as a rite in which Christians can confirm the commitment to the church made for them at baptism.

The confirmation rite is a relatively simple ceremony that is traditionally performed during the mass by the bishop, though modern liturgical renewal has empowered pastors of parishes to confer confirmation. The service includes a homily, usually on the meaning of the sacrament, followed by the renewal of the vows of baptism by the confirmands. The bishop raises his hands over those taking confirmation and prays for the bestowal of the sevenfold gift of the Holy Spirit (according to Isaiah 11:2–3, wisdom, understanding, counsel, strength, knowledge, piety, and fear of the Lord). He then anoints the forehead of each confirmand with chrism (holy oil consecrated at the Maundy Thursday service) and says *Accipe signaculum doni Spiritus Sancti* ("Be sealed with the gifts of the Holy Spirit"). The rite concludes with the eucharistic service and blessing of the congregation. The recipient of confirmation, who is presented by a sponsor of the same sex, traditionally takes a "confirmation name" that will remind the confirmand of this sacrament. Many confirmands choose the name of a saint whose qualities they admire.

RECONCILIATION

The name of the fourth sacrament, reconciliation, or penance as it was once known, reflects the practice of restoring sinners to the community of the faithful that was associated with the earliest discipline of the penitential rite. Those who sinned seriously were excluded from

Holy Communion until they showed repentance by undergoing a period of trial that included fasting, public humiliation, the wearing of sackcloth, and other austerities. At the end of the period, they were publicly reconciled to the church. Although there were some sins, called mortal sins—e.g., murder, adultery, and apostasy—for which certain local churches at certain times did not perform the rite, this did not mean that God did not forgive but only that good standing in the church was permanently lost. Elsewhere it was believed that the rite of penance could be performed only once; relapsed sinners lost good standing permanently. Rigorist sects that denied the power to forgive certain sins were regarded as heretical. The penitential rite involving strict discipline did not endure beyond the early Middle Ages, and there can be no doubt that it was too rigorous for most Christians. In the opinion of many, it did not reflect the forgiveness of Jesus in the Gospels with all fidelity.

It is impossible to assign an exact date of origin for "auricular confession"—i.e., the confessing of faults by an individual penitent to a priest—but it was most likely developed in the 6th century by Irish monks and introduced to the Continent later by Irish and Anglo-Saxon monks. This is the penitential rite that has endured into modern times. It was rejected by most of the Reformers on the ground that God alone can forgive sins. The Roman Catholic Church claims that the absolution of the priest is an act of forgiveness; to receive it, the penitent must confess all

serious (mortal) sins and manifest genuine "contrition," or sorrow for sins, and a reasonably firm purpose to make amends. Following Vatican II, the church began to emphasize penance as a process of reconciliation with the church and as a means of obtaining pardon from God. The priest is seen as a healer aiding in the process, and the penitent sinner is called to conversion and correction of his or her life.

Indulgences, which caused such controversy at the beginning of the Reformation, represent neither instant forgiveness to the unrepentant nor licenses of sin to the habitual sinner. Rather, they are declarations that the church accepts certain prayers and good works, listed in an official publication, as the equivalent of the rigorous penances of the ancient discipline.

ANOINTING OF THE SICK

This sacrament was long known in English as "extreme unction," literally rendered from its Latin name, *unctio extrema*, meaning "last anointing." It is conferred by anointing the forehead and hands with blessed oil and pronouncing a formula. It may be conferred only on those who are seriously ill. Seriousness is measured by the danger of death, but imminent death, however certain, from external causes—such as the execution of a death sentence—does not render one apt for the sacrament. It may be administered only once during the same illness; recovery renders one apt again. Its effects are described as the strengthening of both soul and body. An ancient rite that continues Jesus's ministry of healing, the sacrament is directed against "the remains of sin." Although this is a poorly defined phrase, it was long ago recognized that serious illness saps one's spiritual resources as well as one's physical strength so that one is not able to meet the crisis of mortal danger with all one's powers. In popular belief, anointing is most valuable as a complement to confession or—in case of unconsciousness—as a substitute for it.

Anointing is not the sacrament of the dying—it is the sacrament of the sick. The New Testament passage to which the Roman Catholic Church appeals for this rite (James 5:14–15) does not envisage a person beyond recovery. Postponement until the patient is critically ill (in modern medical terms) means that the sacrament is often administered to unconscious or heavily sedated patients even though the church urges that the sacrament be given, if possible, while the person is still conscious.

MARRIAGE

The inclusion of marriage among the sacraments gives the Roman Catholic Church jurisdiction over an institution that is of as much concern to the state as it is to the church. The church claims complete jurisdiction over the marriages of its members, even though it is unable to urge this jurisdiction in modern secular states. The sacrament in Roman Catholic teaching is administered by

the spouses through the exchange of consent. The priest, whose presence is required, is an authorized official witness; in addition, the church requires two other witnesses. Marriage is safeguarded by a number of impediments that render the marriage null whether they are known or not, and the freedom of the spouses must be assured. This means that the Roman Catholic Church demands an unusually rigorous examination before the marriage, and this in turn means that it is practically impossible to marry on impulse in the Catholic church. All of this is for the purpose of assuring that the marriage so contracted will not be declared null in the future because of some defect.

The rigid Roman Catholic rejection of divorce, which is based on the teachings of Jesus, has been a major cause of hostility toward the church in the modern world. Absolute indissolubility is declared only of the marriage of two baptized persons (Protestants as well as Catholics). The same indissolubility is not declared of marriages of the unbaptized, but the Roman church recognizes no religious or civil authority except itself that is empowered to dissolve such marriages; this claim is extremely limited and is not used unless a Roman Catholic is involved. Declarations of nullity, however, should not be confused with divorce nor be thought of as a substitute for divorce.

The onerous conditions that Roman Catholicism formerly imposed upon non-Catholic partners in "mixed" marriages have been relaxed significantly since Vatican II, particularly as regards written promises that the children will receive religious education in the Roman Catholic faith. The church's former rigidity toward such marriages has also largely disappeared. They may now be celebrated in church during the mass, and a Protestant minister or a Jewish rabbi may share the witness function with the priest.

HOLY ORDERS

This sacrament confers upon candidates the power over the sacred, which means the power to administer the sacraments. The Latin church had long recognized four minor orders (porter, lector, exorcist, acolyte) and four major orders (subdeacon, deacon, priest, bishop). The minor orders represented church services rendered by persons not ordained. In 1972 Pope Paul VI issued the apostolic letter *Ministeria quaedam* ("Certain Ministries"), which abolished the major order of subdeacon and all minor orders and created the lay liturgical ministries of lector and acolyte. Only the major orders are held to be sacramental, but they are regarded as one sacrament within which a tripartite hierarchy of sacramental effects is administered separately. Ordination is conferred only by the bishop; the rite includes the imposition of hands, anointing, and delivery of the symbols of the order. The power of the sacred peculiar to the bishop is shown only in the sacraments of confirmation and orders. Ordination can neither be repeated nor annulled. Priests who are suspended

from priestly powers or laicized (permanently authorized to live as laymen) retain their sacred power but are forbidden to exercise it except in emergencies. The priest is always ordained to a "title," meaning that he is accepted in some ecclesiastical jurisdiction. Lectors and acolytes are instituted by a bishop or by the major superior of a clerical religious institute. Following a calling of the candidates, instruction, and prayer, lectors are presented with a Bible and acolytes with a vessel with bread or wine.

Following Vatican II, much theological discussion was devoted to such issues as the ordination of women, which is a divisive issue within the church and between the church and other Christian denominations. Catholic women do serve in various roles, as lectors, eucharistic ministers, even marriage tribunal officers and altar servers, and a large number of women are lay chaplains. Many traditionalist Catholics, however, have seen the advent of altar girls in 1994 as merely the first salvo in the battle for the complete ordination of women, and John Paul II made it clear to dioceses and bishops that they are under no pressure to use altar girls. Some nuns have also pushed for a larger role in a more "inclusive" church; some of them have even gathered in groups to administer the Eucharist to one another. Other controversial suggestions include the restoration of the permanent diaconate (with the powers to baptize, preach, and administer the Eucharist), to which both married and single men are admitted, and the idea of ordination for

Newly ordained deacons prostate in front of Pope Benedict XVI in St. Peter's basilica in the Vatican, June 20, 2010. The pontiff celebrated a mass for priestly ordination of the deacons of the Roman diocese. Tiziana Fabi/AFP/Getty Images

a fixed period of service. Except for the diaconate, these are radical suggestions in Roman Catholicism.

ORDER OF THE MASS

Catholics are expected to attend mass each Sunday and on various holy days of obligation designated by the church. The mass itself is highly structured and can be difficult for non-Catholics to follow. Typically lasting about an hour, sometimes longer, the mass is generally divided into two parts, the liturgy of the Word and the liturgy of the Eucharist, but in reality five distinct phases are discernable: the introductory rites, the liturgy of the Word, the liturgy of the Eucharist, the communion rite, and the concluding rite. Catholics must stand, sit, kneel, bow,

and make the sign of the cross at various points throughout the mass. Variations in the order of the mass (discussed below) are common depending on certain circumstances and the time of year.

THE INTRODUCTORY RITES

A typical Sunday mass begins with an entrance song, during which the priest, deacon, and ministers, and sometimes altar servers (both altar boys and girls are permissible), lectors, and lay eucharistic ministers (who assist in administering Holy Communion) process to the altar. The priest and deacon then kiss the altar. After greeting the congregation, the priest asks the people to recall their sins and to repent by reciting the penitential rite ("I confess to almighty God...") or a version of it. Unless it is included in the penitential rite, the Kyrie is then spoken ("Lord, have mercy...") followed (except during Christmas and Lent) by the Gloria, an ancient hymn of praise ("Glory to God in the highest, and peace to his people on earth..."). The priest then delivers the opening prayer, to which the congregation responds with "Amen" ("So be it"), thus concluding the first part of mass.

THE LITURGY OF THE WORD

The second phase of the mass, the liturgy of the Word, typically consists of three readings: a reading from the Old Testament, a non-Gospel reading from the New Testament, and a reading from the Gospels; the first two readings are done by a lector (a lay reader), and the Gospel is proclaimed by the deacon. A responsorial psalm and a Gospel acclamation divide the three readings. The priest then delivers the homily, which usually focuses on one of the readings or on that day's special occasion. The public profession of faith follows, which means reciting either the Nicene Creed or the shorter Apostles' Creed. Ending the liturgy of the Word are the general intercessions (the "prayer of the faithful"), in which petitions are offered for the "holy Church, for the civil authorities, for those oppressed by various needs, for all mankind, and for the salvation of the entire world." Specific prayers may also be extended to couples recently married in the church, to persons ordained or confirmed in the church, or to members of the church suffering illness or bereavement.

THE LITURGY OF THE EUCHARIST

The third part of mass, the liturgy of the Eucharist, is the high point of the celebration. While the gifts (donations) of the people are being gathered and brought to the altar, an offertory song is typically sung. Meanwhile, the deacon and assistants prepare the altar. The priest washes his hands, and he offers a prayer of thanks to God (quietly or aloud, if no song is being sung) for the gifts of bread and wine that presently will be changed into Christ's body and blood. He then invites the people to pray that their sacrifice will be acceptable to God, whereupon the people repeat: "May the Lord accept the sacrifice at your hands for the praise and glory of his name, for our good, and the good of all his Church." The eucharistic prayer follows, in which the holiness of God is honoured, his servants are acknowledged, the Last Supper is recalled, and the bread and wine are consecrated. The host and chalice are then elevated into the air by the priest, who sings or recites: "Through him, with him, in him, in the unity of the Holy Spirit, all glory and honour is yours, almighty Father, forever and ever." The people respond with "Amen."

THE COMMUNION RITE

At the start of the communion rite, the priest calls on the people to pray the most universal of Christian prayers—the Lord's Prayer (the "Our Father," the Pater Noster)—whose author, according to the Gospels, was Christ himself. The prayer is said or sung, often while members of the congregation join hands:

> *Our Father, who art in heaven,*
> *Hallowed be thy name;*
> *Thy kingdom come;*
> *Thy will be done on earth as it is*
> *in heaven.*
> *Give us this day our daily bread;*
> *And forgive us our trespasses*
> *As we forgive those who trespass*
> *against us;*
> *And lead us not into temptation,*
> *But deliver us from evil.*

In divergence from Protestant practice, the Catholic church stops the prayer after "deliver us from evil," which is where the original prayer ended before an additional two lines (a doxology) were added about AD 100. At this pause in the prayer the priest says, "Deliver us, Lord, from every evil, and grant us peace in our day..." at which point the people in unison complete the final two lines of the prayer, saying, "For the kingdom, the power, and the glory are yours, now and forever." The deacon then asks members of the congregation to exchange a sign of peace with their neighbours to signify one family in Christ, an act which usually consists of a handshake or a nod while saying "Peace" or "Peace be with you." After the

priest prepares the bread and wine, the people exclaim: "Lord, I am not worthy to receive you but only say the word and I shall be healed." Once the priest has administered Holy Communion to his assistants, the people then file up to the altar, row by row, receiving the bread first (which is placed in their hands or on their tongues by the priest, deacon, or eucharistic minister) and the chalice of wine, if offered, second. (Communion offered in both kinds—bread and wine—has a long and complicated history; beginning in the 12th century, the chalice gradually came to be reserved for the priest alone. Though Communion under both kinds is now allowable at the discretion of the bishop, many churches offer both kinds to the priest's assistants at the altar but offer only the bread to the congregation at large; this is often done merely to ensure an "orderly" administering of Communion to the congregation, and the church teaches that the whole Christ is present in the individual elements of bread and wine.) Upon receiving Communion, the people then return to their seat and kneel in silent prayer while waiting for Communion to end.

THE CONCLUDING RITE

Once Holy Communion is completed and the altar has been cleared, the final part of mass follows: the concluding rite. The priest, after a period of silence for reflection on the "mystery" that has just occurred, offers a final greeting. Church announcements are typically made at this point, a final blessing is then offered, and the people are dismissed, encouraged to "go in peace to love and serve the Lord." Variations on the dismissal include "The mass is ended, go in peace," and "Go in the peace of Christ." Some parishes sing a final song, though this is not required according to the official order of the mass.

EASTERN RITE CHURCHES

An Eastern rite church, also called an Eastern Catholic Church, is any of a group of churches originating in Eastern Europe or in the Middle or Near East that trace their origins to various ancient national or ethnic Christian bodies but have established union or canonical communion with the Roman Apostolic See and, thus, with the Roman Catholic Church. In this union they accept the Roman Catholic faith, keep the seven sacraments, and recognize the pope of Rome as supreme head of the church. They retain, however, all other characteristics—e.g., liturgy, spirituality, sacred art, and especially organization—proper to themselves. The special status of the Catholic churches of the Eastern rite was guaranteed at the time of each rite's union with Rome and was approved again by the decree of the Second Vatican Council, in *De ecclesiis catholicis orientalibus,* promulgated on Nov. 21, 1964. In the late 20th century, the number of Eastern Catholics throughout the world numbered more than 12,000,000.

HISTORY

Eastern Catholics—in contrast to Western, or Latin, Catholics—trace their origins largely to the failure of the ecclesiastical authorities at the Council of Ferrara-Florence in 1439 to unite Christians of the East and West. Stimulated by this unsuccessful beginning, however, and encouraged also by the later missionary activities of such monastic orders as the Jesuits, Dominicans, Franciscans, and Capuchins, the proponents of the goal of the eventual reunion of Eastern and Western Christians began to achieve some elements of success.

The Brest-Litovsk Union of 1596—under which all but two Ukrainian Orthodox bishops accepted, at the demand of their Polish Catholic king, the primacy of the pope—in a substantial way signaled the effective advent of Eastern rite churches. Other smaller groups had united with Rome in previous centuries, but the Ukrainians who were united with Rome at this time were the largest branch of Eastern Catholics to move in that direction. The Union of Uzzhorod (Uzhgorod) in 1646 brought many Ruthenians (or Rusyns) under Rome when 63 Ruthenian Orthodox priests, who represented Ruthenians living under Catholic rule, accepted the authority of Rome while being allowed to maintain their liturgical language (Old Church Slavonic) and customs.

RELATIONSHIP TO OTHER CHURCHES

Eastern Catholic churches correspond in kind to the more numerous Eastern Orthodox churches and the Oriental Orthodox churches (which do not accept the decrees of the ecumenical Council of Chalcedon). Within this fuller context, Eastern Catholics as a group are the smallest segment within Eastern Christianity.

Furthermore, from the viewpoint of the Eastern Orthodox and Oriental Orthodox traditions, Eastern Catholics may be looked upon with suspicion, primarily because of the Latinizing influence found in their ranks. Hence the majority of Orthodox and Eastern independent churches characterize Eastern Catholics as "Uniate" churches. This term was coined by the opponents of the Brest-Litovsk Union. "Uniatism" implies hybridism, or the tendency for Latinization, and hence a betrayal of one's ancient, national tradition. Eastern rite churches would prefer to be considered as united churches rather than Uniate, with its negative implications.

Eastern rite churches make manifest the pluralistic composition of the Roman Catholic tradition. Eastern Catholic rites permit a married clergy and the immediate admission of baptized infants to the sacraments of Holy Communion (the Lord's Supper) and confirmation. In the "Decrees on the Catholic Churches of the Eastern Rite" adopted by the Second Vatican Council (1962–65), the Roman pontiff reaffirmed the pledge of his predecessors to preserve the rites of the Eastern churches. "All the Eastern Rite members should know and be convinced," states the decree, "that they can and should always preserve their legitimate liturgical rite and their established way of life, and that these may not be altered except to obtain for themselves an organic improvement." The Code of Canons of the Eastern Churches was promulgated by Pope John Paul II in 1990; it now complements the 1983 Code of Canon Law for the Latin church.

ORGANIZATION

The supreme head of the Eastern rite churches is the pope. The central organ of the Holy See for them is the Congregation for the Oriental Churches. The prefect of this congregation is the pope himself, and a cardinal proprefect performs the ordinary functions of chairman. The Congregation is competent for the Eastern churches in all matters (except certain specified cases) and has exclusive jurisdiction in specified countries in eastern Europe and the Middle East. The individual Eastern Catholic churches are organized differently according to their historical and ethnic situation, the number of adherents, the degree of evolution, and so on. The following organizational units are found.

Patriarchates comprise a certain number of dioceses of a single rite, under the jurisdiction of a patriarch.

The patriarchs, according to the Eastern canon law, have special rights and privileges; in the general hierarchy they rank with the cardinals according to seniority (following the titular cardinal bishops of the suburban sees of Rome) and before all other bishops. In the late 20th century there were six Eastern Catholic patriarchates, as follows: one of Alexandria, for the Copts; three of Antioch, one each for the Syrians, Maronites, and Greek Melkites; one of Babylonia, for the Chaldeans; and one of Sis, or Cilicia, for the Armenians. The patriarchs of Babylonia and of Sis are called *katholikos*.

Major archiepiscopates are those that govern a certain number of dioceses of their rite but whose territory has not yet been erected into a patriarchate.

Metropolitanates govern ecclesiastical provinces independent of the patriarchates and major archiepiscopates and comprise a number of dioceses. One of them is the metropolis; and its archbishop, the metropolitan, is the head of the whole metropolitanate.

Eparchies correspond to the Latin dioceses. Although they are usually subject to one of the aforementioned higher organizations, a few are immediately subject to the Holy See or to a Latin metropolitan see.

Exarchies correspond to vicariates, and their bishops govern not by ordinary jurisdiction but by delegated authority.

Apostolic administrations concern territories whose administration the Holy See, for certain reasons, has assumed temporarily, entrusting them to the care of a neighbouring bishop or an apostolic administrator.

Ordinariates are the lowest organizational units, found either at an early stage of development, such as a mission, or in small congregations. Usually the head is not a bishop.

THE RITES

The term *rite* in "Eastern Catholic rite" signifies not only liturgical ceremonies but the whole organization of particular churches. In the late 20th century, there were five distinct Eastern rite traditions—the Byzantine, the Alexandrian, the Antiochene, the Chaldean, and the Armenian—each (except the last) with two or more branches.

The Byzantine rite is by far the most significant, affecting the most persons and most territories worldwide (many of the faithful are in the Americas). Its liturgy is based on the rite of St. James of Jerusalem and the churches of Antioch, as reformed by St. Basil and St. John Chrysostom. The liturgy is used by the majority of Eastern Catholics and by the Eastern Orthodox Church (which is not in union with Rome). The Byzantine branches include the Albanians, Bulgarians, Belarusians, Georgians, Greeks, Greek Catholic Melkites, Hungarians, Italo-Albanians, Romanians, Russians, Ruthenians, Slovaks, Ukrainians (or Galician Ruthenians), and Yugoslavs, Serbs, and Croatians.

The Alexandrian rite is found among the Egyptians and the Ethiopians. Its

Coptic liturgy (known as the Liturgy of St. Mark) is derived from the Greek Liturgy of Alexandria, modified by several elements, including the Byzantine rite of St. Basil. Its two branches are the Copts (of Egypt) and the Ethiopians.

The Antiochene rite can be traced to Book 8 of the *Apostolic Constitutions* and to the Liturgy of St. James of Jerusalem. Its branches include the Maronites (constituting the largest single group of Eastern Catholics in the Middle East and throughout the world), the Syrians, and the Malankarese (of India).

The Chaldean rite, though derived from the Antiochene rite, is listed as a separate and distinct rite by the Sacred Congregation for the Eastern Churches. Its branches include the Chaldeans (descended from the Nestorians) and the Syro-Malabarese (descended from the St. Thomas Christians of India).

The Armenian rite, using the liturgical language of classical Armenian, is based on the Greek Liturgy of St. Basil, as modified by elements of the Antiochene rite. It consists of one group, the Armenians, found in the Middle East, Europe, Africa, the Americas, and Australasia.

OLD CATHOLIC CHURCHES

Standing outside the ecclesial jurisdiction of the Roman Catholic Church are several groups of Western Christians who believe themselves to maintain in complete loyalty the doctrine and traditions of the undivided church. These "Old Catholic churches" separated from the see of Rome after the First Vatican Council of 1869–70. Their organizational structures vary, and some of them resemble Protestant denominations rather than Roman Catholicism.

ORIGINS

The promulgation of the doctrine of the infallibility of the pope by the First Vatican Council triggered hostility among some theologians, clergymen, and lay parishioners. The German bishop and church historian J.J.I. von Döllinger refused to assent to the decision of the council and was excommunicated by name. Although he took no part in forming separatist churches, his advice and guidance helped the Old Catholic churches come into being in a number of countries—Germany, Switzerland, Austria, and elsewhere. As no bishop had joined any of these groups, recourse was had to the Jansenist church in Holland, which had maintained a somewhat precarious existence in separation from Rome since the 18th century but had preserved an episcopal succession recognized by Rome as valid though irregular.

The first consecration of the new order was that of Joseph H. Reinkens, who was made bishop in Germany by a sympathetic bishop of the Jansenist Church of Holland, Bishop Heykamp of Deventer, on Aug. 11, 1873. Rather later and for similar reasons, though with a certain national emphasis, the Polish National Catholic Church—an American and Canadian church serving Polish

A Lebanese woman prays February 8, 2004, at the Maronite church of Saint Sharbel in the moun-tain village of Ennaya, northeast of Beirut. Joseph Barrak/AFP/Getty Images

immigrants—was founded in Scranton, Pa., U.S., with Franciszek Hodur as its bishop. The episcopal succession was transmitted to this church in 1907 by Bishop E. Herzog of Switzerland.

ORGANIZATION

In 1889 the Union of Utrecht was formed, and the declaration of Utrecht, issued in that year by the Old Catholic bishops, is the charter of Old Catholic doctrine and polity. Adherents to this union are the Old Catholic Church of the Netherlands, the Old Catholic Church of Germany, the Christian Catholic Church of Switzerland, the Old Catholic Church of Austria, and the Polish National Catholic Church. The Old Catholic churches in Poland, Czechoslovakia, and Yugoslavia suffered severely during and after World War II.

The chief authority in the Old Catholic churches is the conference of bishops. The archbishop of Utrecht exercises a kind of honorary primacy. Each diocese has its synod, with full participation of both clergy and laity in every aspect of the life of the church, including the election of bishops.

THEOLOGICAL POSITION

Döllinger at the start laid down the vocation of the Old Catholic churches in three propositions: (1) "to bear witness *for* the truth and *against* new-fangled errors, especially the disastrous and arbitrary development of new articles of the faith; (2) gradually to bring into being a Church which will be more closely conformed to the ancient undivided Church; (3) to serve as an instrument for a future great reunion of separated Christians and Churches."

Taking these principles as their basis, the Old Catholics deny that they teach anything that is contrary to the doctrine and traditions of the Roman Catholic Church. They accept the Scriptures, the Apostles' and Nicene creeds, and the dogmatic decisions of the first seven ecumenical councils. They uphold the conciliar basis of the church and accord a high place to tradition. They accept seven sacraments as of permanent obligation in the life of the church. The episcopate is accepted as a gift given by God to the church, in which all Catholic bishops share equally, having been admitted thereto by bishops who themselves stand in unbroken historical succession from the time of the Apostles.

Nevertheless, many differences in practice separate Old Catholics from Roman Catholics. By adopting in all countries the use of the vernacular in public worship, the Old Catholics accepted what at the time was regarded as one of the fundamental principles of the Protestant Reformation. Confession to God in the presence of a priest is not obligatory, and celibacy of the clergy was made optional in some Old Catholic churches. Many Old Catholic churches admit women to the priesthood; some bless same-sex marriages.

ECUMENICAL RELATIONSHIPS

The third of Döllinger's principles pledged the Old Catholics from the start to work persistently for Christian union. This was stressed at the first Bonn conference on Christian union, held in 1874, and was repeated at all the international Old Catholic congresses, held at intervals of roughly five years. The *Internationale Kirchliche Zeitschrift* (founded in 1893 as the *Internationale Theologische Zeitschrift*) renders unique service as a reliable and unprejudiced sourcebook on interchurch relationships throughout the world. In 1931, by the agreement of Bonn, full intercommunion was established between the Church of England and the Old Catholic churches; this was followed in 1946 by a similar agreement between the Polish National Catholic Church and the Episcopal Church in the United States of America (ECUSA), which was suspended in 1976 after the latter permitted the ordination of women. Under the papacy of John Paul II, high-level ecumenical discussions took place, especially with the Polish National Catholic Church. In 2003 the Polish National Catholic Church was expelled from the Union of Utrecht because of the church's stance against ordaining women to the priesthood.

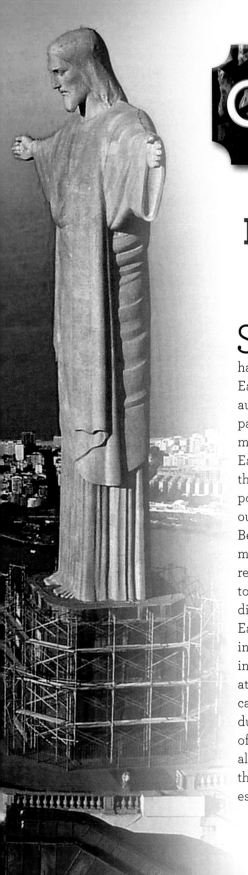

CHAPTER 11

EASTERN CHURCHES

Separated from the West from the Schism of 1054 until the mid-20th century, the Orthodox churches of the East have developed their own way for more than a millennium. Each national church is autocephalous, meaning that it is autonomous and has its own patriarch. The "ecumenical patriarch" of Constantinople is not the Eastern pope but merely the first in honour among equals in jurisdiction. Eastern Orthodoxy interprets the primacy of Peter and therefore that of the pope similarly, denying the right of the pope to speak and act for the entire church by himself, without a church council and without his episcopal colleagues. Because of this polity Eastern Orthodoxy has identified itself more intimately with national cultures and with national regimes than has Roman Catholicism. Therefore the history of church–state relations in the East has been very different from that in the West because the church in the East has sometimes tended toward the extreme of becoming a mere instrument of national policy while the church in the West has sometimes tended toward the extreme of attempting to dominate the state. The history of ecumenical relations between Eastern Orthodoxy and Protestantism during the 20th century was also different from the history of Protestant–Roman Catholic relations. While keeping alive their prayer for an eventual healing of the schism with the Latin Church, some of the Orthodox churches have established communion with Anglicanism and with the

Old Catholic Churches—a movement of Western, largely national churches that broke with Rome after the First Vatican Council—and have participated in the conferences and organizations of the World Council of Churches.

Doctrinal authority for Eastern Orthodoxy resides in the Scriptures, the ancient creeds, the decrees of the first seven ecumenical councils, and the tradition of the church. In addition to the issues mentioned in the discussion of Roman Catholicism above, the chief dogmatic difference between Roman Catholic and Eastern Orthodox thought is on the question of the procession of the Holy Spirit from the Father and from the Son—the Eastern Orthodox churches do not accept the *Filioque* as part of the Nicene Creed. But "orthodoxy," in the Eastern use of the term, means primarily not a species of doctrine but a species of worship. The Feast of Orthodoxy on the first Sunday of Lent celebrates the end of the iconoclastic controversies and the restoration to the churches of the icons, which are basic to Orthodox piety. In Orthodox churches (as well as in the Eastern rite churches that have reestablished communion with Rome), the most obvious points of divergence from general Western practice are the Byzantine liturgy, the right of the clergy to marry before ordination (though bishops may not be married), and the practice of intinction—the administration of the sacrament of the Eucharist by dipping bread in wine and giving both together to the communicant.

EASTERN ORTHODOXY

The various national churches that comprise Eastern Orthodoxy share a rich mystical and spiritual tradition that arose in marked distinction from the Roman Catholic Church and subsequent Western developments. The rise of national churches (with the primate of Constantinople accorded historical and spiritual primacy) and its distinct view of the nature of the Trinity and of the relationship between divinity and humanity are starkly different from those in Catholicism or Protestantism.

DOCTRINE

All Eastern Orthodox creedal formulas, liturgical texts, and doctrinal statements affirm the claim that the Eastern Orthodox Church has preserved the original apostolic faith, which was also expressed in the common Christian tradition of the first centuries.

COUNCILS AND CONFESSIONS

The Orthodox church recognizes seven ecumenical councils—Nicaea I (325), Constantinople I (381), Ephesus (431), Chalcedon (451), Constantinople II (553), Constantinople III (680–681), and Nicaea II (787)—but considers that the decrees of several other later councils also reflect the same original faith (e.g., the councils of Constantinople that endorsed the theology of St. Gregory Palamas in the 14th century). Finally, it recognizes itself as the bearer of an uninterrupted living tradition of true Christianity that is expressed in its worship, in the lives of the saints, and in the faith of the whole people of God.

In the 17th century, as a counterpart to the various "confessions" of the Reformation, there appeared several "Orthodox confessions," endorsed by local councils but in fact associated with individual authors (e.g., Metrophanes Critopoulos, 1625; Petro Mohyla, 1638; Dosítheos of Jerusalem, 1672). None of these confessions would be recognized today as having anything but historical importance. Orthodox theologians, rather than seeking literal conformity with any particular confession, will look for consistency with Scripture and tradition, as it has been expressed in the ancient councils, in the works of the Church Fathers (the early theological authorities of the church), and in the uninterrupted life of the liturgy. Most theologians will not shy away from new formulations if consistency and continuity of tradition are preserved.

What is particularly characteristic of this attitude toward the faith is the absence of any great concern for establishing external criteria of truth—a concern that has dominated Western Christian thought since the Middle Ages. Truth appears as a living experience accessible in the communion of the church and of which the Scriptures, the councils, and theology are the normal expressions. Even ecumenical councils, in the Orthodox perspective, must be accepted by the body of the church in order to be recognized as truly ecumenical. Ultimately, therefore, truth is viewed as its own criterion: there are signs that point to it, but none of those signs is a substitute for a free and personal experience of truth, which is made accessible in the sacramental fellowship of the church.

Because of this view of truth, the Orthodox have traditionally been reluctant to involve church authority in defining matters of faith with too much precision and detail. This reluctance is not due to relativism or indifference but rather to the belief that truth needs no definition to be the object of experience and that legitimate definition, when it occurs, should aim mainly at excluding error and not at pretending to reveal the truth itself that is believed to be ever present in the church.

GOD AND HUMANKIND

The development of the doctrines concerning the Trinity and the Incarnation, as it took place during the first eight centuries of Christian history, was related to the concept of humankind's participation in divine life.

The Eastern (Greek) Fathers always implied that the phrase found in the biblical story of the creation of man (Genesis 1:26), according to "the image and likeness of God," meant that humans are not autonomous beings and that their ultimate nature is defined by their relation to God. In paradise Adam and Eve were called to participate in God's life and to find in him the natural growth of their humanity "from glory to glory." To be "in God" is, therefore, the natural state of humankind. This doctrine is particularly important in connection with the Fathers' view of human freedom. For theologians such as Gregory of Nyssa (4th century) and Maximus the Confessor (7th century), humans are truly free only when they are in communion with God. Otherwise they are only slaves to their body or to "the world," over which, originally and by God's command, he was destined to rule. Thus, the concept of sin implies separation from God and the reduction of humans to a separate and autonomous existence, in which they are deprived of both God's natural glory and freedom.

Freedom in God, as enjoyed by Adam, implied the possibility of falling away from God. This is the unfortunate choice made by Adam and Eve, which led them to a subhuman and unnatural existence. The most unnatural aspect of this new state was death. In this perspective, "original sin" is understood not so much as a state of guilt inherited from Adam and Eve but as an unnatural condition of human life that ends in death. Mortality is what each person now inherits at birth and what leads an individual to struggle for existence, to self-affirmation at the expense of others, and ultimately to subjection to the laws of animal life. The "prince of this world" (i.e., Satan), who is also the "murderer from the beginning," has dominion over humanity. From this vicious circle of death and sin, humans are understood to be liberated by the death and Resurrection of Jesus, which are actualized in baptism and the sacramental life in the church.

The general framework of this understanding of the relationship between God and humankind is clearly different from the view that became dominant in the Christian West—i.e., the view that conceived of "nature" as distinct from "grace" and that understood original sin as an inherited guilt rather than as a deprivation of freedom. In the East humans are regarded as complete when they participate in God; in the West humans are believed to be autonomous, sin is viewed as a punishable crime, and grace is understood as the granting of forgiveness. Hence, in the West the aim of the Christian is justification, but in the East it is rather communion with God and deification (*theosis*). In the West the church is viewed in terms of mediation (for the bestowing of grace) and authority (for guaranteeing security in doctrine); in the East the church is regarded as a communion in which God and the individual meet once again and a personal experience of divine life becomes possible.

CHRIST

The Eastern Orthodox Church is formally committed to the Christology that was defined by the councils of the first eight centuries. Together with the Latin church of the West, it rejected Arianism (a belief in the subordination of the Son to the Father) at Nicaea (325), Nestorianism (a belief that stresses the independence of the divine and human natures of Christ) at Ephesus (431), and Monophysitism (a belief that Christ has only one, divine nature) at Chalcedon (451). The Eastern and Western churches still formally share the tradition of subsequent Christological developments, even though the famous formula of Chalcedon, "one person in two natures," is given different emphases in the East and the West. The stress on Christ's identity with the preexistent Son of God, the Logos of the Gospel According to John, characterizes Orthodox Christology. On Byzantine icons, often depicted around the face of Jesus are the Greek letters о'ω'ν—the equivalent of the Jewish tetragrammaton YHWH, the name of God in the Hebrew Bible. Jesus is thus always seen in his divine identity. Similarly, the liturgy consistently addresses the Virgin Mary as Theotokos (the "one who gave birth to God"), and this term, formally admitted as a criterion of orthodoxy at Ephesus, is actually the only Mariological (doctrine of Mary) dogma accepted in the Orthodox church. It reflects the doctrine of Christ's unique divine person. Mary is venerated solely because she is his mother "according to the flesh."

This emphasis on the personal divine identity of Christ, based on the doctrine of St. Cyril of Alexandria (5th century), does not imply the denial of his humanity. The anthropology (doctrine of humankind) of the Eastern Fathers does not view the individual as an autonomous being but rather implies that communion with God makes the individual fully human. Thus,

the human nature of Jesus Christ, fully assumed by the divine Word, is indeed the "new Adam" in whom the whole of humanity receives again its original glory. Christ's humanity is fully that of every human being; it possesses all the characteristics of the human being— "each nature (of Christ) acts according to its properties," Chalcedon proclaimed, following Pope Leo I—without separating itself from the divine Word. Thus, in death itself—for Jesus's death was indeed a fully human death—the Son of God was the "subject" of the Passion. The theopaschite formula ("God suffered in the flesh") became, together with the Theotokos formula, a standard of orthodoxy in the Eastern church, especially after the second Council of Constantinople (553). It implies that Christ's humanity is indeed real not only in itself but also for God, since it brought him to death on the cross, and that the salvation and redemption of humanity can be accomplished by God alone—hence the necessity for him to condescend to death, which holds humanity captive.

This theology of redemption and salvation is best expressed in the Byzantine liturgical hymns of Holy Week and Easter: Christ is the one who "tramples down death by death," and, on the evening of Good Friday, the hymns already exalt his victory. Salvation is conceived not in terms of satisfaction of divine justice—through paying the debt for the sin of Adam, as the medieval West understood it—but in terms of uniting the human and the divine, with the divine overcoming human mortality and weakness and, finally, exalting man to divine life.

What Christ accomplished once and for all must be appropriated freely by those who are "in Christ"; their goal is "deification," which does not mean dehumanization but the exaltation of humans to the dignity prepared for them at creation. Such feasts as the Transfiguration or the Ascension are extremely popular in the East precisely because they celebrate humanity glorified in Christ—a glorification that anticipates the coming of the kingdom of God, when God will be "all in all." Participation in the deified humanity of Christ is the true goal of Christian life, and it is accomplished through the Holy Spirit.

THE HOLY SPIRIT

The gift of the Holy Spirit at Pentecost "called all men into unity," according to the Byzantine liturgical hymn of the day. Into this new unity, which St. Paul called the "body of Christ," each individual Christian enters through baptism and chrismation (the Eastern counterpart of the Western confirmation) when the priest anoints the Christian with the words "the seal of the gift of the Holy Spirit."

This gift, however, requires a person's free response. Orthodox saints such as Seraphim of Sarov (1759–1833) described the entire content of Christian life as a "collection of the Holy Spirit." The Holy Spirit is thus conceived as the main agent of humanity's restoration to its original natural state through Communion in Christ's body. This role of the Holy Spirit is reflected, very richly, in a variety of liturgical and sacramental acts. Every act of worship usually starts with a prayer addressed to the Holy Spirit, and all major sacraments begin with an invocation to the Holy Spirit. The eucharistic liturgies of the East attribute the ultimate mystery of Christ's presence to a descent of the Holy Spirit upon the worshipping congregation and upon the eucharistic bread and wine. The significance of this invocation (in Greek *epiklēsis*) was violently debated between Greek and Latin Christians in the Middle Ages because the Roman canon of the mass lacked any reference to the Holy Spirit and was thus considered deficient by the Orthodox Greeks.

Since the first Council of Constantinople (381), which condemned the Pneumatomachians ("fighters against the Spirit"), no one in the Orthodox East has ever denied that the Spirit is not only a "gift" but also the giver—i.e., that he is the third person of the Trinity. The Greek Fathers saw in Genesis 1:2 a reference to the Spirit's cooperation in the divine act of creation. The Spirit was also viewed as active in the "new creation" that occurred in the womb of the Virgin Mary when she became the mother of Christ (Luke 1:35); Pentecost was understood to be an anticipation of the "last days" (Acts 2:17) when, at the end of history, a universal communion with God will be achieved. Thus, all the decisive acts of God are accomplished "by the Father in the Son, through the Holy Spirit."

The Trinity, represented by Christ as a human, the Holy Spirit as a dove, and the Father as a hand, Armenian miniature, 1273; in the Topkapı Palace Museum, Istanbul. Ara Guler, Istanbul

THE HOLY TRINITY

By the 4th century a polarity had developed between Eastern and Western Christians in their respective understandings of the Trinity. In the West God was understood primarily in terms of one essence (the Trinity of persons being conceived as an irrational truth found in revelation); in the East the tri-personality of God was understood as the primary fact of Christian experience. For most of the Eastern Fathers, it was not the Trinity that needed theological proof but rather God's essential unity. The Cappadocian Fathers (Gregory of Nyssa, Gregory of Nazianzus, and Basil of Caesarea) were even accused of being tri-theists because of their conception of God as one essence in three hypostases (the Greek term *hypostasis* was the equivalent of the Latin *substantia* and designated a concrete reality). For Eastern theologians, this terminology was intended to designate the concrete New Testament revelation of the Son and the Holy Spirit as distinct from the Father.

Polarization of the Eastern and Western concepts of the Trinity is at the root of the *Filioque* dispute. The Latin word *Filioque* ("and from the Son") was added to the Nicene Creed in Spain in the 6th century. By affirming that the Holy Spirit proceeds not only "from the Father" (as the original creed proclaimed) but also "from the Son," the Spanish councils intended to condemn Arianism, which held that the Son was a created being. Later, however, the addition became an anti-Eastern battle cry, especially after Charlemagne, the Carolingian ruler of the Franks, was crowned emperor of the Romans in 800. The addition was finally accepted in Rome under Frankish pressure. It found justification in the framework of Western conceptions of the Trinity; the Father and the Son were viewed as one God in the act of "spiration" of the Spirit.

Byzantine theologians opposed the addition, first on the ground that the Western church had no right to change the text of an ecumenical creed unilaterally and, second, because the *Filioque* clause implied the reduction of the divine persons to mere relations ("the Father and the Son are two in relation to each other, but one in relation to the Spirit"). For the Greeks the Father alone is the origin of both the Son and the Holy Spirit. Patriarch Photius (9th century) was the first Orthodox theologian to explicitly spell out the Greek opposition to the *Filioque* concept, but the debate continued throughout the Middle Ages.

THE TRANSCENDENCE OF GOD

An important element in the Eastern Christian understanding of God is the notion that God, in his essence, is totally transcendent and unknowable. In this understanding, God can only be designated by negative attributes: it is possible to say what God is not, but it is impossible to say what God is. A purely negative, or "apophatic" theology—the only one applicable to the essence of

God in the Orthodox view—does not lead to agnosticism, however, because God reveals himself personally—as Father, Son, and Holy Spirit—and also in his acts, or "energies." Thus, true knowledge of God always includes three elements: religious awe; personal encounter; and participation in energies, which God freely bestows on creation.

This conception of God is connected with the personalistic understanding of the Trinity. It also led to the official confirmation by the Orthodox church of the theology of St. Gregory Palamas, the leader of Byzantine Hesychasts (monks devoted to divine quietness through prayer), at the councils of 1341 and 1351 in Constantinople. The councils confirmed a real distinction in God, between the unknowable essence and the energies which make possible a real communion with God. The deification of man, realized in Christ once and for all, is thus accomplished by a communion of divine energy with humanity in Christ's glorified humanity.

MODERN THEOLOGICAL DEVELOPMENTS

Until the conquest of Constantinople by the Turks (1453), Byzantium was the unquestioned intellectual centre of the Orthodox church. Far from being monolithic, Byzantine theology was often polarized by a humanistic trend, favouring the use of Greek philosophy, and the more austere and mystical theology of monastic circles. The concern for preservation of Greek culture and for the political salvation of the empire led several prominent humanists to adopt a position favourable to union with the West. The most creative theologians (e.g., Symeon the New Theologian, died 1033; Gregory Palamas, died 1359; Nicholas Cabasilas, died c. 1390), however, were found in the monastic party that continued the tradition of patristic spirituality based upon the theology of deification.

The 16th, 17th, and 18th centuries were the dark age of Orthodox theology. There was no opportunity for any independent theological creativity in any of the major regions of Orthodoxy—the Middle East, the Balkans, and Russia. With no access to formal theological education except in Western Roman Catholic or Protestant schools, the Orthodox tradition was preserved primarily through the liturgy, which retained its richness and often served as a substitute for formal schooling. Most doctrinal statements of this period, issued by councils or by individual theologians, were polemical documents directed against Western missionaries.

After the reforms of Peter the Great (died 1725), a theological school system was organized in Russia. Shaped originally in accordance with Western Latin models and staffed with Jesuit-trained Ukrainian personnel, this system developed in the 19th century into a fully independent and powerful tool of theological education. The Russian theological efflorescence of the 19th and 20th centuries produced many scholars, especially in historical theology—e.g., Philaret Drozdov, Vasily Osepovich Klyuchevsky, Vasily Vasilievich Bolotov, Evgeny Evstigneyevich Golubinsky, and Nikolay Nikanorovich Glubokovsky. Independently of the official theological schools, a number of laymen with secular training developed theological and philosophical traditions of their own and exercised a great influence on modern Orthodox theology—e.g., Alexey Stepanovich Khomyakov, Vladimir Sergeyevich Solovyev, and Nikolay Aleksandrovich Berdyayev. Others, such as Pavel Florensky and Sergey Nikolayevich Bulgakov, became priests. A large number of the Russian theological intelligentsia—e.g., Bulgakov and Georges Florovsky—emigrated to western Europe after the Russian Revolution (1917) and played a leading role in the ecumenical movement.

With the independence of the Balkans, theological schools were also created in Greece, Serbia, Bulgaria, and Romania. Modern Greek scholars contributed to the publication of important Byzantine ecclesiastical texts and produced standard theological textbooks. The Orthodox diaspora—the emigration from eastern Europe and the Middle East—in the 20th century contributed to modern theological development through their establishment of theological centres in western Europe and America.

Orthodox theologians reacted negatively to the new dogmas proclaimed by Pope Pius IX: the Immaculate Conception of Mary (1854), which held that Mary was conceived without sin, and papal infallibility (1870), which held that, under certain conditions, the pope cannot err when teaching on matters of faith and morals. In connection with the dogma of the Assumption of Mary, proclaimed by Pope Pius XII (1950), which held that Mary was raised to heaven in both body and soul, the objections mainly concerned the presentation of such a tradition in the form of a dogma.

In contrast to the trend toward social concerns evident in Western Christian thought since the late 20th century, Orthodox theologians have generally emphasized that the Christian faith is primarily a direct experience of the kingdom of God, sacramentally present in the church. Without denying that Christians have a social responsibility to the world, they consider this responsibility as an outcome of the life in Christ. This traditional position accounts for the remarkable survival of the Orthodox churches under the most contradictory and unfavourable of social conditions, but to Western eyes it often appears as a form of passive fatalism.

WORSHIP AND SACRAMENTS

With its spiritual significance and rich variety, the worship of the Orthodox church represents one of the most significant factors in the church's continuity and identity. It helps to account for the survival of Christianity during the many centuries of Muslim rule in the Middle East and the Balkans, when the liturgy was the only source of religious knowledge or experience. Since liturgical practice was practically the only religious expression legally authorized in the Soviet Union, the continuous existence of Orthodox communities in the region was also centred almost exclusively around the liturgy. The concept that the church is most authentically itself when the congregation of the faithful is gathered together in worship is a basic expression of Eastern Christian experience. Without that concept it is impossible to understand the fundamentals of church structure in Orthodoxy, with the bishop functioning in his essential roles as teacher and high priest in the liturgy. Similarly, the personal experience of participation in divine life is understood in the framework of the continuous liturgical action of the community.

THE ROLE OF THE LITURGY

According to many authorities, one of the reasons why the Eastern liturgy has made a stronger impact on the Christian church than has its Western counterpart is that it has always been viewed as a total experience, appealing simultaneously to the emotional, intellectual, and aesthetic faculties of humans. The liturgy includes a variety of models, or symbols, using formal theological statements as well as bodily perceptions and gestures (e.g., music, incense, prostrations) and the visual arts. All are meant to convey the content of the Christian faith to the educated and the noneducated alike. Participation in the liturgy implies familiarity with its models, and many of them are conditioned by the historical and cultural past of the church. Thus, the use of such an elaborate and ancient liturgy presupposes catechetical preparation. It may require an updating of the liturgical forms themselves. The Orthodox church recognizes that liturgical forms are changeable and that, because the early church admitted a variety of liturgical traditions, such a variety is also possible today. Thus, Orthodox communities with Western rites now exist in western Europe and in the Americas.

The Orthodox church, however, has always been conservative in liturgical matters. This conservatism is in particular due to the absence of a central ecclesiastical authority that could enforce reforms and to the firm conviction of the church membership as a whole that the liturgy is the main vehicle and experience of true Christian beliefs. Consequently, reform of the liturgy is often considered as equivalent to a reform of the faith itself. However inconvenient this conservatism may be, the Orthodox liturgy has preserved many essential Christian values transmitted directly from the experience of the early church.

Throughout the centuries the Orthodox liturgy has been richly embellished with cycles of hymns from a wide variety of sources. Byzantium (where the present Orthodox liturgical rite took shape), while keeping many biblical and

A Ukrainian Orthodox priest waves incense while celebrating a mass at the Kiev-Pecherskaya Lavra monastery in Kiev, during a service on November 3, 2009. Sergei Supinsky/AFP/Getty Images

early Christian elements, used the lavish resources of patristic theology and Greek poetry, as well as some gestures of imperial court ceremonial, in order to convey the realities of God's kingdom.

Normally, the content of the liturgy is directly accessible to the faithful because the Byzantine tradition is committed to the use of any vernacular language in the liturgy. Translation of both Scriptures and liturgy into various languages was undertaken by the medieval Byzantines, as well as by modern Russian missionaries. Liturgical conservatism, however, leads de facto to the preservation of antiquated languages. The Byzantine Greek used in church services by the modern Greeks and the Old Church Slavonic still preserved by all the Slavs are at least as distant from the spoken languages as is the language of the King James Version of the Bible—used in many Protestant churches—from modern English.

THE EUCHARISTIC LITURGIES

The liturgies attributed to St. John Chrysostom and St. Basil the Great are the eucharistic liturgies most generally used in Orthodox worship. Both acquired their present shape by the 9th century, but it is generally recognized that the wording of the eucharistic "canon" of the liturgy of St. Basil goes back to the 4th century and may be the work of St. Basil himself. The liturgy of St. James—composed about the 4th century and largely similar to that of St. Basil—is used occasionally, especially in Jerusalem. During the period of Lent a service of Communion, with elements (bread and wine) reserved from those consecrated on the previous Sunday, is celebrated in connection with the evening service of vespers; it is called the "liturgy of the presanctified" and is attributed to St. Gregory the Great.

The liturgies of St. John Chrysostom and of St. Basil differ only in the text of the eucharistic canon: their overall structures, established in the High Middle Ages, are identical and begin with an elaborate rite of preparation (*proskomidē*). A priest on a separate "table of oblation" disposes on a paten (plate) the particles of bread that will symbolize the assembly of the saints, both living and dead, around Christ, the "Lamb of God." Then follows the liturgy of the catechumens, which begins with a processional entrance of the priest into the sanctuary with the Gospel ("little entrance") and which includes the traditional Christian "liturgy of the word," the reading from the New Testament letters and the Gospels as well as a sermon. This part of the liturgy ends with the expulsion of the catechumens, who, until they are baptized, are not admitted to the sacramental part of the service. (If no catechumens are present, the expulsion is symbolic.) The Liturgy of the Faithful includes another ceremonial procession of the priest into the sanctuary. He carries the bread and wine from the table of oblations to the altar ("great entrance"). This is followed here—as in the West—with the recitation of the Nicene Creed, the eucharistic canon, and the Lord's Prayer and Communion prayer. The bread used for the Eucharist is ordinary leavened bread; both elements (bread and wine) are distributed with a special spoon (*labis*).

THE LITURGICAL CYCLES

One of the major characteristics of the Byzantine liturgical tradition is the wealth and variety of hymnodical texts marking the various cycles of the liturgical year. A special liturgical book contains the hymns for each of the main cycles. The daily cycle includes the offices of Hesperinos (vespers), Apodeipnon (Compline), the midnight prayer, Orthros (matins), and the four canonical "hours"—offices to be said at the "first" (6:00 AM), "third" (9:00 AM), "sixth" (12:00 noon), and "ninth" (3:00 PM) hours. The liturgical book covering the daily cycle is called the *Hōrologion* ("The Book of Hours"). The Paschal (Easter) cycle is centred on the Feast of Feasts—i.e., the feast of Christ's Resurrection. It includes the period of Great Fast (Lent), preceded by three Sundays of preparation and the period of 50 days following Easter. The hymns of the Lenten period are found in the *Triōdion* ("Three Odes") and those of the Easter season in the *Pentēkostarion* (called the "Flowery Triodion"). The weekly cycle is the continuation of the Resurrection cycle found in the *Triōdion* and the *Pentēkostarion*; each week following the Sunday after Pentecost (50 days after Easter) possesses its own musical tone, or mode, in accordance with which all the hymns of the week are sung. As described in the *Octoechos* ("The Book of Eight Tones"), there are eight tones whose composition is traditionally attributed to St. John of Damascus (8th century). Each week is centred around Sunday, the day of Christ's Resurrection.

The Easter and weekly cycles clearly dominate all offices of the entire year and illustrate the absolute centrality of the Resurrection in the Eastern understanding of the Christian message. The date of Easter, set at the Council of Nicaea (325), is the first Sunday after the full moon following the spring equinox. Differences between the East and the West in computing the date exist because the Orthodox church uses the Julian calendar for establishing the date of the equinox (hence a delay of 13 days) and also because of the tradition that Easter must necessarily follow the Jewish Passover and must never precede it or coincide with it.

The yearly cycle includes the hymns for each of the 366 days of the calendar year, with its feasts and daily commemoration of saints. They are found in the 12 volumes of the *Menaion* ("Book of Months"). From the 6th to the 9th century the Byzantine church experienced its golden age of creativity in the writing of hymns by outstanding poets such as John of Damascus. In more recent times hymn writing has generally followed the accepted patterns set by those authors but rarely has it reached the quality of its models. Since the Eastern Orthodox tradition bans instrumental music, or accompaniment, the singing is always a cappella, with only a few exceptions admitted by some parishes in the United States.

THE SACRAMENTS

Contemporary Eastern Orthodox catechisms and textbooks all affirm that the church recognizes seven *mystēria* ("sacraments"): baptism, chrismation, Communion, holy orders, penance, anointing of the sick, and marriage. Neither the liturgical book called *Euchologion* ("Prayer Book"), which contains the texts of the sacraments, nor the patristic tradition, however, formally limits the number of sacraments. They do not distinguish clearly between the "sacraments" and such acts as the blessing of water on Epiphany Day or the burial service or the service for the tonsuring of a monk that in the West are called *sacramentalia*. In fact, no council recognized by the Orthodox church ever defined the number of sacraments. It is only through the "Orthodox confessions" of the 17th century, which was directed against the Protestant Reformation (which recognized only two, baptism and Communion), that the number seven has been generally accepted.

Russian Orthodox priests pray during a traditional Orthodox Epiphany celebration in New Jerusalem Voskresensky Monastery on January 19, 2010, in Istra, Russia. Believers cleanse themselves with holy and pure water blessed by a cleric on Epiphany. Epsilon/Getty Images

The underlying sacramental theology of the Orthodox church is based, however, on the notion that the ecclesiastical community is the unique *mystērion*, of which the various sacraments are the normal expressions. The church interprets each sacramental act as a prayer of the entire ecclesiastical community, led by the bishop or his representative, and as God's response, based upon Christ's promise to send the Holy Spirit upon the church. These two aspects of the sacrament exclude both magic and legalism: they imply that the Holy Spirit is given to free people and call for their responses. In the *mystērion* of the church

the participation of humans in God is effected through their "cooperation" or "synergy"; to make this participation possible once more is the goal of the Incarnation.

Baptism and Chrismation

Baptism is normally performed by triple immersion as a sign of the death and Resurrection of Christ; thus, the rite appears essentially as a gift of new life. It is immediately followed by chrismation, performed by the priest who anoints the newly baptized Christian with "Holy Chrism" (oil) blessed by the bishop. Baptized and chrismed children are admitted to Holy Communion. By admitting children immediately after their baptism to both chrismation and Communion, the Eastern Christian tradition maintains the meaning of baptism as the beginning of a new life nourished by the Eucharist.

The Eucharist

There never has been, in the East, much speculation about the nature of the eucharistic mystery. Both canons presently in use (that of St. Basil and that of St. John Chrysostom) include the "words of institution" ("This is my Body" and "This is my Blood"), which are traditionally considered in the West as the formula necessary for the validity of the sacrament. In the East, however, the culminating point of the prayer is not in the remembrance of Christ's act but in the invocation of the Holy Spirit, which immediately follows:

> Send down Thy Holy Spirit upon us and upon the Gifts here spread forth, and make this bread to be the precious Body of Thy Christ.

Thus, the central mystery of Christianity is seen as being performed by the prayer of the church and through an invocation of the Spirit. The nature of the mystery that occurs in the bread and wine is signified by the term metabolē ("sacramental change"). The Western term

transubstantiation occurs only in some confessions of faith after the 17th century.

Orders

The Orthodox church recognizes three major orders—the diaconate, the priesthood, and the episcopate. It also recognizes two minor orders—the lectorate and the subdiaconate. All ordinations are performed by a bishop normally during the eucharistic liturgy. The consecration of a bishop requires the participation of at least two or three bishops, as well as an election by a canonical synod.

Penance

The sacrament of penance in the early church was a solemn and public act of reconciliation, through which an excommunicated sinner was readmitted into church membership. It has evolved, however, into a private act of confession through which every Christian's membership in the church is periodically renewed. The practice and the rite of penance vary in the Orthodox church today. In the churches of the Balkans and the Middle East, it fell into disuse during the four centuries of Turkish occupation but was gradually restored in the 20th century. In Greek-speaking churches only certain priests, especially appointed by the bishop, have the right to hear confessions. In Russia, on the contrary, confessions remained a standard practice that was generally required before communion. General or group confession, introduced by John of Kronshtadt, a Russian spiritual leader of the early 20th century, is also occasionally practiced.

The rite of confession in the *Euchologion* retains the form of a prayer, or invocation, said by the priest for the remission of the penitent's sins. In the Slavic ritual a Latin-inspired and juridical form of personal absolution was introduced in the 17th century by Petro Mohyla, metropolitan of Kiev. In general Orthodox practice, however, confession is generally viewed as a form of spiritual healing rather than as a tribunal. The relative lack of legalism reflects the Eastern patristic understanding of sin as an internal passion and as an enslavement. The external sinful acts—which alone can be legally tried—are only manifestations of humanity's internal disease.

Anointing of the Sick

Anointing of the sick is a form of healing by prayer. In the Greek church it is performed annually for the benefit of the entire congregation on the evening of Holy Wednesday in church.

Marriage

Marriage is celebrated through a rite of crowning, performed with great solemnity and signifying an eternal union, sacramentally "projected" into the kingdom of God. Orthodox theology of marriage insists on its sacramental eternity rather than its legal indissolubility. Thus, second marriages, in cases of either widowhood or divorce, are celebrated through a subdued penitential rite, and men who have been married more than once are not admitted to the priesthood. Remarriage after divorce is tolerated on the basis of the possibility that the sacrament of marriage was not originally received with the consciousness and responsibility that would have made it fully effective; according to this view, remarriage can be a second chance.

ORIENTAL ORTHODOXY

There is another branch of Orthodoxy in the "East"—not only in the Middle East but also in Africa, the Caucasus, and India—that was largely overlooked by the broader stream of Christianity (whether Roman Catholic, Eastern Orthodox, or Protestant) until the 20th century. The reason for this stretches far back into Christian history, even further back than the East-West Schism of 1054. Only in the mid-20th century were official attempts made to mend this rift.

In 451 the Council of Chalcedon promulgated the statement—received as orthodox by Rome and Constantinople and subsequently upheld by Eastern Orthodox and Western Christians—that the one person of Jesus Christ consists of two natures, one divine and one human, both equally present. This statement intended to put to rest two alleged heresies: one attributed to Nestorius of Constantinople that Christ had radically separate human and divine natures and one of monophysitism, the belief that Christ had only one single, divine nature. However, churches in Armenia, Egypt, Syria, India, and Ethiopia held that the Christological statement agreed upon at Chalcedon tended dangerously toward the former pole and risked professing the idea of a fundamental gap between Christ's divinity and his humanity. These churches held to the position of St. Cyril of Alexandria, which proclaimed "one incarnate nature of the Word." The Roman and Eastern Orthodox churches denounced them as monophysite heretics for this, but these pre-Chalcedonian, or non-Chalcedonian, churches—known centuries later as "Oriental Orthodox churches"—protest that their position is one of miaphysitism. They neither emphasize the difference between the humanity and the divinity present in the person of Jesus Christ nor teach that Christ's divinity is more important than (or cancels out) his humanity. Following St. Cyril, they profess that both divinity and humanity are equally present within a single (hence the Greek prefix *mia*-) nature in the person of Christ through the mystery of the Incarnation.

These miaphysite churches of the Oriental Orthodox communion— the Armenian Apostolic Church, the Coptic Orthodox Church of Alexandria, the Syriac Orthodox Patriarchate of Antioch and All the East, the Malankara (Indian) Orthodox Church, the Ethiopian Tewahedo Orthodox Church, and, since 1998, the Eritrean Tewahedo Orthodox Church—have mended much of the schism between themselves and the Eastern Orthodox and Western churches. Despite both Christological and liturgical differences, they are no longer held to be heretical; they are held by these other churches to be Christians in good standing, even though they do not share full communion with these Chalcedonian churches. Moreover, they participate in ecumenical endeavours and are members of the World Council of Churches. They stand in loose communion with each other, sharing a common background as representatives of one of the oldest forms of Christianity. What follows is a brief survey of the diversity of Oriental Orthodoxy with a view of the churches in Armenia, Egypt, Syria, and Ethiopia.

ARMENIAN APOSTOLIC CHURCH

The Armenian Apostolic Church is seen by many as the custodian of Armenian national identity. According to tradition, Armenia was evangelized by the apostles Bartholomew and Thaddeus. Armenia became the first country to adopt Christianity about 300 CE, when St. Gregory the Illuminator converted the Arsacid king Tiridates III. The new Armenian church soon struck a course independent of the founding church at

Caesarea Cappadociae (now Kayseri, Turkey), though it developed in close relationship with the Syrians, who provided it with scriptures and liturgy and much of its basic institutional terminology. In 506 at the Council of Dvin, the Armenian church rejected the Christological statement approved by the Council of Chalcedon (451). It remained in contact and communion with the other pre-Chalcedonian churches in the Caucasus, the Middle East, and Asia that did not offer allegiance to Rome or to Constantinople.

Gregory the Illuminator, the first head of the Armenian church, and his early successors had their residence at Ejmiadzin. It was moved to Dvin from 485 to 927 and then was located variously until 1293, when the catholicosate (the church's highest ecclesiastical administrative office) was transferred to the Cilician capital, Sis (now Kozan, Turkey), where it remained after the fall of Cilicia to the Muslim Mamlūks of Egypt. In the 15th century Gregory IX Musabegian rejected efforts to transfer the see (ecclesiastical jurisdiction) to eastern Armenia in order to withdraw it from Roman influence. A synod of 17 bishops deposed him, and the monk Kirakos was elected catholicos at Ejmiadzin in 1441, the first in a long line of prelates bearing the title "Catholicos of All Armenians."

The Armenian Apostolic Church comprises four sees. Two are catholicosates, at Ejmiadzin and Cilicia (now based in Antelias, Lebanon). There are also two patriarchates, at Constantinople (now Istanbul, Turkey) and Jerusalem, respectively. The catholicos of Ejmiadzin is generally recognized as the head of the whole church and bears the title "Supreme Patriarch and Catholicos of All Armenians." The catholicos at Cilicia, who bears the title "Catholicos of the Great House of Cilicia," owes the catholicos of Ejmiadzin spiritual allegiance but retains administrative autonomy. Relationships between the catholicoses have on occasion been strained by political tensions. Whereas the supreme catholicos resides in Armenia, Armenian nationalists (Dashnaks) tend to support the see of Cilicia. This division is reflected among North American Armenians.

The patriarchates of Constantinople and Jerusalem are of relatively recent origin and recognize the supremacy of Ejmiadzin. The patriarchate of Jerusalem was founded early in the 14th century when the monastery of St. James in Jerusalem proclaimed its bishop Sargis an independent patriarch. The patriarchate of Constantinople was created in 1461 by the Ottoman sultan Mehmed II, who appointed a local bishop to be the religious leader of the entire Armenian community in the Ottoman Empire. Because the territory involved included the majority of Armenians, the patriarch of Constantinople, while owing spiritual allegiance to Ejmiadzin, was effectively the most powerful prelate in the Armenian church until the end of the Ottoman Empire after World War I. Alongside other Oriental Orthodox churches, it participated since the late 20th century in dialogues with both the Roman Catholic and Eastern Orthodox churches in efforts to resolve doctrinal disputes dating back to the Council of Chalcedon. Many of these issues have been resolved.

COPTIC ORTHODOX CHURCH OF ALEXANDRIA

The people of Egypt before the Arab conquest in the 7th century identified themselves and their language in Greek as "Aigyptios" (Arabic *qibt*, Westernized as Copt). When Egyptian Muslims later ceased to call themselves Aigyptioi, the term became the distinctive name of the Christian minority. In the 19th and 20th centuries they began to call themselves Coptic Orthodox in order to distinguish themselves both from Copts who had converted to Roman Catholicism and from Eastern Orthodox, who are mostly Greek.

In the 4th and 5th centuries a theological conflict arose between the Copts and the Greek-speaking Romans, or Melchites ("Emperor's Men"), in Egypt. The Melchites recognized the outcome of Chalcedon. The Coptic church, however, did not and became one of the Eastern churches denounced as monophysite heretics by the Roman Catholic and Eastern Orthodox churches. After the Arab conquest of Egypt in the 7th century, the Copts ceased speaking Greek, and the language barrier added to the controversy. Various attempts at compromise by the Byzantine emperors came to naught. Later, the Arab caliphs, although they tended to favour those who adopted Islam, did not interfere much in the church's internal affairs. The *jizya*, the tax levied upon non-Muslims living in an Islamic state, was abolished in the 18th century.

Arabic is now used in the services of the Coptic Orthodox Church for the lessons from the Bible and for many of the variable hymns; only certain short refrains that churchgoing people all understand are not in Arabic. The service books, using the liturgies attributed to St. Mark, St. Cyril of Alexandria, and St. Gregory of Nazianzus, are written in Coptic (the Bohairic dialect of Alexandria), with the Arabic text in parallel columns.

The Coptic Orthodox Church developed a democratic system of government after the 1890s. The patriarch and the 12 diocesan bishops, with the assistance of community councils in which the laity is well represented, regulate the finances of the churches and schools and the administration of the rules relating to marriage, inheritance, and other matters of personal status. When the patriarch dies, an electoral college, predominantly of laymen, selects three duly qualified monks at least 50 years of age as candidates for the office of patriarch. Among these three, the final choice is made by lot after prayer. The highest-ranking bishop is the patriarch of Alexandria, who resides in Cairo; he is called the pope and claims apostolic authority for his office from St. Mark. The church has its own primary and secondary schools in many places in Egypt, as well as a strong Sunday-school movement for the religious education of children unable to go to Coptic schools. There is an Institute of Coptic Studies in Cairo, a theological college connected with the institute, and a Coptic museum. There are Coptic Orthodox churches in Jerusalem and in other areas of the Holy Land, built in the 19th and 20th centuries, as well as a Coptic bishopric in Khartoum, Sudan. The church also has a small presence in North America, Australia, and the United Kingdom.

SYRIAC ORTHODOX PATRIARCHATE OF ANTIOCH AND ALL THE EAST

In the 5th and 6th centuries a large body of Christians in Syria repudiated the patriarchs of Antioch who had

Pope Shenouda III (C), 86 years old, the 117th Pope of the Coptic Orthodox Church of Alexandria and poses with Coptic archbishops for a photograph at the Abbassiya Cathedral of Saint Marcos in Cairo, Egypt, on June 8, 2010. Khaled Desouki/AFP/Getty Images

supported the Council of Chalcedon (451) both in its affirmation of the dual nature (both human and divine) of Jesus Christ and in its denunciation of monophysitism, the doctrine that Christ has only a divine nature. Contrary to the allegations of their detractors, the Syrian and other miaphsyite Christians did not deny Christ's human nature or emphasize his divine nature. The Syrian Christians severed relations with the Western churches, which had branded them monophysites, and set up their own patriarchs of Antioch in opposition to the Chalcedonian patriarchs, whom the Syrians called Melchites.

Because of the instrumental role of St. Jacob Baradaeus, bishop of Edessa (died 578), in organizing their community, they have historically been called Jacobites, though they reject this name because they trace their founding to the Apostle Peter rather than to Baradaeus. The Syrian Christians were also called Syriani because their doctrine was associated with the Syriac language after it had died out among Greek-speaking people; the Greek Orthodox Syrians, on the other hand, were known as Rūmī (Arabic: "Roman").

After the Arab conquest of Syria (7th century), each church in the Caliphate and in Muslim states generally was treated as a *millet*, or religious community, governed by its own laws and courts under its own clergy. The Syriani were recognized as the West Syrian *millet* (the East Syrian *millet* being the Assyrians, or Nestorians). Since the 17th century, when a minority of the West Syrians were united with Rome and became the Syrian Catholic Church, the rest have been known as Syrian Orthodox, although they remained distinct from the Chalcedonian "Greek Orthodox" Christians of the area. In 2000 the Syrian Orthodox Church adopted its present name, which contains the word *Syriac* in order to distinguish itself from the Syrian Catholic Church. Their liturgical language is the literary Syriac of Edessa, which they preserve as a living tongue; it is a close relative of the Aramaic spoken by Jesus Christ and his Apostles.

The Syriac Orthodox patriarch of Antioch and All the East has very seldom lived in Antioch itself; his usual residence was the monastery of Dayr al-Za'farān (Deyrulzafaran) near Mardin, near Diyarbakır in eastern Turkey. During World War I most Orthodox left Turkey, and their patriarch moved to Ḥimṣ (1921) and then to Damascus (1957). They now live mainly in Syria, Lebanon, Iraq, and Turkey, with smaller numbers in Jordan, Egypt, and the United States. In the first decade of the 21st century, the church claimed more than 1.4 million members.

ETHIOPIAN ORTHODOX TEWAHEDO CHURCH

Ethiopia was Christianized in the 4th century AD by two brothers from Tyre— St. Frumentius, later consecrated the first

Ethiopian bishop, and Aedesius. They won the confidence of King Ezana at Aksum (a powerful kingdom in northern Ethiopia) and were allowed to evangelize. Toward the end of the 5th century, nine monks from Syria, probably non-Chalcedonian, are said to have brought monasticism to Ethiopia and encouraged the translation of the Scriptures into the Ge'ez language. The Ethiopian church followed the Coptic (Egyptian) church in rejecting the Christological decision issued by the Council of Chalcedon in 451 CE. The term *Tewahedo* in the name means "unity" in Ge'ez and expresses the church's miaphysite belief.

In the 7th century the conquests of the Muslim Arabs cut off the Ethiopian church from contact with most of its Christian neighbours. Contact with the outside Christian world was maintained through the Ethiopian monastery in Jerusalem.

Beginning in the 12th century, the patriarch of Alexandria appointed the Ethiopian archbishop, known as the *abuna* (Arabic: "our father"), who was always an Egyptian Coptic monk; this created a rivalry with the native *itshage* (abbot general) of the strong Ethiopian monastic community. Attempts to shake Egyptian Coptic control were made from time to time, but it was not until 1929 that a compromise was effected: an Egyptian monk was again appointed *abuna,* but four Ethiopian bishops were also consecrated as his auxiliaries. A native Ethiopian *abuna,*

Basil, was finally appointed in 1950, and in 1959 an autonomous Ethiopian patriarchate was established. When Eritrea gained independence from Ethiopia in 1993, it appealed to Pope Shenouda III, the patriarch of the Coptic Orthodox Church of Alexandria, for autocephaly. This was granted in 1994; the Ethiopian church assented in 1998 to the independence of the new Eritrean Orthodox Tewahedo Church.

The Amhara and Tigray peoples of the northern and central highlands have historically been the principal adherents of the church, and the church's religious forms and beliefs have been the dominant element in Amhara culture. Under the Amhara-dominated Ethiopian monarchy, the Ethiopian Orthodox Tewahedo church was declared to be the state church of the country, and it was a bulwark of the regime of Emperor Haile Selassie. Upon the abolition of the monarchy and the institution of socialism in the country beginning in 1975, the Ethiopian Orthodox church was disestablished, its patriarch was removed, and the church was divested of its extensive landholdings. The church was placed on a footing of equality with Islam and other religions in the country, but it nevertheless remained Ethiopia's most influential religious body.

The clergy is composed of priests and deacons, who conduct the religious services and perform exorcisms, and *debtera,* who, though not ordained, perform the music and dance associated with church services and learn church lore. Ethiopian Christianity places considerable emphasis on the Hebrew Bible. Further, the church recognizes a wider canon of scripture that includes such texts as the apocalyptic Book of Enoch. Circumcision is almost universally practiced; the Saturday Sabbath (in addition to Sunday) is observed by some devout believers; the ark is an essential item in every church; and rigorous fasting is still practiced. There are theological seminaries in Addis Ababa and Harer. Monasticism is widespread, and individual monasteries often teach special subjects in theology or church music. Each community also has its own church school, which until 1900 was the sole source of Ethiopian education. The liturgy and scriptures are typically in Ge'ez, though both have been translated into Amharic, the principal modern language of Ethiopia. In the early part of the 21st century, the church claimed more than 30,000,000 adherents in Ethiopia.

CHAPTER 12

PROTESTANT CHURCHES

The name *Protestant* first appeared at the Diet of Speyer in 1529, when the Roman Catholic emperor of Germany, Charles V, rescinded the provision of the Diet of Speyer in 1526 that had allowed each ruler to choose whether to administer the Edict of Worms. On April 19, 1529, a protest against this decision was read on behalf of 14 free cities of Germany and six Lutheran princes who declared that the majority decision did not bind them because they were not a party to it and that if forced to choose between obedience to God and obedience to Caesar they must choose obedience to God. They appealed either to a general council of all Christendom or to a synod of the whole German nation. Those who made this protest became known to their opponents as Protestants, and gradually the label was applied to all who adhered to the tenets of the Reformation, especially to those living outside Germany. In Germany the adherents of the Reformation preferred the name *evangelicals* and in France *Huguenots*.

The name was attached not only to the disciples of Martin Luther (*c.* 1483–1546) but also to the Swiss disciples of Huldrych Zwingli (1484–1531) and later of John Calvin (1509–64). The Swiss Reformers and their followers in Holland, England, and Scotland, especially after the 17th century, preferred the name *Reformed*.

In the 16th century *Protestant* referred primarily to the two great schools of thought that arose in the Reformation, the Lutheran and the Reformed. In England in the early 17th century, the word was used to denote "orthodox" Protestants as opposed to those who were regarded by Anglicans as unorthodox, such as the Baptists or the Quakers. Roman Catholics, however, used it for all who claimed to be Christian but opposed Catholicism (except the Eastern churches). They therefore included Baptists, Quakers, and Catholic-minded Anglicans under the term. Before the year 1700 this broad usage was accepted, though the word was not yet applied to Unitarians. The English Toleration Act of 1689 was entitled "an Act for exempting their Majesties' Protestant subjects dissenting from the Church of England." But the act provided only for the toleration of the opinions known in England as "orthodox dissent" and conceded nothing to Unitarians. Throughout the 18th century the word *Protestant* was still defined in relation to the 16th-century Reformation. In the 19th century it referred also to a diversity of new movements that defined themselves in distinction from the traditional Protestant churches. In the 20th and early 21st centuries, it has largely been used as a general term referring to Christian churches that are not Roman Catholic, Old Catholic, Eastern Orthodox, or Oriental Orthodox. It includes not only traditional Protestant churches but newer traditions such as Evangelicalism, fundamentalism, and Pentecostalism, though even these terms are somewhat porous.

LUTHERANISM

The question "What is Lutheran theology?" is not easily answered. Martin Luther himself was not a systematic thinker, and his colleague Philipp Melanchthon became for many his authentic interpreter, raising at once the charge that Melanchthon had distorted Luther's thought.

TEACHINGS

The doctrinal controversies in 16th-century Lutheranism are indicative of the difficulty of defining precisely what it means to be "Lutheran." Nonetheless, Luther's own thought has always been the guiding force in the delineation of Lutheran theology. The two major Lutheran confessional statements of the 16th century, the Augsburg Confession of 1530 and the Formula of Concord of 1576, have traditionally been thought to explicate Luther's teachings.

Since the introduction of Lutheranism in European countries was not centrally directed, the emergence of Lutheran theology took place variously. Thus, not all Lutheran churches formally accepted the Formula of Concord. Authority in Lutheranism is understood as fidelity to the confessional documents that constitute authentic exposition of biblical teaching. Lutheranism has no formal teaching office comparable to that of the Roman Catholic Church.

JUSTIFICATION

Following St. Augustine, Western Christian theologians until the 16th century conceived the redemptive act of divine grace as taking place within the context of willful human collaboration. This centuries-old consensus of divine and human cooperation was sharply rejected by Martin Luther, who maintained that the apostle Paul denied human participation in the process of salvation. Accordingly, the Augsburg Confession notes, people "are justified freely on account of Christ through faith when they believe that they are received into grace and their sins forgiven on account of Christ, who by his death made satisfaction for our sins"; God "imputes [this faith] as righteousness in his sight." This affirmation, on which "the church stands and falls," has received a variety of interpretations since the 16th century. In the 19th and 20th centuries, Lutheran theologians sought to express the teaching in new ways, always insisting that it represented an authentic interpretation of the apostle Paul. Thus, Paul Tillich interpreted justification through faith as the condition of being accepted despite one's unacceptability.

SCRIPTURE AND TRADITION

Foremost among Lutheran teachings is the insistence, shared with all Protestant traditions, that the Bible is the sole source of religious authority. Lutherans subscribe to the three ancient ecumenical Christian creeds together with the 16th-century Lutheran confessional statements. All Lutheran churches affirm the Augsburg Confession; some, notably those in Germany and the United States, additionally affirm the confessional writings found in the Book of Concord. The Formula of Concord designated the Bible as the "sole and most certain rule" for judging Christian teachings. This position was in marked contrast to the Catholic affirmation of both Scripture and tradition. Luther never accepted the Catholic insistence that church tradition was merely making explicit what was already found implicitly in Scripture.

The new centrality of the Bible had dramatic consequences. Luther understood the need for a Bible in the German vernacular, for only if the Bible was accessible could its teachings be appreciated. Luther's example of making available a vernacular Bible was followed by reformers throughout Europe, such as William Tyndale in England. Catholic theologians promptly recognized the powerful weapon Luther had created and undertook to provide vernacular translations of their own. None of them, however, possessed the literary cogency of Luther's translation or of the translation produced early in the 17th century under the direction of King James I of England.

CHURCH, SACRAMENTS, AND MINISTRY

In a famous definition, the Augsburg Confession speaks of the church as the "congregation of saints [believers] in which the gospel is purely taught and the sacraments rightly administered." Luther regarded the true church as essentially invisible, which means that its authority is found not in a formal structure but in fidelity to Scripture. It is in no way identical to the visible (empirical) church organization. Although the visible church is prone to be as weak and sinful as any other human institution, God works in it insofar as it is faithful to his word. During the periods of orthodoxy and Pietism, the notion of the invisibility of the church was understood to mean that God alone knows who among the assembled Christians are true believers. In the 19th century the relationship of the visible and invisible church received much attention in Lutheran theology, partly under the influence of a dynamic Catholicism, with some Lutheran theologians bestowing great importance on the visible church and the sacraments and ritual. These tendencies were exemplified in the thought of Wilhelm Löhe. A more democratic understanding of the church was promulgated in North America by the Missouri Synod theologian C.F.W. Walther. The most influential conception of the visible church was the historical-evolutionary doctrine of the German theologian Albrecht Ritschl, who saw the institutional church as the actualization of the Kingdom of God progressively realized in history.

The Lutheran confessions recognize two sacraments, baptism and the Lord's Supper. According to Lutheran teaching, the sacraments are acts instituted by Christ and connected with a divine promise. Faith is necessary for a salvatory reception of the sacrament. Thus, Lutherans reject the notion that the sacraments are effective *ex opere operato* (operative apart from faith) or that they are only symbolic actions.

The Lutheran affirmation that in the Lord's Supper Christ is bodily present "in, with, and under bread and wine" proved to be the great divisive issue of the 16th century. The Lutheran teaching of the "real" presence left open the question of whether Christ is present in the bread and wine because he is present everywhere, ubiquitously, as some Lutherans contend, or because he promises to be specifically present in the elements. In either case, Lutherans reject the Roman Catholic doctrine of transubstantiation, which asserts that the bread and wine are transformed into the literal body and blood of Christ, as an inappropriate use of philosophical categories to express biblical truth. Most Lutheran churches allow participation in the Lord's Supper to all baptized Christians who affirm the real presence of Christ in the elements of the bread and wine. Late 20th-century Lutheran theology, notably that of Wolfhart Pannenberg, sought to steer away from the elements of the bread and wine and to emphasize the notion of the Lord's Supper as a meal with the resurrected Jesus.

The ministry is understood as preaching and the administration of the sacraments. Unlike the ministry of the Roman Catholic Church, however, it does not entail a special status for the minister. Lutherans affirm the priesthood of all believers, according to which every baptized Christian may carry out, when properly called, the functions of ministry. While preaching and administration of the sacraments ordinarily is done by "rightly called" (ordained) ministers, Lutherans allow laypersons to carry out these functions when properly authorized.

Lutheran churches have not insisted on uniformity of the liturgy or even on uniformity of church structure. There have been Lutheran bishops in Scandinavia ever since the 16th century, whereas in Germany and North America other designations for such supervisory positions have been used. The title of bishop is accepted in the ELCA but not in the Missouri or the Wisconsin synod.

In 1970 both the LCA and the ALC approved the ordination of women, a practice carried over into the ELCA. The ordination of women is accepted by all Lutheran churches in Europe and North America except the Missouri and Wisconsin synods. Women were first ordained in Denmark in 1948. In Norway the parliament decreed the ordination of women in 1938, an act fiercely resisted by the overwhelming majority of bishops (the first woman was not ordained, however, until 1961). Most German Lutheran churches endorsed the change soon after the Norwegian decree.

CHURCH AND STATE

Lutheran theology has understood the relationship between church and state in terms of God's two ways of ruling in the world (two "realms" or "kingdoms"). The distinction is similar to that made by St. Augustine between the City of God and the City of the World. Luther argued that God governs the world in two ways: through orders of creation, such as government and marriage, which stem from God's desire that all people everywhere live in peace and harmony, and through his Word and Gospel, though these apply only to Christians. These two domains of power and grace are interdependent because the Gospel itself cannot preserve societal peace and justice, and civil government cannot effect salvation. Although this conception allowed North American Lutherans to accept the separation of church and state in the United States and elsewhere, it also meant that Lutheranism, unlike Calvinism, made little effort to "Christianize" the social and political order. Historically, this entailed the autonomy of the secular realm, even a certain subservience of the religious to the secular. Quite consistently, when the German peasants staged an uprising in 1524–25, Luther forcefully argued that social and political demands cannot be justified by the Gospel.

Lutheran theology stressed obedience to government as a Christian duty and did not, as did Reformed theology, produce a fully developed doctrine of resistance against tyrannical governments. Luther advocated resistance only if the preaching of the Gospel was in jeopardy. This principle was first put to the test in the middle of the 16th century, when the Lutheran city of Magdeburg successfully resisted Emperor Charles V's reintroduction of Catholicism.

Nazi totalitarianism caught German Lutheranism unprepared to offer a clear rationale for opposing tyranny. The weakness of Lutheran theology on this point became evident during the period of Nazi rule. Thus, when the government decreed racially exclusionary laws, which had implications for the churches, most Lutheran theologians conceded that it had the authority to do so under the divine order. The impact of Nazi Germany and other totalitarian regimes led some Lutheran church leaders, such as the German theologian Dietrich Bonhoeffer and the Norwegian bishop Eivind Berggrav, to reconsider the traditional Lutheran view.

ETHICS

Lutheran ethical teaching has been described as centring on faith active in

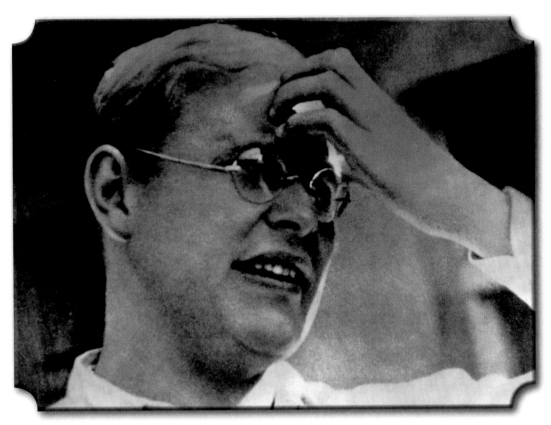

Dietrich Bonhoeffer in the 1930s. Authenticated News/Archive Photos/Getty Images

love, which means that the believer makes moral choices in freedom, without pre-set rules and laws. Lutheranism has thus eschewed the notion of a specifically Christian ethos but has insisted that the place of ethical endeavour is the common ordinary life, in which Christian believers are called upon to serve their neighbours. This ethical teaching, therefore, emphasized the sacredness of all human activities and maintained that an ethical life should be pursued apart from legalistic rules in what Martin Luther called "Christian freedom."

WORSHIP AND ORGANIZATION

Although Luther retained the basic structure of the mass and liturgy, he introduced significant changes in the worship service, primarily of a theological nature, in writings such as the *German Mass* of 1526. The emphasis in the traditional mass on the reiteration of the sacrifice of Jesus was replaced by an emphasis on thanksgiving. Luther saw the sacrament of the altar (the Lord's Supper) not as an autonomous form of the Gospel but as a proclamation of it. Therefore, he retained only the recitation of the words of institution ("In the night in which he was betrayed, Jesus...") from the prayer of thanksgiving. Because of the importance placed on the Bible, the sermon occupied the pivotal place in worship.

LITURGY AND MUSIC

In the early 21st century, most Lutheran churches followed essentially the same order of worship. It consisted of two main parts, Word (Liturgy of the Word) and the Lord's Supper, both understood as the proclamation of the Gospel. The liturgical movement in the 20th century, which sought to restore the active role of the laity in church services, affected Lutheranism by deemphasizing the didactic sermon and increasing the frequency of the celebration of the Lord's Supper. Other liturgical revisions (in Sweden in 1942, in Germany in 1954, and in North America in 1941, 1958, and 1978) increased the uniformity of Lutheran worship beyond national boundaries. Although traditionally only confirmed members received the Communion elements, in 1970 both the Lutheran Church in America and the American Lutheran Church endorsed participation in the Lord's Supper for baptized younger children, even for those who have not been confirmed. In the decades following the reform, a tendency emerged in the ELCA to allow even young children to receive the bread and wine.

Other rites of the Lutheran churches are baptism, confirmation, ordination, marriage, and burial. Lutherans practice infant baptism. In confirmation (which usually occurs between the ages of 10 and 15), the individual publicly professes the faith received in baptism.

Lutheranism made an important contribution to Protestant hymnody, which not only conveyed the evangelical teaching but also allowed for increased popular participation in worship. Many of the well-known Lutheran hymns come from the 16th and 17th centuries, notably "A

Mighty Fortress Is Our God," by Martin Luther, "O Sacred Head Now Wounded," by Paul Gerhardt, and "Wake, Awake, for Night Is Flying," by Philipp Nicolai. American Lutherans have been heir to this heritage, but since the 19th century they have also embraced the hymnody of Anglo-Saxon Protestantism. Hymns from the 20th century, such as those by the German composer Hugo Distler, have been adopted somewhat more sparingly, though in the early 21st century, as evidenced by the new ELCA hymnal and worship book, *Evangelical Worship*, a persistent effort was under way to make Lutheran hymnody contemporary and multicultural.

ORGANIZATION

The polity of the Lutheran churches differs between Scandinavia and Germany, with North American Lutheranism and Lutheran churches on other continents reflecting both traditions. The Church of Sweden, which ended its status as a state church in 2000, has maintained the episcopal office (and with it episcopal succession), and its local congregations have considerable freedom to appoint their own pastors. The Danish Church first rejected then reintroduced the episcopal office. In Norway the ties between church and state had traditionally been closer than in the other Scandinavian countries, with the parliament exercising a major voice in church affairs, but in 2006 the General Synod of the Church of Norway agreed that church and state

should separate in Norway. Since 1869 the Finnish Church has been independent of state control but is supported by public funds.

Until the end of World War I, the administrative affairs of the Lutheran churches in Germany were handled by government offices, with the ruler exercising important power as *summepiskopus*, or presiding bishop, a system of church governance that emerged from the Reformation. With the establishment of the Weimar Republic, the regional Lutheran churches (*Landeskirchen*) adopted new constitutions that in some provinces placed the congregations under a superintendent and a general synod while in others they were placed under a bishop. These *Landeskirchen* consisted of 15 Lutheran and 12 Prussian Union synods along with one Reformed synod. These churches were united in 1922 in the German Evangelical Church Federation (Deutscher Evangelischer Kirchenbund). For Lutherans the concurrent existence of both Lutheran churches and churches of the Prussian Union in the federation was highly problematic, since it posed the question of the federation's theological viability. Confessional Lutherans insisted on the creation of an Association of Evangelical Lutheran Churches (ELKD; Evangelisch-Lutherische Kirche Deutschlands).

After the end of World War II, the Lutheran, Prussian Union, and Reformed *Landeskirchen* organized the Evangelical Church in Germany (Evangelische Kirche in Deutschland, EKD), under the leadership of bishops Theophil Wurm and Hans Meiser and Pastor Martin Niemöller. The member churches of the EKD adopted the Declaration of Barmen, with its expression of the communalities of the Lutheran and Reformed traditions, as a foundational statement. To safeguard Lutheran confessional concerns, the United Evangelical Lutheran Church of Germany (Vereinigte Evangelisch-Lutherische Kirche Deutschlands, VELKD) was established in 1948 as the federation of Lutheran regional churches. By the late 20th and early 21st century, efforts had begun to integrate the VELKD more fully into the EKD.

Despite the division of Germany into four Allied zones of occupation at the end of World War II, the EKD encompassed both East and West Germany. The creation of the East German and West German states in 1949 initially did not mean the end of the EKD. In 1968 pressure from the East German government forced the East German churches to leave the EKD and establish their own East German Evangelical federation (United Evangelical Lutheran Church in the German Democratic Republic).

East German Lutherans, living in a society that was hostile to Christianity and intermittently persecuted Christians, sought to avoid confrontations with the state, even when it decreed an all but mandatory "youth consecration," which was to replace confirmation. In contrast to communist Poland, where the Catholic Church did not shy from outright confrontation with the regime, East German Lutherans were determined to cooperate

with the state whenever possible while at the same time affirming the need for the church to be the church. This strategy was expressed in the slogan "church within socialism." By the late 1970s a rapprochement with the communist regime had begun to take place. Nonetheless, membership in the Lutheran churches declined significantly in the roughly half-century of communist rule in East Germany. When the German Democratic Republic began to experience a series of human rights demonstrations in 1988 and 1989, Lutheran pastors and churches were in the forefront of the demand for greater civil liberties, thus playing an important role in the eventual disintegration of the East German state. The unification of Germany in 1990, however, had little impact on church membership, as the downward trend begun during communist rule continued. In the early 21st century less than 20 percent of the population of the former German Democratic Republic belonged to a Christian church.

In the United States the polity of the Lutheran churches is congregational, but in a complex form in which congregations yield some authority to synods on regional and national levels. Elected heads are called presidents in some Lutheran bodies, such as the Lutheran Church–Missouri Synod and the Wisconsin Synod Lutheran Church, while the Evangelical Lutheran Church of America uses the term *bishop* for its 65 synodical leaders. It also has a "presiding bishop," elected to a six-year term, who guides churchwide activities and initiatives. An assembly of all member churches meets every two years and is the legislative body of the ELCA. Besides these larger Lutheran church bodies, there are a number of smaller Lutheran churches both in Europe (e.g., the Evangelical Lutheran [Old Lutheran] Church in Germany) and in the United States (e.g., the Church of the Lutheran Confession or the Apostolic Lutheran Church), which have greater congregational autonomy.

A global association of Lutheran churches was first established in the Lutheran World Conventions, which met at Eisenach in 1923 and in Copenhagen in 1929. In 1947 it assumed permanent form as the Lutheran World Federation (LWF), an umbrella organization of the various national Lutheran churches. The LWF has no authority to speak for worldwide Lutheranism and mainly serves as a forum for intra-Lutheran discussion and ecumenical consultation with other churches. The LWF took the lead in ecumenical conversations with the Roman Catholic Church, which led to a "Joint Declaration" on justification, signed by representatives of the Roman Catholic Church and the LWF in 1999. The document declared that no substantive theological differences exist between the positions of the two churches on the topic. However, among Lutheran theologians, especially in Germany, the "Joint Declaration" evoked intense criticism for being unfaithful to the Lutheran tradition, even as the Roman curia also recorded reservations about the document, which nonetheless is understood as a milestone in Lutheran-Catholic relations.

The most exciting development of the 20th century was the dramatic expansion of Lutheranism beyond its European (and North American) homelands. Of the 65 million Lutherans who belonged to the LWF at the beginning of the 21st century, there were roughly 39 million in Europe, 5 million in North America, and 20 million in Asia and Africa. This new geographical diversity has created the same challenge for Lutheranism as it has for other global but originally European churches: that of maintaining traditional European and North American leadership in thought and practice as more and more adherents are found in other parts of the world. In the early 21st century there were about 30 Lutheran church bodies, with some 15 million members altogether, in Africa and more than 40 churches, with some 8 million members, in Asia.

REFORMED AND PRESBYTERIAN CHURCHES

Reformed churches consider themselves to be the Roman Catholic Church reformed. Calvin in his *Institutes* spoke of the holy Catholic church as mother of all the godly. Heinrich Bullinger in the Second Helvetic Confession made it clear that Reformed churches condemn what is contrary to ecumenical creeds.

PRESBYTERIAN AND REFORMED CHURCHES

Protestant bodies that owe their origins to the reformatory work of John Calvin and his associates in various parts of Europe are often termed *Reformed*, particularly in Germany, France, and Switzerland. In Britain and in the United States they have usually taken their name from their distinctive polity and have been called Presbyterian. They are distinguished from both Lutheranism and Anglicanism by the thoroughness of their separation from Roman Catholic patterns of liturgy, piety, and even doctrine. Reformed theology has tended to emphasize the sole authority of the Bible with more rigour than has characterized the practice of Anglican or Lutheran thought, and it has looked with deeper suspicion upon the symbolic and sacramental traditions of the Catholic centuries. Perhaps because of its stress upon biblical authority, Reformed Protestantism has sometimes tended to produce a separation of churches along the lines of divergent doctrine or polity, by contrast with the generally inclusive or even latitudinarian churchmanship of the more traditionalistic Protestant communions. This understanding of the authority of the Bible has also led Reformed Protestantism to its characteristic interpretation of the relation between church and state, sometimes labeled theocratic, according to which those charged with the proclamation of the revealed will of God in the Scriptures (i.e., the ministers) are to address this will also to civil magistrates. Puritanism in England and America gave classic expression to this view. As the church is "reformed according to the Word of God," so the lives of the individuals in the church are to conform to the Word of God; hence the Reformed tradition has assigned great prominence to the cultivation of moral uprightness among its members.

TEACHINGS

Interpretations of the early Church Fathers and decrees and canons of councils "were not to be despised, but we modestly dissent from them when they are found to set down things differing from, or altogether contrary to, the Scriptures."

DOCTRINES

Universal articles of Christian faith, such as the doctrines of the Trinity, the humanity and divinity of Christ, and the sin of man and the saving work of Christ, are affirmed in Reformed faith. Reformed churches share with Lutheran and other Protestant communions the concept of justification by grace through faith as central to the Gospel. The essence of faith is God's forgiving love coming as a gift through Jesus Christ. As with Lutherans, the true treasure of the church is this good news of the grace of God. Scripture is the authoritative witness of the good news, but, as was stated in the Westminster Confession, "authority thereof is from the inward work of the Holy Spirit, bearing witness by and with the word in our hearts." Calvin said: "There is no doubt that faith is a light of the Holy Spirit through which our understandings are enlightened and our hearts are confirmed in a sure persuasion." Such understanding is shared by Lutheran and Reformed Christians.

THE CHURCH AND THE SACRAMENTS

Calvin tried unsuccessfully to mediate between the Lutherans and Zwinglians, holding that Zwingli had been more concerned to show how Christ was not present than how he was and affirming, with Luther, the real presence of the resurrected Christ in communion. In the 1980s Lutheran and Reformed churches in Europe and the United States came to recognize each other's ministries of word and sacrament.

Both Calvin and Martin Bucer, more than Luther, were concerned to keep the "profane" from receiving communion. This encouraged the development of church discipline, and the use of elders to oversee discipline within the parish became a feature of Reformed church life. In the struggle to maintain that discipline, Calvin's successor, Theodore Beza, asserted that the presbyterian form of government was ordained by Christ.

SCRIPTURE AND TRADITION

Before the Reformation, humanists rejected arguments that appealed to the authority of church tradition. They made the authority of Scripture central in the church. Following them, Reformed Christians insisted that no authority in the church was on a level with Scripture; by Scripture all tradition was to be judged.

THE SOVEREIGNTY OF GOD AND DOUBLE PREDESTINATION

There has been no argument in Reformed theology about the positive side of the doctrine of predestination concerning the election of those whom God wills to save. Difference of opinion, however, arose over whether God determines who is reprobated. Bullinger did not believe that it was God's will that "one of these little ones should perish." He maintained that Christians should always hope for the best for all. Calvin affirmed "double" predestination, meaning that both reprobation and election are within the active will of God. His reason found this appalling but scriptural. To call God, thereby, unjust was to judge One who is the very standard of justice.

In his *Institutes* Calvin discussed predestination in the context of the love and grace of Jesus Christ. Later theologians expounded predestination more abstractly as an aspect of God's sovereignty. Arminianism rose in protest to this. The defenders of double predestination thought that Arminianism would cut the nerve of the Protestant doctrine of justification by grace alone and lead people back to popery. Hence, at Dort in 1618, double predestination was affirmed as Reformed orthodoxy.

WORSHIP AND ORGANIZATION

In the Reformation earlier liturgies were modified by using the vernacular, removing anything that implied the reenacting of sacrifice in the mass, providing for congregational confession, and emphasizing the preaching of the word. The singing of Psalms became characteristic of Reformed worship. While most Reformed churches today use a broad spectrum of vocal music, some hold exclusively to Psalms.

LITURGY

Stress on preaching reached its peak among English Puritans. Some clergy preached two hours on a text from the Hebrew Scriptures on Sunday morning, preached another two hours on a New Testament text in the afternoon, and devoted the evening to discussion of the day's sermons with the congregation. Calvin held that the Eucharist should be celebrated weekly, though others believed that it was too sacred for such frequent use. Care was taken to instruct participants and to prepare them for confession. The Eucharist was served around a table.

Since the 20th century attention has been given to relating worship to the social and material needs of human beings as well as to communicating the word to human hearts and minds. At the Iona Community in Scotland, for example, where worship is directed to those intending to work in economically deprived areas, and at the Taizé Community in France new forms of worship are being developed. In recent years there has been emphasis upon celebration in response to the good news of God, a greater appreciation of the arts in worship than in the past, and a concern for inclusive language.

RELIGIOUS EDUCATION

The requirements of Reformed life have demanded an educated clergy and an informed laity. Besides academic training for pastors, the early practice was for them to meet often and for one to interpret Scripture and for the others to engage in critical discussion. Queen Elizabeth I suppressed the custom in England, for she believed that four sermons a year were quite enough and that gatherings of pastors might be subversive.

Lay education was accomplished through preaching the word and teaching the catechism, such as Calvin's Little Catechism, which was designed for teaching the young. Others, such as the Westminster Larger Catechism, were used to instruct pastors and teachers. More recently catechetical instruction has given way to inductive forms of education, with emphasis on the age level at which instruction takes place. There is also concern to relate the Christian faith to the daily life of the larger community.

PRESENT ORGANIZATION

In Presbyterian churches a local congregation is ruled internally by a session moderated by the pastor and composed of laity (elders) elected from the congregation. A presbytery formed of pastors and elders representing each congregation rules over local congregations on a district level. In other Reformed churches the district association has less power and the local congregation more than in Presbyterian churches. In Hungarian Reformed churches a presiding bishop moderates the presbytery.

Beyond the district level are regional synods or conferences and national assemblies. These bodies are usually composed of an equal number of clergy and laity. Since 1875 there has been a World Alliance of Reformed Churches, which was joined in 1970 at Nairobi, Kenya, by the International Congregational Council to form the World Alliance of Reformed Churches (Presbyterian and Congregational). There are about 160 member denominations. Although a few Reformed groups still have a special relationship to the government of their nation, there is little difference in practice between established and free Reformed churches.

SOCIAL ETHICS

Reformation leaders were involved in the total life of their communities. Calvin's relation to the education, health and welfare services, refugee settlement, industry, finance, and politics of Geneva is well documented. The historian R.H. Tawney, impressed by this, has called Calvin a "Christian socialist." The English Puritans believed that if they could reshape the political and church life of the nation, God's blessing would come upon the land instead of war, famine, and pestilence. Concern to achieve greater social justice for humankind has been normative among Presbyterian and Reformed churches. Such concern in the past has been seen as resulting sometimes in petty

rules and harsh administration, but in new forms that concern is still a living force.

TYPES OF REFORMED PIETY

In Zwingli, Calvin, William the Silent, and Oliver Cromwell, a classic type of Reformed piety was manifest. Those persons saw themselves as God's instruments in redeeming human affairs, even at cost to themselves, and they had high expectations of others. Living under God's mercy, they showed little fear of the powers of this world and were ready to make choices on a pragmatic basis.

In a less heroic mold were Reformed Christians who did not expect to change history but who encouraged the development of godliness in those about them, beginning with themselves. The increasing emphasis in the late 16th century upon the personal experience of saving faith helped the Reformed tradition to become a nursery for Pietism in the late 17th and 18th centuries. Along with a more confessional orthodoxy and a more rationalistic liberalism, such Pietism remains to the present. A new style of worldly Christianity is emerging with Christ, standing for and with the oppressed, as the model.

CONGREGATIONALISM

Throughout their history, Congregationalists have shared the beliefs and practices of the more liberal mainline Evangelical Protestant churches of the English-speaking world.

TEACHINGS

The English historian Bernard Manning once described their position as decentralized Calvinism, in contrast to the centralized Calvinism of Presbyterians. That description contains much truth about their doctrines and outlook through the early 19th century, but it underestimates the Congregational emphasis on the free movement of the Spirit, which links the Congregationalists with the Quakers and partly explains their reluctance to give binding authority to creedal statements. They have not been slow to produce declarations of faith, however. In addition to the Savoy Declaration, the Cambridge Platform, and the Kansas City Creed, lengthy statements have also been made both by the United Church of Christ and by the English Congregationalists. No great authority is claimed for any of these, and in recent generations most Congregationalists have regarded the primitive confession, "Jesus is Lord," as a sufficient basis for membership.

Similarly, Congregationalists have always stressed the importance of freedom. Even in the days of Cromwell, they were tolerant by the standards of the time. They contributed greatly in the 18th century to the establishment of the rights of minorities in England through the activities of the Protestant Dissenting deputies, who had the right of direct access to the monarch. Both in England and in America, the long-faced and repressive Puritan of tradition owes as much to the caricatures of opponents as to actual fact.

PRACTICES

Congregationalism has always considered preaching important because the Word of God as declared in Scripture is regarded as constitutive of the church. Baptism and the Lord's Supper are considered to be the only sacraments instituted by Christ. Infants are baptized, normally by sprinkling. The Lord's Supper is normally celebrated once or twice a month and has not always been given a central place in the Congregationalist service, often following a preaching service after a brief interval during which many of the congregation leave. In recent times, the unity of sermon and sacrament as parts of the same service has been emphasized much more strongly. Traditionally, public prayer is extempore, but from the 20th century service books and set forms have increasingly been used. Since the 18th century and the work of the great Congregationalist hymn writer Isaac Watts, hymns have featured prominently in Congregational worship. The English compilation *Congregational Praise* (1951) worthily maintained the tradition. Congregationalists do not see the need to make the sign of the cross or to invoke the assistance of saints; Jesus Christ, they believe, is their only mediator.

POLITY

Congregationalism is unique in its emphasis on the spiritual autonomy of each congregation. The congregation, however, is not thought of as any casual gathering of Christians but as a settled body, with a well-defined constitution and offices, that has ordered itself according to the New Testament's understanding of the nature of the church. Congregationalists believe that no earthly place could be more fully a church than one possessing the Bible, the sacraments, a properly called and appointed minister and deacons, and members who have made a genuine Christian profession. It follows that, as the church is responsible to God for its life in that place, so it must have the freedom to discern and obey God's will for itself, with no interference from outside. Although this view respects the rights of individual conscience, it does not promote spiritual individualism; it is rather an attempt to treat the visible and corporate character of the church as concretely as possible.

It has always been recognized that this principle does not involve ecclesiastical isolation. But the nature of the precise relationship between the churches and the associations and councils through which the churches express their communion has often caused uneasy debate. In the 19th century, thinking about this relation was affected by the individualism of the age, whereas in the more centralized and mobile 20th century the positive role of councils was stressed. The authentic Congregational principle would appear to be that, whatever adaptations of organization may be necessary in changing circumstances, responsibility and the freedom to fulfill it must always be as specific and personal as possible.

According to Congregationalists, "the crown rights of the Redeemer" (Christ) are impugned whenever the state or a prelacy imposes its will on the church. Consequently, the idea of the "gathered" church is integral to Congregationalism, even though the extent to which the idea can be applied to churches with large formal memberships remains a problem for modern Congregationalists. The idea of the gathered church entails that the primary agent in church foundation is not human but divine. Rejecting the Anglican territorial conception of the church, according to which all residents of a particular neighbourhood should be counted as members, Congregationalists insist that it is the duty and privilege of the believer to discover who else in the vicinity is called by Christ and then to walk together with them in church order, which is thought as a matter not of organization but of common lifestyle. Church members are granted equal rights and are expected to exercise them in the church meeting, a regular gathering, usually monthly, that addresses matters pertaining to the particular church's life such as admission of members and election of officers. Church meetings have not always been very vigorous, and, especially in the United States, many of their powers have been delegated to officers or committees, but efforts have been made to restore them to their important place.

Congregational ministers are ordained through acceptance for training by the churches acting together and then by the call from a particular church to act as its minister. The churches corporately set standards for training, which, particularly in the United States and Canada, is frequently conducted in interdenominational seminaries or universities. This training is open to women, as are all offices in the Congregational church, which ordained its first woman in 1917.

Until new patterns were established by mergers, nearly all Congregational churches formed associations or unions on local, provincial, or national levels. Superintendent ministers or moderators have been appointed to oversee the churches of the association, but their role is not that of diocesan bishops, since they are not regarded as the sources of ecclesiastical order and have no formal authority over independent churches. It is a Congregational principle that the service of the Word and the sacraments, rather than one's place in a system of ecclesiastical administration, confers authority on a minister.

Churches are financed mainly by the contributions of members. There are substantial denominational funds to finance pensions and stipends for missionary work, but even these depend heavily on contributions from the churches as well as on endowments.

CONGREGATIONALISM IN THE 21ST CENTURY

Although Congregationalism has not succeeded in establishing itself as one of the major forms of churchmanship, its ideas and practices have greatly influenced the modern world. It has flourished in smaller cities and in the suburbs of larger cities, where, especially in the 19th century, it played a prominent role in civic, educational, and cultural life. Congregationalism has also been a major factor in shaping the institutions and the general culture of the United States and, to a lesser degree, of Britain and the Commonwealth, particularly in the 19th century. In the 20th century, however, Congregationalism lost much of its influence because of increasing geographic mobility, greater centralization of business organizations, and decreasing continuity of lifestyle between one generation and the next. The number of Congregational churches has also declined, and most of them are now part of the Reformed family of churches; there were roughly 2.4 million Congregationalists worldwide at the start of the 21st century. Whether what is distinctive in Congregationalism can be effectively maintained under the pressures of modern urban mobility in more centrally organized churches is still to be seen.

ANGLICANISM

The Anglican Communion holds to the faith as expounded by the Scriptures and by the early Church Fathers. It respects the authority of the state but does not submit to it, and it equally respects the freedom of the individual. The Anglican Communion does not seek to evade the challenges of the world or to live a life separate from it. Basing its doctrines on the Bible, the Anglican Communion allows a remarkable latitude of interpretation by both clergy and laity.

TEACHINGS

What has come to be known as the Lambeth Quadrilateral defines the essential beliefs of Anglicanism.

DOCTRINAL VIEWS

First suggested by an American, William Reed Huntington, in 1870, the Quadrilateral states four elements essential to the Anglican conception of Christian identity—the Bible, the Nicene Creed, baptism and Holy Communion, and the episcopate. The Lambeth Conference of 1930 further clarified the nature of Anglicanism when it described the Anglican Communion as

a fellowship within the One Holy Catholic and Apostolic Church, of those duly constituted Dioceses, Provinces or Regional Churches in communion with the See of Canterbury, which uphold and propagate the...faith and order as they are generally set forth in the Book of Common Prayer...; promote within each of their territories a national expression of Christian faith, life and worship; and are bound together not by a central legislative and executive authority, but by mutual loyalty sustained

through the common counsel of the Bishops in conference.

The Church of England, the oldest of the Anglican national churches, also holds close to the spirit of the Thirty-nine Articles. This doctrinal statement was drawn up by the clergy of Canterbury in the mid-16th century and approved by Elizabeth I in 1571. Nevertheless, subscription to the articles is not required of the laity, and adherence by the clergy is expected only in a general way. Other churches or councils of the Anglican Communion take different views of the articles, but none regards them as having, for example, the status of the historic statements of belief set forth in the Apostles' Creed or the Nicene Creed, nor do they accord them the status given to other 16th-century doctrinal statements, such as the Augsburg Confession of the Lutheran churches or the Westminster Confession of the Reformed and Presbyterian churches.

THE MINISTRY

Anglicans accept a threefold order of ministry, consisting of bishops, priests or presbyters, and deacons. Although they hold to the view of succession from the Apostles, they are not committed to any particular theory regarding the conveyance of that ministry. Anglicans attempt to balance the clerical point of view with forms of authority that include the laity. Even bishops are rarely able to function without the advice and consent of other clergy and laity.

WORSHIP AND ORGANIZATION

Worship is the centre of Anglican life. Anglicans view their tradition as a broad form of public prayer, and they attempt to encompass diverse Christian styles in a traditional context.

ANGLICAN WORSHIP

Although *The Book of Common Prayer* is the most apparent mark of Anglican identity, it has undergone many revisions and wears national guises. The prayer book of 1662 represents the official version in the Church of England, but a 1928 version is commonly used. In 2000 the church introduced *Common Worship*, a modernized collection of services and prayers, as an official alternative to the 1662 prayer book.

Outside England a few Anglicans still rely upon the English prayer book of 1662, but most have their own versions, increasingly in languages other than English. All forms hold to the essential, historic elements of the prayer book but incorporate local idioms. In recent years there has been a recovery of ancient liturgical styles and vestments as well as an increased emphasis on the Eucharist as the central act of Christian worship. Experimental rites have appeared in different parts of the Anglican world. Change in Anglican worship has meant increased variety, new roles for the laity, and a tendency toward freedom of expression while retaining the essence of the church's traditional forms.

COMPREHENSIVENESS IN DOCTRINE AND PRACTICE

Often said to be the middle way between Roman Catholic and Protestant churches, the Anglican Communion is comprehensive in matters of doctrine and practice. While asserting the importance of the apostolic succession of bishops and *The Book of Common Prayer*, it nevertheless allows a considerable degree of flexibility in most doctrinal and liturgical matters. Thus, within the Communion there are several schools of thought and practice, including High Church, Anglo-Catholic, Low Church or Evangelical, and others. The various churches of the Anglican Communion, though autonomous, are bound together by a common heritage and common doctrinal and liturgical concerns, and there has always been a considerable amount of interchange of ecclesiastical personnel.

AUTHORITY AND STRUCTURE

The Anglican Communion consists of autonomous national churches that are bound together by intangible links best described as ties of loyalty between the see of Canterbury and each other. Although the archbishop of Canterbury is respected throughout the Communion and his words carry great moral authority, he exercises no jurisdiction over any part of the Communion other than the diocese of Canterbury and the Church of England as a whole through the authority vested in synods and convocations.

Like a family, the Anglican Communion changes its form and shape, growing larger when new provinces (areas of jurisdiction) are formed and smaller when schemes of union with non-Anglican churches are consummated.

The basic unit of the Anglican Communion is the diocese, a geographic area over which a bishop presides. Dioceses generally form part of a larger unit known as a province, but even these are far from uniform in configuration. A province may, for example, be part of an autonomous church: the Anglican Church of Australia has five provinces and that of Canada four; the Churches of England and Ireland have two each; and the Episcopal Church in the United States of America (ECUSA) has nine. Some provinces, however, include whole countries, such as Japan, Kenya, Uganda, and Tanzania. Other provinces cover a number of countries, such as the provinces of Southern Africa, West Africa, Central Africa, the West Indies, and the Southern Cone of America. On occasion, one diocese covers a whole country or even several countries, such as the diocese of Polynesia.

Variations occur in the titles of the heads of the various provinces or national churches. England has two archbishops (Canterbury and York), known as metropolitans, as does Ireland. Canada has a primate (who has no province) and four metropolitans. Australia has five archbishops, one of whom—while having jurisdiction over a province—is known as the primate. The church

of Japan and that of Brazil each have a primate who also has a diocese, and the United States has a presiding bishop and a primate, both without a diocese. To complicate organizational matters, the Scottish Episcopal Church has a primus (primate), and the ECUSA has presidents (who are elected for three-year periods) of its nine provinces.

Several branches of the church exist apart from provincial or national churches, though usually in reliance upon either the Church of England or the ECUSA. A number of dioceses in Central America, as in Guatemala, Honduras, Nicaragua, and El Salvador, participate in the ECUSA, though with the goal of eventual autonomy in a Central American province. The church in Hong Kong, once a special adjunct to the Council of Churches of East Asia, now constitutes a province, and Bermuda is an extraprovincial see of the Church of England. In some areas, such as China, India, and Pakistan, Anglicans have participated in the creation of ecumenical forms of church union.

BAPTIST CHURCHES

Initially, Baptists were characterized theologically by strong to moderate Calvinism. The dominant continuing tradition in both England and the United States was Particular Baptist. By 1800 this older tradition was beginning to be replaced by evangelical doctrines fashioned by the leaders of the evangelical revival in England and the Great Awakening in the

United States. By 1900 the older Calvinism had almost completely disappeared, and Evangelicalism was dominant. The conciliatory tendency of Evangelicalism and its almost complete preoccupation with "heart religion" and the experience of conversion largely denuded it of any solid theological structure, thereby opening the door to a new theological current that subsequently became known as modernism. This was an attempt to adjust the Christian faith to the new intellectual climate, made large inroads among the Baptists of England and the United States during the early years of the 20th century, and Baptists provided many outstanding leaders of the movement, including Shailer Mathews and Harry Emerson Fosdick. Many people regarded these views as a threat to the uniqueness of the Christian revelation, and the counterreaction that was precipitated became known as fundamentalism, a movement emphasizing biblical literalism.

CONTENTS OF FAITH

As a result of the controversy that followed, many Baptists developed a distaste for theology and became content to find their unity as Baptists in promoting denominational enterprises. By 1950, outside the South, both modernists and fundamentalists were becoming disenchanted with their positions in the controversy, and it was from among adherents of both camps that a more creative theological encounter began to take place. While the majority of Baptists remained nontheological in their interests and concerns, there were many signs that Baptist leadership was increasingly recognizing the necessity for renewed theological inquiry.

The unity and coherence of the Baptists is based on six distinguishing, although not necessarily distinctive, convictions they hold in common.

1. The supreme authority of the Bible in all matters of faith and practice. Baptists are non-creedal, and their ultimate appeal always has been to the Scriptures rather than to any confession of faith that they may have published from time to time to make known their commonly accepted views.

2. Believer's baptism. This is the most conspicuous conviction of Baptists. They hold that if baptism is the badge or mark of a Christian, and if a Christian is a believer in whom faith has been awakened, then baptism rightly administered must be a baptism of believers only. Furthermore, if the Christian life is a sharing in the life, death, and resurrection of Christ, if it involves a dying to the old life and a rising in newness of life, then the act of baptism must reflect these terms. The sign must be consonant with that which it signifies. It is for this latter reason that Baptists were led to insist upon immersion as the apostolic form of the rite.

3. Churches composed of believers only. Baptists reject the idea of a territorial or parish church and insist that a church is composed only of those who have been gathered by Christ and who have placed their trust in him. Thus the membership of a church is restricted to those who—in terms of a charitable judgment—give clear evidence of their Christian faith and experience.

4. Equality of all Christians in the life of the church. By the doctrine of the priesthood of all believers Baptists not only understand that the individual Christian may serve as a minister to other members but also that each church member has equal rights and privileges in determining the affairs of the church. Pastors have special responsibilities, derived from the consent of the church, which only they can discharge, but they have no unique priestly status.

5. Independence of the local church. By this principle Baptists affirm that a properly constituted congregation is fully equipped to minister Christ and need not derive its authority from any source, other than Christ, outside its own life. Baptists, however, have not generally understood that a local church is autonomous in the sense that it is isolated and detached from other churches. As individual Christians are bound to pray for one another and to maintain communion with one another, so particular churches are under similar obligation. Thus, the individual churches testify to their unity in Christ by forming associations and conventions.

6. Separation of church and state. From the time of founder John Smyth, Baptists have insisted that a church must be free to be Christ's church, determining its own life and charting its own course in obedience to Christ without outside interference. Thus Smyth asserted that the

magistrate is not by virtue of his office to meddle with religion or matters of conscience, to force and compel men to this or that form of religion or doctrine, but to leave Christian religion free to every man's conscience.

Baptists were in the forefront of the struggle for religious freedom in both England and the United States. They cherished the liberty established in early Rhode Island, and they played an important role in securing the adoption of the "no religious test" clause in the U.S. Constitution and the guarantees embodied in the First Amendment.

Few Baptists have been willing to become so sectarian as to deny the Christian name to other denominations.

CONFESSION OF FAITH

A confession of faith is usually more extensive than a creed. It is a formal statement of doctrinal belief ordinarily intended for public avowal by an individual, a group, a congregation, a synod, or a church. The medieval Christian Church did not attempt an official codification of its doctrine. The creeds inherited from antiquity (Nicene Creed) or formulated in the early Middle Ages (Apostles' Creed, Athanasian Creed) were used in liturgical worship to confess the Christian faith. Certain doctrinal points were defined by councils as a result of doctrinal controversies. A decree on the seven sacraments issued by the Council of Ferrara-Florence in 1439 was a statement concerning one important part of the doctrinal system. But there was still no codification of doctrine. Nor did the heretical movements in the Middle Ages produce comprehensive declarations of faith.

The Reformation in the 16th century led to the formulation of declarations aiming at a definition of all the main points of the doctrinal system. Most of these documents were compiled with the purpose of expressing the church's doctrine; a few of them originally served other purposes but were soon given the rank of doctrinal standards. The first confessional documents of the Reformation were the drafts preceding the Augsburg Confession of 1530. This example set by the Lutherans was followed by the other Reformation churches, and it was even followed by the Council of Trent (1545–63), whose decrees and canons, together with the Professio fidei Tridentina *of 1564, were a codification of Roman Catholic doctrinal tenets. Other important Protestant confessions include the Lutheran Schmalkald Articles (1537), Formula of Concord (1577), and Book of Concord (1580); the Reformed Helvetic Confessions (1536, 1566), Gallican Confession (1559), Belgic Confession (1561), Heidelberg Catechism (1563), and Canons of Dort (1619); the Presbyterian Westminster Confession (1648); and the Anglican Thirty-nine Articles (1571).*

With the exception of the Southern Baptists, most Baptists cooperate fully in interdenominational and ecumenical bodies, including the World Council of Churches.

WORSHIP AND ORGANIZATION

Baptist worship is hardly distinguishable from the worship of the older Puritan denominations (Presbyterians and Congregationalists) of England and the United States. It centres largely on the exposition of the Scriptures in a sermon and emphasizes extemporaneous, rather than set, prayers. Hymn singing also is one of the characteristic features of worship. Communion, received in the pews, is customarily a monthly observance.

Baptists insist that the fundamental authority, under Christ, is vested in the local congregation of believers, which admits and excludes members, calls and ordains pastors, and orders its common life in accord with what it understands to be the mind of Christ. These congregations are linked together in cooperative bodies—regional associations, state conventions, and national conventions—to which they send their delegates or messengers. The larger bodies, it is insisted, have no control or authority over a local church; they exist only to implement the common concerns of the local churches.

The pattern of organization of the local church has undergone change during the 20th century. Traditionally the pastor was the leader and moderator of the congregation, but there has been a tendency to regard the pastor as an employed agent of the congregation and to elect a lay member to serve as moderator at corporate meetings of the church. Traditionally the deacons' functions were to assist the pastor and to serve as agents to execute the will of the congregation in matters both temporal and spiritual; there has been a tendency, however, to multiply the number of church officers by the creation of boards of trustees, boards of education, boards of missions, and boards of evangelism. Traditionally decisions were made by the congregation in a church meeting, but there has been a tendency to delegate decision making to various boards. The relationship of local churches to the cooperative bodies has undergone similar change, which has occasioned ongoing discussion among all Baptist groups.

METHODIST CHURCHES

Methodism is marked by an acceptance of the doctrines of historical Christianity; by an emphasis on doctrines that indicate the power of the Holy Spirit to confirm the faith of believers and to transform their personal lives; by an insistence that the heart of religion lies in a personal relationship with God; by simplicity of worship; by the partnership of ordained ministers and laity in the worship and administration of the church; by a concern for the underprivileged and the improvement of social conditions; and (at least in its British form) by the formation of small groups for mutual encouragement and edification.

TEACHINGS

All Methodist churches accept the Scriptures as the supreme guide to faith and practice. Most welcome the findings of modern biblical scholarship, though the fundamentalist groups among them do not. The churches follow the historical creeds and believe that they are part of the tradition of the Protestant Reformation. They emphasize the teaching of Christian perfection, interpreted as "perfect love," which is associated with John Wesley, who held that every Christian should aspire to such perfection with the help of the Holy Spirit.

Methodist churches affirm infant baptism. They also regularly receive the sacrament of the Lord's Supper, in which they believe Christ to be truly present, though they have no precise definition of the manner of his presence. They believe that they are integral parts of the one, holy, catholic, and apostolic church and that their ministers are true ministers of Word and sacrament in the church of God.

Worship and Organization

Methodist worship everywhere is partly liturgical and partly spontaneous.

Patterns of Service

The general pattern was established by John Wesley, who regularly used the Anglican *Book of Common Prayer* (which he adapted for use in the United States) and conducted services that included extemporaneous prayer. This tradition continued in British Methodism into the 20th century, when it underwent change. The practice of Anglican morning prayer was eliminated first, and during the Liturgical Movement, when Roman Catholic and Protestant churches revised their liturgies, Anglican Holy Communion was dropped. The Liturgical Movement also influenced the *Methodist Service Book* (1975) in Britain and, in the United States, the *Book of Worship* (1965), the *Ordinal* (1980), and the *United Methodist Hymnal*, subtitled *The Book of United Methodist Worship* (1988). The reforms provided new opportunity for congregational participation. The Sunday service, or Holy Communion, restores the traditional fourfold pattern—the offering of bread and wine, the thanksgiving, the breaking of the bread, and the sharing of the elements. Nonliturgical services, which constitute the majority, claim to be spontaneous but are not. In British but not in American Methodism, many services are conducted by lay preachers.

Hymns are important in all branches of Methodism. The most important hymns of British Methodism are those of Charles Wesley, which are mingled with many contemporary hymns as well as those from other traditions. In *Hymns and Psalms* (1983), certain changes were made to eliminate overtones that Methodists considered sexist. American books contain fewer hymns by Wesley.

Polity

In the churches of the British tradition, the annual Conference is the supreme authority for doctrine, order, and practice. All ministers have equal status, but the president and secretary of the Conference, the chairmen of districts, the secretaries of divisions, and superintendents exercise special duties. District affairs are regulated by Synods, circuits by Circuit Meetings, local societies by Church Councils.

The American tradition is episcopal; the bishops are elected by the Jurisdictional Conferences, which, like the General Conference, meet every four years. Each diocese has an annual Conference and District Conferences, each with its superintendent. The dioceses are combined into five jurisdictions that cover the country. A minister is ordained first a deacon, then an elder.

There are Methodist churches in most European countries. Those in Italy and Portugal are of English origin, those in

Germany of mixed English and American origin. Methodist churches in the rest of Europe are derived from American Methodism, though they exhibit many similarities in spirituality to the English type. Many Methodist churches in Latin America, Africa, and Asia (Taiwan, South Korea, and the Church of South India, a united church also including Anglicans, Congregationalists, and Presbyterians) are also similar in structure and worship to American Methodist churches.

PENTECOSTALISM

Pentecostalism is a religious movement that gave rise to a number of Protestant churches in the United States in the 20th century. It is unique in its belief that all Christians should seek a postconversion religious experience called baptism with the Holy Spirit. Recalling the Holy Spirit's descent upon the first Christians in Jerusalem on the day of Pentecost, or Shabuoth (Acts of the Apostles 2–4), this experience appears to have been common in the Christian movement during its first generations.

Baptism with the Holy Spirit is also believed to be accompanied by a sign, the gift of tongues. This "speaking in tongues" occurs as glossalalia (speech in an unknown language) or xenoglossy (speech in a language known to others but not the speaker). Speaking in tongues is considered one of the gifts of the Spirit described by St. Paul the Apostle (1 Corinthians 12), and Pentecostals believe that those baptized by the

Holy Spirit may receive other supernatural gifts that purportedly existed in the early church: the ability to prophesy, to heal, or to interpret speaking in tongues. Faith healing is also part of the Pentecostal tradition, which reflects patterns of faith and practice characteristic of the Baptist and Methodist-Holiness churches—the Protestant denominations from which most of the first generation of Pentecostals came. Like them, Pentecostals emphasize conversion, moral rigour, and a literal interpretation of the Bible. However, Pentecostals never formed a single organization; instead individual congregations came together to found the various denominations that constitute the movement today.

THE ORIGINS OF PENTECOSTALISM

Although Pentecostals trace their origin to the Apostles, the modern-day Pentecostal movement has its roots in the late 19th century, a time of mounting indifference to traditional religion. Denominations that were known for revivalistic fervour became subdued. Emotional modes of religious expression—enthusiastic congregational singing, spontaneous testimonies, prayer in unison, and extemporaneous sermons on simple biblical themes by lay preachers—gave way to ordered, formal worship services that were conducted by "reverends," ministers trained in homiletics (preaching skills), who were influenced by higher biblical criticism. Lecture centres and elegant sanctuaries replaced camp meetings and crude wood-frame tabernacles.

As the large popular Protestant denominations became the churches of the upper-middle class, people of limited means began to feel out of place. They yearned to return to a "heart religion" that would satisfy their spiritual desires and their emotional, psychological, and physical needs. Pentecostalism, like its precursor, the Holiness movement (based on the belief that a second work of grace following conversion would "sanctify" Christians and remove the desire to sin), fulfilled these needs for churchgoers and nonchurchgoers alike. Moreover, Pentecostal churches, though open to all levels of society, spoke to the special needs of the disaffected.

Notwithstanding the charismatic outbursts in some 19th-century Protestant churches, the watershed of contemporary Pentecostalism came in the early 20th century at Bethel Bible College, a small religious school in Topeka, Kansas. The college's director, Charles Fox Parham, one of many ministers who was influenced by the Holiness movement, believed that the complacent, worldly, and coldly formalistic church needed to be revived by another outpouring of the Holy Spirit. He instructed his students—many of whom already were ministers—to pray, fast, study the Scriptures, and, like the Apostles, await the blessings of the Holy Spirit.

On Jan. 1, 1901, Agnes Oznam became the first of Parham's students to speak in an unknown tongue. Others soon had the same experience, and Parham claimed that glossolalia was the "initial evidence" that one had been truly baptized with the Holy Spirit. Parham and his students understood these recurrences of Pentecost prophetically, interpreting them as signs of the imminence of the last days, or Endtime. Imbued with this sense of urgency, they set out on an evangelical mission.

Their initial efforts were unsuccessful, and the movement nearly collapsed as it encountered disbelief and ridicule. In 1903 its fortunes were revived when Parham returned to the practice of faith healing. Borrowed from several Holiness churches, notably the Christian and Missionary Alliance, faith healing became a hallmark of Pentecostalism. Parham was the first in a long line of Pentecostal evangelists (Mary B. Woodworth-Etter, Charles Price, Aimee Semple McPherson, and, more recently Oral Roberts, Kathryn Kuhlman, and Benny Hinn) who taught that Christ's atonement provides deliverance from sickness and is, therefore, the privilege of all who have the requisite faith. Attracting new converts, the movement enjoyed success in the American South and Southwest, especially in Texas, Alabama, and Florida. In Texas alone, 25,000 people had embraced the Pentecostal faith by 1905, according to Parham. Kansas and Missouri also became hotbeds for Pentecostalism.

Wider national and international expansion, however, resulted from the Azusa Street revival that began in 1906 at the Apostolic Faith Gospel Mission at 312 Azusa Street in Los Angeles. Its leader,

Aimee Semple McPherson. Topical Press Agency/Getty Images

William Seymour, a one-eyed Holiness church pastor and former member of the African Methodist Episcopal church, had been exposed to Parham's teachings at a Bible school in Houston, Texas. Under Seymour's guidance, the old frame building on Azusa Street became a great spiritual centre that for many years attracted rich and poor, blacks and whites, Anglos and Latinos, as well as many preachers whose own ministry had become staid.

Spiritually energized and convinced that they had been charismatically endowed, scores of men and women from Azusa and other Pentecostal churches began extolling the reality of speaking in tongues. Pentecostal Christians were linked only by an amorphous "spiritual union," in part because no thought was given to forming a separate "Pentecostal" branch of the Christian church. As members of the historic Protestant churches embraced Pentecostal beliefs and practices, they did so without any intention of withdrawing from their own churches. They merely wanted to be agents of reform and revival, helping to rid their churches of formalism and worldliness. They strove to transform their congregations into Spirit-filled communities like those described in the New Testament book Acts of the Apostles. Moreover, they fully expected the prophetically promised "latter rain" (from the Book of Joel, an outpouring of the Spirit of God before the final judgment) to fall upon their churches and make them wholly Pentecostal.

In one or two cases churches did sever their mainstream ties and become Pentecostal (e.g., the transformation of the Christian Union to the Church of God, headquartered in Cleveland, Tennessee). But the triumphant conquest of the Protestant churches by Pentecostal ideas during those early years never materialized. In fact, the movement became the object of widespread opposition. Pastors who endorsed Pentecostal practices were relieved of their pulpits; missionaries who were sympathetic toward the charismatic movement lost their financial support; and parishioners speaking in tongues were expelled from their churches. Resolutions were passed and anathemas (the harshest form of excommunication) were pronounced against Pentecostals in traditional churches. Charismatic Christians found it increasingly difficult to practice their faith within the institutional framework of conventional Protestantism; consequently, many Pentecostals withdrew from their churches to form new ones.

By the beginning of World War I, new congregations had emerged as storefront missions, small tabernacles in sparsely populated rural areas, and upper-story lofts in squalid urban neighbourhoods. These modest dwellings, found across North America, housed poor but lively groups of Pentecostal believers under such names as the Pentecostal, Apostolic, Latter Rain, or Full Gospel churches. Although many Pentecostals were wary of administrative institutions and unwilling to subject themselves to external ecclesiastical control, various divisive issues drove them into denominational fellowships.

In 1913 a new doctrine challenged the consensus theology that Pentecostals had inherited from their Protestant forebears. R.E. McAlister, following the formula for baptism found in Acts of the Apostles rather than that in The Gospel According to Matthew, taught that water baptism in the early church was not done according to the familiar Trinitarian formula (i.e., in the name of the Father, the Son, and the Holy Spirit) but in the name of Jesus Christ alone. McAlister's teaching led to the emergence of the Apostolic, or "Jesus Only," movement. Among the Pentecostal churches that adhere to this non-Trinitarian theology are the United Pentecostal Church International and the Church of the Lord Jesus Christ of the Apostolic Faith. As the movement spread, however, Trinitarian Pentecostals banded together to prevent the spread of what they considered heresy.

Even before McAlister's teaching, the issue of Holiness divided members of the new faith. Parham, Seymour, and other early Pentecostals came from the Holiness tradition that taught Christians to seek "sanctification." They built upon that heritage and taught that the baptism of the Holy Spirit was for people who had already experienced sanctification. On the other hand, Pentecostals from Baptist backgrounds disagreed and taught that the baptism of the Holy Spirit was for every believer. This doctrinal division drove Pentecostals into two warring camps. The Holiness Pentecostal belief is represented by such groups as the International Pentecostal Holiness Church; among the groups that emerged from a Baptist background are the Christian Church of North America and the International Church of the Foursquare Gospel.

Although Pentecostal fellowships generally emerged as the result of doctrinal differences, nonreligious factors, such as the outbreak of World War I, also contributed to their development. For example, the majority of Pentecostals were pacifists when the war started, but they and even those who were not pacifists found themselves without a voice in Washington, D.C., on matters of armed service. The Assemblies of God, an organization of independent Trinitarian Pentecostals, was founded in Hot Springs, Arkansas, in 1914 in response to the need for better relations between the churches and the government. Racial issues also affected the Pentecostal movement. For instance, the Azusa revival was led by an African American minister who welcomed worshipers regardless of their race, and the first formal Pentecostal denomination, the Pentecostal Assemblies of the World, was organized as an interracial fellowship (and remained such). This liberal racial attitude bred controversy, however, and as Pentecostalism spread into the Deep South the movement became segregated along the same racial lines as had the older denominations.

INTERNATIONAL GROWTH OF PENTECOSTALISM

Inspired by Acts of the Apostles 2:1–13, which speaks of God pouring out his Spirit in the last days, many Pentecostals believe that their revival is a sign of the Endtime, and hence a call to bring the world to salvation before Christ's Second Coming. Like the Apostles who spoke to people from many nations in their own tongues on the first Pentecost, Pentecostals believe that speaking in tongues facilitates the conversion of the world's peoples. Thus, Pentecostalism developed into an international missionary effort almost immediately. The movement spread first among ethnic communities in North America and was quickly transferred to Europe. By the end of 1906, missionary work had begun in Norway, and in 1907 it reached the rest of Scandinavia and Germany, Italy, and Holland. Latinos who took part in the Azusa Street revival helped spread the movement to Mexico, and a vital Spanish-speaking church movement developed there and in the southwestern United States. The Assemblies of God and the Church of God developed large Spanish-language branches, and completely new autonomous denominations formed in both Mexico and Puerto Rico. From these groups, Pentecostalism spread into the rest of Latin America, where it became especially popular in the latter decades of the 20th century.

Pentecostal missionaries reached South Africa in 1907 and found a home in the mission established only a few years earlier by representatives of the Christian Catholic church, an American church that emphasized healing. They were joined in 1914 by Assemblies of God missionaries. Nicholas B.H. Bhengu, a former Lutheran who joined the Assemblies of God, was the first great African-born Pentecostal evangelist. With the emergence of the African Independent church movement after World War II, Pentecostalism became a mass movement across sub-Saharan Africa.

Pentecostalism grew throughout the 20th century in North America, even though it was dismissed by mainstream denominations and denounced as heresy by conservative Evangelical groups that rejected the notions of faith healing and speaking in tongues. As segments of the movement became comfortable in their new faith and settled into less spontaneous worship, speaking in tongues and faith healing became somewhat routinized. In reaction to the loss of fervour, revitalization efforts periodically appeared that generally led to the creation of new Pentecostal denominations, more than 100 of which now exist. The growth of Pentecostalism in the late 20th century was not limited to its traditional constituency, however, and included members from the larger Protestant and Roman Catholic churches. This success with mainstream Protestants and Roman Catholics in the 1970s was one of the more important events in Pentecostal history and led to the formation of Charismatic (from Greek *charis*, "gift") fellowships in most of the major American denominations. While many welcomed the new life these fellowships represented, denominational leaders saw them as disruptive. As a result, most Charismatic members of mainline churches left to form new denominations.

Although statistics on Pentecostalism are difficult to obtain, it has been estimated that there are more than 10 million Pentecostals in the United States, including 5.5 million members of the Church of God in Christ and 2.5 million members of the Assemblies of God. There are a number of African and Latin American Pentecostal denominations claiming more than a million members. The Assemblies of God probably constitutes the largest Pentecostal denomination worldwide with more than 25 million members and with congregations in more than 150 countries.

CHRISTIAN FUNDAMENTALISM

Christian fundamentalism is a movement in American Protestantism that arose in the late 19th century in reaction to theological modernism, which aimed to revise traditional Christian beliefs to accommodate new developments in the natural and social sciences, especially the advent of the theory of biological evolution. In keeping with traditional Christian doctrines concerning biblical interpretation, the mission of Jesus Christ, and the role of the church in society, fundamentalists affirmed a core of Christian beliefs that included the historical accuracy of the Bible, the imminent and physical Second Coming of Jesus Christ, and Christ's Virgin Birth, Resurrection, and Atonement. Fundamentalism became a significant phenomenon in the early 20th century

and remained an influential movement in American society into the 21st century.

Fundamentalist worship practices, which are heavily influenced by revivalism, usually feature a sermon with congregational singing and prayer, though there can be considerable variation from denomination to denomination. Although fundamentalists are not notably ascetic, they do observe certain prohibitions. Most fundamentalists do not smoke, drink alcoholic beverages, dance, or attend movies or plays. At most fundamentalist schools and institutes, these practices are strictly forbidden.

ORIGINS

During the 19th century, major challenges to traditional Christian teachings arose on several fronts. Geologic discoveries revealed that the Earth was far older than the few thousand years suggested by a literal reading of the biblical book of Genesis. The work of Charles Darwin (1809–82) and his colleagues established that human beings as a species had emerged over millions of years through a process of evolution, rather than suddenly by divine fiat. Social scientists and philosophers influenced by Herbert Spencer (1820–1903) advocated a parallel theory of progressive social evolution that refuted the traditional religious understanding of human sin, which was predicated on the notion that, after the fall from grace, the human condition was corrupt beyond repair. Meanwhile, some ministers in various denominations ceased to emphasize the conversion of individuals to the religious life and instead propounded a "social gospel" that viewed progressive social change as a means of building the kingdom of God on Earth.

A more direct challenge to traditional Christianity came from scholars who adopted a critical and historical approach to studying and interpreting the Bible. This perspective, known as modernism, treated the books of the Bible—especially the first five (the Pentateuch)—not as simple documents written by a single author but as complex texts constructed by multiple authors from several older sources. Although modernism offered a solution to many problems posed by seemingly contradictory biblical passages, it also raised severe doubts about the historical accuracy of the biblical text, leading scholars to revise the traditional history of the biblical era and to reconsider the nature of biblical authority.

The issue of biblical authority was crucial to American Protestantism, which had inherited the fundamental doctrine of *sola Scriptura* (Latin: "Scripture alone") as enunciated by Martin Luther (1483–1546) and other 16th-century Reformers. Thus, any challenge to scriptural integrity had the potential to undermine Christianity as they understood and practiced it. In response to this challenge, theologians at the Princeton Theological Seminary argued for the verbal (word-for-word) inspiration of Scripture and affirmed that the Bible was not only infallible (correct when it spoke on matters of faith

and morals) but inerrant (correct when it spoke on any matters, including history and science).

As the theologians at Princeton developed their new approach, John Nelson Darby, one of the earliest leaders of the Plymouth Brethren (a British free church movement emphasizing biblical prophecy and the Second Coming of Christ), introduced a very different theological perspective, called dispensationalism. First taught to the Brethren in the mid-19th century, dispensationalism maintained that history is divided into distinct periods, or "dispensations," during which God acts in different ways toward his chosen people. The present period, according to dispensationalism, was one of expectant waiting for the imminent return of Jesus Christ. Dispensationalists believed in an apocalyptic millennialism that foretold the Rapture (the bodily rescue of the chosen by God) and the subsequent cataclysmic events of the Last Days, such as the persecutions by the Antichrist and the Battle of Armageddon.

Although most Protestant churches rejected the broad teachings of the Plymouth Brethren, many accepted the "premillennialism" of Darby's followers. They believed that the next important event in human history would be the coming of Christ to justify and redeem his people and establish them in leadership over a millennial (thousand-year) kingdom.

Singular interest in the Second Coming—an issue promoted by William

Miller (1782–1849) and the Adventist churches in the 1830s and '40s—inspired a popular movement through the Niagara Bible Conference, held every summer at Niagara-on-the-Lake, Ontario. Initiated by James Inglis, a New York City Baptist minister, shortly before his death in 1872, the conference continued under James H. Brookes (1830–97), a St. Louis, Missouri, Presbyterian minister and editor of the influential millennial periodical *The Truth*. Other early millennial leaders included George C. Needham (1840–1902), a Baptist evangelist; William J. Erdman (1834–1923), a Presbyterian minister noted for his skill as a biblical exegete; and William R. Nicholson (1822–1901), who left the Episcopal Church in 1873 and later became a bishop in the Reformed Episcopal Church. Near the end of the century, the millennial movement attracted other prominent leaders, such as Adoniram J. Gordon (1836–95), a Baptist minister in Boston; and Maurice Baldwin (1836–1904), the bishop of Huron in the Church of England in Canada.

The millenarians associated with the Niagara Conference also sponsored public conferences in major cities beginning in 1878, such as the International Prophetic Conferences in New York City. Chicago evangelist Dwight L. Moody (1837–99) provided an influential platform for millennial expression in his Northfield, Massachusetts, conferences. Millennialists were also active in the late 19th-century missionary revival that was eventually institutionalized as the Student Volunteer Movement.

DOCTRINAL AND INSTITUTIONAL DEVELOPMENT

During the last years of the 19th century, the millennial movement was divided over issues of prophetic interpretation, but Brookes managed to hold the dissident factions together. Within a few years of his death, however, the Niagara Conference was abandoned.

THE LATE 19TH TO THE MID-20TH CENTURY

Even before Brookes's death, tensions between millennialists and modernists had reached unprecedented levels. In the 1890s several liberal ministers and professors were subjected to church trials on charges of heresy and apostasy; the most famous such trial involved Charles A. Briggs (1841–1913), a minister of the Presbyterian Church who had denounced the idea of verbal inspiration in an address at the Union Theological Seminary in New York City in 1891. Briggs was convicted of heresy and suspended from the ministry in 1893. In response, the seminary dropped its official connection to the Presbyterian Church, and Briggs became an Episcopalian. Briggs's colleagues Henry Preserved Smith (1847–1927) and A.C. McGiffert (1861–1933) suffered similar experiences, prompting them to join Congregationalist churches.

Continuing conservative militancy led to the founding of the American Bible League in 1902 and the subsequent publication of *The Fundamentals: A*

Testimony to the Truth (1910–15), a series of 12 booklets comprising articles by conservative leaders from across the country. The series, which would eventually give the conservatives their name, attacked modernist theories of biblical criticism and reasserted the authority of the Bible, affirming all the theological principles that conservatives felt were being denied by modernist spokespersons. Financed by two wealthy Presbyterian laymen, *The Fundamentals* was freely distributed to millions of pastors throughout the world.

After a hiatus during World War I, conflict between conservatives and modernists was renewed in 1918. A number of conservative conferences in New York City and Philadelphia led to the formation of a larger and more comprehensive organization in 1919, the World's Christian Fundamentals Association. The 1919 conference placed planks in a platform on which the fundamentalist movement would stand for years to come. Conservative-fundamentalist leaders reiterated the creedal basis of the movement and called for the rejection of modernism and related trends, especially the teaching of the theory of evolution. They turned away from the universities (almost totally controlled by administrations and faculties hostile to the fundamentalist position) and placed their faith in the more recently founded Bible institutes. Finally, they denounced the unitive and cooperative spirit exemplified in the Federal Council of the Churches of Christ in America and threatened schism if this type of spiritual decline persisted.

By this time, the modernist position had gained a foothold in Episcopal, Congregational, Methodist Episcopal, American Baptist, and Presbyterian denominations in the North. The stage was set for major confrontations during the 1920s, and it remained to be seen only whether the modernists could be forced out of their denominations. Discord among northern Baptists was focused at their annual conventions. In 1920 a group of Baptists calling themselves the National Federation of Fundamentalists began holding annual preconvention conferences on Baptist fundamentals. When their attempts to carry their views into the convention failed to make immediate progress, the more militant among them founded the Baptist Bible Union. Eventually the militants left the denomination to form several small fundamentalist churches, while the remainder stayed to constitute a permanent conservative voice within the American Baptist Convention (now the American Baptist Churches in the U.S.A.).

The most serious phase of the conservative-modernist controversy erupted among the Presbyterians. Conservatives had imposed a set of doctrines upon the denomination in 1910, declaring that the Christian faith required belief in the inerrant inspiration of the Bible, Christ's Virgin Birth, and his Atonement, Resurrection, and miracle-working power. In 1922 a New York minister, Harry Emerson Fosdick (1878–1969), protested the activities of conservatives in foreign-mission fields in a widely reproduced sermon titled "Shall the Fundamentalists Win?" The conservatives in the denomination forced Fosdick, a Baptist serving the First Presbyterian Church of New York City, out of his pastorate. He was soon reestablished in the independent Riverside Church.

In the midst of these debates, an event in the Deep South made visible the intense division that had entered American religious life. Fundamentalists, believing that the Bible could not be reconciled with Darwin's theory of evolution, lobbied their state legislatures to ban the teaching of evolution in the public schools; they were joined in this effort by many others who were not fundamentalists. The state of Tennessee passed such a statute, which was challenged in the courts in 1925 at the instigation of the American Civil Liberties Union. John T. Scopes (1900–70), a science teacher in the small town of Dayton, offered to serve as the defendant against the charge of having taught evolution. Two of the foremost figures of that decade, William Jennings Bryan (1860–1925), a Presbyterian fundamentalist and three-time Democratic presidential candidate, and Clarence Darrow (1857–1938), a defense counsel in

Clarence Darrow, defence lawyer (right), questions William Jennings Bryan, director of the prosecution, about the Bible during the Scopes "Monkey Trial," Dayton, Tennessee, in July 1925. Hulton Archive/Getty Images

notable criminal trials, served as the assistant prosecuting attorney and the lead defense attorney, respectively. Scopes was found guilty and fined, though his conviction was later overturned on the technicality that the fine had been excessive. The law forbidding the teaching of evolution in Tennessee was upheld in 1925 and repealed in 1967.

By the end of the 1920s, fundamentalists had lost control of the major denominations and had given up hope of recapturing them, at least in the foreseeable future. Although most remained in their denominations, some broke away to form their own churches. In 1932 a number of Baptists left the Northern Baptist Convention and established the General Association of Regular Baptist Churches; four years later, the Princeton theologian J. Gresham Machen (1881–1937) headed a group of fundamentalists that created the Orthodox Presbyterian Church. Other fundamentalists joined one of the smaller churches that preached biblical literalism and premillennialism—such as the Christian and Missionary Alliance, the Plymouth Brethren, and the Evangelical Free Church—or one of the many independent Bible churches that arose during that period.

Having also lost control of the denominational seminaries, the fundamentalists regrouped around a set of independent Bible institutes and Bible colleges. Many of these schools, such as the Moody Bible Institute in Chicago and the Bible Institute of Los Angeles (now Biola University), not only provided instruction to their students but assumed many of the duties formerly performed by denominational institutions. They published periodicals, broadcast from their own radio stations, held conferences, and maintained a staff of extension speakers. Indeed, they operated much like a denominational headquarters, providing a bond between otherwise isolated congregations.

The establishment of new fundamentalist denominations in the 1930s brought to the fore long-standing divisions within the fundamentalist movement that had been held in check while they concentrated on a common enemy. One of the most divisive issues for Presbyterians was the question of premillennialism and postmillennialism. While Machen defended the more conventional postmillennialism of the Princeton theology, the opposite view was taken by New Jersey minister Carl McIntire, who later founded the rival Bible Presbyterian Church.

McIntire was the focus of a second divisive issue: separatism. He argued that fundamentalists must not only denounce modernist deviations from traditional Christian beliefs but also separate themselves from all heresy and apostasy. This position entailed the condemnation of conservatives who chose to remain in fellowship with more liberal members of their denominations. In 1942 McIntire gathered the independents who accepted his position into the American Council of Christian Churches.

The fundamentalists' denunciation of modernist theology and their censure of church-related institutions of higher learning often led them to reject contemporary education; this in turn contributed to the impression of many outsiders that fundamentalism was essentially anti-intellectual. At the same time, the fundamentalists' withdrawal from larger denominations and their decrying of certain trends in contemporary society conveyed the impression that they were opposed to science and culture. By the end of the 1930s, the largest segment of the fundamentalist movement, believing that a conservative restatement of faith, representing the best of conservative scholarship, was compatible with contemporary intellectual culture, distanced itself from the separatists. They dropped the fundamentalist label, which they left to the separatists, and formed the so-called "neo-Evangelical" movement. *Christianity Today* was founded as their major periodical. Their new intellectual centre, Fuller Theological Seminary, was opened in Pasadena, California; many of the schools formerly identified with fundamentalism, such as the Moody Bible Institute, also moved into the Evangelical camp. A new ecumenical organization, the National Association of Evangelicals, was organized in 1942.

THE MID-20TH CENTURY TO THE PRESENT

Although fundamentalism was pushed to the fringe of the Christian community by the new Evangelical movement, it continued to grow as new champions arose. The Baptist Bible Fellowship, formed in 1950, became one of the largest fundamentalist denominations; Jerry Falwell, subsequently a prominent televangelist, emerged as the movement's leading spokesperson in the 1970s. Liberty University, founded by Falwell in Lynchburg, Virginia, in 1971; Bob Jones University, founded as Bob Jones College in College Point, Florida, by Bob Jones, Sr., in 1927 (the school relocated to Cleveland, Tennessee, and then to Greenville, South Carolina, in 1947); and Regent University, founded by the televangelist Pat Robertson in 1978, were the movement's main intellectual centres. Television, which provided direct access to the public, assisted the careers of a number of fundamentalist religious leaders; in addition to Falwell, they included Tim LaHaye, head of a pastorate in San Diego and coauthor of a popular series of novels based on the Revelation to John.

In the 1960s, religious conservatives and fundamentalists became involved in a renewed controversy over the teaching of evolution in the public schools. Defending the doctrine of creationism—the view that the account of the Creation presented in Genesis is literally correct—they sought again to ban the teaching of evolution or to require the teaching of the Genesis account wherever evolutionary theory was taught. Some fundamentalists also attempted to require the teaching of so-called "creation science," or "scientific creationism," which presumed to present the Genesis account as a legitimate scientific alternative to evolution. In the

1990s some creationists advocated the teaching of a doctrine known as "intelligent design," according to which the diversity and complexity of living things are impossible to explain except by positing the existence of an intelligent creator. In the late 20th and early 21st centuries, creationists were elected to various local and state boards of education, some of which subsequently enacted measures requiring the teaching of intelligent design. In some cases the measures were blocked by the courts or were repealed, and some creationists lost their seats to emboldened defenders of evolution.

In 1979 Falwell founded the Moral Majority, a civic organization that crusaded against what it viewed as negative cultural trends, especially legalized abortion, the women's movement, and the gay rights movement. It also lobbied for prayer in public schools, increased defense spending, a strong anticommunist foreign policy, and continued American support for the State of Israel. The Moral Majority led a new generation of fundamentalists beyond simply denouncing cultural trends and back into an engagement with contemporary life in the political arena. Falwell cooperated with nonfundamentalists on common secular causes but remained aloof from the major fundamentalist organizations. Meanwhile, the Evangelicals campaigned on many of the same issues, thus blurring the boundaries between the two movements.

By the 1980s fundamentalists had rebuilt all the institutional structures that had been lost when they separated from the older denominations. As early as 1941, fundamentalist groups had come together in the American Council of Christian Churches, and in 1948 they joined with like-minded Christians around the world to create the International Council of Christian Churches. In the late 1960s the American Council attempted to move beyond the leadership of Carl McIntire, who had dominated it for more than a quarter of a century. It withdrew from the International Council to help form the World Council of Bible Believing Churches. In the late 20th century, some fundamentalists even began to engage in discussions with conservative members of the Roman Catholic Church, traditionally regarded by fundamentalists as a non-Christian cult. Protestant fundamentalists and conservative Catholics found common ground on a variety of issues, including abortion and school prayer.

From the late 1980s, fundamentalists sought to build on the success of the Moral Majority and like-minded groups. In 1988 Robertson ran unsuccessfully for president of the United States. Shortly afterward he founded the Christian Coalition, which succeeded the Moral Majority as the leading organization of the movement and became closely associated with the Republican Party. Fundamentalists were strong supporters of President George W. Bush and played an important role in the election of Republicans at all levels of government. They also continued to promote conservative positions on various questions of social policy.

At the start of the 21st century, fundamentalist teachings were not significantly different from what they were at the time of the Niagara Conference. Fundamentalists still believed in the inerrancy and infallibility of the Bible and rejected critical biblical scholarship and the many new translations of the Bible to which such scholarship gave rise. A significant percentage of the movement continued to use the King James Version of the Bible exclusively.

EVANGELICALISM

Any of the classical Protestant churches or their offshoots is called an Evangelical church. Since the late 20th century, however, the term has applied to churches that stress the preaching of the gospel of Jesus Christ, personal conversion experiences, Scripture as the sole basis for faith, and active evangelism, or the winning of personal commitments to Christ. The word *evangelical* comes from the Greek (*euangelion*) and Latin (*evangelium*) words for "good news," which evolved into the word *gospel*.

The 18th-century religious revival that occurred in continental Europe (the Pietist movement), in Great Britain (the Methodist revival), and in North America (the Great Awakening) was generally referred to as the Evangelical revival. These movements emphasized conversion experiences, reliance on Scripture, and missionary work rather than the sacraments and traditions of the established churches. An Evangelical party also developed within the Church of England that, unlike the Methodists, did not leave the church. The growing strength of the movement and the awareness of their shared interests led Evangelicals from several denominations and countries to form the Evangelical Alliance in London in 1846.

In the United States in the mid-20th century, the term was applied to a group that emerged out of the ongoing fundamentalist controversy. Earlier in the century, an intense conflict developed between the modernists (liberals) and fundamentalists (conservatives) in several of the larger Protestant denominations. Some fundamentalists left their old churches to found new ones when it became evident that they had lost control of the governing boards of their denominations. Many of those who left called for a separation from modernism, which they saw as heresy (denial of fundamental Christian beliefs) and apostasy (rejection of the Christian faith). This demand for separation led to a break with conservatives who remained within the established denominations. It also meant a break with church-sponsored institutions of higher learning (from which many of the defectors had graduated) and the founding of new colleges and seminaries committed to fundamentalism—actions that seemed to indicate a denial of the legitimacy of modern scholarship. By the late 1930s, conservatives still in the older denominations and those who left but remained friendly (especially Baptists and Presbyterians) made common cause

GREAT AWAKENING

The "Great Awakening" was a religious revival in the British American colonies mainly between about 1720 and the '40s. It was a part of the religious ferment that swept western Europe in the latter part of the 17th century and early 18th century, referred to as Pietism and Quietism in continental Europe among Protestants and Roman Catholics and as Evangelicalism in England under the leadership of John Wesley (1703–91).

A number of conditions in the colonies contributed to the revival: an arid rationalism in New England, formalism in liturgical practices, as among the Dutch Reformed in the Middle Colonies, and the neglect of pastoral supervision in the South. The revival took place primarily among the Dutch Reformed, Congregationalists, Presbyterians, Baptists, and some Anglicans, almost all of whom were Calvinists. Preachers emphasized the "terrors of the law" to sinners, the unmerited grace of God, and the "new birth" in Jesus Christ. One of the great figures of the movement was George Whitefield, an Anglican priest who was influenced by John Wesley but was himself a Calvinist. Visiting America in 1739–40, he preached up and down the colonies to vast crowds in open fields because no church building would hold the throngs he attracted. Jonathan Edwards was the great academic and apologist of the Great Awakening. A Congregational pastor at Northampton, Mass., he preached justification by faith alone with remarkable effectiveness. He also attempted to redefine the psychology of religious experience and to help those involved in the revival to discern what were true and false works of the Spirit of God.

The Great Awakening stemmed the tide of Enlightenment rationalism among a great many people in the colonies. One of its results was division within denominations, for some members supported the revival and others rejected it. The revival stimulated the growth of several educational institutions, including Princeton, Brown, and Rutgers universities and Dartmouth College. The increase of dissent from the established churches during this period led to a broader toleration of religious diversity, and the democratization of the religious experience fed the fervour that resulted in the American Revolution.

against the separatist position. Although they maintained a commitment to fundamental Christian beliefs, they also declared their willingness to engage in a dialogue with the academy and society. To distinguish themselves from the separatists, they chose to be called Neo-Evangelicals, soon shortened to Evangelicals.

The new Evangelicals prospered because of the personalities they attracted and the institutions they created. They soon found a champion in a young Baptist evangelist, Billy Graham. Graham's oratorical skills, combined with his refusal to deviate from his preaching mission and to involve himself in theological controversies, did much to legitimize Evangelicals with the public. Simultaneously, Carl F.H. Henry and other theologians provided the movement with intellectual sophistication. The zeal and commitment of the movement was institutionalized in a periodical, *Christianity Today*; a new ministerial training school, Fuller Theological Seminary, in Pasadena, California; and a liberal arts college, Wheaton College, in suburban Chicago. In 1942 Evangelical leaders created some organizational unity with the formation of the National Association of Evangelicals.

The movement experienced significant international growth in the decades following World War II and became an important force in world Christianity. Developing a sense of international and interdenominational unity, Evangelicals formed the World Evangelical Fellowship (WEF) in 1951 (three years after the founding of the World Council of Churches). More than 110 regional and national organizations and some 110 million people are affiliated with the WEF, now headquartered in Singapore.

As the Evangelical community emerged, a series of vocation- and interest-based organizations made up of doctors, scientists, athletes, and others was established. Chapters of the Inter-Varsity Christian Fellowship and Campus Crusade for Christ formed on hundreds of college campuses to offer religious support similar to that provided by various Protestant and Roman Catholic organizations. Both the American Scientific Affiliation and the Evangelical Theological Society hold meetings and publish a journal to examine trends in science, theology, and cultural studies.

While Evangelicalism has grown into a significant cultural force, separatist fundamentalism has also flourished. Carl McIntire, an early leader of the movement, contributed greatly to this growth. He conducted a radio broadcast, *The Twentieth Century Reformation Hour*, and helped found the American Council of Christian Churches (ACCC) and the International Council of Christian Churches (ICCC). In 1969 the ICCC and ACCC broke off relations after the latter moved to end McIntire's dominance of its administration. The World Council of Bible Believing Churches and the American Christian Action Council (now the International Council of Christian Churches in America) emerged as a result of the schism. In the 1980s McIntire's leadership of American fundamentalism gave way to that of Baptist televangelist Jerry Falwell.

Although fundamentalists have often appeared on radio and television, they have been overshadowed by Evangelicals in those media. Before World War II, Evangelicals used the radio to bring their message to an American audience; after the war, they established the Far East Broadcasting Company and Trans World Radio, the first of a number of stations to broadcast internationally. Oral Roberts, Billy Graham, and other evangelists were among the first to see the potential of television. By 1960, the first Christian television network, the Christian Broadcasting Network, was chartered, and later the Trinity Broadcasting Network and

LeSea Broadcasting formed to provide programming for the Evangelical community.

Since the 1980s the Evangelical movement has greatly expanded. The reconciliation of conservatives from the Reformed tradition (Presbyterian and Baptist) with those from the Methodist tradition (Holiness and Pentecostal) was an important step in the growth of the movement. These two groups had been bitter rivals but joined forces against the perceived secularization of American culture. Holiness and Pentecostal churches joined the National Association of Evangelicals and the World Evangelical Fellowship. Evangelicals have also broadened their intellectual horizons. While continuing to affirm that the Bible is the Word of God, many Evangelicals have been open to contemporary trends in critical biblical scholarship, found means to accommodate a belief in biological evolution, and developed a consciousness of the role of culture in shaping theological perspectives.

DISCIPLES OF CHRIST

The Disciples of Christ denomination was founded in the early 19th century by Alexander Campbell. It placed radical emphasis upon the autonomy of the individual congregation. The Disciples had held together during the controversy over slavery and through the Civil War, when major American denominations had divided. In the postwar years, however, the Disciples also suffered schism, eventually breaking into two denominations: Churches of Christ and the Christian Churches (Disciples of Christ). In the early 21st century, the Churches of Christ claimed more than one million members and the Christian Churches (Disciples of Christ) claimed about 690,000.

CONTROVERSY AND SEPARATION

New developments in response to growing urbanization and sophistication brought two sharply divergent responses. The conservatives regarded such developments as unauthorized "innovations," while the progressives (pejoratively termed *digressives*) looked on them as permissible "expedients." Discord first arose over the "society principle" involving general missionary work. Alexander Campbell's biblical view of the church had kept pushing him toward a general church organization, but he could never find a convincing biblical text to support his proposals. Frontier independence and pragmatic popular biblicism prevailed. The "society principle" seemed to its advocates a legitimate solution: entertaining no ecclesiastical pretensions as a secular corporation, the missionary society provided a means by which individual Disciples could work in voluntary cooperation. But the opponents saw in it a repudiation of the Bible as the determining rule of practice.

The introduction of musical instruments (reed organs) into Christian worship led to many local disputes.

Other innovations added occasion for controversy—the infringement of the "one-man pastoral system" on the local ministry of elders, introduction of selected choirs, use of the title Reverend, and lesser issues.

In 1889 several rural churches in Illinois issued the Sand Creek Declaration, withdrawing fellowship from those practicing "innovations and corruptions." In 1904 a separate "preacher list" issued unofficially by some conservative leaders certified their preachers for discounts on railway tickets. The Federal Religious Census of 1906 acknowledged the separation between Churches of Christ and Disciples of Christ (who commonly used the name Christian Churches) even though many congregations did not decide which they were for some years. The crucial issue centred on the manner of understanding biblical authority. Both conservatives and progressives accepted the New Testament as the only rule for the church. The conservatives, heavily concentrated in the South, applied a strict construction to Scripture; this required a specific New Testament precept to authorize any practice. The progressives tended toward a broader construction, accepting as expedient such measures as they found harmonious with Scripture or not in conflict with it.

TEACHINGS

Alexander Campbell summarized his theology in *The Christian System* (1835), the most influential book in shaping Disciples thought. In it he outlined a commonsense biblical doctrine against the complex theories of the schools and the sects. He emphasized reliance on the Bible and insisted on going to the sources. Relying on John Locke, "The Christian philosopher," Campbell perceived the grounds for Christian faith in historical events and objective evidence (recorded in Scripture) rather than in mysticism or subjective religious "experience." He therefore repudiated the Calvinist (and revivalist) concept of miraculous conversion and the similar concept of miraculous call to the ministry. Debates on these issues, as well as on the damnation of unbaptized infants, which Disciples denied, led them to think of themselves as anti-Calvinist.

The general framework of their thought nevertheless followed Reformed (Calvinist) lines, modified by the influence of British Independents (the originally Scottish Glasites—or Sandemanians—in practice a strictly New Testament sect, and the Congregationalists). Disciples shared the orthodox Protestant emphasis on the authority of Scripture. Their classic biblical position differs from that of other Protestants in being a product of the early 19th rather than of the 16th or 17th century.

Early Disciples understood their uniqueness to lie in the rigour, precision, and simplicity with which they set forth the biblical basis for the unity of all Christians. Campbell distinguished sharply between Old and New Covenants (the Hebrew Bible, or Old

Testament, and the New Testament), limiting to the latter any authority for "the original faith and order" of the church. Only explicit apostolic teaching or precedent belonged in the realm of faith, of the essential; all else, however logical or helpful, fell in the area of opinion and consequently of Christian liberty. Thus they rejected creeds as tests of fellowship; they believed such tests usurped the sole authority of the New Testament and set forth demands not found there. The popular Disciples' bias against theology as a divisive preoccupation with human opinions—as well as Alexander Campbell's early protest against ecclesiastical institutions as unwarranted by Scripture and threatening to freedom—also was inferred from the New Testament.

WORSHIP AND ORGANIZATION

After fruitless attempts to derive a stated order of worship from the New Testament, Disciples settled into an informal but relatively stable pattern composed of hymns, extemporaneous prayers, Scripture, sermon, and breaking of bread. Except for its omission of the Decalogue, the public confession of sin, and the creed, it resembled classic Reformed (or Presbyterian) worship, especially in its austerity of spirit. In the second half of the 19th century it took over more of the mood of popular revivalism, which still prevails among Churches of Christ and the independent Christian Churches.

Because many churches in the 19th century had the services of a preacher only occasionally but regularly observed the Lord's Supper (communion) after the Bible School (Sunday School) hour, the breaking of bread came to precede the sermon, which was simply added on when a preacher was present. At the table two local elders presided, one offering a prayer of thanksgiving for the bread and the other for the cup. The minister now commonly presides, but the elders ordinarily offer the prayers.

Christian Worship: A Service Book (1953), a semiofficial manual for voluntary use, exerted wide influence in restoring and stabilizing the typical pattern, with an emphasis on use of scriptural sentences throughout. The influence of the Liturgical Movement brought greater use of responsive readings, litanies, and affirmations of faith, as well as closer accommodation to the historical pattern of the liturgy—all demonstrated in the 1987 "resource for Christian worship," *Thankful Praise.*

Campbell regarded immersion and "the breaking of bread" (i.e., baptism and communion) as ordinances of Christ. While the insistence on believer's baptism alone separated Disciples from the "paedobaptists" (those advocating baptism of children), weekly communion served as a universal element in their worship and tempered their rationalist bent. Despite their memorialist doctrine (that communion is a commemoration of Christ's Last Supper involving no miracle of transubstantiation), they understood the service as present communion with their Lord.

Campbell saw the biblically authorized ministry as that of elders and deacons, ordained by the congregations, and of evangelists, who served the church at large. Since the 1950s congregations have commonly elected women to diaconate and eldership, and Disciples have long ordained women as ministers. By the 1980s fully one-third of their seminarians were women.

The Design recognizes "the order of the ministry," consisting of ordained ministers and licensed ministers. Since restructure, the General Assembly has established policies and criteria for the order of ministry, which are interpreted and applied by regional commissions.

INTERNAL DIFFERENCES

The divisions in the movement expressed varying attitudes toward Scripture as the norm of faith and practice: Churches of Christ construing it strictly, Disciples more loosely. Many who introduced organs in worship held the same view of biblical authority as those who refused to do so; their interpretation simply led to a different conclusion about the use of musical instruments in apostolic times. They provided the constituency for the "independent" Christian Churches, whereas Disciples tended to find more and more flexibility in the principle of expediency.

Beginning in the early 19th century as a revolution occurred in the scholarly understanding of the biblical documents and the nature of their authority, the Churches of Christ generally held steadfastly to older views of Scripture, as the independents also tended to do, while Disciples accepted the approach of critical scholarship. At the beginning of the 20th century, the most influential Disciples scholar was J.W. McGarvey, a champion of the traditional doctrines and view of the Bible and an opponent of the musical instrument in worship. Early in the century Herbert L. Willett, E.S. Ames, and C.C. Morrison led in a liberal reformulation of the plea, emphasizing a pragmatic and reasonable approach to faith, the repudiation of creeds, an openness to the scientific world view, and a commitment to Christian unity. Neoorthodoxy held less appeal for most Disciples, but William Robinson gained attention for his emphasis on biblical doctrine.

TRENDS SINCE THE MID-20TH CENTURY

With the rapid growth of seminaries and religion faculties and extensive ecumenical involvement, Disciples enjoyed a theological renaissance in the 1950s. During the heyday of biblical theology some of them worked out a contemporary formulation of the tradition within the ecumenical context. A Panel of Scholars, appointed by two of the national agencies, published three volumes of papers in 1963 reflecting the new mood.

The institutional developments leading to restructuring were accompanied by a reformulation of the doctrine of the church. The founders had spoken of the Church of Christ as a local congregation; they recognized no other organization as a church. The new generation of Disciples could no longer deny the churchly character of the institutions that had been developed. The Design speaks of three manifestations of the Christian Church—congregational, regional, general (United States and Canada). The name that they adopted—the Christian Church (Disciples of Christ)—they found to have been dictated by their history. They saw that church manifesting itself organizationally "within the universal body of Christ" and committed to "responsible ecumenical relationships." In 1962 Disciples entered the Consultation on Church Union and in 1985 an ecumenical partnership with the United Church of Christ. They gave a cordial reception to the World Council of Churches document *Baptism, Eucharist and Ministry* (1982), even while recognizing problems posed by their eldership for the emerging consensus. In the immediate decades after restructure no major theological controversy arose. Resurgent fundamentalism and Evangelicalism on the larger scene had little impact.

SOCIAL ISSUES

On social questions Disciples have held positions characteristic of the American denominations of English background. With regard to the issue of slavery Campbell prevented schism by admitting that Scripture and civil law permitted slavery, though, as a matter of personal opinion, he favoured emancipation. During the Civil War a number of leading Disciples, especially in the Border States, espoused pacifism on biblical grounds.

Disciples representatives to the National Council of Churches and the World Council of Churches have supported those organizations' general stand on social issues. Since the second half of the 20th century, though a moderate conservatism obtained at the grassroots, ministers, seminaries, general units, and General Assembly placed social issues high on their agenda, with vocal sympathy for liberation theology. In 1969 the General Assembly called for a 20 percent presence of ethnic minorities on church policy-making bodies, even though the combined number of Native American, black, Hispanic, and Asian-American Disciples fell well below that figure. In 1990 the General Assembly approved the Alverna Covenant, a statement urging Disciples to make an "ecologically responsible lifestyle" a Christian commitment.

SOCIETY OF FRIENDS (QUAKERS)

The customs of the Society of Friends (also known as the Quakers) and the exclusion of Friends from many professions in England concentrated their secular achievements. Plainness meant that painting, music, and the theatre were proscribed. For a century, trust in the

Inward Light inhibited the foundation of colleges (though in the 19th century American Friends founded colleges such as Earlham, Haverford, and Swarthmore; and individual Friends founded Bryn Mawr College, Cornell University, and Johns Hopkins University). Friends' schools emphasized science; the chemist John Dalton, the geneticist Francis Galton, the anthropologist E.B. Tylor, the astronomer Arthur Eddington, and Joseph Lister, discoverer of antisepsis, were Friends. In trade Friends were trusted and got customers; they trusted one another and extended credit; thus the many successful Quaker firms and banks, of which Barclay's and Lloyd's are the best known. Friends also pioneered in inventions, developing the puddling process for iron and the safety match and promoting the first English railroad line.

TEACHINGS

The "public testimonies" of Friends from the very beginning included the plain speech and dress and refusal of tithes, oaths, and worldly courtesies. To these was added in a few years an explicit renunciation of participation in war; within the next century bankruptcy, marriage out of meeting, smuggling, and dealing in or owning slaves also became practices for which an unrepentant Friend would be disowned. These latter, especially those relating to slavery, became matters for discipline because a comparative minority of Friends persuaded the rest that they were inconsistent with Friends' principles.

But not all social concerns were corporate in this sense or were enforced by sanctions. Friends' relief work, for example, has usually arisen from an individual response to suffering, often as the result of war. From the time of the American Revolution Quakers have been active in ministering to refugees and victims of famine—so much so that the entire Society of Friends is sometimes taken for a philanthropic organization; yet this work, recognized in 1947 by the award of the Nobel Peace Prize to the American Friends Service Committee and the (British) Friends Service Council, has mobilized many non-Quakers and thus exemplifies the interaction between the Quaker conscience and the wider world.

Yet the Society of Friends is grounded in the experience of God, out of which philanthropic activities may flow. There have always been Friends whose concerns went well beyond what meetings were willing to adopt. Most Friends were not abolitionists before the American Civil War; they probably did not approve of the Underground Railroad nor share the early feminist views of Lucretia Mott and Susan B. Anthony. (Most of the early suffragist leaders in America were Quakers.) The two American presidents of Quaker background were both Republicans: Herbert Hoover and Richard M. Nixon. Often the issue has been the relationship between private witness and public policy. Some Quaker pacifists make an absolute personal stand against war (for example, by

This image shows the marriage of founder of Pennsylvania William Penn and Hannah Callowhill at a Quaker meeting at the Friends' Meeting House, Bristol, England in January 1696. Spencer Arnold/Hulton Archive/Getty Images

refusing to register for selective service and thus forfeiting conscientious objectors' status); others are more willing to sacrifice absolute purity by working for an alleviation of international tensions even at the cost of less rigorous application of their principles.

THE INWARD LIGHT

Trust in the Inward Light is the distinctive theme of Quakerism. The Light should not be confused with conscience or reason; it is rather that of God in everyone, which allows human beings an immediate sense of God's presence and will for them. It thus informs conscience and redirects reason. The experience of hearkening to this inner Guide is mystical, but corporate and practical. Meetings to worship God and await his word (always open to anyone who wishes to come) are essential to Quaker faith and practice. Although the inward Seed can work in a solitary person, Friends do not meditate like monks, isolated in their cells. It is in the pregnant silence of the meeting of true waiters and worshipers that the Spirit speaks. Sometimes the meeting is too dull or worldly for any message to be heard, and sometimes there are altogether silent meetings. Although these are spiritually beneficial to the participants, ideally someone has reached a new understanding that demands to be proclaimed. He or she—for Friends have always given women equality in worship—speaks or prays and thus ministers to the meeting, which weighs this "testimony" by its own experiences of God. Friends historically have rejected a formal or salaried clergy as a "hireling ministry." If God can provide his own living testimony, the Bible and the learning necessary to read it can take a subordinate place, and creeds and outward sacraments can be dispensed with altogether. But despite their emphasis on silent waiting and their distrust of "creaturely" activity, Friends are no more habituated to passive than to solitary meditation. Often the "opening" of the Inward Light is a "concern" for the sufferings of others and a mandate laid upon the conscience to take action to alleviate that suffering. Such concerns typically are laid before a meeting and thoroughly considered; there must be a consensus for any corporate action. But slow as such action sometimes is, Friends have taken the lead in opposing slavery, brutality in prisons and insane asylums, oppression of women, militarism, and war.

POLITY

Insofar as George Fox was the founder of Quakerism, he was so chiefly because of the system of meetings for church business that he established in the years immediately after 1667, which essentially stands today. Most important is the monthly meeting, which considers all applications for membership, in some localities manages Friends' properties, and acts on members' concerns. Generally, in the United States each congregation has a monthly meeting; in England and in some parts of the United States several meetings for worship combine in monthly meeting. Several monthly meetings form quarterly meetings, which are combined in yearly meetings.

This array is less hierarchical than it sounds. Any Friends can attend any meeting, which tries to remain open to the concerns or the service they can perform (much in the spirit of a meeting for worship). There is an official, the clerk, but the responsibility of the clerk is not to preside in a parliamentary manner but rather to feel for a "sense of the meeting," which draws together the thinking of the meeting to the point of action.

Though Friends have no ordination, they have always given a special place to Recorded Ministers (or Public Friends). Recorded Ministers are those whose testimony in local meetings has been officially recognized; they are free to "travel in the ministry" by visiting other meetings, should they be led to do so. Pastoral meetings maintain their

Recorded Ministers, who also do much of the work of seeing to the relief of the poor, care of properties, and discipline of erring members. Ministers have usually had their own meetings together, and in most yearly meetings executive responsibility had been taken by a meeting like the Meeting for Sufferings in London (these are also called Representative meetings or committees or Permanent boards). London Meeting for Sufferings in the 17th century served as a political pressure group, lobbying Parliament for relief from persecution, coordinating legal strategy, and using the press for public appeals; in the 19th century they broadened their concerns to respond to sufferings everywhere.

Quakerism and World Christianity

The cause of schisms in the past—the tension between entire reliance on the Inward Light and the profession of orthodox Christian doctrines—remains unresolved. As it has divided Friends among themselves, it has also tended to separate them from other Christians. The London Yearly Meeting in 1940 declined to join the World Council of Churches out of uneasiness with its creedal basis, though some U.S. groups of Friends sent delegates to the first meeting of the council in 1948. Looked at in the context of Christendom as a whole, Friends offer a distinctive opportunity for spontaneity of worship, fellowship in mysticism, and proving mystical insight in labour for a suffering world. Many alienated from institutional Christianity have found this combination attractive; they may well feel more comfortable identifying themselves as Friends than as Protestants or even as Christians. This may make it more difficult for Quakerism to be subsumed into a reunited Christian church; but the faith of most Friends has always been that of Schweitzer in *The Quest of the Historical Jesus*: as "we do the work of Christ we shall come to know who he is."

CHAPTER 13

MISSIONS AND ECUMENISM

In the early 21st century, about one-third of the world's people claimed the Christian faith. Christians thus constituted the world's largest religious community and embraced remarkable diversity, with churches in every nation. Christianity's demographic and dynamic centre had shifted from its Western base to Latin America, Africa, Asia, and the Pacific region, where more than half the world's Christians lived. This trend steadily accelerated as the church declined in Europe. The global extent of Christianity represented a new phenomenon in the history of religions. This was largely the fruit of mission. Yet the diversity of expressions of that Christian faith led to attempts at outreach between the various churches and denominations in order that theological and liturgical differences could be overcome, that past schisms could be mended, and that the pain caused by these ruptures could be alleviated. Such efforts at ecumenism emerged when the early church began to grow but intensified in the 20th and early 21st centuries.

MISSIONS

This was the fruit of mission. The word *mission* (Latin: *missio*), as a translation of the Greek *apostolē*, "a sending," appears only once in the English New Testament (Galatians 2:8). An apostle (*apostolos*) is one commissioned and sent to fulfill a special purpose.

Dancers from Keali'i Ka'apunihonua Ke'ena A'o Hula, perform at the conclusion of mass in honor of the 19th century Saint Damien at the Cathedral of Our Lady at Peace, in Honolulu, Hawaii, in November 1, 2009. AFP/Getty Images

BIBLICAL FOUNDATIONS

The roots of mission, Christians have believed, lie in God's active outreach to humanity in history—as a call to those able to fulfill the divine purpose, among them Abraham, Moses, Jonah, and Paul. The New Testament designated Jesus as God's apostle (Hebrews 3:1). Jesus's prayer in The Gospel According to John includes the words "As thou didst send me into the world, so I have sent them into the world.... [I pray also] for those who believe in me through their word, that they may all be one...so that the world may believe that thou hast sent me" (John 17:18, 20–21). Moreover, the "Great Commission" of Jesus declares: "Go therefore and make disciples of all nations, baptizing them in the name of the Father and of the Son and of the Holy Spirit, teaching them to observe all that I have commanded you; and lo, I am with you always, to the close of the age" (Matthew 28:19–20; compare Mark 16:15, Luke 24:47, John 20:21–22, and Acts 1:8).

THE HISTORY OF CHRISTIAN MISSIONS

The Christian mission, the church, and Christianity—each distinguishable, but inseparably related—have experienced four major transitions in their history.

FIRST TRANSITION, TO AD 500

The new missionary faith made its first major transition as it emerged from Palestine and spread throughout the Mediterranean world. The apostle Paul became the missionary to the Gentile world. With help from Barnabas and a local network of coworkers, many of them women, he evangelized Asia Minor and southern Greece and eventually reached Rome. Dominated politically by the Roman Empire, the new religion benefited from the stability the empire provided and the language its elite shared—common, or koine, Greek. Alexandrian Jews had translated (250 BCE) the Hebrew Bible into koine Greek for dispersed Greek-speaking Jews. The New Testament writers also wrote in koine Greek. In that largely literate empire early Christians used and widely distributed the Hebrew Scriptures.

Several factors brought growth to the faith. From the beginning laypeople—both men and women—conducted the largest part of mission. Congregations grew in homes used as churches. Although the house was owned by the husband, the wife was its mistress, and women throughout the empire opened their homes to newly forming churches. Most evangelization occurred in the daily routine as men and women shared their faith with others. Christianity's monotheism, morality, assurance of eternal life with God, and ancient Scriptures attracted many to the faith.

Christians daily encountered members of other religions—gnosticism and the mystery and philosophical cults. In the 2nd and 3rd centuries external and internal pressures drove the young church to strengthen itself through creating a structured ministry, formulating beliefs in creeds, and producing a canon of Scripture. That process established critical institutions for the early Christian movement. The major thrust of the early church-mission sprang from the conviction that Christians and congregations were fulfilling a mission and ministry begun in Jesus Christ. Baptism provided induction into the vibrant company of "God's own people" (1 Peter 2:9-10), which many in the empire gradually accepted.

Rome, however, declared Christianity an illegal religion, in part because Christians refused to engage in emperor worship, and persecutions ensued. In the persecutions so many Christians bore witness (Greek: *martyria*) that the word *martyr* quickly evolved into its current meaning. Christian faith—not least that of young women such as Blandina, Perpetua, and Felicity—made an impact, and many who beheld that witness became Christian. In 313 when the new emperor, Constantine, declared the persecutions ended, Christians probably constituted 10 percent of the empire's population.

By 315 many who saw advantage in belonging to Constantine's new faith poured into the churches. The result was striking: small congregations of convinced Christians serving God's outreach in the world became large churches with many nominal members whose instruction and needs had to be met. As multitudes entered the churches, the need for outreach to others was much reduced, and most churches shifted from an outward thrust to an inward focus upon themselves. Mission and service became the province of priests, deacons, and, increasingly, monks.

At the same time, mission beyond the frontiers of the empire continued. Ulfilas (c. 311–c. 382), Arian bishop and apostle to the Goths, translated the Bible into their tongue. Martin of Tours (c. 316–397) served in Gaul, and Patrick (c. 389–c. 461) laboured in Ireland. In Malabar, South India, a church of ancient tradition, demonstrably present since the 3rd century, held the apostle Thomas to be its founder. Frumentius (d. c. 380) from Tyre evangelized in Ethiopia and became the first patriarch of its church. In the 5th century Nestorians pushed into Central Asia and began a mission that eventually reached the capital of China.

In its first 500 years Christianity achieved remarkable missionary and theological acculturation. Through the first four ecumenical councils (325–451), and in the Nicene Creed (on the Trinity) and Definition of Chalcedon (on Christology), the church had stated its faith with meaning for the Greek and Latin worlds.

By the close of the period Jerome's Latin translation of the Bible, the Vulgate, had appeared, and Christianity had become the official religion of the empire. The first great transition of the Christian mission—from Judaic Palestine to the Mediterranean world—had ended.

SECOND TRANSITION, TO AD 1500

Rome's urban and literate world quickly disappeared under the barbarians' westward onslaught. These conquerors established themselves as the new ruling elite; however, they recognized in missionary monks the bearers of a new faith and preservers of a higher civilization. The mission thrust of these monks contrasted sharply with that of the tiny persecuted church in the first three centuries. Then, except for the conversions of the city-state of Edessa, in AD 200, and Armenia, declared a Christian nation in AD 300, people joined the new faith individually. In this second transition whole peoples followed their sovereigns into the new faith.

Christianity expanded in the Byzantine Empire as well as in the remnants of the

In AD 563, Irish missionary Saint Columba (c. 521–597), known as the Apostle of Caledonia, sailed with his twelve disciples to the island of Iona on the west coast of Scotland. Columba worked to convert the Picts to Christianity. Hulton Archive/Getty Images

Western Empire, but it experienced a widening breach, and a split of the Eastern and Western churches occurred in 1054. Yet the major result of this 1,000-year mission was the creation of European civilization. Its emergence marked the second great transition of the faith.

Western Mission

The medieval mission began with the baptism of Clovis, king of the Franks, and his soldiers, traditionally dated to 496 though it may have occurred as late as 508. The first Germanic king to be baptized by a Catholic bishop rather than an Arian one (through the influence of Clotilda, Clovis's Catholic wife, according to Gregory of Tours), he helped to turn the tide against the Arians.

Irish Celtic Christianity differed from that on the Continent. It was organized into communalized groups under an abbot and nurtured intense missionary conviction and outreach. It did not recognize Rome's authority. The abbot Columba (c. 521–597) built a monastery on Iona, off Scotland's western coast, as a base for mission to Scotland and northern England.

From it Aidan (d. 651) traveled to Lindisfarne, off England's northern coast, where he and a successor, Cuthbert (634/635–687), helped evangelize Northumbria. Moving southward, the Celtic monks might have evangelized all of Britain, but midway they met Roman missionaries. Other Celtic *peregrini*, or "wanderers," evangelized on the Continent.

Papal Mission

Pope Gregory I the Great (reigned 590–604), who possessed the mind of both a statesman and a theologian, greatly magnified papal spiritual power and temporal involvement. In 596 he sent Augustine of Canterbury and some 40 monks on a mission to England—the first papally sponsored mission. Augustine's missionaries reached England's southern coast in 597. King Aethelberht of Kent and his wife, Bertha, a Christian, enabled them to make their base at Canterbury. Within the year the king and 10,000 subjects had received baptism. Roman missionaries moving northward met the Celts, and at the Synod of Whitby in 664 the Celts accepted Roman jurisdiction and religious practices, including the method of determining the date of Easter each year.

Inspired by Irish missionary enthusiasm, the English Christians evangelized northern Europe. Outstanding in this effort were Willibrord (658?–739), "Apostle to the Frisians" (Friesland, Holland, and Belgium), and Wynfrid, renamed Boniface (c. 675–754), one of the greatest of all Roman missionaries. In central and southern Germany Boniface established Benedictine monasteries for evangelization. With full papal trust and Carolingian support he strengthened and reformed the Frankish church.

Boniface also saw the need for women in mission. From England he recruited Lioba (d. 782) and entrusted her with developing Benedictine monasteries for women. Despite her outstanding and unique achievements, the movement ended with her death, and Roman Catholic women reentered mission service only in the 19th century. But the Christian wives of pagan kings, who led their husbands into the faith and through them hastened the Christianizing of whole peoples, also contributed to its spread.

In the 8th and 9th centuries, Carolingian rulers mixed military conquest and missionary activity, establishing the faith in pagan territories as they expanded the boundaries of their empire. Charlemagne imposed Christianity and his political authority over numerous peoples, including the Avars and Saxons. His son, Louis the Pious, sent a mission to the Danes in 826, and later emperors built upon this precedent.

In 955 the Holy Roman emperor Otto I defeated the Magyars and brought them to Christian faith. Later, Hungary's first king, Stephen (reigned 1000–38), made the country a Christian land. From the Holy Roman Empire, Catholic outreach into Bohemia took root under King Wenceslas I (c. 907–929), with evangelization complete by about AD 1000. In Poland, Mieszko I, under the influence of his wife, accepted baptism in 966 or 967. His reign saw the beginning of the evangelization of the country, which continued under his able son, Boleslaw.

Early attempts at evangelization in Denmark and Sweden were made by a German monk, Ansgar (801–865). Canute (d. 1035), Danish king of England, of Denmark, and of Norway, was probably raised as a Christian and determined that Denmark should become a Christian country. The archbishop of Canterbury consecrated bishops for him, and he saw his goal realized before he died. Olaf I Tryggvason (reigned 995–c. 1000) was baptized by a Christian hermit, returned to Norway and was accepted as king, and sought to make his realm Christian—a task completed by King Olaf II Haraldsson (reigned 1016–30), later St. Olaf. Olaf I also presented Christianity to a receptive Iceland. Leif Eriksson took the faith to Greenland's Viking settlers,

SYNOD OF WHITBY

The Synod of Whitby marked a vital turning point in the development of the church in England. It was a meeting held by the Christian Church of the Anglo-Saxon kingdom of Northumbria in 663/664 to decide whether to follow Celtic or Roman usages. Though Northumbria had been mainly converted by Celtic missionaries, there was by 662 a Roman party, which included Queen Eanfled, Bishop Wilfrid, and other influential people. The Celtic party was led by the bishops Colman and Cedd and Abbess Hilda. Two accounts of the synod survive, in Bede's Ecclesiastical History of the English People *and in the life of Wilfrid by the monk Eddi. King Oswiu decided in favour of Rome because he believed that Rome followed the teaching of St. Peter, the holder of the keys of heaven. The decision led to the acceptance of Roman usage elsewhere in England and brought the English Church into close contact with the Continent.*

who quickly accepted it. After several efforts Sweden became Christian during the reign of Sverker (c. 1130–56). Sweden's Eric IX controlled Finland and in 1155 required the Finns to be baptized, but only in 1291, with the appointment of Magnus, the first Finnish bishop, was evangelization completed.

Eastern and Nestorian Missions

The gradual disappearance of Roman political authority from the Western Empire strengthened the temporal power of the bishop of Rome. In the Byzantine Empire the patriarch of Constantinople remained under the political control of the Christian emperor. Cultural, political, philosophical, and theological differences strained relations between the two cities, and in 1054 the papal legate and the patriarch of Constantinople excommunicated each other.

One reflection of growing difficulties lay in counterclaims to pursue mission in and hold the allegiance of border areas between the two jurisdictions. Rostislav of Great Moravia sought help from the emperor, who (presumably through the patriarch) in about 862 sent two brothers, Constantine (later called Cyril; c. 827–869) and Methodius (c. 825–884), from Constantinople to Moravia. They provided Scriptures and liturgy in the mother tongue of each people evangelized and trained others in their methods. This missionary competition was repeated in Bulgaria when its khan, Boris I, sought to convert to Christianity.

Receiving missionaries from both Rome and Constantinople, Boris ultimately accepted the jurisdiction of the patriarch in Constantinople for the church in Bulgaria.

Constantinople's greatest mission outreach was to areas that later became Russia. In the 10th century the Scandinavian Rus controlled the areas around Kiev. Undoubtedly influenced by his Christian grandmother Olga and by a proposed marriage alliance with the Byzantine imperial family, Vladimir I (c. 956–1015) of Kiev, from among several options, chose the Byzantine rite. Baptized in 988, he led the Kievans to Christianity. His son Yaroslav encouraged translations and built monasteries.

From 1240, and for the next 200 years, the Mongol Golden Horde was suzerain over Russia but generally allowed freedom to the church. For Russians the church proved to be the one means through which they could express national unity. They moved the metropolitanate from Kiev to Moscow, and their church became and remained the largest of the Orthodox bodies, protector and leader for the others. When Constantinople fell to the Ottoman Turks in 1453, Moscow became "the third Rome" and accepted for itself the mystique, dynamism, and messianic destiny of the first Rome—a reality essential to understanding Russian Orthodoxy and nationalism.

East of the Euphrates River, Nestorians and Jacobites maintained headquarters in Persia for eastern outreach. The more numerous Nestorians developed a far-flung mission network throughout Central Asia. The Persian bishop A-lo-pen reached China's capital, Ch'ang-an (modern Xi'an), in 635 and founded monasteries to spread the Christian faith. By the end of the Tang dynasty (618–907), however, the Nestorian community had disappeared.

In 1289 the pope—responding to a request made 20 years earlier by Kublai Khan that 100 Christian scholars be brought by the Polo brothers to China—sent one Franciscan, Giovanni da Montecorvino (1247–1328). He reached Dadu (modern Beijing) in 1294 and launched a small but successful mission. In 1342 Giovanni dei Marignolli arrived with 32 other missionaries, but their work flourished for less than 25 years because the succeeding Ming dynasty excluded foreigners. Twice Christianity had entered and disappeared from China.

The Rise of Islam

Between Muhammad's death in 632 and the defeat of Muslim forces at Poitiers by Charles Martel's Franks in 732, Arab Muslims had taken the Middle East and Egypt, then swept across North Africa, turned northward through Spain, and ventured briefly into southwestern France. Within a century Islam had taken control of more than half of Christendom.

The Iberian reconquest, which began as a traditional war of conquest, became a crusade against Islam and fused an Iberian Catholicism that Spain and Portugal later transplanted around the globe. In the early 21st century its members represented nearly half the world's Roman Catholics. The Crusades (1095–1396) produced among many Christians an adversarial approach to those of other faiths. Ramon Llull (c. 1235–1316) pursued a different way. He studied Arabic and sought through dialogue and reason the conversion of Muslims and Jews.

As a result of the second great transition the faith of the Mediterranean world had become that of all Europe and had largely created its civilization. Christendom had lost half of its territory to Islam, but Europe had become the new centre of the Christian faith.

THIRD TRANSITION, TO AD 1950

By 1500 Europe was bursting with new energy and achievement, and from it Christianity spread worldwide. Iberian monks in the 16th century spanned the globe, and later Protestant missionaries did the same.

Roman Catholic Missions, 1500–1950

In the 15th century European nations began a process of exploration and colonization that brought them more fully into contact with the rest of the world and facilitated the spread of Christianity. Motivated in part by Christian zeal, Portugal's Prince Henry the Navigator (1394–1460) launched exploratory voyages along the western coast of Africa. Papal grants in 1454 and 1456 gave Henry all lands, power over the missionary bishops therein, and trading rights south of the Tropic of Cancer. In 1494, following Columbus's successful voyages for Spain, the pope granted Spain all territory west of 47° W longitude (eastern Brazil). Under royal patronage (*patronato real*, or *padroado*), monarchs of both nations accepted responsibility for evangelizing the newly found peoples. Franciscans, Dominicans, Augustinians, and, from 1542, Jesuits staffed the resulting missions. Finally, by 1600, other great powers, including France and the Protestant countries of England, Holland, and Denmark, began to establish and evangelize overseas empires.

When the Europeans arrived in the Americas, the native population south of the Rio Grande numbered some 35 million but in North America there were at most 1.2 million people. The great majority of European males entering Latin America were unmarried and quickly produced a mestizo, or mixed, population. European settlers, who expected to instruct the indigenous population in the faith and protect them, instead enslaved or cruelly exploited them. Bartolomé de Las Casas (1474–1566) championed their cause but, ironically, favoured increasing the already growing number of African slaves.

Despite its weaknesses, the Roman Catholic mission gained vast numbers for the faith as Franciscans and Dominicans traveled widely and built mission churches. Although limits were placed on the ordination of Native Americans and much evangelization appeared to be an integral part of military conquest, the indigenous and mestizo populations of Mexico and South America, who intermingled traditional and Christian beliefs, thought of themselves as Roman Catholics. The best known example of such missionary success is that of Juan Diego (1474–1548), an Aztec convert whose visions of the Virgin Mary (Our Lady of Guadalupe) contributed to the conversion of Mexico.

Evangelization in French North America followed a somewhat different course. In 1534 Jacques Cartier claimed New France (Canada) for his homeland. A century later French missionaries began to enter the territory. In their work these missionaries sought to reshape Indian life as little as possible.

Some of the most productive missions, however, appeared in Asia, chiefly through the work of the Jesuits. Under a papal commission the Jesuit missionary Francis Xavier (1506–52) reached Goa in 1542. He established Christian communities in India, built a college in Goa for training priests, began a prospering mission in Japan, and died off the coast of China while hoping to enter that land. Despite his death, there were about 300,000 Christians in Japan by 1600. Christianity was afterward proscribed in Japan, many Christians were martyred, and the Japanese sealed themselves off from the West.

China also was closed to foreigners, but the Italian Jesuit missionary Matteo Ricci (1552–1610) arrived in 1582 and eventually reached the capital. His efforts brought success, and other Jesuits followed. An edict of toleration was proclaimed in 1692. Ricci's conviction that the honouring of ancestors and Confucius was a social rite that could be accommodated within the church produced the Chinese Rites Controversy (1634–1742). It brought bitter opposition from Dominicans and Franciscans. Attempts at papal intervention at the beginning of the 18th century angered the emperor. The Chinese forced missionaries to leave the country and persecuted Christians. Yet by 1800 some 250,000 remained, and since the 16th century the church has been continuously present in China.

In India Jesuits were welcomed to the court during the reign of the Mughal emperor Akbar (1556–1605). The noted Jesuit Roberto de Nobili (1577–1656) sought points of agreement between Hinduism and Christianity as a means of evangelization, but this caused difficulty with the church. The missionaries also worked among India's existing Christian communities. In 1599 the Roman Catholic Church brought the South Indian Christians (Nestorians) into its fold, but in 1653 about 40 percent of the Syrian, or Thomas, Christians revolted and linked themselves with the Jacobites. Nevertheless, the Roman Catholics

Indian women take part in a special mass to mark the beginning of Mother Teresa's birth centenary celebration at a cathedral dedicated to Mother Teresa at Baruipur on the outskirts of Kolkata on August 23, 2010. Deshakalyan Chowdhury/AFP/Getty Images

retained a solid base of Christians on which to build.

To provide knowledgeable oversight and to coordinate policy, in 1622 Pope Gregory XV established the Sacred Congregation for the Propagation of the Faith (Propaganda Fide). It provided a library for research and a school for training priests and missionaries, assigned territories, and directed ecclesiastical matters overseas. The Foreign Missionary Society of Paris (1663), directed exclusively toward outreach to non-Christian peoples, sought to produce rapidly an indigenous secular clergy (i.e., one not bound to a religious order), and focused its efforts on Vietnam, Cambodia, Laos, and Thailand.

With the suppression of the Jesuits (1773–1814) and the decline of Spanish and Portuguese influence, Roman Catholic missions found themselves at low ebb, but French and other European missionaries steadily took up the slack. Between 1800 and 1950 new vigour paralleled that seen in Protestantism and brought new orders—such as the Society of the Divine Word (1875) and the Catholic Foreign Missionary Society of North America (1911) of Maryknoll fathers and sisters—and voluntary societies to promote and support missions. The missionary force remained overwhelmingly European.

Protestant Missions, 1500s–1950

Protestant missionaries have been reaching out to the world for converts since the early days of the Reformation.

Early Protestant Missions

Protestant missions emerged well after Martin Luther launched the Reformation in 1517; Protestants began to expand overseas through migration, notably to North America. European colonization of North America aroused interest in Native Americans, and the Virginia and Massachusetts charters enjoined their conversion. The mission of John Eliot (1604–90) to the Pequot Iroquois and that of the Thomas Mayhew family encouraged the formation of supporting societies in Britain. Individual Anglicans formed the Society for Promoting Christian Knowledge (SPCK; 1698) and the Society for the Propagation of the Gospel in Foreign Parts (SPG; 1701), whose chaplains were also to spread the Gospel among non-Christians. The Dutch East India Company trained ministers in Leiden to serve their employees in Indonesia and Ceylon (Sri Lanka), but they were also encouraged to catechize and baptize local people.

The German Lutheran Pietists were the first Protestant group to launch church-supported continuing missions from the Continent. Philipp Jakob Spener (1635–1705) and August Hermann Francke (1663–1727) at the University of Halle trained Bartholomäus Ziegenbalg (1683–1719) and Heinrich Plütschau (1678–1747). From 1706 they served the Danish mission of King Frederick IV at Tranquebar, in South India. Also trained at Halle, Nikolaus Ludwig, Count von Zinzendorf (1700–60), received Moravian refugees at his Herrnhut estate and in 1732 molded them into a missionary church. Their small, self-supporting communities spread from Greenland to South Africa.

William Carey's *Enquiry into the Obligations of Christians, to Use Means for the Conversion of the Heathens* (1792) became the "charter" for Protestant missions and produced the Baptist Missionary Society. In 1793 Carey went to India. His first letter to an England stirred by the Evangelical Revival resulted in the formation of the London Missionary Society (1795). The Scottish Missionary Society (1796) and the Netherlands Missionary Society (1797) soon appeared. Anglican evangelicals organized the Church Missionary Society (1799), and many others followed. Like the SPCK and SPG, they were founded not by churches but as autonomous societies supported chiefly by denominational constituencies. Similarly, in Europe these organizations were usually created geographically— such as the Basel (1815), Berlin (1824), and Leipzig (1836) societies.

With separation of church and state in the United States, American churches made plain that mission was the responsibility of each Christian. Most denominations developed their own boards or societies. The American Board of Commissioners for Foreign Missions (1810) was the first, and the pattern of denominational societies spread. These missions centred on the new immigrants and those following the westward-moving frontier until 1890, but from that time they turned their attention to areas abroad. In 20th-century "overseas" missions, English-speaking participants represented from 80 to 89 percent, and North Americans about 67 percent, of all Protestant missionaries.

Women have not only provided the major support for mission in the modern era but also early recognized the need to found their own societies and send their own missionaries. In much of the world, because of local customs, women missionaries could perform services for other women and for children, especially in medicine and education, that men could not undertake. Their greatest impact was in the production of vast corps of able and educated women, especially in Asia, who played major roles in the professions and in church leadership.

Missions to Asia

In the early 19th century in India, William Carey, Joshua Marshman, and William Ward—the Serampore trio—worked just north of Calcutta (now Kolkata). Their fundamental approach included translating the Scriptures, establishing a college to educate an Indian ministry, printing Christian literature, promoting social reform, and recruiting missionaries for new areas as soon as translations into that area's language were ready. These efforts were followed by those of Alexander Duff (1806–78), who established the pattern for an entire educational system, including colleges, in India. By the 1860s education for women had advanced and nurses' training had begun; the vast majority of Indian nurses also have been Christian. The education of women physicians began at the turn of the century. The Vellore Medical College is a monument to the missionary physician Ida Scudder (1870–1959).

Missionaries also returned to China and other parts of East Asia in the 19th century. Following the Opium Wars of 1842–44 and 1858–60, China was opened to Westerners. Although there had been a Roman Catholic presence in China since the 16th-century Jesuit mission, the arrival of Christianity in the 19th century had a profound impact on Chinese culture and history. The Taiping Rebellion (1850–64), which nearly toppled the Qing, or Manchu, dynasty and took an estimated 20 million lives, was led by Hong Xiuquan, who was influenced by Christian teachings and thought that he was Jesus's younger brother. The Boxer Rebellion of 1899–1900 brought death to thousands of Chinese Christians and several hundred missionaries. Yet Protestant schools, colleges, and hospitals offered educational opportunities and attracted Chinese youth to the Christian faith. With the fall of the Qing dynasty in 1911/12, Sun Yat-sen, a Christian favouring parliamentary government, became the provisional president. The Christian influence in China, particularly in education, was significant. In 1949, when the People's Republic of China was formed, Christians represented only 1 percent of the Chinese population, but they exercised an influence out of all proportion to their size.

Christianity's fortunes in the second half of the 20th century were mixed. The Chinese government expelled all missionaries in 1950–51, confiscated churches, and brought pressure on Christians. During the Cultural Revolution (1966–76) no churches or other religious bodies could operate. Christians continued to exist in China, but they suffered grievously. From 1976, as the government allowed some churches to open, Christians reemerged throughout the country. Roman Catholic and Protestant churches were filled, and in varied ways "silent" house-churches testified that the underground church had been dynamically growing. In the early 21st century the church in China, despite persecution and lingering tensions between the Vatican and the Chinese government, is considerably larger and stronger than it was in 1949.

Koreans baptized as Roman Catholics in China returned in 1784 but remained underground when their faith was soon proscribed. A handful of American Presbyterians and Methodists entered Korea in 1884, and the faith they planted flourished through the 20th century, despite Korea's long wartime devastation. Unlike other Asian countries, Korea did not experience Christianity's arrival with Western imperialism but rather saw that faith as reinforcing Korean nationalism against Japanese imperialism from 1910 to 1945. Christian evangelization in Korea enabled the church to grow in less than a century to about one-third of the country's population. Evangelistic and self-supporting Korean churches were known throughout Asia for their effective promotion of Bible study. Helen Kim, a Korean graduate of Ewha College, built that institution into the world's largest women's university, and Sun Myung Moon founded the Unification Church, which teaches a unique Christian theology.

Missions to South East Asia and the Pacific

Missionaries also evangelized regions throughout Southeast Asia and the Pacific. The first missions to Vietnam were undertaken in the 16th and 17th centuries by Dominicans and Jesuits from Portugal and France. A more permanent presence, which led to French military intervention, was established in the 18th and 19th centuries. In the early 21st century, some 9 percent of the population of Vietnam was Christian.

Dutch chaplains established churches in Indonesia in the 17th century. In the mid-19th century, the German Rhenish Missionary Society enabled the Batak Church of Sumatra to grow in size and strength and to provide leadership for the nation. Other strong churches developed in various parts of the predominantly Muslim country.

The vast Pacific Ocean, with tiny, scattered island kingdoms among the Polynesian, Micronesian, and Melanesian peoples, early attracted missionaries. Most of them were laypeople of deep Christian faith. It was the effort of the Christian islanders, however, that achieved virtually total evangelization of the Pacific.

Missions to Africa and South America

Although Christianity had existed in Ethiopia since the 4th century, much of Africa remained a mission field into the 20th century. Protestant missionaries were working in most of the West and Central African colonial nations in the 19th century, but in some parts of East Africa mission began only in the 20th century. After Ghana gained freedom in 1957, many former colonies were granted independence. Cataclysmic change appeared everywhere: in building new nations; rapid shifts from a rural to an urban population; coping with the massive problem, especially in cities, of some 2,500 languages; and developing literacy. Amid all this, Christianity grew with increasing rapidity. By the early 21st century more than half of the sub-Saharan African population was Christian. African independent, or indigenous nonwhite, churches proliferated, and several of the largest ones joined the World Council of Churches.

In the 19th century Evangelical churches were begun in Latin America by Protestant missionaries who were largely from the United States but also in some instances from Britain and Germany. Most of these churches have remained small. The exception was the explosion of Pentecostalism throughout the region, with heaviest concentration in Brazil, Chile, and Mexico. Evangelicals also have gained members in Central America.

Missionary Associations

Protestants discovered the need for cooperation and unity. As tiny minorities in lands of other religions, new Christians and missionaries together saw that denominational separatism hindered evangelization. Four streams led to the cooperation and unity reflected in the World Missionary Conference (WMC) held in Edinburgh in 1910. First, missionary "field" conferences affirmed comity (separation of spheres of work), cooperation in Bible translation and missionary councils, and shared sponsorship in major enterprises such as hospitals and colleges. A second stream involved missionary conferences in England and the United States from 1854 to 1900. A third force flowed through the missionary concern of the international student Christian and missionary movements. The fourth stream arose in the West from continuing interdenominational conferences of mission leaders to face common concerns and forge common policies. Among others, these included the Continental European Missions Conference (1866) and the Foreign Missions Conference of North America (1893).

The Edinburgh conference was unique—a landmark and watershed for all that was to follow. Largely Western in membership, but with 17 Asian delegates,

it created a Continuation Committee that in 1921 became the International Missionary Council (IMC). The IMC consisted of a worldwide network of Christian councils and the Western cooperative agencies. In 1961 the IMC became the Division of World Mission and Evangelism of the World Council of Churches (WCC). In 1971 the Division underwent further restructuring but maintained its relationship with the WCC and in the late 20th and 21st century sponsored a series of ecumenical conferences on world mission.

Orthodox and Nondenominational Missions

Virtually the entire outreach of the Russian Orthodox mission extended to the peoples of the vast Russian Empire across Asia. Its outstanding missionaries included the linguist and translator Nicholas Ilminsky (d. 1891) and Ivan Veniaminov (1797–1879), who in 1823 went as its first missionary to the Aleutian Islands. Veniaminov eventually became Metropolitan Innocent of Moscow, and in 1870 he founded the Russian Orthodox Missionary Society. The Russian Orthodox Church opened a mission to Japan in 1854 and in 1941 turned over all church property to its members.

For some decades the church appointed missionaries to its highest posts. Tikhon (1865–1923), who in 1917 became the first patriarch in two centuries, and Sergius (Stragorodsky; 1867–1944), who followed him in that post, had both served missions abroad. Following the 1917 Revolution, Russian missions came to an end, and after the fall of communism in Russia in 1991 the country itself became the focus of missionaries from various Christian churches.

Nondenominational faith missions viewed J. Hudson Taylor's China Inland Mission (1865; after 1965 called the Overseas Missionary Fellowship) as the great prototype. Missions such as these often sought to work in areas unoccupied by other missionaries, guaranteed no salaries, and left financial support in God's hands; but most bodies made their financial needs known to a wide constituency. Their chief aim has been to proclaim the Gospel and eschew the provision of social services. These societies joined together in the Interdenominational Foreign Mission Association (IFMA; 1917). Since the 1960s they have cooperated with the Evangelical Foreign Missions Association (EFMA; 1945), the missionary arm of the National Association of Evangelicals (1943), and, at the international level, with the World Evangelical Fellowship (1952). Membership in the Association grew most rapidly in the 1950s, and by the 1980s, despite slower growth, numbered 38 member organizations. Since the 1960s IFMA has worked on a variety of projects with the Evangelical Fellowship of Mission Agencies, and in the late 20th century it addressed a variety of social issues, including an educational program concerned with AIDS, as part of its mission.

FOURTH TRANSITION, FROM 1950

During the third transition, Christianity had spread worldwide from a base in Europe. As a result of the fourth transition, more Christians lived in Asia, the Pacific Islands, Africa, and Latin America than in the old Christendom, part of a long-term, continuing shift in Christianity's numerical and vivifying centre. The growing churches brought new life and dynamism to the faith, along with new theologies and concerns.

The growth of the world Christian community kept pace with the 20th-century population explosion, and in the fastest-growing areas the growth rate in numbers of Christians was almost three times greater than the general population increase. The majority of the world's Christians lived in non-Western nations: a universal Christian church had come into being.

In this transition two issues were especially prominent. First, the church found itself engaged with those of traditional or new religions and those for whom ideologies had become religions. In that setting the Roman Catholic Church and the Orthodox and Protestants in the World Council of Churches affirmed evangelization to be essential but also engaged in dialogue with other religions to promote better understanding between the different faiths. This effort brought with it much dissent and tension.

Second, "Third World theologies" often provoked angry debate. The underlying questions concerned the identification of what was essentially Christian in Western Christianity and theology and whether Western church structures and theologies were universally normative. But the most basic question asked how Christians of all races could manifest unity.

Another force was the worldwide growth in the number of Pentecostals and charismatics. They formed new churches, appeared in traditional churches, and found outlet in many nonwhite indigenous bodies. Pentecostals and charismatics were most heavily concentrated in Latin America and Africa but also experienced growth in Asia and in the West. They forced theological reflection—perhaps best developed by Roman Catholics—on the doctrine of the Holy Spirit and on authority within the church.

The Second Vatican Council (1962–65) was the most important ecclesiological and missiological event for Roman Catholics since the 16th century. Theologically it set itself within the dynamics of the faith's fourth transition. The council's Decree on the Church's Missionary Activity (*Ad Gentes*) built theologically on the council's foundational document, the "Dogmatic Constitution on the Church" (*Lumen Gentium*; "Light of the Nations"), which insisted upon evangelization but presented a larger understanding of God's grace for those outside the church, and urged missionaries to pursue dialogue.

After Vatican II the situation changed, as the very definition of missionary activity was transformed and the duties of all Christians to undertake evangelical work was emphasized. The new evangelism emphasized the importance of bearing witness to Christ, which includes efforts to spread the Gospel and to promote the church's teachings on human dignity. The former missionary churches were placed more and more in the hands of local peoples, and the bishops in regional councils took over leadership of evangelization formerly held by missionary orders. In the decades following Vatican II, the church's mission was conducted with greater sensitivity toward other cultures, and church leaders emphasized interreligious dialogue. In 1986 Pope John Paul II invited world religious leaders to Assisi to pray for peace, and he subsequently prayed at a synagogue and a mosque. The pope offered further guidance on missions in his encyclical *Redemptoris missio* (Dec. 7, 1990; "The Mission of Christ the Redeemer"), renewing the church's commitment to mission and calling for the evangelization of lapsed Christians and non-Christians alike.

SCRIPTURE TRANSLATIONS

The translation of the Holy Scriptures has constituted a basic part of mission. During the Middle Ages few could read the Latin Bible, and vernacular versions of the Bible, in part or whole, appeared at times throughout the period. The most important of these was the so-called Wyclif Bible, an English translation compiled in 1382. Within 80 years of the invention of printing in the West, however, Reformation leaders such as Luther and Calvin focused on the Word of God. Their cardinal principle remained that each should be able to read the Bible in his own tongue. The printing press greatly aided Protestantism, and Roman Catholicism used it effectively as well.

Translations of the Bible became more numerous and widespread beginning in the 16th century. One of the earliest and most important was Luther's German translation. The first official Roman Catholic translation of the Bible, the Douai-Rheims Bible, appeared in two stages: in 1582, the New Testament was published, and in 1609–10, the Old Testament appeared. In 1611, the most influential English Bible, the King James Version, was published at the commission of James I. Modern English translations were produced in the 20th century by Roman Catholic and Protestant scholars. Translations into other European languages were first made in the 16th and 17th centuries, and in the 19th century Holy Scripture was translated into various African and Asian languages.

In the 20th century printed Christian Scriptures became available in the mother tongues of almost 99 percent of the world's people. That unprecedented accomplishment marks the greatest achievement in the history of written communications. Bibles were available in nearly 325 languages, complete New Testaments in nearly 700 languages, and some portion of the Scriptures in 1,800 other languages. The translation effort, most of which has occurred during the past 200 years, has in many cases reduced a language to writing for the first time. The effort involved the production of grammars and dictionaries of these languages as well as scriptural translations, and an additional benefit has been the written preservation of the cultural heritage by native speakers of the language.

Bible societies, including the United Bible Societies (1946), have coordinated and aided the translation work of missionaries in this task for almost 200 years. Wycliffe Bible Translators (1936) concentrated its work among the language groups having the smallest numbers of speakers. From 1968, Roman Catholics and the United Bible Societies have coordinated their efforts and cooperated in translation and production wherever possible.

ECUMENISM

The word *ecumenism* comes from a family of Classical Greek words: *oikos*, meaning a "house," "family," "people," or "nation"; *oikoumenē*, "the whole inhabited world"; and *oikoumenikos*, "open to or participating in the whole world." Like many biblical words, these were invested with Christian meaning. The *oikoumenē* describes the place of God's reconciling mission (Matthew 24:14); the unity of the Roman Empire (Luke 2:1) and of the kingdoms of the earth (Luke 4:5); and the world destined to be redeemed by Christ (Hebrews 2:5). The vision of one church serving

God in the world came to reflect a central teaching of the early Christian faith.

In later centuries the word *ecumenical* was used to denote church councils (e.g., Nicaea, Chalcedon) whose decisions represented the universal church, in contrast to other councils that enjoyed only regional or limited reception. The honorary title of ecumenical patriarch was given to the Greek Orthodox patriarch of Constantinople in the 6th century because his see was located in the capital of the *oikoumenē* and his leadership was accepted as primus inter pares (first among equals) in the faith and mission of the whole church. The Apostles', the Nicene, and the Athanasian creeds are called ecumenical because they witness to the faith of all Christians. Since the 19th century the term *ecumenism* has denoted the movement of the renewal, unity, and mission of Christians and churches of different traditions "so that the world may believe."

Ecumenism is a vision, a movement, a theology, and a mode of action. It represents the universality of the people of God and affects the way Christians think about their faith, the church, and the world. Ecumenism is a long process that draws Christians together, uniting their life and mission and bringing the Body of Christ and the human community closer to the fulfillment of God's purposes. Those involved in ecumenism participate in ideas, activities, and institutions that express a spiritual reality of shared love in the church and the human community. Ecumenism is characterized by the work of officially organized ecumenical bodies, the confessing and witnessing of Christians in local places, and the spirituality and actions of those who live together in love and prophetic proclamation. Far more than a program or an organization, ecumenism is, according to the British ecumenist Oliver S. Tomkins, "something that happens to the soul of Christians."

Any unity worthy of this vision cannot be identified with political or spiritual coercion, strategies of dominance or superiority, calls for "a return to the mother church," or expectations of monolithic uniformity or a superchurch. The weapons of faith are not those of force or intolerance; neither can divisions be overcome nor authentic unity manifested by syncretism, a least-common-denominator theology, or a casual friendliness. Ecumenism accepts the diversity of God's people, given in creation and redemption, and strives to bring these confessional, cultural, national, and racial differences into one fully committed fellowship.

Ultimately the purpose of ecumenism is to glorify the triune God and to help the one missionary church to witness effectively and faithfully among all peoples and nations. In the second half of the 20th century Christians confessed new dimensions of this vocation, especially in relation to what divides the churches. Progress was made on historical theological issues that have divided Christians through the centuries—baptism, the Eucharist, and ministry.

But equally divisive among Christians are the divisions of the human family: racism, poverty, sexism, war, injustice, and differing ideologies. These issues are part of the agenda of ecumenism and bring a particular context, dynamic spirit, and urgency to the pursuit of Christian unity as well as of justice and peace. The church's unity becomes essential for the renewal and unity of the human family. Through its unity the church becomes a sign, the first fruits of the promised unity and peace among God's peoples and the nations.

THE BIBLICAL PERSPECTIVE

The unity of the church and of all creation is a dominant motif in the Bible. This witness begins in the Old Testament, or Hebrew Scriptures, not the New Testament. As attested in the Bible, God established a covenant with the Hebrew people and gathered the disparate tribes into one religious nation, Israel, taking steps to overcome the alienation between God and humans and to reconcile God's people. The tradition of ancient Judaism, therefore, was based on the reality of the one people of God. Their unity was an expression of their monotheistic faith, the oneness of God (Yahweh). According to Genesis, God created the world as one cosmos, an ordered unity determined by one single will in which all creatures are responsive to the purposes of the Creator. Yahweh chose Israel from all the nations of the world and entered into covenant with its people. Whenever men and women sinned and alienated themselves from God and from one another, God acted to bring about their reconciliation. Israel's mission was to preserve the faithfulness and unity of all God's people and to prepare them for the realization of the Kingdom of God.

The vision of unity is central to the Gospel of Jesus Christ and the teachings of his Apostles. Those who confess Jesus as Lord and Saviour are brought together in a new community: the church. The New Testament writers assumed that to be "in Christ" is to belong to one fellowship (Greek: *koinōnia*). Jesus clearly gave the mandate when at the Last Supper he offered his high-priestly intercession, praying that the disciples and all those who believe in him "may all be one; even as thou, Father, art in me, and I in thee...so that the world may believe that thou hast sent me" (John 17:21). This unity was demonstrated in the miracle of Pentecost (Acts 2) and other actions that established the primitive church—e.g., the epoch-making Council of Jerusalem (Acts 15), which negotiated conflicts between Jewish and Gentile Christians.

The early church nevertheless had many tensions and conflicts that called for ecumenical proclamations and pleas from the Evangelists and Apostles. Tensions arose between Jewish Christian churches and Gentile Christian churches, between Paul and the enthusiasts. Peter and Paul disagreed strongly over whether Gentiles had to fulfill Jewish requirements in order to be welcome at the Lord's Supper (Eucharist). As revealed in the New Testament, the young church clearly faced the challenge of theological aberrations: Colossians refutes gnosticism; the Johannine Epistles warn against Docetism; 2 Peter and Revelation attack false prophets.

Diversity, however, did not create schism nor allow a break in fellowship. There were no denominations or divided communities, as were to develop later in the church's history. Division among Christians is a denial of Christ, an unthinkable distortion of the reality of the church. Amid their diversity and conflicts the early Christians remained of "one accord," visibly sharing the one Eucharist, accepting the ministries of the whole church, reaching out beyond their local situation in faith and witness with a sense of the universal community that held all Christians together. As Paul taught the Ephesians, God's ultimate will and plan is "to unite all things in him [Christ], things in heaven and things on earth" (chapter 1, verse 10).

THE HISTORY OF ECUMENISM

While unity is given in Christ, two diametric forces appear in the history of the church. One is the tendency toward sectarianism and division; the other is the conviction toward catholicity and unity. Ecumenism represents the struggle between them. Some of the schisms were theological conflicts foreshadowed in the apostolic church; others were internal quarrels related to liturgical differences, power politics between different patriarchates or church centres, problems of discipline and piety, or social and cultural conflicts. Nevertheless, according to the American historian John T. McNeill, "the history of the Christian Church from the first century to the 20th might be written in terms of its struggle to realize ecumenical unity."

EARLY CONTROVERSIES

A long and continuing trail of broken relations among Christians began in the 2nd century when the gnostics presented a serious doctrinal error and broke fellowship. Quartodecimanism, a dispute over the date of Easter, pitted Christians from Asia Minor against those from Rome. Montanism—which taught a radical enthusiasm, the imminent Second Coming of Christ, and a severe perfection, including abstinence from marriage—split the church. The Novatians broke fellowship with Christians who offered sacrifices to pagan gods during the persecutions of the Roman emperor Decius in AD 250. In the early 4th century the Donatists, Christians in North Africa who prided themselves as the church of the martyrs, refused to share communion with those who had lapsed (i.e., who had denied the faith under threat of death during the great persecutions of Diocletian and Galerius). They remained a powerful force in Africa into the 5th century and survived into the 7th despite opposition from church and state. This schism—like many since—reflected regional, national, cultural, and economic differences between the poor, rural North African Christians and the sophisticated, urban Romans.

In each century leaders and churches sought to reconcile these divisions and to manifest the visible unity of Christ's church. But in the 5th century a severe break in the unity of the church took place. The public issues were doctrinal consensus and heresy, yet in the midst of doctrinal controversy alienation was prompted by political, cultural, philosophical, and linguistic differences. Tensions increased as the church began to define the relationship between God the Father and God the Son and later the relation between the divine and human elements in the nature and person of Jesus Christ. The first four ecumenical councils—at Nicaea (AD 325), Constantinople (381), Ephesus (431), and Chalcedon (451)—defined the consensus to be taught and believed, articulating this faith in the Nicene Creed and the Chalcedonian Definition, which stated that Jesus is the only begotten Son of God, true man, and true God, one person in "two natures without confusion, without change, without division, without separation." Two groups deviated doctrinally from the consensus developed in the councils. The Nestorians taught that there are two distinct persons in the incarnate Christ and two natures conjoined as one; Monophysites taught that there is one single nature, primarily divine. Several churches refused to accept the doctrinal and disciplinary decisions of Ephesus and Chalcedon and formed their own communities. These pre-Chalcedonian, or non-Chalcedonian, churches, including the Oriental Orthodox churches, became great missionary churches and spread to Africa and throughout Central, South, and East Asia.

THE SCHISM OF 1054

The greatest schism in church history occurred between the church of Constantinople and the church of Rome. While 1054 is the symbolic date of the separation, the agonizing division was six centuries in the making and the result of several different issues. The Eastern Church sharply disagreed when the Western Church introduced into the Nicene Creed the doctrine that the Holy Spirit proceeds not from the Father alone—as earlier Church Fathers taught—but from the Father and the Son (Latin: *Filioque*). When the Roman Empire was divided into two zones, Latin-speaking Rome began to claim superiority over Greek-speaking Constantinople; disputes arose over church boundaries and control (for example, in Illyricum and Bulgaria). Rivalry developed in Slavic regions between Latin missionaries from the West and Byzantine missionaries from the East, who considered this territory to be Orthodox. Disputes over authority became even more heated in the 11th century as Rome asserted its primacy over all churches. Lesser matters related to worship and church discipline—for example, married clergy

(Orthodox) versus celibacy (Roman Catholic) and rules of fasting and tonsure—strained ecclesial relations. The tensions became a schism in 1054, when the uncompromising patriarch of Constantinople, Michael Cerularius, and the uncompromising envoys of Pope Leo IX excommunicated each other. No act of separation was at this time considered final by either side. Total alienation came a century and a half later, as a result of the Crusades, when Christian knights made military campaigns to save Jerusalem and the Holy Land from the Muslims. In 1204 the Fourth Crusade was diverted to attack and capture Constantinople brutally. Thousands of Orthodox Christians were murdered; churches and icons were desecrated and undying hostility developed between East and West.

Even so, certain leaders and theologians on both sides tried to heal the breach and reunite East and West. In 1274, at the second Council of Lyon, agreement was reached between the two churches over several key issues—Orthodox acceptance of papal primacy and the acceptance of the Nicene Creed with the *Filioque* clause. But the agreements were only a rushed action conditioned by political intrigue. As a result, reunion on these terms was fiercely rejected by the clergy and laity in Constantinople and other Orthodox provinces. A second attempt at reunion came at the Council of Ferrara-Florence that met in Italy in 1438 and 1439. A formula of union was approved by both delegations, but later it was rejected by rank-and-file Orthodox Christians.

THE REFORMATION

The next dramatic church division took place during the Reformation in the West in the 16th century. Like other schisms, this one does not yield to simple analysis or explanation. The Reformation was a mixture of theology, ecclesiology, politics, and nationalism, all of which led to breaks in fellowship and created institutional alienation between Christians throughout Western Christendom. In one sense it was a separation, especially a reaction against the rigid juridical structures of medieval Roman Catholicism and its claim to universal truth and jurisdiction. In another sense, however, the Reformation was an evangelical and ecumenical renewal of the church as the Body of Christ, an attempt to return to the apostolic and patristic sources in order, according to Calvin, "to recover the face of the ancient Catholic Church." All the continental Reformers sought to preserve and reclaim the unity of the church.

Once the separation between the Roman Catholic and new Protestant churches was complete, people on both sides tried to restore unity. Roman Catholics such as Georg Witzel and George Cassander developed proposals for unity, which all parties rejected. Martin Bucer, celebrated promoter of church unity among the 16th-century leaders, brought Martin Luther and his colleague Philipp Melanchthon into dialogue with the Swiss Reformer Huldrych Zwingli at Marburg, Germany, in 1529.

In 1541 John Calvin (who never ceased to view the church in its catholicity), Bucer, and Melanchthon met with Cardinal Gasparo Contarini and other Roman Catholics at Ratisbon (now Regensburg, Germany) to reconcile their differences on justification by faith, the Lord's Supper, and the papacy. Another attempt was made in 1559, when Melanchthon and Patriarch Joasaph II of Constantinople corresponded, with the intention of using the Augsburg Confession as the basis of dialogue between Lutheran and Orthodox Christians. On the eve of the French wars of religions (1561), Roman Catholics and Protestants conferred without success in the Colloquy of Poissy. It would seem that the ecumenical projects of theologians and princes in 16th-century Europe failed unequivocally, but they kept alive the vision and the hope.

ECUMENISM IN THE 17TH AND 18TH CENTURIES

Throughout the 17th and 18th centuries storms of contention and division continued to plague the churches of Europe. During these two centuries there was an eclipse of official, church-to-church

A scene from the Conversations at Marburg, October 1529. Various leaders of the Reformation met in an attempt to reconcile the growing theological differences especially between Martin Luther and Huldreich Zwingli (standing centre right), the leader of the Swiss Reformation. The conference ended without agreement. Henry Guttmann/Hulton Archive/Getty Images

attempts at unity. Instead, ecumenical witness was made by individuals who courageously spoke and acted against all odds to propose Christian unity.

In England, John Dury, a Scots Presbyterian and (later) an Anglican minister, "a peacemaker without partiality," traveled more extensively than any other ecumenist before the 19th century. He negotiated for church unity in his own country and in Sweden, Holland, France, Switzerland, and Germany. Richard Baxter, a Presbyterian Puritan, developed proposals for union, including his Worcestershire Association, a local ecumenical venture uniting Presbyterians, Congregationalists, and Anglicans.

Efforts were undertaken in Germany and Central Europe as well. The German Lutheran George Calixtus called for a united church between Lutherans and Reformed based on the "simplified dogmas," such as the Apostles' Creed and the agreements of the church in the first five centuries. Count Nicholas von Zinzendorf applied his Moravian piety to the practical ways that unity might come to Christians of all persuasions. The philosopher Gottfried Wilhelm Leibniz worked tirelessly for union between Protestants and Roman Catholics, writing an apologia interpreting Roman Catholic doctrines for Protestants. John Amos Comenius, a Czech Brethren educator and advocate of union, produced a plan of union for Protestants based upon the adoption of a scriptural basis for all doctrine and polity and the integration of all human culture.

Orthodox Christians also participated in the search for union. Metropolitan Philaret of Moscow and the Russian Orthodox theologian Aleksey S. Khomyakov expressed enthusiasm for ecumenism. Cyrillus Lukaris, Orthodox patriarch of Alexandria and later of Constantinople, took initiatives to reconcile a divided Christendom. People throughout Europe held tenaciously to the dream of ecumenism, although no attempt at union was successful.

19TH-CENTURY EFFORTS

A worldwide movement of evangelical fervour and renewal, noted for its emphasis on personal conversion and missionary expansion, stirred new impulses for Christian unity in the 19th century. The rise of missionary societies and volunteer movements in Germany, Great Britain, the Netherlands, and the United States expressed a zeal that fed the need for church unity. Enduring the harmful results of Christian divisions in different countries, Protestant missionaries in India, Japan, China, Africa, Latin America, and the United States began to cooperate.

In 1804 the British and Foreign Bible Society, an interdenominational Protestant organization, came into existence to translate the Scriptures into the world's vernaculars and distribute the translations throughout the world. This was followed, 40 years later, by the founding of two important Christian organizations in England: the Young Men's

Christian Association (1844) and the Young Women's Christian Association (1855). Their international bodies, the World Alliance of YMCAs and the World YWCA, were established in 1855 and 1894, respectively. The Evangelical Alliance, possibly the most significant agent of Christian unity in the 19th century, held a unique place among the volunteer associations of the age. Founded in London in 1846 (the American section was established in 1867), the alliance sought to draw individual Christians into fellowship and cooperation in prayer for unity, Christian education, the struggle for human rights, and mission.

Also pivotal in the 19th century were advocates for the visible unity of the church. In the United States, where the most articulate 19th-century unity movements were heard, the witness to the unity and union was led by three traditions. The Lutherans Samuel Simon Schmucker and Philip Schaff pleaded for "catholic union on apostolic principles." Among Episcopalians, the visionaries for unity included Thomas Hubbard Vail, William Augustus Muhlenberg, and William Reed Huntington, who proposed the historic "Quadrilateral" of the Scriptures, the creeds, the sacraments of baptism and the Lord's Supper, and episcopacy as the keystone of unity. Thomas Campbell and his son, Alexander, and Barton Warren Stone, members of the church of the Disciples of Christ, taught that "the Church of Christ on earth is essentially, intentionally and constitutionally one." Ecumenism was enflamed in the hearts of 19th-century Christians and in the next century shaped the churches as never before.

ECUMENISM SINCE THE START OF THE 20TH CENTURY

The 20th century experienced a flowering of ecumenism. Four different strands—the international Christian movement, cooperation in world mission, Life and Work, and Faith and Order—developed in the early decades and, though distinctive in their emphases, later converged to form one ecumenical movement.

The modern ecumenical era began with a worldwide movement of Christian students, who formed national movements in Great Britain, the United States, Germany, Scandinavia, and Asia. In 1895 the World Student Christian Federation, the vision of American Methodist John R. Mott, was established "to lead students to accept the Christian faith" and to pioneer in Christian unity. The World Missionary Conference at Edinburgh (1910) inaugurated another aspect of ecumenism by dramatizing the necessity of unity and international cooperation in fulfilling the world mission of the church. In 1921 the International Missionary Council (IMC) emerged, bringing together missionary agencies of the West and of the new Christian councils in Asia, Africa, and Latin America for joint consultation, planning, and theological reflection. The Life and Work movement was pledged to practical Christianity and common action by focusing the Christian conscience on international relations and social, industrial, and economic problems. Nathan Söderblom, Lutheran archbishop of Uppsala, inspired world conferences on Life and Work at Stockholm (1925) and Oxford (1937). The Faith and Order movement, which originated in the United States, confronted the doctrinal divisions and sought to overcome them. Charles H. Brent, an Episcopal missionary bishop in the Philippines, was chiefly responsible for this movement, although Peter Ainslie, of the Disciples of Christ, shared the same vision and gave significant leadership. World conferences on Faith and Order at Lausanne (Switzerland; 1925), Edinburgh (1937), Lund (Sweden; 1952), and Montreal (1963) guided the process of theological consensus building among Protestants, Orthodox, and Roman Catholics, which led to approval by the Faith and Order Commission of the World Council of Churches of the historic convergence text *Baptism, Eucharist, and Ministry* (1982).

The World Council of Churches (WCC) is a privileged instrument of the ecumenical movement. Constituted at Amsterdam in 1948, the conciliar body includes more than 300 churches—Protestant, Anglican, and Orthodox—which "confess the Lord Jesus Christ as God and Saviour according to the Scriptures and therefore seek to fulfill together their common calling to the glory of the one God, Father, Son, and Holy Spirit." Its general secretaries have been among the architects of modern ecumenism: Willem Adolph Visser 't Hooft

(the Netherlands), Eugene Carson Blake (United States), Philip Potter (Dominica), Emilio Castro (Uruguay), Konrad Raiser (Germany), and Samuel Kobia (Kenya). The witness and programs of the WCC include faith and order, mission and evangelism, refugee and relief work, interfaith dialogue, justice and peace, theological education, and solidarity with women and the poor. What distinguishes the WCC constituency is the forceful involvement of Orthodox churches and churches from the developing world. Through their active presence the WCC, and the wider ecumenical movement, has become a genuinely international community.

Roman Catholic ecumenism received definitions and momentum at the Second Vatican Council (Vatican II; 1962–65), under the ministries of Popes John XXIII and Paul VI, and through the ecumenical diplomacy of Augustin Cardinal Bea, the first president of the Secretariat for Promoting Christian Unity. The church gave the ecumenical movement new hope and language in the "Decree on Ecumenism" (1964), one of the classic ecumenical teaching documents. Another result of Vatican II was the establishment of a wide variety of international theological dialogues, commonly known as bilateral conversations. These included Roman Catholic bilaterals with Lutherans (1965), Orthodox (1967), Anglicans (1967), Methodists (1967), Reformed (1970), and the Disciples of Christ (1977). Topics identified for reconciling discussions include baptism, the Eucharist, episcopacy and papacy, authority in the church, and mixed marriage.

Critical to modern ecumenism is the birth of united churches, which have reconciled formerly divided churches in a given place. In Asia and Africa the first united churches were organized in China (1927), Thailand (1934), Japan (1941), and the Philippines (1944). The most heralded examples of this ecumenism are the United Church of Canada (1925), the Church of South India (1947), and the Church of North India (1970). Statistics of other united churches are revealing. Between 1948 and 1965, 23 churches were formed. In the period from 1965 to 1970, unions involving two or more churches occurred in the West Indies (in Jamaica and Grand Cayman), Ecuador, Zambia, Zaire (now the Democratic Republic of the Congo), Pakistan, Madagascar, Papua New Guinea, the Solomon Islands, and Belgium. Strategic union conversations were undertaken in the United States by the nine-church Consultation on Church Union (1960) and by such uniting churches as the United Church of Christ (1957), the Presbyterian Church (U.S.A.) (1983), and the Evangelical Lutheran Church in America (1988).

Spiritual disciplines play a key role in ecumenism, a movement steeped in prayer for unity. During the Week of Prayer for Christian Unity, celebrated every year (January 18–25), Christians from many traditions engage in prayer, Bible study, worship, and fellowship in anticipation of the unity that Christ wills.

CHAPTER 14

CHRISTIANITY AND WORLD RELIGIONS

The global spread of Christianity through the activity of European and American churches in the 18th, 19th, and 20th centuries has brought it into contact with all other existing religions. Meanwhile, since the beginning of the 19th century, the close connection between Christian world missions and political, economic, technical, and cultural expansion has, at the same time, been loosened.

After World War II, the former mission churches were transformed into independent churches in the newly autonomous Asian and African states. The concern for a responsible cooperation of the members of Christian minority churches and its non-Christian fellow citizens became the more urgent with a renaissance of the Asian higher religions in numerous Asian states.

Missionaries of Asian religions have moved into Europe, the Americas, and Australia. Numerous Vedanta centres have been established to introduce Hindu teachings within the framework of the Ramakrishna and Vivekananda missions. In 1965, the Hare Krishna movement was founded in the United States, attracting followers to its version of Vaishnava Hinduism. South Asian Theravada (Way of the Elders) Buddhism and the Mahayana (Greater Vehicle) Buddhism, particularly that of Japan (largely Pure Land and Nichiren but also Zen) and Tibet, founded meditation centres, community centres, and meditation or other spiritual retreats. This influence has penetrated Europe and North America on several fronts, whether in the form of a spontaneously received flow of religious ideas and methods of meditation through literature and philosophy, through developments in psychology and psychotherapy, or through institutions at which Americans could develop a personal practice of meditation and participate in the life of the sangha (community). As a result, since the latter part of the 20th century, Christianity has found itself forced to enter into a factual discussion with non-Christian religions.

There has also been a general transformation of religious consciousness in the West since the middle of the 19th century. Until about 1900, knowledge of non-Christian world religions was still the privilege of a few specialists. During the 20th century, however, a wide range of people studied translations of source materials from the non-Christian religions. The dissemination of the religious art of India and East Asia through touring exhibitions and the prominence of the Dalai Lama as a political and religious figure have created a new attitude toward the other religions in the broad public of Europe and North America. In recognition of this fact, numerous Christian institutions for the study of non-Christian religions have been founded: e.g., in Bangalore, India; in Bangkok, Thailand; in Kyōto, Japan; and in Hong Kong, China.

The readiness of encounter or even cooperation of Christianity with

Many churches have made efforts to reach out to other faiths. Here, Tibetan spiritual leader the Dalai Lama holds an Easter Egg presented by Orthodox Archbishop Zossima (right) as he visits the Orthodox Church of the Icon of Kazan Virgin in Elista, Russia, November 30, 2004. Tatyana Makeyeva/AFP/Getty Images

non-Christian religions is a phenomenon of modern times. Until the 18th century, Christians showed little inclination to engage in a serious study of other religions. Even though contacts with Islam had existed since its founding, the first translation of the Qur'an (the Islamic scriptures) was issued only in 1141 in Toledo by Peter the Venerable, abbot of Cluny. Four hundred years later, in 1542/43, Theodor Bibliander, a theologian and successor of the Swiss Reformer Zwingli, edited the translation of the Qur'an by Peter the Venerable. He was subsequently arrested, and he and his publisher could be freed only through the intervention of Luther.

Christian exposure to Asian religions also was delayed. Although the name *Buddha* is mentioned for the first time in Christian literature—and there only once—by Clement of Alexandria about 200 CE, it did not appear again for some 1,300 years. Pali, the language of the Buddhist canon, remained unknown in the West until the early 19th century, when the modern Western study of Buddhism began.

The reasons for such reticence toward contact with foreign religions were twofold: (1) The ancient church was significantly influenced by the Jewish attitude toward contemporary pagan religions. Like Judaism, it viewed the pagan gods as "nothings" next to the true God; they were offsprings of human error that were considered to be identical with the wooden, stone, or bronze images that were made by humans. (2) Besides this, there was the tendency to identify the pagan gods as evil demonic forces engaged in combat with the true God. The conclusion of the history of salvation, according to the Christian understanding, was to be a final struggle between Christ and his church on one side and Antichrist and his minions on the other, culminating with the victory of Christ.

CONFLICTING CHRISTIAN ATTITUDES

Christianity faced greater challenges when it encountered Islam and the religions of East Asia. When Islam was founded in the 7th century, it considered the revelations of the Prophet Muhammad to be superior to those of the Old and New Testaments. Christianity also fought Islam as a Christian heresy and saw it as the fulfillment of the eschatological prophecies of the Apocalypse concerning the coming of the "false prophet" (Revelation to John). The religious and political competition between Christianity and Islam led to the Crusades, which influenced the self-consciousness of Western Christianity in the Middle Ages and later centuries.

In China and Japan, however, missionaries saw themselves forced into an argument with indigenous religions that could be carried on only with intellectual weapons. The old Logos theory prevailed in a new form founded on natural law, particularly among the Jesuit theologians who worked at the Chinese emperor's court in Peking (now Beijing). The Jesuits also sought to adapt indigenous religious traditions to Christian rituals but were

Christian, Muslim and Jewish scholars attend the openning session of the Sixth Doha Conference for Interfaith Dialogue in Doha Qatar, on May 13, 2008. Karim Jaafar/AFP/Getty Images

forbidden from doing so by the pope during the Chinese Rites Controversy.

Philosophical and cultural developments during the Enlightenment brought changes in the understanding of Christianity and other world religions. During the Enlightenment, the existence of the plurality of world religions was recognized by the educated in Europe, partly—as in the case of the German philosopher Gottfried Wilhelm Leibniz—in immediate connection with the theories of natural law of the Jesuit missionaries in China. Only in the philosophy of the Enlightenment was the demand of tolerance, which thus far in Christian Europe had been applied solely to the followers of another Christian denomination, extended to include the followers of different religions.

Some missionaries of the late 18th and the 19th centuries, however, ignored this knowledge or consciously fought against it. Simple lay Christianity of revivalist congregations demanded that a missionary denounce all pagan "idolatry." The spiritual and intellectual argument with non-Christian world religions simply did not exist for this simplified theology, and in this view a real encounter of Christianity with world religions did not, on the whole, occur in the 18th and 19th centuries.

CONCLUSION: CONTEMPORARY VIEWS

The 20th century experienced an explosion of publicly available information concerning the wider religious life of humanity, as a result of which the older Western assumption of the manifest superiority of Christianity ceased to be plausible for many Christians. Early 20th-century thinkers such as Rudolf Otto, who saw religion throughout the world as a response to the Holy, and Ernst Troeltsch, who showed that, socioculturally, Christianity is one of a number of comparable traditions, opened up new ways of regarding the other major religions.

During the 20th century, most Christians adopted one of three main points of view. According to exclusivism, there is salvation only for Christians. This theology underlay much of the history outlined above, expressed both in the Roman Catholic dogma *extra ecclesiam nulla salus* ("outside the church no salvation") and in the assumption of the 18th- and 19th-century Protestant missionary movements. The exclusivist outlook was eroded within advanced Roman Catholic thinking in the decades leading up to the Second Vatican Council and was finally abandoned in the council's pronouncements. Pope John Paul II's outreach to the world's religions may be seen as the practical application of the decisions of Vatican II. Within Protestant Christianity there is no comparable central authority, but most Protestant theologians, except within the extreme Fundamentalist constituencies, have also moved away from the exclusivist position.

Since the 20th century many Roman Catholics and Protestants have moved toward inclusivism, the view that, although salvation is by definition Christian, brought about by the atoning work of Christ, it is nevertheless available in principle to all human beings, whether Christian or not. The Roman Catholic theologian Karl Rahner expressed the inclusivist view by saying that good and devout people of other faiths may, even without knowing it, be regarded as "anonymous Christians." Others have expressed in different ways the thought that non-Christians also are included within the universal scope of Christ's salvific work and their religions fulfilled in Christianity.

The third position, which appealed to a number of individual theologians, was pluralism. According to this view, the great world faiths, including Christianity, are valid spheres of a salvation that takes characteristically different forms within each—though consisting in each case in the transformation of human existence from self-centredness to a new orientation toward the Divine Reality. The other religions are not secondary contexts of Christian redemption but independent paths of salvation. The pluralist position is controversial in Christian theology because it affects the ways in which the doctrines of the person of Christ, atonement, and the Trinity are formulated.

Christians engage in dialogue with the other major religions through the World Council of Churches' organization on Dialogue with People of Living Faiths and Ideologies and through the Vatican's Secretariat for Non-Christians, as well as through a variety of extra-ecclesiastical associations, such as the World Congress of Faiths. A multitude of interreligious encounters have taken place throughout the world, many initiated by Christian and others by non-Christian individuals and groups.

GLOSSARY

anathema A ban or curse solemnly pronounced by ecclesiastical authority and accompanied by excommunication.

antinomian One who holds that under the gospel dispensation of grace the moral law is of no use or obligation because faith alone is necessary to salvation.

apologetics A branch of theology devoted to the defense of the divine origin and authority of Christianity.

autocephalous Independent of external and especially patriarchal authority—used especially of Eastern national churches.

bull A solemn, sealed papal letter.

casuistry A resolving of specific cases of conscience, duty, or conduct through interpretation of ethical principles or religious doctrine.

Christology Theological interpretation of the person and work of Christ.

deism A movement or system of thought advocating natural religion, emphasizing morality, and in the 18th century denying the interference of the Creator with the laws of the universe.

dogma A doctrine or body of doctrines concerning faith or morals formally stated and authoritatively proclaimed by a church.

epistemology The study or a theory of the nature and grounds of knowledge, especially with reference to its limits and validity.

gnosticism The thought and practice of various cults of early Christian centuries distinguished by the conviction that matter is evil and that emancipation comes through gnosis, or esoteric knowledge of spiritual truth.

hagiography An idealizing or idolizing biography of a saint or other venerated person.

heresy An opinion or doctrine contrary to church dogma.

hypostasis The substance or essential nature of an individual.

iconoclast A person who destroys religious images or opposes their veneration.

kerygma The apostolic proclamation of salvation through Jesus Christ.

latitudinarian Tolerant of variations in religious opinion or doctrine.

Logos The divine wisdom manifest in the creation, government, and redemption of the world and often identified with the second person of the Trinity.

Manichaeism A syncretistic religious dualism founded by Mani, a third-century Persian prophet, which taught the release of the spirit from matter through asceticism.

monochristic Character that strongly accented the centrality of Christ at the expense of some cultural ties.

Monophysite In Christianity, one who believed that Jesus Christ's nature remains altogether divine and not human, even though he has taken on an earthly and human body with its cycle of birth, life, and death.

Monothelite Any of the 7th-century Christians who maintained that Christ had only one will.

Parousia The Second Coming of Christ.

Pentecostalism A charismatic religious movement that gave rise to a number of Protestant churches in the 20th century and that is unique in its belief that all Christians should seek a post-conversion religious experience called baptism with the Holy Spirit.

polemic An aggressive attack on or refutation of the opinions or principles of another.

schema A mental codification of experience that includes a particular organized way of perceiving cognitively and responding to a complex situation or set of stimuli.

schism Formal division in or separation from a church or religious body.

soteriology The theological study of salvation; especially as effected by Jesus Christ.

syncretistic The combination of different forms of belief or practice.

synoptic Of or relating to the first three Gospels of the New Testament.

Theism A philosophical and theological belief that all things are dependent on and distinct from a supreme being who may be referred to as God; rational approach to question of the existence of God based on evidence of human experience.

theodicy Defense of God's goodness and omnipotence in view of the existence of evil.

tropological Of, relating to, or involving biblical interpretation stressing moral metaphor.

Unitarianism Religious disposition promoting the idea that God is one single being and stressing reason and experience rather than dogma or emotion in beliefs.

BIBLIOGRAPHY

HISTORY OF THE CHRISTIAN CHURCH

Broad overviews are found in Owen Chadwick, *The Pelican History of the Church*, 6 vol. (1960–70, reprinted 1985–86); Kenneth Scott Latourette, *A History of Christianity*, rev. ed., 2 vol. (1975); and John McManners (ed.), *The Oxford Illustrated History of Christianity* (1990, reissued 2001).

Guides to the first centuries include W.H.C. Frend, *The Rise of Christianity* (1984, reprinted 1986); Robert M. Grant, *Augustus to Constantine: The Thrust of the Christian Movement into the Roman World* (1970, reissued 2004); Rodney Stark, *The Rise of Christianity: A Sociologist Reconsiders History* (1996); Wayne A. Meeks, *The First Urban Christians: The Social World of the Apostle Paul* (1983); and Adolf Harnack, *The Mission and Expansion of Christianity in the First Three Centuries*, trans. from the German and ed. by James Moffat, 2 vol. (1904, reprinted 1998; also published as *The Mission and Expansion of Christianity in the First Three Centuries*, 1908, reissued 1972).

Discussions of special topics are presented in Henry Chadwick, *Early Christian Thought and the Classical Tradition: Studies in Justin, Clement, and Origen* (1966, reprinted 1984); Robin Lane Fox, *Pagans and Christians* (1986, reprinted 1995); Wayne A. Meeks, *The First Urban Christians: The Social World of the Apostle Paul*, 2nd ed. (2003); and J.M. Hussey, *The Orthodox Church in the Byzantine Empire* (1986, reissued 1990).

In addition to the relevant volumes of the histories cited above, the church in the Middle Ages and the Reformation is treated in Peter R.L. Brown, *The Rise of Western Christendom: Triumph and Diversity, AD 200–1000*, 2nd ed. (2003); John Bossy, *Christianity in the West, 1400–1700* (1985); Richard A. Fletcher, *The Barbarian Conversion: From Paganism to Christianity* (1999); Joseph H. Lynch, *The Medieval Church: A Brief History* (1995); Diarmaid MacCullough, *The Reformation: A History* (2004); Steven Ozment, *The Age of Reform (1250–1550): An Intellectual and Religious History of Late Medieval and Reformation Europe* (1980); and J.M. Wallace-Hadrill, *The Frankish Church* (1983).

Modern church history is covered in the general histories cited above; in the works cited in the sections below on Christian missions and ecumenism; and in Kenneth Scott Latourette, *Christianity in a Revolutionary Age: A History of Christianity in the Nineteenth and Twentieth Centuries*, 5 vol. (1958–62, reissued 1973); and Glen T. Miller, *The Modern Church: From the Dawn of the Reformation to the Eve of the Third Millennium* (1997).

CHRISTIAN DOCTRINE

Walter Kasper, *The God of Jesus Christ*, trans. by Matthew J. O'Connell (1984, reissued 1989; originally published in German, 1982). Albert Schweitzer, *The Quest of the Historical Jesus: A Critical Study of Its Progress from Reimarus to Wrede*, trans. by W. Montgomery et al., 3rd ed. (1954, reissued 2001; originally published in German, 1906); and Edward Schillebeeckx, *Christ, the Sacrament of the Encounter with God*, trans. by Paul Barrett (1963, reprinted 1977; originally published in Dutch, 1960). Yves M.J. Congar, *I Believe in the Holy Spirit*, trans. by David Smith, 3 vol. (1983, reissued 1997; originally published in French, 1979–80). Karl Rahner, *The Trinity*, trans. by Joseph Donceel (1970, reissued 1997; originally published in German); and Michael O'Carroll, *Trinitas: A Theological Encyclopedia of the Holy Trinity* (1987), are useful introductions to the contemporary understanding of the persons of the Trinity.

Reinhold Niebuhr, *The Nature and Destiny of Man: A Christian Interpretation*, 2 vol. (1941–43, reissued 1996); and Wolfhart Pannenberg, *What Is Man?: Contemporary Anthropology in Theological Perspective* (1970, reissued 1975; originally published in German, 1962).

The history and nature of Christian eschatology is examined in Rudolf Bultmann, *History and Eschatology* (1957; also published as *The Presence of Eternity: History and Eschatology*, 1975); Jürgen Moltmann, *Theology of Hope: On the Ground and the Implications of a Christian Eschatology* (1967, reissued 1993; originally published in German, 1964); and Frederic J. Baumgartener, *Longing for the End: A History of Millennialism in Western Civilization* (1999; reissued 2001).

CHRISTIAN MISSIONS

Kenneth Scott Latourette, *A History of the Expansion of Christianity*, 7 vol. (1937–45, reissued 1971), is a pioneering classic. Stephen Neill, *A History of Christian Missions*, 2nd ed. rev. by Owen Chadwick (1986), is a lively, engaging work. Pope Paul VI, *On Evangelization in the Modern World* (1975), addresses post-Vatican II debates. Andrew Walls, *The Missionary Movement in Christian History* (1996), is another useful study.

ECUMENISM

Introductions to the topic are provided by Thomas Fitzgerald, *The Ecumenical Movement: An Introductory History* (2004); Jeffrey Gros, Eamon McManus, and Ann Riggs, *Introduction to Ecumenism* (1998); Constantin G. Patelos (ed.), *The Orthodox Church in the Ecumenical Movement: Documents and Statements, 1902-1975* (1978); and Hans-Ruedi Weber, *Asia and the Ecumenical Movement, 1895-1961* (1966).

CHRISTIANITY AND WORLD RELIGIONS

The most comprehensive survey of Christian attitudes toward the world religions is Paul F. Knitter, *No Other Name?* (1985). A wide range of views is represented in John Hick and Brian Hebblethwaite (eds.), *Christianity and Other Religions: Selected Readings*, rev. ed. (2001); and Gerald H. Anderson and Thomas F. Stransky (eds.), *Christ's Lordship and Religious Pluralism* (1981). The classic modern statement of a conservative position is that of Hendrick Kraemer, *The Christian Message in a Non-Christian World*, 3rd ed. (1956, reissued 1969). Hans Küng et al., *Christianity and the World Religions: Paths of Dialogue with Islam, Hinduism, and Buddhism*, trans. by Peter Heinegg (1986; originally published in German, 1984), represents a contemporary Roman Catholic standpoint. The pluralistic option is expressed in, for example, John Hick, *A Christian Theology of Religions: The Rainbow of Faiths* (1995).

INDEX

E

F